Nicholas Hagger has written more than 30 books on history, literature and philosophy, including a study of the founding, rise and fall of civilizations. He has lectured at universities in Baghdad, Iraq; Tokyo, Japan (where he was a Professor); and Tripoli, Libya. He has followed a career in education, and travelled widely. For seven years he owned the house in Suffolk in which the Jamestown settlement is thought to have been planned, and he was involved in the discovery of a skeleton which was thought to be that of Bartholomew Gosnold. He has appeared many times on radio and television, and has written articles in newspapers on the subject of the founding and expansion of America, and on global governance and the rise of a new world state.

GW00567348

## By the Same Author

The Fire and the Stones
Selected Poems
The Universe and the Light
A White Radiance
A Mystic Way
Awakening to the Light
A Spade Fresh with Mud
The Warlords
Overlord
A Smell of Leaves and Summer
The Tragedy of Prince Tudor
The One and the Many
Wheeling Bats and a Harvest Moon
The Warm Glow of the Monastery Courtyard
The Syndicate
The Secret History of the West
The Light of Civilization
Classical Odes
Overlord, one-volume edition
Collected Poems 1958–2005
Collected Verse Plays
Collected Stories
The Secret Founding of America
The Last Tourist in Iran
The Rise and Fall of Civilizations
The New Philosophy of Universalism
The Libyan Revolution
Armageddon
The World Government

# THE SECRET AMERICAN DREAM

### The Creation of a
### New World Order with
### the Power to Abolish War,
### Poverty and Disease

## NICHOLAS HAGGER

WATKINS PUBLISHING
LONDON

This edition published in the UK 2011 by
Watkins Publishing, Sixth Floor, Castle House,
75–76 Wells Street, London W1T 3QH

1 3 5 7 9 10 8 6 4 2

Designed and typeset by Jerry Goldie
Printed and bound by Imago in China

British Library Cataloguing-in-Publication Data Available

ISBN: 978-1-907486-53-1

www.watkinspublishing.co.uk

# New World Order

'[George H.W.] Bush said: "My vision of a New World Order foresees a United Nations with a revitalized peace-keeping function."…. The term "New World Order," in the sense that Bush used it, meant that American superpowerdom would underpin a peace enforced by the UN, and would police it. During the 1990s the term came to have a second meaning: a world government imposed by the Syndicate, led by "Rothschilds" and "Rockefellers," which would corner all the world's natural resources including gas and oil, convey them through pipelines to ports and sell them round the world. Piping would replace arms sales as the principal way of raising revenue for Syndicate multinationals.' (pp.128–9)

# World State

'If it was always Obama's intention to take the eighth path rather than the seventh path – the path of bringing the prospect of the American Dream to all humankind rather than handing the world to commercial *élites* for their own gain – then he would have to bring in a World State that, although technically (seman-tically) a new world order, would be very different from the Syndicate's New World Order…. The concept of a World State has emerged from the attempts to create a New World Order by the Syndicate…. It has become increasingly clear that there needs to be a supranational authority with legal power to declare war illegal…. A new supranational authority should confine itself to limited federal goals and leave the day-to-day activities of civilizations and nation-states as they are…. The supranational authority would secure peace; provide access to the Earth's natural resources and energy without Syndicate manipulation; have a unified approach toward environmental problems; work to end disease and famine; provide financial stability without Syndicate manipulation; and eliminate poverty in an affordable way…. These last two goals can be afforded out of a "peace dividend" that would accrue with the abolition of war.' (pp.184, 185, 190–1)

'America must choose one of three courses after this war: narrow nationalism, which inevitably means the ultimate loss of our own liberty; international imperialism, which means the sacrifice of some other nation's liberty; or the creation of a world in which there shall be an equality of opportunity for every race and every nation. I am convinced the American people will choose, by overwhelming majority, the last of these courses.'

Wendell Willkie, *One World*, 1943[1]

To the memory of the philosopher Immanuel Kant, who dreamt of perpetual peace and knew it could not be achieved in his lifetime; to Francis Fukuyama, who will see that I have located an unenduring World State within the rise and fall of civilizations; and to President Obama, who has it in his power to request the UN General Assembly to vote to set up a World Constitutional Convention that will establish a partial World State and the secret American Dream (see p.229).

# CONTENTS

# LIBERTY'S DREAM

Liberty has come to represent much of what America stands for. Her statue was unveiled in the US in 1886 as a gift from the people of revolutionary France to the people of revolutionary America. 'Miss Liberty' or 'Lady Liberty' is a representation of Libertas, ancient Rome's goddess of freedom from slavery, oppression, and tyranny.

She wears a Roman *stola* (a long outer garment) and a Roman facial expression. Her head is modeled on the Graeco-Roman sun-god Helios, a version of the sun-god Apollo as shown on a marble tablet in the archaeological Museum of Corinth, Greece. She has the seven-spiked rays of Sol's radiate solar crown. These seven spikes represent the seven seas and seven continents.[1] She is moving forward. Her right foot is raised and her left foot tramples broken shackles.[2] Her torch represents enlightenment, and the keystone she holds represents knowledge and shows the date of the United States' Declaration of Independence in Roman numerals: July IV, MDCCLXXVI.

The Colossus of Rhodes, erected between 292 and 280BCE and one of the Seven Wonders of the World, also represented the sun-god Helios.[3] It is shown in a 16th-century engraving by Maerten van Heemskerck holding a torch[4] to guide ships into harbor in the dark. The torch in this engraving was based on what is believed to be the genuine dedication text for the Colossus of Rhodes: 'To you, O Sun, the people of Dorian Rhodes set up this bronze statue reaching to Olympus, when they had pacified the waves of war and crowned their city with the spoils taken from the enemy. Not only over the seas but also on land did they kindle the lovely torch of freedom and independence.'[5]

Like the Colossus of Rhodes (if this dedication is genuine), Liberty functioned as a lighthouse, and from 1886 to 1902 it shone an electric light that could be seen on board ship for 24 miles (39km). One and a half times the height of the Colossus of Rhodes – 151 feet (46m) from base to torch as against 107 feet (33m) – Liberty was the first image that immigrants saw as they steamed into New York to begin their new lives. To them, Liberty was a guarantee of personal liberty from oppression, of a prospect of freedom. Emma Lazarus wrote these haunting lines in her sonnet, 'The New Colossus,' which was written during fund-raising for the pedestal of the Statue of Liberty in 1883:

> 'Not like the brazen giant of Greek fame,
> With conquering limbs astride from land to land;
> Here at our sea-washed, sunset gates shall stand
> A mighty woman with a torch, whose flame
> Is the imprisoned lightning, and her name
> Mother of Exiles. From her beacon-hand
> Glows world-wide welcome; her mild eyes command
> The air-bridged harbor that twin cities frame.
> "Keep, ancient lands, your storied pomp!" cries she
> With silent lips. "Give me your tired, your poor,
> Your huddled masses yearning to breathe free,
> The wretched refuse of your teeming shore.
> Send these, the homeless, tempest-tossed to me,
> I lift my lamp beside the golden door!"'

The first two lines refer to the Colossus of Rhodes. The bronze plaque in the pedestal omits the comma after 'Keep' in line 9.[6]

The 'American Dream' is one of prosperity for all within the American democracy. For many it has been the prospect of an escape from misery and persecution in Europe and of a new life in which they would be able to stand on their own feet. The phrase was first expressed in 1931 by James Truslow Adams, who in his book *The Epic of America* wrote: 'The American Dream is that dream of a land in which life should be better and richer and fuller for every man, with opportunity for each according to opportunity or achievement.... It is not a dream of motor cars and high wages merely, but a dream of social order in which each man and each woman shall be able to attain to the fullest stature of which they are innately capable, and be recognized by others for what they are, regardless of the fortuitous circumstances of birth or position.'[7]

It has been the dream of countless immigrants who came to the United States in the 19th and 20th centuries seeking a prosperous life. It looked back to the 1776 Declaration of Independence, which proclaimed all men's 'inalienable rights' including 'Life, Liberty and the pursuit of Happiness.' For many, seeing the Statue of Liberty as their ship approached American shores represented a fresh start in a free society where all had the opportunity to succeed, regardless of their past. For arriving immigrants, Liberty with her torch embodied the American Dream.

The American Dream emerged during bouts of expansion which culminated in the rise of the United States to superpowerdom and a global role. Not since the Roman Empire has one nation-state dominated the world to such an extent. There is a feeling abroad that America controls an empire, defined by the *Concise Oxford Dictionary* as 'an extensive group of states or countries under a single supreme authority, especially an emperor.'

The Greek model of empire which the Athenians put into practice was that of a city-state holding colonies in subjugation. The Roman model of empire was more ecumenical. It spread the benefits of Roman citizenship without enslaving the inhabitants of colonies. The American model of empire was the Roman one rather than the Greek one, under a presidency akin to the Roman Caesars' imperial rule. It is no accident that Liberty is based on a Roman lady, Libertas, rather than a Greek one.

Yet empire is what the Founding Fathers stood against. They proclaimed liberty in the Declaration of Independence. This meant liberty from religious persecution, the principle that drove the Separatists to board the *Mayflower* in 1620, and liberty from the colonialism of the British Empire. From the outset, the United States sided with revolutionary countries that opposed colonialism. One of these was France, which fraternally gave the United States the Statue of Liberty. Having crowned Napoleon Emperor in 1804 and having been under a Second Empire from 1852 until 1870, France was now a Third Republic and against all emperors, who were regarded as arbitrary despots. (It should be pointed out that the French Third Republic went on to establish colonial rule in Tunisia in 1881 and Indo-China in 1884–7.)

Today the United States sides with the oppressed and downtrodden, the victims of tyrannical empires. Ideologically, the United States commands an anti-empire:

a network of nation-states that have broken free from their colonial masters. And so Donald Rumsfeld, US Secretary of Defense, when questioned by an *Al-Jazeera* correspondent, stated on February 25, 2003: 'We're not a colonial power. We've never been a colonial power. We don't take our force and go around the world and try to take other people's real estate or other people's resources, their oil. That's just not what the United States does. We never have and we never will. That's not how democracies behave. That's how an empire-building Soviet Union behaved but that's not how the United States behaves.'[8] He also asserted on April 29, 2003: 'We don't seek empires, we're not imperialistic, we never have been, I can't imagine why you'd even ask the question.'[9]

President George W. Bush agreed: 'We're not an imperial power, as nations such as Japan and Germany can attest. We are a liberating power, as nations in Europe and Asia can attest, as well.'[10] Nevertheless, the fact remains that Liberty runs what can only be described as a loose, Roman-style empire: 'an extensive group of states.'

Whether or not America has a formal empire, it has undergone a number of expansions during its growth. Each one is a strand, and they appear to be intertwined like seven strands of spaghetti tangled in a small bowl. Each strand is actually a path, and now America has reached a crossroads. President Obama has tried to bring change in place of the policies of the Bush era. Yet there is a profound sense in the world that no one is sure where America is going, what the future will bring.

What should America's direction be now? This book is about the course America will take – has begun to take – in the immediate future. It is about what America will do next and how it can benefit all the world's citizens. To understand the new direction America is taking we need to consider the past direction, or differing directions, it has already taken, the route which has brought us to this point. We need to review America's past dealings with the outside world. We will then see that its next direction is emerging both as a reaction against, and as a continuity with, what has already happened.

The first three parts of this book identify seven bouts or strands of expansion that are behind the rise of the United States to superpowerdom. Each has its own individual characteristic, and each is of a different kind. Part One tells when Liberty's empire apparently began: in the late 1890s when the US founded a colonial empire with what was widely understood to be Christian zeal and an embracing of what Kipling called the 'White Man's burden.' It carries us forward to America's subsequent isolationism and interventionism and on to America's Cold-War hegemony. Part Two tells when Liberty's empire really began: further back in time with the federal unification that was encouraged by Freemasonry, and the ensuing westward expansion that built the United States. Part Three brings the story up to date by focusing on America's world empire and supremacy, which have been covertly backed by commercial *élites*.

Each of the seven bouts of expansion represented an attempted direction. The seven expansions are like the seven radiate spikes of Liberty's crown. These seven directions can all in theory be continued by the Obama Administration. Examining each in turn will make it clear why a new direction is needed now, one that leads on from these past efforts.

It is as though America has reached a 'double crossroads' shaped like an eight-pointed star. There is such a place in Denmark, in the Gribskov Forest not far from Copenhagen, where eight radial paths meet at Stjernen. ('Stjerne' is 'star' in Danish, and associations include 'many-pointed star' and 'eight-pointed asterisk'.) The paths were made for huntsmen from 1680 to 1690 by King Christian V, who had spent time at the court of Louis XIV, the 'Sun-King,' at Versailles.

The Danish philosopher Søren Kierkegaard wrote of the intersection in *Stages on Life's Way* (1845):

> 'There is in Gribskov a place called the Eight Roads' Nook; only he finds it who seeks it worthily, for no map gives it. The name itself also seems to hold a contradiction, for how can the collision of eight roads make a nook?... It really has eight roads, but is still very lonesome; off-place, hidden.... Eight roads and no traveler!'[11]

The intersection inspired the choice in *Either/Or: A Fragment of Life*, which came out two years earlier. I tried to find the spot in 1987, but discovered that the intersection amid high beeches can only be reached on foot and is not marked on most maps.

If one imagines that seven of the radial forest paths symbolize the seven directions America has tried, the question is: where does the eighth way lead? This is addressed in Part Four of this book, where it becomes clear that distancing ourselves from the directions of the past helps us to identify America's future direction.

I was impelled to chart America's future course by my research when owner of Otley Hall in Suffolk, England, where the 1607 Jamestown Settlement is thought to have been planned. In May 2001 I was visited by the First Lady of Virginia, Roxane Gilmore, who had led some 20 Americans to Ipswich to request that Jamestown and Ipswich become sister-cities. That evening I was invited to meet her husband, the Governor of Virginia, at the US Embassy in London. I gave him a copy of my study of 25 civilizations, *The Fire and the Stones*, to present to George W. Bush. In my dedication to President Bush at the front of the book I wrote that the 21st century belonged to America. I knew exactly what I meant. I did not mean that it belonged to American supremacy and the pre-emptive strikes that succeeded 9/11, which stunned the world just over three months later.

A few years later my book *The Secret Founding of America*, this book's prede- cessor, narrated the planting and founding of America to coincide with the 400th anniversary of the Jamestown Settlement in 2007. It followed the inter- play between early Christianity and Freemasonry in the growth of the North-American civilization, which culminated in attempts by self-interested *élites* to found a federal New World Order in our time and absorb civilizations and nation-states, including the United States itself. I subsequently wrote my second poetic epic, *Armageddon*, about the War on Terror and the New World Order's commercial gain from US military activities. I followed this up with *The World Government*, a philosophical approach in the tradition of Kant's *Perpetual Peace*. It advanced a political Universalism that would counterbalance and control the *élites* pressing for a New World Order. I became convinced that America has a hitherto-undisclosed agenda, which will soon be revealed and to which my present title alludes.

It is completely understandable that in his first year of office Obama did not fully disclose his program. Any president elected on a ticket of 'change' would have done the same. For a new president to carry a program through requires the win- ning of substantial support, precise timing, and political savvy. Obama's way forward has been necessarily enmeshed in the dictates of political strategy. A program cannot be fully blazoned across the US press until mid-term has been reached, by which time the necessary support can be presumed to have been built.

The word 'secret' in my title in no way impugns Obama or suggests underhand deviousness on his part. The *Concise Oxford Dictionary* defines 'secret' as 'kept or meant to be kept private, unknown or hidden from all but a few,' and the practical requirements of political strategy have meant that a full understanding of the ambitious breadth of his way forward has been confined to a few within his inner circle. (The same was true of the 'neoconservative' program during Bush's presidency.)

My title also alludes to, and turns around, the title of *The Secret Founding of America*. In that work 'secrecy' had a negative connotation: the secrecy of Freemasonry's hidden role in the founding of the federal Union and of *élites* with Masonic links pressing to hijack America's destiny for their own ends. In this work 'secrecy' has a positive connotation: a hitherto-much-hinted-at but less-than-fully-disclosed role that when fully disclosed (as we shall see in Part Four) will receive the admiration and applause of the entire world. Between them the titles of the two books convey how a secret agenda in its negative sense is being transmuted into an ambitious ideal for all humankind that is still understandably undeclared, veiled in secrecy in a positive sense.

To many observers America's current stance is bewildering. While writing my previous works I saw that their bewilderment had much to do with the contradictions of the seven past paths in relation to America's coming destination.

My cumulative consideration of America's role in these works placed me in the center of the 'Star crossroads,' and I researched the way forward Obama is planning for America. I was fascinated that Obama has said, 'No one nation can or should try to dominate another nation.'[12] And yet Obama sent 30,000 additional troops to fight in Afghanistan.

In the work I presented to President Bush, *The Fire and the Stones*, I see each civilization in terms of a rainbow which appears to have seven bands. These bands are only differentiated through the refraction of light in raindrops, and in the human eye, as they are part of a unified spectrum. In that work, I saw these seven bands as the essential ingredients of every civilization: the vision of reality that inspires the genesis of each civilization; alternative inspirations; a civilization's religion, which eventually degenerates into coteries; the stones (temples, cathedrals, mosques) which are inspired by the vision of reality and are later destroyed; the peoples who join the civilization and contribute to its cultural unity, and the seceders who later cause cultural disintegration; a foreign military threat which brings foreign cults; and the secularizing State which expands into empire.

When I was writing this passage in *The Fire and the Stones*, which identified 25 civilizations, I had a crystal hanging in my window and in the morning sun it cast

THE SECRET AMERICAN DREAM

25 rainbows on my desk and carpet, which represented my 25 civilizations and their sevenfold bands. In the North-American civilization it is possible to perceive these bands as also representing the seven bouts of expansion since the planting of the first settlements. The eighth band is the entire unified spectrum which embraces all seven differentiated components: the unified rainbow that thrusts upward toward the arch, as does the North-American civilization now.

I see the Statue of Liberty, the Colossus that is America, standing beside the upward curve of a rainbow which represents the apparently differentiated seven directions the North-American civilization has tried. Liberty's empire spans the globe, but has been notoriously difficult to describe. In fact many authors describe just one of the bands of the unified rainbow. I resolved to see Liberty's rainbow as a whole and to follow its rise.

To define America's new direction we must first distinguish it from America's past directions. To see America's way forward we must go back to when Liberty's empire apparently began, somewhere near the base of the curve of the thrusting North-American civilization; distinguish its expansion; identify America's mission; and chart its stunning and continuing rise.

# PART ONE

# When Liberty's Empire *Apparently* Began: The Rise of American Hegemony

# CHAPTER 1

# LIBERTY'S COLONIAL EMPIRE

In any consideration of the future of the *Pax Americana* and of America's global empire in the 21st century one fundamental question must be asked: can America ever be said to have had an empire, and if so when did it begin?

The generally accepted story of America's expansion into empire is that it began with the Spanish–American War of 1898. By then several of Europe's powers already had empires – the British, the French, the Germans, the Belgians, the Dutch, the Italians, and earlier the Portuguese and the Spanish, the Austro-Hungarians, the Russians, and the Ottoman Turks – and the notion of empire was firmly entrenched in the international arena.

This notion had met with the disapproval of libertarian Americans. Before the 1890s most Americans believed, as they had since the Revolution, that America should remain aloof from European affairs. The Revolution and War of Independence had expelled the British from the United States and most Americans were content to benefit from America's economic growth since the Civil War in a mindset of isolation, and ignore Europe's imperial ambitions.

## The Spanish–American War of 1898

By 1898 a depression ended that had left many US farmers in distress, and industrialists and farmers alike were looking for new outlets for industrial and agricultural production. Darwin's theory of the survival of the fittest, a term he took from Herbert Spencer, referred to the survival of those best adapted to, and therefore most fit for, their environment. The theory was widely misinterpreted as referring to the strongest, and a feeling spread in some parts of the United States that the outside world was a jungle in which only the strongest would survive. The United States should therefore build up its sea power and develop a large navy that had bases throughout the world.

Religious leaders saw an opportunity to export Christianity to remote Pacific territories and they promoted Christian universalism in the belief that Americans should 'take up the White Man's burden.' ('The White Man's Burden' was the title of a poem by Kipling about the duty of white men to civilize those less fortunate; the poem's subtitle related to the Pacific: 'The United States and the Philippine Islands.') They felt that the US Navy should carry Christianity and America's superior culture to backward peoples.

Christianity had been brought to America as Catholicism, Anglicanism, and Puritanism by the first settlers, and had been transmuted into evangelical Protestantism by the Great Awakening of the 1740s and by later evangelical developments. America had a new messianic Christianity to spread throughout the world.

## Cuba

There had been clamor for intervention in Spanish-ruled Cuba since 1895. The depression had caused a decline in Cuban sugar exports to the United States and Cuban rebels had attempted a revolution against Spanish rule in that year. The Spanish clamped down, and Cuban refugees to the US circulated stories of Spanish atrocities. The United States was naturally on the side of the Cuban revolutionaries, who yearned for liberty from the Spanish Empire, and there was widespread support for intervention.

In December 1897 the US battleship *Maine* was sent to Havana Harbor to 'protect US citizens and property.' On February 15, 1898, an explosion sank the USS *Maine* in Havana Harbor; 266 Americans were killed and a further eight subsequently died from injuries.[1]

A US naval court of inquiry later found that the explosion had been caused by a submarine mine. It was suggested that the battleship had been sabotaged by the Spanish, and soon the incident was widely blamed on Spain.

On April 9, Spain announced an armistice. However, the US declared Cuba's right to independence and demanded Spain's withdrawal. In mid-April Congress authorized President William McKinley, who had taken office in March 1897, to

3

use the armed forces to expel the Spanish from Cuba. Spain broke off diplomatic relations with the US and on April 23 declared war. On April 25 the US Congress declared that a state of war had existed between the US and Spain since April 20.[2]

So began the Spanish–American War of 1898. One of the US's principal objectives was to win control of Spanish possessions in the Caribbean – Cuba and Puerto Rico – and in the Pacific: the Philippines and Guam.[3] On April 27, US ships bombarded the Spanish fortifications at Matanzas Bay on Cuba's north coast.

The US Army had been weakened by the Civil War and had little manpower. President McKinley put out a call for 1,250 volunteers to fight for the United States. An American expeditionary force of 1,060 volunteers and 1,258 horses and mules – the first US Volunteer Cavalry, a regiment that soon came to be known as the 'Rough Riders' – made its way to Tampa, Florida, bound for Cuba. In fact four of the twelve companies and almost all the horses and mules were left behind at Tampa. Those who traveled were led by Lieutenant-Colonel Theodore Roosevelt.

In May 1898 a Spanish fleet under Admiral Pascual Cervera was located in Santiago harbor on the southern coast of Cuba. US naval squadrons under Rear Admiral William T. Sampson and Commodore Winfield S. Schley blockaded the harbor entrance, and US troops including the Rough Riders landed east of the city and fought battles at El Caney and San Juan Hill on July 1.

On July 3 Admiral Cervera tried to sail his squadron out of the harbor and came under heavy fire from the US fleet. His ships were beached, and many were burned or sunk. Two weeks later Spain surrendered Santiago de Cuba. On July 16 an armistice was signed by the US and Spanish forces at the Arbol de La Paz, a large ceiba tree. The city surrendered to General William Shafter on July 17.

The US naval victory off Cuba ensured that the Spanish ceased to oppose the US Navy in the New World. The US Navy's reputation was now very high. However, the Spanish–American War was not over yet.

### Guam

Guam had been under Spanish control since 1668 but had recently been neglected by the Spanish. The captain of the cruiser USS *Charleston*, then in Honolulu en route to Manila, was brought sealed orders from the US Navy Department on the SS *City of Pekin*.

The orders said: 'On your way, you are hereby directed to stop at the Spanish Island of Guam. You will use such force as may be necessary to capture the port of Guam, making prisoners of the governor and other officials and any armed force that may be there. You will also destroy any fortifications on said island and any Spanish naval vessels that may be there, or in the immediate vicinity. These operations at the Island of Guam should be very brief and should not occupy more than one or two days.'

Captain Henry Glass arrived off Guam on June 20, and noticed that the only ship in the harbor was a Japanese trading vessel. There were no Spanish ships. The inhabitants gathered on the shores of Piti and gazed at the cruiser and its three accompanying transports. The *Charleston* fired thirteen times at the ancient Spanish fortress. There was no return of fire.

On shore, Captain Pedro Duarte Anducar of the Spanish Marine Corps remarked that the cruiser must be saluting the fort. He sent a messenger to the Spanish governor, Juan Marina, to send artillery to Piti so that he could return the salute. Meanwhile he and a few others, including an interpreter, put out in a boat and climbed aboard the cruiser to welcome the visitors.

Captain Glass told them that war had been declared between the US and Spain and that they were now prisoners-of-war. Shocked, the party went into the captain's cabin to discuss the surrender of the island.[4]

The Spanish governor sent a letter to Piti, saying: 'If you give any assistance to the American men of war, you will be executed tomorrow morning on the beach.' He also sent a letter to Glass agreeing that the island should be occupied by the Americans.

Realizing that the Spanish governor was trying to trick him, Glass resorted to a counter-trick. He issued an ultimatum, landed at the harbor of Piti under a flag of truce and gave the Spanish governor half an hour to reply. He then took the Spanish officials prisoner, and flew the American flag over the fortification. The Spanish governor protested that he had been tricked by the flag of truce.

Meanwhile, a US troop convoy bound for the Philippines had captured the Spanish-owned Wake Island on July 4, 1898.

### Hawaii

The American–Spanish fighting off the Philippines had made Hawaii's strategic location for warfare in the Philippines important to US interests.

In early 1893 the United States had approved the overthrow of the queen of Hawaii by local revolutionaries. It had resulted in a provisional government ruling the Hawaiian islands in transition to an expected US annexation. President Benjamin Harrison sent a treaty of annexation to the Senate. His successor, President Grover Cleveland withdrew it and the revolutionaries formed an independent Republic of Hawaii. It voluntarily joined the United States in 1898 with full citizenship for its residents.

On July 7, 1898, Cleveland's successor McKinley signed the Newlands Resolution (named after Congressman Francis G. Newlands), officially annexing Hawaii to the United States. A formal ceremony was held on the steps of the Iolani Palace, Honolulu, during which the Hawaiian flag was lowered and the American flag raised.

The annexation, which took place through legislation rather than warfare, had been expected since the overthrow of Queen Liliuokalani in 1893. However, Hawaii did not become a state in the Union until March 18, 1959.

## Puerto Rico

As soon as Cuba surrendered the United States dispatched its fleet to Puerto Rico, Spain's last island in the Caribbean.

On March 10, two prominent leaders of the Puerto-Rican section of the Cuban Revolutionary Party had written to US President McKinley requesting that Puerto Rico should be included in any intervention that was planned for Cuba. They provided the US Government with information on the Spanish military presence on the island.[5]

Puerto Rico was protected by Spanish ships. On May 12, 1898 the US Navy had bombarded the capital, San Juan (not to be confused with San Juan Hill in Cuba), and imposed a blockade on the harbor. This marked the First Battle of San Juan.

On June 22 two Spanish ships, the cruiser *Isabel II* and the destroyer *Terror*, had opened fire on the USS *Saint Paul* in an unsuccessful attempt to break the blockade in what came to be known as the Second Battle of San Juan. In a Third Battle of San Juan on June 28 two American cruisers fought a squadron of Spanish warships.

A US land offensive began on July 25, when an American expeditionary force of 3,300 infantry soldiers landed at Guánica. They fought off the Spanish at Yauco and on August 1 seized control of Fajardo. On August 5 they took Guayama after a battle and advanced to Coamo. They captured the Silva Heights near San Germán and defeated the Spanish at Asomante. Fighting continued until August 13.

*The Philippines*

Meanwhile Commodore George Dewey had been ordered to leave Hong Kong with his Asiatic squadron 'to capture or destroy the Spanish fleet,' which was then in Philippine waters.

On May 1, 1898, Dewey fought a Spanish flotilla in Manila harbor in the Philippine Islands. The Spanish fleet was anchored in the harbor, and in the engagement there were 381 Spanish casualties against fewer than ten Americans. Manila was bombarded and was eventually occupied by the US Army on August 13.

The Battle of Manila Bay had finally turned the United States into a naval power. The Spanish–American War was completely over when Manila fell.

# Peace Agreement

On August 13, President McKinley and French Ambassador Jules Cambon, acting for the Spanish Government, signed an armistice whereby Spain relinquished its sovereignty over Cuba, Puerto Rico, and the Philippines.

Unaware that a peace protocol (a preliminary peace treaty) had been signed between Spain and the United States in Washington DC the previous day, Admiral Dewey and the US commanders began a bombardment of Fort San Antonio de Abad in the Philippines at 9:30 a.m. Full surrender took place on August 14.

A more detailed agreement was worked out in Paris in October. Under the terms of the Treaty of Paris, Spain withdrew from Cuba, recognized Cuba's independence, and ceded Puerto Rico and Guam. Along with Guam Spain ceded the Northern Mariana Islands.[6]

The Treaty of Paris also stipulated that the Philippines should be ceded to the United States. There was a dispute as to how this should be achieved. US businessmen wanted to acquire the entire Philippine archipelago and make it a base for trade with the countries of the Far East, and despite Spanish objections there was clamor for the US flag to be flown in Manila. In the end President McKinley forced Spain to sell the Philippines to the United States for $20 million.

The Treaty of Paris was signed on December 16, 1898, and marked the end of the Spanish Empire in the Caribbean and the Pacific.

America's empire in the Caribbean and Pacific, which was principally wrested from Spain in the late 1890s, also included a number of island groups, and it is worth presenting the full picture:

- Cuba (1899–1902, 1906–8) – under US protection via the 1898 Treaty of Paris with Spain, now independent except for the lease of Guantanamo Bay naval base;
- Guam – acquired in 1898 via the Treaty of Paris, now an organized, unincorporated US 'territory' (a region under the jurisdiction of the US federal government);
- Hawaii – annexed July 7, 1898 but became a 'territory' in 1900 and eventually a state in 1959;
- Puerto Rico – acquired in 1898 via the Treaty of Paris, now a US commonwealth (an insular dependent territory that is organized and self-governing but not incorporated within the United States, whereas a 'state' is incorporated and a 'territory' is subject to US jurisdiction and sovereignty, has delegated powers, but lacks full protection of the US Constitution);
- The Philippines (1898–1946) – acquired by the US via the 1898 Treaty of Paris, which led to the Philippine–American War (see below, p.10); now independent after Treaty of Manila (1946);
- American Samoa – acquired as a *de facto* colony and established in December 1899 by the Treaty of Berlin between the United States, Britain, and Germany; now an officially unorganized, although self-governing, US territory;
- United States Minor Outlying Islands – eleven insular, largely uninhabited US possessions acquired from Spain between 1856 and 1912, including the Spanish Wake Island in 1898, all of which are now unincorporated territories of the United States (i.e. not within the limits of any state and not admitted as states) except for Palmyra Atoll, the sole incorporated territory of the United States (i.e. part of the United States and having an organized government, authorized by an Organic Act passed by the US Congress);
- Northern Mariana Islands – ceded by Spain in 1898; became a US commonwealth on March 24, 1976, as the Mariana Islands;
- Panama Canal Zone – leased 1903–79 under the Hay–Bunau-Varilla Treaty; part of Panama since 1999 following the Torrijos–Carter Treaties;
- US Virgin Islands – purchased from Denmark in 1917 when the United States feared the islands might be seized and turned into a German submarine base; now an organized, unincorporated US territory.

## Reluctant Benevolent Imperialists

Now anti-imperialist isolationists opposed American domination in the Caribbean and Pacific. They complained that America should never control and govern distant alien peoples such as the inhabitants of the Philippines as the American Revolution had been founded on the right to self-determination and liberty from foreign colonialism.

The Anti-Imperialist League was founded on June 15, 1898 in Boston, Massachusetts to oppose the acquisition of the Philippines by the United States. Supporters of the League argued that imperialist policy countered the political doctrines of the 1776 Declaration of Independence, Washington's 1796 Farewell Address, and Lincoln's 1863 Gettysburg Address.[7]

The League can have swung enough votes in the Senate to defeat the Treaty of Paris. However, the leader of the Democrats, William Jennings Bryan, urged his party to support the Treaty so that he could make imperialism the main issue of the 1900 presidential campaign. This strategy backfired on Bryan as McKinley was re-elected.

In fact, imperialism had more or less run its course. McKinley's administration took the view that the Constitution only applied to America's insular possessions in a limited way, and its position was confirmed by the Supreme Court. There were immediate moves to dissolve the new empire. The American people could now claim to be reluctant imperialists.

### Cuba, Hawaii, Puerto Rico

Under the Teller Amendment to the war resolution, which had been enacted on April 19, 1898, Congress declared that the United States would not annex Cuba. Congress did annex the Hawaiian Islands on July 7, 1898, as we have seen, but made it a 'territory' in 1900, so that it was only within the American colonial empire for a short while. Puerto Rico was given limited self-government in 1900. Under the 1917 Jones Act (Puerto Rico) it became a territory and its inhabitants received full American citizenship. Puerto Rico's self-government was limited by the US-appointed governor's veto.

## The Philippines

The American attitude toward the Philippines at first seemed more ambivalent. President McKinley made a direct appeal to the people of the Philippines in a proclamation of December 21, 1898:

> 'It should be the earnest wish and paramount aim of the military administration to win the confidence, respect, and affection of the inhabitants of the Philippines by assuring them in every possible way that full measure of individual rights and liberties which is the heritage of free peoples, and by proving to them that the mission of the United States is one of benevolent assimilation substituting the mild sway of justice and right for arbitrary rule. In the fulfilment of this high mission, supporting the temperate administration of affairs for the greatest good of the governed, there must be sedulously maintained the strong arm of authority, to repress disturbance and to overcome all obstacles to the bestowal of the blessings of good and stable government upon the people of the Philippine Islands under the free flag of the United States.'[8]

'Benevolent assimilation' was what America claimed to be practicing, replacing arbitrary rule with mild justice and the free way of life of America: Liberty's values of individual rights and liberties. However, this benevolence appeared to be contradicted by events on the ground.

The Treaty of Paris had transferred Philippine sovereignty from Spain to the United States, and as we have seen Manila had been occupied by the United States on August 13. However, the transfer was not accepted by the revolutionary leaders who controlled the country outside Manila. The young revolutionary leader, Emilio Aguinaldo returned from exile in Hong Kong and led a bloody war between Filipino revolutionaries who had fought Spanish colonial rule since 1896, and the US Army. There was shooting on the outskirts of Manila from time to time.

In May 1899 Corporal Sam Gillis wrote to his parents:

> 'We make everyone get into his house by seven p.m. and we only tell a man once. If he refuses we shoot him. We killed over 300 natives the first night. They tried to set the town on fire. If they fire a shot

from a house we burn the house down and every house near it, and shoot the natives, so they are pretty quiet in town now.'[9]

During the next spring, American troops thrust into the Central Luzon Plain and drove Aguinaldo into the northern mountains. Aguinaldo was captured in 1901 and persuaded to appeal to Filipinos to stop fighting and accept American sovereignty.

There continued to be guerrilla warfare in the Philippines, and there was fighting on the island of Samar in 1901. Enraged by a guerrilla massacre of American troops, General Jacob F. Smith launched a ferocious campaign of retaliation.

In 1901 General Smith issued orders: 'I want no prisoners. I wish you to kill and burn, the more you kill and burn the better it will please me. I want all persons killed who are capable of bearing arms in actual hostilities against the United States.' Major Littleton 'Tony' Waller demanded 'to know the limit of age to respect.' He was told, 'Ten years of age.' Everyone over ten was to be killed.[10] Smith was subsequently court-martialed and forced to retire.

On December 7, 1901, General J. Franklin Bell proclaimed: 'The United States Government, disregarding many provocations to do otherwise, has for three years exercised an extraordinary forbearance and patiently adhered to a magnanimous and benevolent policy towards the inhabitants of the territory occupied by this brigade.'[11]

However, in 1900 Mark Twain, a leader and founding member of the Anti-Imperialist League, wrote:

> 'I have read carefully the Treaty of Paris and I have seen that we do not intend to free, but to subjugate the people of the Philippines. We have gone there to conquer not to redeem. It should, it seems to me, be our pleasure and duty to make those people free, and let them deal with their own domestic questions in their own way. And so I am an anti-imperialist. I am opposed to having the eagle put its talons on any other land.'[12]

As soon as the Philippine insurrection ended in 1901, the Philippines were granted partial self-government under the Philippine Organic Act of 1902, and this became almost complete home rule under the 1916 Philippine Autonomy Act (Jones Law).

After 1902 the Americans saw the Filipino guerrillas as bandits. A thousand guerrillas fought until late 1903 under Simeón Ola. Guerrillas resisted the US Army on Samar from 1904 to 1906, burning villages that had been pacified. In Patangas Province south of Manila, guerrillas commanded by Macario Sakay evaded capture until 1906. From then on America controlled the Philippines despite having granted partial self-government, and possessed the islands until 1946.

Historians are divided as to how benevolent this early US imperialism was. The military historian Max Boot proposes that the United States altruistically went to war with Spain to liberate Cubans, Puerto Ricans, and Filipinos from Spanish tyranny.[13] He argues that in the Philippines the United States set up a constabulary, worked with local officials and made a priority of holding fair elections 'because once a democratically-elected government was installed, the Americans felt they could withdraw.'[14]

The historian Samuel Flagg Benis, on the other hand, argues that expansionism during the Spanish–American War was a short-lived imperialistic impulse and 'a great aberration in American history,' a very different form of territorial growth from that of earlier US history.[15]

The US armed forces saw themselves as benevolently bringing democracy and freedom to the Philippines, and their peaceful occupation (as they saw it) was jarred by personal encounters between colonists and natives bent on violent resistance. Many in the US armed forces seemed to have been unprepared for, and bewildered by, the uprising. The Filipinos had opposed the tyrannical Spanish, and must therefore surely side with their liberators. The utter incomprehension, and no doubt naivety, of the US democracy-bringers may explain the angry and violent reaction of generals such as Jacob F. Smith, and may in turn explain how their ideal of benevolence sometimes turned into military suppression.

The United States now applied its aspirations to benevolence and altruism to China. The United States was now a major Pacific power and poised to exploit the Chinese market. However, Britain, France, Russia, and Japan had spheres of influence extending from Manchuria to southern China. On September 6, 1899, Secretary of State John Hay, in a so-called 'Open-Door Note,' asked the powers with interests in China to permit equal trade and investment within their Chinese sphere of influence. The 1900 Chinese Boxer

Rebellion protested at foreign influence. Hay then circulated a second Open-Door Note proclaiming that it was American policy to preserve Chinese territorial and political integrity.

It should be pointed out that the Open-Door Notes and US declarations on Chinese territorial integrity were not completely altruistic. They were at least in part a response to fears that the colonial powers in China would annex their 'spheres of influence' as full-blown colonies. This in turn might restrict the freedom of other nations – particularly the United States – to trade in those regions. US policy in China had a strong element of self-interest in its intentions.

However, the United States never enforced this policy, although it mediated in the Russo-Japanese War of 1905 to protect the Open-Door policy and to maintain a balance of power in the Far East. And in 1915 President Woodrow Wilson intervened to protect Chinese independence from Japan. Under the 1922 Nine-Power Treaty of Washington all nine nation-states with Chinese interests (China, the United States, Japan, Britain, France, Italy, Belgium, the Netherlands, and Portugal) promised to respect the Open-Door policy.

## US Interventions in Latin America

The United States continued to intervene in Latin America for at least another decade following the 1898 Treaty of Paris.

### Panama

The focus now returned to Central America, and to the desirability of cutting a canal to link the Caribbean and the Pacific. Theodore Roosevelt, who became US President in 1901, became convinced that a US-controlled canal across Central America was a vital strategic interest of the United States.

When the USS *Maine* was destroyed in Cuba on February 15, 1898, the USS *Oregon* was dispatched from San Francisco to replace her. The voyage around Cape Horn took 67 days but would have taken only three weeks via Panama – a third of the time. American imperial interests in the Far East made a direct trade route a pressing need, and Americans in the Far East added to the clamor for a canal.

Now Roosevelt reversed an earlier decision to cut a canal in Nicaragua and supported the cutting of a canal across the Panama isthmus.

Under the 1850 Clayton–Bulwer Treaty, the British Government had acquired joint rights with the United States to dig a Panama Canal. Britain surrendered these rights under the 1901 Hay–Pauncefote Treaty. A French company owned a right of way across the isthmus and sold it to the United States. However Colombia, of which Panama was then a part, refused to ratify the 1903 Hay–Herran Treaty between the United States and Colombia, which would have granted the United States a perpetual lease on a six-mile-wide strip across Panama through which a canal could have been constructed.

In 1903 Roosevelt supported a Panamanian revolution engineered by officials of the French company to secure the independence of Panama from Colombia. With support from the US Navy, which sent the USS *Nashville* into Panamanian waters, the Republic of Panama proclaimed its independence on November 3, 1903. Under the Hay–Bunau-Varilla Treaty signed on November 18, 1903, the new republic allowed the United States to control the Panama Canal Zone. Under the terms of this treaty, the US paid $10 million to acquire control of the Zone on February 23, 1904. The Panama Canal was duly constructed and opened in 1914.

While the Panama Canal was being built, the United States was wary of action in Latin America by European powers, particularly the German Empire, which might conflict with American interests in the region. In the early 20th century it therefore began interfering in many Central American and Caribbean republics.

### Venezuela, Dominican Republic
The first was Venezuela. In 1902–3 Britain, Germany, and Italy blockaded Venezuela to recover debts, and the United States forced Germany to allow the Hague Court to adjudicate. The Dominican Republic had defaulted on foreign debt, and from March 30, 1903, to March 28, 1905, the United States occupied the republic and acted as receiver so as to meet outstanding payments.

In 1904 Roosevelt announced a new Latin-American policy in his annual address to Congress: the Americans would take action to ensure that no Latin-American states gave cause for European intervention. This new policy in Latin America extended the Monroe Doctrine of December 2, 1823, which had forbidden European use of force in the New World. The Monroe Doctrine had been invoked in 1845 by President James K. Polk and in 1881 with regard to Panama. This new policy of 1904 was known as the Roosevelt Corollary to the Monroe Doctrine. Roosevelt now announced that 'chronic wrong-doing or an impotence which results in a general loosening of the ties of civilized society may... require intervention by some civilized nation.'[16]

### Santo Domingo, Nicaragua, Cuba

In 1905 Roosevelt intervened in Santo Domingo, the capital of the Dominican Republic, and in two years put the nation's affairs in good order. Shortly after that US Marines landed in Nicaragua to prevent civil war. They ran the country for a while to promote stability in the Caribbean – and the United States was denounced by the Central-American Court of Justice for curtailing Nicaragua's sovereignty. In 1906–9 the United States administered Cuba to prevent a civil war.

Roosevelt's successor, William Howard Taft, previously Roosevelt's Secretary of War, adopted a policy known as 'Dollar Diplomacy' to replace European creditors in the Caribbean with American bankers.[17] In 1913 President Woodrow Wilson agreed to pay reparation to Colombia for US involvement in the Panamanian Revolution. The plan was defeated in the Senate.

### Haiti, Dominican Republic

Wilson promoted a pan-American non-aggression pact but this was opposed by some Latin-American governments. Wilson was concerned to protect American security, and fearing European intervention in chaotic Haiti he imposed a protectorate and pro-American government on the island in 1915. US Marines occupied Haiti and ran it until 1930. In 1916 Wilson then imposed a military occupation on the former Spanish colony of the Dominican Republic. This lasted eight years. He made Nicaragua a protectorate of the United States, and purchased the Danish Virgin Islands for $25 million in 1916 to prevent them from being transferred from Denmark to Germany.

### Mexico

Two years earlier the United States intervened in the Mexican Revolution and occupied the north of Mexico.

A military usurper, Victoriano Huerta, had murdered President Francisco Madero and been recognized by most European governments. President Wilson supported Madero's successor, Venustiano Carranza. US troops seized the port of Veracruz in April 1914 to cut off Huerta's supplies and revenues, and Carranza occupied Mexico City in August 1914.

The revolutionary forces then split into those loyal to Carranza and those who supported his rival, General Pancho Villa. Carranza won the ensuing civil war in the summer of 1915, but Villa then attacked Columbus, New Mexico, on March 9, 1916.

A retaliatory and punitive US expedition under General John J. Pershing pressed deep into Mexico, and there were skirmishes between Mexican and US troops. In April 1917 Wilson recognized Carranza's regime and then ignored all attempts to persuade him to intervene further in Mexico.

The full picture of America's interventions in Latin America is as follows:

- 1901 – the Platt Amendment made Cuba a protectorate of the United States, restricting the Cuban Government's financial freedom and taking Guantanamo Bay as a US base while reserving the right to intervene in Cuban affairs;
- 1903 – US customs receivership in Haiti;
- 1903 – United States backed the independence of Panama from Colombia to build the Panama Canal;
- March 30, 1903–March 28, 1905 – US occupation of the Dominican Republic;
- 1904 – Roosevelt's Corollary to the Monroe Doctrine, stating that the United States would intervene to protect its interests in the Western hemisphere if Latin American governments proved unstable;
- 1905 – US intervention in Santo Domingo;
- March 28, 1905–1941 – US protectorate of Dominican Republic;
- 1906–9 – US military rule over Cuba under Governor Charles Edward Magoon;
- 1909 – United States-backed rebellion in Nicaragua forced the resignation of President José Santos Zelaya;
- 1914–16 – Mexican Revolution, during which US troops occupied the north and Veracruz;
- 1915–34 – US occupation of Haiti;
- 1923–8 – US Marines occupied the main cities of Nicaragua.

The received view, then, is that America's interventions in the Pacific, Caribbean, and Latin America were not inspired by American colonial ambitions, but rather by American impatience at the poor self-government in these regions.

America's growing imperialism was not of the Greek type – Athenian-style control of colonies – which the European nation-states, including Britain, had followed. It was rather of the Roman type: seeking to bring benefits to the world, not aristocratically holding foreign nation-states in bondage for the benefit of the home country but conveying an ecumenical vision, democratically seeking eventual equality for all nation-states so that each became a 'common wealth,' a *res publica*.[18] Liberty's Roman associations can be seen in retrospect to have been extremely appropriate.

America's posture was that while being fundamentally reluctant to intervene in the affairs of other nation-states, it had to step into power vacuums when it felt its way of life was threatened, including its interests invested in the stability of the Panama Canal. This posture was confirmed by the lack of an American standing army in the early 20th century. America in fact decolonized and voluntarily abandoned the Philippines.

By banning further European colonization in the New World and European intervention in Western governments, the Monroe Doctrine had turned the Western hemisphere into a US protectorate. The United States made sure that no European intervention challenged its supremacy in that area. In the first decade of the 20th century, it seemed inconceivable that America would be drawn into intervening in Europe not once, but twice in fairly quick succession.

## CHAPTER 2

# LIBERTY'S INTERRUPTED ISOLATION:

## Interventions in Europe

There is considerable support for the view that the American colonial empire that extended from Puerto Rico to the Philippines and spanned 10,000 miles (16,000km) was reluctant and altruistic, and designed to improve the rights and liberties of the inhabitants rather than bring profit to the mother country.

Such an altruistic view had long been held by Americans, many of whom believed that the whole world should share the benefits of American liberty. America turned away from colonizing the Philippines and swiftly returned to isolationism. America's isolationist mindset was interrupted and finally broken by the foreign interventions in two world wars that gave America control of Europe.

### US Intervention in the First World War

We need to look closely at how the United States was sucked into the First World War.

At its outbreak in 1914, most Americans were neutral and their instinct was to avoid involvement unless American rights and interests were violated. America had historical links with Germany, which had provided the Great Seal of the United States[1] and many immigrants, German Americans whose names were German. President Woodrow Wilson reflected this mood by proclaiming American neutrality in August 1914 and by appealing to Americans two weeks later to be 'impartial in thought as well as in action.'

Initially there was friction between America and the British. The British naval blockade of Germany turned back American exports of food and raw materials bound for Germany. The US State Department protested, and the British Government cited blockade precedents established by the United States during the Civil War.

An Anglo-American agreement was reached under which the United States became the chief provider of food and raw materials for the British and French war machines. The Allied governments borrowed more than $2 billion from the United States to finance this war trade. America would have no difficulty in remaining neutral so long as the war was restricted to the land mass of Europe.

## German Submarine Warfare

However, Germany decided to target Allied shipping – the Allied blockade – with a new weapon: the submarine. In February 1915 the German Admiralty announced that all Allied ships would be torpedoed without warning, including neutral merchant vessels in British waters. Wilson replied that Germany would be held to account if its submarines destroyed any American ships and lives. Germany gave guarantees about American ships, but Americans traveling on Allied ships were still at risk.

Germany attacked Allied shipping. On May 7, 1915, a German submarine sank the British Cunard liner *Lusitania* off the southern coast of Ireland without warning, killing nearly 1,200 passengers including 128 Americans. President Wilson appealed to Germany to halt attacks on unarmed passenger ships on humane grounds. But in August 1915 a German submarine sank the British liner *Arabic*, again without warning. Wilson threatened to break off diplomatic relations with Germany unless such attacks stopped, and Germany promised not to attack unarmed passenger ships without warning.

But in March 1916 a submarine torpedoed a cross-Channel ferry, the twin-screw steamship *Sussex*, drowning approximately 50 people. Wilson again threatened to break off diplomatic relations if Germany did not stop attacking liners and merchantmen without warning, and again Germany promised to comply – so long as the United States forced the British to observe international law in their blockade.

Many Allied ships sailing into American ports were now armed to resist submarine attack. Wilson tried to broker an agreement that such ships would disarm in return for a German promise not to attack them. The British Government rejected this idea. Wilson gave the impression that he would hold Germany to account if any American passenger was killed on armed ships, and there were moves in Congress to ban American citizens from traveling on armed ships, which Germany might consider legitimate targets. In fact, Wilson had not intended to make an issue of armed ships. In December 1915 he called for an expansion of the US armed forces.

In early 1916 he sent his adviser, Colonel House, to Europe to try and negotiate a basis for peace. House had already visited Europe for this purpose at the beginning of 1915, without success. Now the British Government refused to co-operate and intensified its blockade. Wilson became convinced that both sides were fighting for the domination of Europe and for spoils. On December 18, 1916, Wilson asked both sides to state their terms for peace and he called for both sides to attend a peace conference, which he would chair.

Then on January 9, 1917, Germany announced a submarine blockade of Britain. There would be an all-out submarine war against all ships, neutral or armed, to prevent food from reaching Britain. The German Government knew that it was provoking America, but hoped to starve Britain into submission before the United States could mobilize its fleet.

Wilson was forced to end his neutrality by a German blunder. The German Foreign Ministry tried to enlist the support of both Japan and Mexico in the event of America's deciding to enter the war. Germany offered President Carranza of Mexico an inducement: 'An understanding...that Mexico is to reconquer the lost territories in Texas, New Mexico and Arizona.' The German Foreign Minister, Arthur Zimmermann, sent a telegram to his ambassador in Mexico via the State Department's cable system, and it was intercepted by the British, decoded, and passed to the United States. This threat to America's southern states drew Wilson further into the war, and he had to abandon his policy of neutrality.[2]

President Wilson reacted to news of intensified submarine warfare by breaking off diplomatic relations with Germany on 3 February 1917. He said he would only take action if American ships were sunk. In March he armed all American ships to deter submarine attacks. In spite of this, German submarines sank several American ships, and on April 2, 1917, Wilson asked Congress to recognize that the United States and the German Empire were in a state of war. War was declared on April 6, 1917.

From April to December 1917 American mobilization was on a voluntary basis. From December 1917 the US Government took control, nationalizing railroads, establishing a war industries board, rationing food and fuel, building a large fleet, and preventing strikes. The United States declared war on Austria-Hungary, Germany's ally, on December 7, 1917. All opposition to the war was crushed under the Espionage Act of 1917 and the Sedition Act of 1918. The American economy had been prepared for total war.

The American intervention was decisive. US ships helped the British to overcome the submarine blockade by the autumn of 1917. An American Expeditionary Force of 1.2 million men under General Pershing arrived in France by September 1918, tilted the balance on the Western Front, and helped end the war in November 1918, a year earlier than American military planners had expected.

## Peace Settlement

After the war Wilson attempted a peace settlement that would eliminate the causes of future wars and establish machinery to maintain peace. On January 22, 1917, in a speech to the Senate, he had called for 'peace without victory' to be enforced by a 'league of nations' that the United States would join and support. He had failed to persuade Britain and France to support him in issuing a common statement of war aims, to 'make the world safe for democracy.'

On January 8, 1918, in a speech to Congress, Wilson had set out his Fourteen Points. He wanted to replace the diplomacy of alliances that had led to past wars with open diplomacy. He called for: freedom of the seas; a settlement of colonial claims; disarmament; removal of trade barriers; and a league of nations to protect the territorial integrity of member nation-states. There were plans for the restoration of Belgium, help for the Russians in their civil war, an independent Poland, the return of Alsace-Lorraine to France, and self-determination for the Austro-Hungarian and Ottoman peoples.

Germany responded to Wilson's vision. With American troops making headway for the Allies, the German Government appealed to Wilson for an armistice based on the Fourteen Points and other presidential announcements.

The Allies agreed to peace on this basis, but the British would not agree to the freedom of the seas, seeing it as a threat to their naval supremacy which affirmed that 'Britannia rules the waves.' The British and French demanded that Germany should pay reparations for damage to civilian property.

A peace conference opened in Paris in January 1919, and there were demands that Germany should pay the full cost of the war, which Wilson adopted. Wilson had co-operated with the Allies by sending US troops, an American Expeditionary Force, to Russia and Siberia to defend parts of the USSR against Germany and Japan in 1918–20. Wilson prevented the dismemberment of Germany and inserted the Covenant of the League of Nations into the Versailles Treaty.

The Versailles Treaty was presented in the US Senate in July 1919. Speedy ratification was predicted, but 16 isolationist Senators were opposed to American membership of the League of Nations. Then a majority of the Republican Senators, led by Henry Cabot Lodge, added 14 isolationist reservations to the Treaty, including one that stated that the United States had no obligations under Article X of the Covenant, which guaranteed the terrestrial integrity and independence of the League's member nation-states. They insisted that the President must ask Congress for consent to use US armed forces in support of the Covenant.

Wilson said the reservations nullified the Treaty, and in September he toured the West to win support for ratification. The tour ended with Wilson breaking down and suffering a stroke on October 2.

There were now two entrenched and irreconcilable positions – the sick Wilson's and Lodge's – and the two-thirds majority for ratification failed to materialize when the Senate voted on November 19, 1919, and again on March 19, 1920.

Wilson wanted the ensuing presidential campaign to be a referendum on the League of Nations. In fact, the Democrats were beaten by the Republican Warren G. Harding.

## Renewed US Isolationism

In his Inaugural Address, Harding announced that the United States would not be entangled in European affairs, and, distancing himself from the Allies, he made separate peace treaties with Germany, Austria, and Hungary in August 1921.

The United States did not sign the Treaty of Versailles or become a member of the League of Nations. It embarked on 20 years of isolationism. America had won the First World War for the Allies and, refusing to be worried by the Bolshevik threat, had turned round, gone home, and busied itself with the economic prosperity that had returned by 1923 and lasted until the stock-market crash of 1929. Then America was preoccupied with the Great Depression, President F.D. Roosevelt's recovery program, and the New Deal.

On the face of it, America had been drawn into the First World War by the sinking of the *Lusitania* and the German submarine threat to American ships, and by the need to protect its interests against the prospect of German attempts to detach three southern states. America was isolationist and reluctant to become embroiled in Europe once the immediate job of defeating Germany was done. Hence its unwillingness to join the League of Nations, which it had designed, and to follow through Woodrow Wilson's idealistic attempt to secure a peace that would never again be broken. Having won the war, America had already lost the peace.

And yet the events of the Spanish–American War and the First World War had turned America into a great power. As Walter Lippman wrote in 1926: 'We continue to think of ourselves as a kind of great, peaceful Switzerland, whereas we are in fact a great, expanding world power.... Our imperialism is more or less unconscious.'[3] America was already an empire in denial.

The American writer Roland Hugins eloquently stated this denial in 1916:

'The truth is that the United States is the only high-minded Power left in the world. It is the only strong nation that has not entered on a career of imperial conquest and does not want to enter on it.... There is in America little of that spirit of selfish aggression which lies at the heart of militarism. Here alone exists a broad basis for "a new passionate sense of brotherhood, and a new scale of human values." We have a deep abhorrence of war for war's sake; we are not enamored of glamor or glory. We have a strong faith in the principle of self-government. We do not care to dominate alien peoples, white or colored; we do not aspire to be the Romans of tomorrow or the "masters of the world." The idealism of Americans centers in the future of America, wherein we hope to work out those principles of liberty and democracy to which we are committed. This political idealism, this strain of pacifism, this abstinence from aggression and desire to be left alone to work out our own destiny, has been manifest from the birth of the republic. We have not always followed our light, but we have never been utterly faithless to it.'[4]

# US Intervention in the Second World War

We also need to look closely at how America was sucked into the Second World War.

## The End of Neutrality

During the New-Deal years America sought security through isolation. Congress passed neutrality laws which were designed to keep the United States out of any new war. Thus, the Neutrality Act of 1935 banned arms shipments to both aggressor and victim when Italy invaded Ethiopia, and another law of 1936 banned arms shipments to both sides in the Spanish Civil War.

However, President Franklin D. Roosevelt, Theodore Roosevelt's fifth cousin, was alarmed by Japan's conquests in Asia and began rebuilding the US Navy in 1934. When Japan invaded north China in 1937 Roosevelt did not proclaim neutrality and munitions were sold to both sides. In December 1937, Japanese planes sank the US gunboat *Panay* in the Yangtze River. Roosevelt accepted Japanese apologies and compensation, but as war spread in Asia tried to set up a system of collective security within the Western hemisphere.

American neutrality ended with the outbreak of the Second World War. When Germany invaded Poland in 1939 and the Second World War began, Roosevelt summoned Congress to revise the Neutrality Act. The Fourth Neutrality Act allowed Britain and France to buy munitions on a cash-and-carry basis.

When France fell in 1940, leaving only Britain opposing Germany, Roosevelt supplied 50 ageing US destroyers to Britain in return for 99-year leases on British bases from Newfoundland to British Guyana. Re-elected in 1940, Roosevelt strengthened his support for Britain and was accused by isolationists, who believed that the safety of the nation was more important than any foreign war, of leading the United States into war while interventionists complained that he was too slow in entering the conflict.

Imperial denial at this time was caught by Henry Luce, proprietor of *Time* and *Life* magazines before the United States entered the war. He urged Americans

'to seek and to bring forth a vision of America as a world power, which is authentically American.... America as the dynamic center of ever-widening spheres of enterprise, America as the training center of the skilled servants of mankind, America as the Good Samaritan, really believing again that it is more blessed to give than to receive, and America as the powerhouse of the ideals of Freedom and Justice – out of these elements surely can be fashioned a vision of the Twentieth Century…, the first great American Century.'[5]

The sentiment echoed Roosevelt's anti-imperialism. He told his son in 1943: 'The colonial system means war.'

The Battle of Britain prompted American rethinking. If Germany and Italy established hegemony in Europe and Africa and Japan swept through East Asia, the Western hemisphere might be next. By the autumn of 1940 many Americans believed the Axis should be defeated.

The United States continued building up its defenses and sending supplies. Selective conscription was introduced with the Burke–Wadsworth Act of 1940, and the British were allowed to buy munitions and pay for them later under the Lend-Lease Act of 1941. In August 1941 Roosevelt met Churchill off Newfoundland and announced a set of war aims that was known as the Atlantic Charter: national self-determination, economic opportunity, freedom from fear and want, freedom of the seas (previously in Wilson's Fourteen Points and vetoed by the British), and disarmament.

America was again sucked into the war by German submarines, which attacked one American destroyer in September 1941 and another in October. The United States was now in an undeclared war with Germany.

America's relations with Japan deteriorated. In January 1940 the United States had canceled its 1911 commercial treaty with Japan, but American companies continued to sell Japan materials for its war with China. In September 1940 Japanese troops had invaded French Indo-China to establish bases from which the East Indies (the islands east of India, especially the Malay archipelago) could be attacked. The United States banned the supply of scrap iron and steel to Japan. In the same month Japan retaliated by signing an agreement with Germany and Italy. From spring 1941 to the end of the year Japan negotiated with the United States, which imposed sanctions on Japan in July. Japan prepared for war on the assumption that the negotiations would fail.

By November 1941 the United States was expecting a Japanese attack but professed to think it would be directed against the East Indies or the Philippines.

On December 7, 1941, Japanese planes bombed Pearl Harbor in Hawaii, destroying or damaging 15 ships and 188 planes and inflicting 3,435 casualties. On December 8, 1941, Congress declared war on Japan.

Three days later Germany and Italy, Japan's partners in the 'Axis,' the triple alliance of September 1940, declared war on the United States. Congress voted unanimously to reciprocate, and did likewise when Bulgaria, Hungary, and Romania also declared war. Now 15 million Americans went into military uniform.

## America's World Role

War increased American productivity and living standards. Personal incomes rose by a third. Congress kept a check on war agencies and military expenditure through the Senate War Investigating Committee led by Harry S. Truman. The US Government tried to control war production.

American factories doubled their output, producing 6,500 naval vessels, 296,400 planes, and 86,330 tanks. American technology developed advanced radar and sonar, and built an atomic bomb more quickly than the enemy (at a cost of $2 billion). Taxes paid for 41 per cent of the war, and with the total cost of the war to the Federal Government put at $321 billion, the national debt jumped from $49 billion in 1941 to $259 billion in 1945.

America's intervention gave the country a world role. In December 1941 Roosevelt and Churchill formed a grand wartime alliance, the United Nations, which 46 nations eventually joined. Their conference brought America out of isolation.

In 1943 six international conferences developed America's new world role. At Casablanca in January, Roosevelt and Churchill decided to invade Italy and insist on unconditional surrender. At Washington, DC, in May they decided to intensify the bombing of Germany. In Quebec in August they decided to invade German-occupied France. In Moscow in October, Secretary Hull agreed to establish a 'United Nations Organization' after the war. At Cairo in November, Roosevelt, Churchill, and Chiang Kai-shek of China affirmed a post-war settlement in East Asia. At Tehran in November, Roosevelt, Churchill, and Stalin agreed plans to invade France.

The invasion of France took place in June 1944. Strengthened by American troops, the Allies landed in Normandy and by the end of August they had taken most of France. The US intervention was decisive.

At Dumbarton Oaks, Washington, DC, in August, representatives of the United States, Britain, the USSR, and China agreed a charter for the United Nations Organization, or UN. In September, Roosevelt met Churchill and agreed a post-war strategy for dealing with Germany. Roosevelt was re-elected for a fourth term with Truman as his Vice-President, and at Yalta in February 1945 Roosevelt, Churchill, and Stalin agreed to enforce Germany's unconditional surrender; to split Germany into zones of occupation; and to establish democratic regimes in Eastern Europe.

The Yalta Conference in fact paved the way for the rise of Soviet power in Eastern Europe. Stalin agreed to enter the war against Japan in return for concessions in East Asia.

Roosevelt was unwell throughout the Yalta discussions, and died on April 12. But by then the war was won. Truman, Roosevelt's successor, oversaw the final collapse of German armed forces and the fall of Berlin before Hitler could succeed in building an atomic bomb.

On April 25, the UN was established at a conference in San Francisco. In July, Truman met Stalin, Churchill, and, following Churchill's defeat in the British general election, his successor Clement Attlee. They agreed a peace settlement for Europe and how to proceed against Japan.

Following the liberation of the Philippines from Japan in 1944–5, the US invasions of Iwo Jima in February–March 1945 and Okinawa in April–June had prepared the way for an invasion of Japan. However, before that could happen Truman authorized the dropping of atomic bombs, developed under the so-called 'Manhattan Project,' on Hiroshima and Nagasaki.

A shocked Emperor Hirohito, who was regarded by the Japanese people as a god, ordered his generals to stop fighting. On September 2, Japan surrendered on the US battleship *Missouri*.

America was now the leading great power, the only one to possess the atomic bomb. In June 1946 the United States proposed international control of atomic energy through the United Nations. However, the Soviet Union did not accept this and insisted the United States should destroy its atomic weapons. US forces demobilized. From a total strength of just over 16 million[6] in 1941–5 there were massive reductions. By the end of 1946 the US Army was down to 1.5 million, and the Navy down to 700,000.

The United States, the sole atomic power and conqueror of Hitler, no longer gave the impression of being run by reluctant imperialists. After the First World War the Americans had gone home and become isolationist. After the Second World War they remained in Europe.

There was much to do of an international nature. The new United Nations was being shaped, and America was one of the five permanent members of the Security Council with a permanent world role. The US Atomic Energy Commission was set up in 1946 to control the development and production of nuclear weapons and to direct research and development of peaceful uses of nuclear energy.

America had a very visible role in the reconstruction of Europe. In 1918 the United States had ignored the threat of Bolshevism, but with Stalin swallowing up the regimes of Eastern Europe (which under the Yalta agreement were supposed to be 'democratic' – a term that the communists who took power eagerly adopted to disguise new tyrannies), America heeded the Soviet threat and stayed on in Europe and elsewhere in the world. Truman recognized that this was no time to return home and be isolationist.

As we have seen, the American empire that had been wrested from Spain had been altruistic in handing rights and liberties to the oppressed former inhabitants of the Spanish Empire and to the inhabitants of poorly-governed Latin-American countries whose disorder threatened America's interests. However, the American intervention in two world wars had proved decisive and had correspondingly enhanced America's reputation as a great power, particularly its intervention in the Second World War and its development of an atomic bomb. America was now the leader of the Free (non-Soviet) World.

American leadership of the Free World did not contradict its early revolutionary principles. Rather, it dovetailed with them. For during the Second World War, America had defeated the tyrannies of Hitler, Mussolini, and Tojo and had brought rights and personal liberties to their oppressed peoples. And America was keeping an eye on the tyranny of Stalin, which still oppressed the people of the USSR and Soviet-occupied Europe. In a sense, as long as the Soviet tyranny of America's former ally menaced, the Second World War had not finished. America's leadership was linked to Liberty's new role as world leader of the free, democratic United Nations.

Liberty's empire now spanned the Atlantic and had a European base in Germany and a Pacific base in Japan, the two largest defeated nations. In Europe, the United States occupied the southern portion of Germany's Western Sector (later West Germany) from 1945–55, and a portion of Austria. In the Pacific, the United States occupied Japan. Fittingly, the supreme commander of the Allied powers in Japan, General Douglas MacArthur, was the son of General Arthur MacArthur, the American commander in the Philippines during the fighting from early 1900 to mid-1901.

Liberty's empire had developed from the colonial empire of 1898 and was already global. As a result of the Second World War, it was poised for hegemony.

# CHAPTER 3

# LIBERTY'S IMPERIAL HEGEMONY

America now progressed from leading allies to being in charge of a hegemony which broadly covered half the world. 'Hegemony' in Greek means 'leadership,' 'especially by one State of a confederacy' (*Oxford English Dictionary*). A 'confederacy' is 'a league or alliance, especially of confederate states,' which are states 'joined by an agreement or treaty.' 'A hegemony' has come to mean a confederacy of states under the leadership of a great power, and has the force of 'empire' as much as 'leadership.'

There are several examples in history of the leadership and dominance of one state over a group of others. The term hegemony was first used of the predominance of a particular Greek city-state over other city-states. At different times it was applied to Athens, Sparta, and Thebes. In more modern times it came to be used of the predominance of a nation or group of nations. For example, Britain is said to have had hegemony over, and a hegemony of, a confederacy of nation-states that passed within its colonial empire from the end of the Napoleonic Wars (1815) to the outbreak of the First World War (1914). This hegemony imposed a *Pax Britannica* on the world for about a hundred years, and when it disintegrated it left a void waiting to be filled. After the Second World War two superpowers emerged, the United States and the Soviet Union, both of whom exercised hegemony over hegemonies as leaders of conflicting groups of allied nation-states within their respective spheres of influence.

# The Cold War between Two Hegemonies

The two post-war hegemonies were established by the acquisition and possession of the atomic bomb.

The Soviet Union opposed a US proposal that atomic energy should be controlled by the UN and insisted that the United States destroy its nuclear weapons. However, it then engaged in nuclear research and spied on the American nuclear program. On August 29, 1949, Soviet scientists exploded their first atomic bomb. The two Western allies now had parity in ability to destroy each other, and America had to accept that there were now two superpowers.

US hegemony was expressed in 'an agreement or treaty' that involved 'confederate states.' In June 1948 the US Senate had passed the Vandenberg Resolution (named after Senator Arthur Vandenberg), which authorized negotiations that led to the signing of the North Atlantic Treaty of April 1949. This created the North Atlantic Treaty Organization (NATO). Soviet hegemony was expressed in a similar 'agreement or treaty' with its 'confederate states': the Warsaw Pact of 1955.

The tensions between the Soviet Union and the Western allies after the Second World War are commonly described as the 'Cold War.' The first use of this term is frequently ascribed to Bernard Baruch, a US presidential adviser who said in a speech on April 16, 1947, 'Let us not be deceived: we are today in the midst of a cold war.'[1] In fact the term had first been used by George Orwell in his essay 'You and the Atomic Bomb,' which was published in the British newspaper *Tribune* on October 19, 1945. He warned of a 'peace that is no peace,' which he called a 'permanent "cold war."'[2] In *The Observer* of March 10, 1946, Orwell wrote that 'after the Moscow conference last December, Russia began to make a "cold war" on Britain and the British Empire.' It is likely that Baruch had read Orwell's article in *The Observer*.

The Cold War between the two hegemonies gave America the impetus to dominate its sphere of influence and to spread its hegemony. The Cold War was an open yet restricted war fought by proxies in local conflicts with limited weapons, deliberately localized and limited because both sides feared setting off a nuclear holocaust.

The Cold War began as a threat to the West in 1946 when the Soviet Union supported communist guerrillas in Greece, alarming Turkey. On March 5, 1946, Churchill spoke of an 'iron curtain' separating Eastern and Western Europe: 'From

Stettin in the Baltic to Trieste in the Adriatic, an iron curtain has descended across the Continent.'

## Truman Doctrine, Marshall Plan

In the spring of 1947 the Truman Administration set out to contain communist expansionism. In March 1947 the British Government said it could no longer afford to oppose Soviet-backed guerrillas in Greece and Turkey, and Truman asked Congress for funds to help Greece and Turkey to resist communism. Congress allocated $400 million.

Truman stated what came to be known as the Truman Doctrine: 'I believe that…it must be the policy of the United States to support free peoples who are resisting attempted subjugation by armed minorities or by outside pressures.'

In June 1947 the Marshall Plan, named after Secretary of State George C. Marshall, provided for the economic rehabilitation of Europe in the face of a growing communist threat. The Marshall Plan covered 16 nations and western Germany. The United States pumped in $13 billion in five years through the Economic Co-operation Administration and revived the economy of Western Europe.

The Marshall Plan reduced the influence of West-European communist parties. Truman was re-elected in 1949, and in his Inaugural Address he proposed giving similar aid and technical assistance to underdeveloped nations.

The Marshall aid for western Germany provoked the Soviet Union, which blockaded the land and water routes across East Germany into West Berlin. Truman ordered planes to fly food and supplies into Berlin, and the blockade ended in spring 1949.

## NATO

It was at this point that NATO was set up in April 1949 under the North Atlantic Treaty. Twelve nations took part. (Greece and Turkey joined later.) The Treaty created a defense force to resist Soviet aggression under its first Supreme Commander, General Dwight D. Eisenhower, the leader of the Allied armed forces that had triumphed over Germany. NATO had a collective defense policy, its basis being that 'an armed attack against one or more' member states 'shall be considered an attack against them all' (Article 5). NATO implemented the Truman Doctrine.

## Soviet Empire

The Soviet empire had spread worryingly between 1939 and 1949. In the empire's west the Soviet Union had taken Eastern Poland (1939), Estonia, Latvia, Lithuania and parts of Eastern Finland (1940), Bessarabia and North Bukovina (from Romania, 1940) and Ruthenia (from Hungary, 1945); and in the east it had taken Tannu Tuva (1944), and Sakhalin and the Kurile Islands (from Japan, 1945). The Soviet Union then took Albania and Yugoslavia (1945–6), Bulgaria (1946), Petsamo/Nautsi (from Finland, 1947), Czechoslovakia (1946–8), Poland (1947–8), Hungary (1947–9), Romania (1947) and East Germany (1948–9).

In the east the Soviet Union had formed pro-Soviet satellites in North Korea (1948) and China (1949). It had backed insurgents in India, Burma, and Indonesia (1948), in the Philippines (1948–54) and in Malaya (1948–60). Indo-China was a worry: a liberation struggle against the French, which began in 1946, was to end in the establishment of North Vietnam (1954). All these countries were within the Soviet hegemony by 1949 and the north of Vietnam was occupied by pro-Soviet Viet Minh communists who wanted national independence.[3]

In a sense the Second World War was still continuing, with the Soviet Union having replaced Germany as aggressor, initially in Europe and the Pacific, and the United States mobilizing its hegemony and the nations of the Free World – those nation-states in the United Nations not under the Soviet hegemony – to block the further expansion of Soviet Communism throughout the world.

America now had a world role as leader of its confederacy of nations and of the Free World. The United States sought to keep world peace before an advancing tide of communism, and the fragile world peace it maintained was known as the *Pax Americana.*

## China

The fall of China to the Communists gave huge cause for concern. Truman had sent General George C. Marshall to China in December 1945 to prevent war between Chiang Kai-shek's Nationalists and Mao Tse-tung's Communists.

However, war ensued and in 1947 the Communists were making progress. Truman had sent General A.C. Wedmeyer to report on the situation. Wedmeyer advised that military personnel and supplies should be sent immediately. Truman had asked Congress for $570 million to aid Chiang Kai-shek. Congress voted $400 million, of which only $125 million could be spent on supplies. In 1949, the inadequately-supplied Nationalists fell and withdrew to Taiwan.

There were now fears that communist expansion would be unstoppable, especially after the Soviet Union became an atomic power by exploding an atomic bomb. Truman began a new drive to persuade impoverished nations to support the United States. In January 1950 he asked the US Atomic Energy Commission to develop a hydrogen bomb, which would be more powerful than the existing atomic bombs and would in theory make America the leading superpower.

### Korean War

The Korean War further enmeshed the United States into its global role. On June 25, 1950, armed forces from the Democratic People's Republic of Korea (North Korea), with the support of the Soviet Union, advanced south across the 38th parallel, the border with the Republic of Korea (South Korea), intensifying the communist insurgency in East Asia.

The US Government referred the invasion to the UN. Despite a Soviet veto the Security Council adopted a resolution calling on all UN Members to resist the invasion. General Douglas MacArthur commanded the UN force.

Communist China entered the war and drove the UN force back. On December 16, 1950, Truman declared a national emergency and put the United States on a war footing. MacArthur had a secret desire to expand the war. His view was that once war broke out, politics had failed and the military had to take over.[4] The previous October, MacArthur had wanted to use nuclear weapons to wipe out 'the seat of Bolshevism.'[5] Alarmed, Truman recalled MacArthur on April 11, 1951, and replaced him with General Matthew B. Ridgway.

Armistice talks began in July 1951 and an armistice was eventually signed on July 27, 1953. There was an attempt to reunite Korea but it failed at Geneva in June 1954.

The United States was now concerned to protect Oceania from communist attacks. With the Chinese invading South Korea, the United States had strengthened occupied Japan. Australia and New Zealand had co-operated with the United States during the Second World War – Australian territory had been invaded by the Japanese, notably at Port Moresby in New Guinea, and Australia itself had been attacked by Japanese planes – and they sent troops to fight alongside NATO in Korea. They were reluctant to finalize a peace treaty with Japan that would allow for Japanese rearmament, as the United States wanted, but relented when the Americans accepted an Australian and New-Zealand proposal for a three-way security treaty with the United States. The ANZUS Treaty was signed in San Francisco on 1 September 1951 and came into force in April 1952. It guaranteed the territorial integrity and political independence of Australia and New Zealand, and, by implication, of the Pacific region.

The United States finally concluded a peace treaty with Japan, formally ending the Second World War, on September 8, 1951. It was signed by 49 nations and under its provisions US troops could be stationed indefinitely in Japan. The United States also signed a defense pact with the Philippines. On July 2, 1952, the US Senate approved a peace agreement between the western allies and West Germany. The Iron Curtain now separated Eastern and Western Europe, and America was locked into its world role in Europe and the Pacific.

## Suez and Hungary

General Eisenhower was elected President in 1952. For the first two years of his Administration at home a senatorial subcommittee chaired by Senator Joseph McCarthy interrogated Americans for alleged communist allegiance. This heightened the feeling of Americans that they were involved in their world role and that they could not be isolationists.

Despite (or perhaps because of) his wartime record Eisenhower sent John Foster Dulles on diplomatic missions to promote peace, and proposed the international control of atomic weapons and aerial inspections of military installations, but his suggestions were not adopted. In 1955 the Big-Four Powers met in Geneva to reduce Cold-War tension, but tension persisted.

In 1955 Eisenhower had a heart attack and in June 1956 he was operated on for ileitis. Though recuperating from surgery, he took a strong line in October when Soviet tanks invaded Hungary to suppress an anti-communist revolution and, almost immediately afterward, Britain, France, and Israel colluded in an attack on the Suez Canal, recently seized and nationalized by the Egyptian president, Colonel Nasser. Eisenhower insisted that his allies should end their Suez adventure. Its abrupt cessation extended American influence, and therefore hegemony, throughout the Middle East.

## Cold-War Competition

America's lead in the arms race and image as the main superpower suffered a reverse in October 1957 when the Soviet Union launched the first artificial Earth satellite, *Sputnik*. For a while the balance of power seemed to have shifted to the Soviet Union. Then in January 1958 the US Army launched an Earth satellite. The arms race between the two superpowers had now developed into a space race.

A succession of events in 1958 brought the United States to the brink of war. In July US troops were sent to Lebanon to prevent the overthrow of the Lebanese Government by pro-Soviet forces. In August, Communist China bombarded the offshore islands of Quemoy and Matsu, bringing China face to face with the United States, which was treaty-bound to defend the Nationalists who had occupied these islands along with Taiwan. In November the Soviet Union threatened to blockade Berlin again. On December 31, pro-Soviet rebels under Fidel Castro seized the government of Cuba.

Cold-War tension was further heightened in May 1960 when a US–Soviet summit in Paris ended prematurely. The Soviet leader, Nikita Khrushchev, ratcheted up the tension by walking out because a US U-2 reconnaissance plane had been shot down over Soviet territory. The 1960 US presidential election was won by the youthful John F. Kennedy, who in his Inaugural Address called for a worldwide struggle against tyranny, poverty, disease, and war.

## Cuba and Détente

In Kennedy's first year of office, forces trained and supplied by the United States invaded Cuba in a *débâcle* that ended ignominiously in the Bay of Pigs.

In Vienna, Kennedy met Khrushchev, who was indignant that the United States, as he saw it, had invaded an island in the Soviet sphere of influence and under its hegemony.

In October 1962, Kennedy learned that the Soviet Union had installed on Cuba ballistic missiles that could attack the United States and posed a real threat. Kennedy blockaded Cuba to prevent further missiles being added and insisted that the Soviet Union should withdraw the existing ones. For five days there was a stand-off and the United States seemed to be on the brink of war. Then the Soviet Union agreed to dismantle its missile bases.

This direct confrontation between the two hegemonies or blocs had terrified the world, and America now led the way toward *détente*, an easing of strained relations that was the context for the events of the next 17 years.

In August 1963 a nuclear test-ban treaty was signed in Moscow by representatives of the United States, the Soviet Union, and Britain. All testing apart from underground tests would be abolished so that the Earth's atmosphere would not be contaminated. France and China (soon to detonate its first nuclear bomb) did not sign and thus complicated the disarmament process.

The confrontation over Cuba may have cost Kennedy his life. On November 22, 1963, he was assassinated in Dallas. There were suspicions that his alleged assassin, Lee Harvey Oswald, was acting on Soviet orders to pay Kennedy back for humiliating the Soviet Union over Cuba. But other groups also had a motive: international central bankers who had not taken kindly to Kennedy's signing of executive Order No. 11110, which attempted to strip the 'Rothschildian' (see pp.107–8) Federal Reserve Bank of its power to issue currency against silver bullion in the US Treasury's vault; the Mafia, who were incensed at Kennedy's courageous drive to put them out of business; and even friends of Marilyn Monroe, who had had an affair with Kennedy and had died – some said she had been murdered – in August 1962 after Kennedy ended the relationship.

### American Defeat in Vietnam

Despite the context of *détente* with the Soviet Union, America's international hege- monistic role widened under President Lyndon B. Johnson, Kennedy's successor.

Johnson focused on South-East Asia, where since 1961 the United States had been helping South Vietnam defend itself against the communist Viet Cong, who were aided by North Vietnam. The US involvement in South Vietnam escalated: there was a rapid increase in military supplies and advisers.

In February 1965 the Soviet premier Aleksey Kosygin – Chairman of the Council of Ministers in the 'collective leadership' that had ousted Khrushchev in October 1964 and a man who actually favored *détente* – visited Hanoi and authorized a massive supply of Soviet arms to North Vietnam. Johnson increased the number of US troops sent to South Vietnam – there were 500,000 by 1968 – and he ordered the bombing of North-Vietnamese military targets while per- sistently offering a peace settlement in the spirit of *détente*.

UN efforts to secure peace failed and in the winter of 1967–8 casualties mounted. Despite massive US bombing in North Vietnam, the Communists maintained their attacks and on January 30, 1968, disregarding a truce for the Tet (lunar new year) holiday, they mounted an offensive against all urban areas of South Vietnam.

Many Americans felt that the war could not be won militarily, and isolation- ist feelings returned.

*Détente* was further strained in Europe. The United States faced another confrontation with the Soviet Union in August 1968, when Soviet tanks invaded Czechoslovakia to crush the 'Prague-Spring' liberalization movement. Leonid Brezhnev, Secretary-General of the Communist Party of the Soviet Union under the 'collective leadership,' formulated the 'Brezhnev Doctrine,' which justified the invasion of Czechoslovakia by its Warsaw-Pact partners. Under this doctrine the Soviet Union and the community of socialist nations had the right to intervene if, in their judgment, one of them pursued policies that threatened the common interest. It was a collective defense policy that was not dissimilar to NATO's: 'an armed attack against one or more...shall be considered an attack against them all.'

Demoralized in Vietnam and alarmed by events in Czechoslovakia, in November 1968 Johnson ended the bombing of North Vietnam.

America widened the fighting in South-East Asia in an attempt to stabilize territory adjoining South Vietnam and to make possible a policy of 'Vietnamization' in Vietnam itself: transferring the fighting from American troops to the South Vietnamese. It has to be said that 'Vietnamization' was a recognition that America probably could not win the war and a way of withdrawing troops before a military defeat.

In 1970 the fighting spread into Cambodia, and in 1971 the United States invaded Laos. By early 1972 American troops in South Vietnam had been reduced from 500,000 in 1968 to just 70,000.

The war was already lost when Johnson's successor Richard Nixon and his national security adviser Henry Kissinger began peace talks in Paris. In April 1972 the North Vietnamese, armed by – and acting as proxies for – the Soviet Union, launched an invasion of South Vietnam. Nixon broke off the peace talks and resumed the bombing of North Vietnam.

Eventually, led by Kissinger, America resumed the Paris peace talks and signed a cease-fire agreement on January 27, 1973. Under its terms the United States would withdraw from South Vietnam, but the North Vietnamese would not withdraw.

The Americans withdrew in 1973, leaving the South Vietnamese to defend South Vietnam. Saigon fell to North-Vietnamese forces on April 30, 1975. The last vestiges of American presence were airlifted from the embassy compound as the North Vietnamese closed in.

Vietnam was now unified as one communist state. Laos and Cambodia also became communist states, as the Lao People's Democratic Republic and the

People's Republic of Kampuchea respectively. So ended 12 years of fighting, which had taken 58,000 American lives.

America was deeply demoralized. 1973, the year it withdrew from South Vietnam, was also the year of the Watergate affair when the White House engaged in illegal activities under the cloak of national security. By the end of the year Nixon had resigned and been replaced by Gerald Ford, who proved to be a caretaker president.

America suffered a tremendous loss of confidence after what had amounted to, and was widely perceived to be, a communist victory in South Vietnam.

## Souring of Détente

Besides expanding in Latin America and Asia, the Soviet empire and hegemony had expanded in Africa during the 1960s. There were Marxist or semi-Marxist governments in Guinea (1960), Mali (1960–68), Algeria (1962), Tanzania (1964), Ghana (1964–8), Sudan (1964–71), and Somalia (1969).

There was further pro-Soviet expansion in Chile (1970). In addition, the Soviet Union had intrigued and installed, often through proxies, anti-Western governments in Egypt (1952), Iraq (1958), Indonesia (1960–65), Uganda (1966), Peru (1968), and Libya (1969).

Despite the spread of the Soviet empire in Latin America, Asia, Africa, and Europe, America under Nixon and Kissinger continued to work for *détente*, improved relations with the Soviet Union. Nixon's new policy brought about Strategic Arms Limitation Talks (SALT), which led to a treaty with the Soviet Union that virtually terminated anti-ballistic-missile systems. In July 1971 Kissinger visited Peking (now known as Beijing) to improve Sino-American relations. In 1972 Nixon visited China and Moscow.

The United States was still in confrontation with the Soviet Union as the Arab–Israeli 'Yom Kippur War' of October 1973 demonstrated. The two hegemonies supported opposite sides in this war: the United States supported Israel and the Soviet Union the Arabs. The ensuing cease-fire made possible later improvements in Israeli–Egyptian relations.

In 1976 Jimmy Carter, a little-known Democrat, became President. He promoted human rights in relation to South Korea, Iran, Argentina, South Africa, and Rhodesia (later Zimbabwe). But he came up against a Soviet leadership that was intensifying the Cold War.

During the 1970s Brezhnev had become more and more powerful and in May 1977 he emerged as leader when Nikolay Podgorny was dismissed from the three-man 'collective leadership.' Under Brezhnev's influence the Soviet Union supported more revolutions that established Marxist- and Moscow-aligned satellites in Africa: the People's Democratic Republic of Yemen (from 1969), Somalia (1974–7), Guinea-Bissau, Angola and Mozambique (1975–6), and Ethiopia (1977). There was also an anti-Western regime in the Malagasy Republic (1972).

This new Soviet activity in Africa soured *détente*. However (or in consequence), the United States re-established full diplomatic relations with China on January 1, 1979, and negotiated a peace treaty between Egypt and Israel on March 26, 1979. America under Carter was pursuing a central role in working for world peace.

### Iran

America's world role was tested by Iran. There had been a revolution in Iran in 1978, and the Shah had fled. The Islamic Republic of Iran was proclaimed on February 1, 1979, under Ayatollah Khomeini.

The US Government threatened to seize $7.9 billion of Iranian assets in the United States. To increase his leverage on the West, in November Khomeini encouraged hard-line students to seize the US embassy in Tehran. They held 52 hostages for 15 months, against the return of the dying Shah.[6] Carter tried to rescue the hostages in April 1980. The attempt failed when a helicopter crashed into the desert, and the hostages were not released until Carter left office in January 1981.

Only six years after the fall of Saigon, America, leader of its hegemony, had been humiliated in the eyes of the world.

## Victory of the US Hegemony

The period from 1979 to 1985 is sometimes called the Second Cold War as the intensity of confrontation again approached the level experienced in 1962 during the Cuba crisis.

The thinking of the Soviet Union at this time can be gauged from thousands of military documents found at bases of the former East-German army, the Nationale Volksarmee (NVA), after the fall of the Berlin Wall. They reveal[7] a communist invasion plan: Warsaw-Pact tanks would push forward into Western Europe on five fronts, conquer West Germany, Denmark, the Netherlands and

Belgium, and reach the French border in 13–15 days. They would then push through France and reach the Spanish border within 30–35 days.

Moving at such speed made the use of tactical nuclear and chemical weapons obligatory, and thus a Warsaw-Pact training exercise in 1980 supported the advance of the first front with 840 tactical nuclear weapons. The plan was a modernized and bolder version of Hitler's blitzkrieg of 1940: racing behind a spearhead of tanks and tactical nuclear weapons. About 8,000 medals were minted to reward the bravery of invading troops. The seized documents confirmed that the West's fears during the Cold War were justified.

## American Regime Change

In the middle of the Iran crisis, in December 1979, 75,000 Soviet troops invaded Afghanistan, which adjoins Iran, to support the recently-installed Marxist government there. Soviet troops remained in Afghanistan for ten years. The United States mobilized against the Soviet troops by funding and arming the anti-government Afghan guerrillas known as the *mujahideen.*

It fell to Ronald Reagan, Carter's successor, to restore America's image. He accelerated a military build-up begun by Carter, but in foreign affairs his first term was unpromising. His aid to 'Contra' rebels failed to depose the left-wing Sandinista regime in Nicaragua. Relations with the Soviet Union deteriorated when he called it an 'evil empire.' He sent US Marines to the Lebanon, where 260 were killed in an attack in 1983. He was criticized for invading Grenada, at a cost of 42 American lives, in order to control Cuban influence. Relations with China deteriorated until the state visits of 1984.

During the Cold War the United States made covert attempts to depose many pro-Soviet regimes. It was accused of attempting regime change in the communist states of Eastern Europe and the Soviet Union (1945–89), Iran (1953), Guatemala (1954), Cuba (1959 onward), Turkey and the Democratic Republic of the Congo (1960), Iraq (1963), Brazil (1964), the Republic of Ghana (1966), Iraq again (1968), Chile (1973), Afghanistan (1973–4), Argentina (1976), Afghanistan again (1978–80s), Iran again and Turkey (1980) and Nicaragua (1981–90).

## Fall of the Berlin Wall

The Cold War ended after Mikhail Gorbachev became Secretary-General of the Communist Party and chief Soviet leader. His liberalizing reforms introduced *glasnost* ('openness'), which from 1985 increased freedom of the press and the transparency of state institutions; and *perestroika* ('restructuring'), which in June 1987 permitted private ownership and foreign investment.

The Soviet reforms dominated Reagan's second term. In 1987 Reagan negotiated an intermediate-range nuclear-forces treaty with the Soviet Union. This resulted in the destruction of two classes of weapons based in Europe. Thanks to Gorbachev, relations between the United States and the Soviet Union improved and there were promises of reductions in armed forces based in Europe.

It was arguably Reagan's vision that ended the Cold War. In a speech at the Brandenburg Gate on June 12, 1987, he challenged Gorbachev to tear down the Berlin Wall: 'General-Secretary Gorbachev, if you seek peace, if you seek prosperity for the Soviet Union and Eastern Europe, if you seek liberalization; come here to this gate! Mr Gorbachev, open this gate! Mr Gorbachev, tear down this wall!'[8]

Just over two years later Gorbachev obliged. The tearing-down and opening of the Berlin Wall on November 9, 1989, when the East-German Government announced – under pressure from Gorbachev and after weeks of unrest – that all GDR citizens could visit West Germany and West Berlin, ended the division of Europe and led to the end of communism.

## Collapse of Communism

The Soviet empire was demonstrably reeling. Between May 1988 and February 1989, Soviet forces withdrew from Afghanistan. There was a universal perception that after ten years of war the Soviet army had been ground down and defeated. Europe sensed its moment. From October 1989 a revolution swept across Central and Eastern Europe. It overthrew the Soviet-style states in East Germany, Poland, and Czechoslovakia, and in Bulgaria and Romania (where the dictator Ceausescu was shot). Gorbachev agreed that Soviet troops should be withdrawn from these countries on a phased basis.

The Hungarian regime was not overthrown but from 1987 had been encouraged by Gorbachev, who had renounced the Brezhnev Doctrine, to move to democracy under a reformist Communist government. Other political parties ceased to be banned in February 1989. In September 1989 Hungary decided to allow thousands of East Germans to leave for the West, triggering the East-German crisis and the revolutionary chain of events that began that October.

On December 3, 1989, Reagan's successor, George H.W. Bush, declared the Cold War over at the Malta summit. Meanwhile, the Berlin Wall was repeatedly attacked and vandalized. On June 13, 1990, the East-German military began the official dismantling of the Wall. By the summer of 1990 Gorbachev agreed to German reunification, which was formally concluded in October 1990. Gorbachev's concept of a 'common European home' had now begun to happen.

But the USSR itself was now collapsing. Gorbachev's policy of *glasnost* had dissolved the repressive glue that held the Soviet Union together, and in February 1990 the Communist Party surrendered its 73-year-old monopoly on state power. Following unrest in the Central-Asian republics, Lithuania unilaterally declared its independence from the Soviet Union in March 1990, and Gorbachev mounted an economic blockade, which temporarily forced the republic back into the Soviet fold. In January 1991 the United States and the Soviet Union, the two former rivals, were partners in the Gulf War against Iraq, long an ally of the Soviet Union.

Later that year the USSR was weakened by a failed anti-reformist *coup*, and with Soviet republics, including Russia itself, threatening to secede, the Soviet Union was officially dissolved on December 25, 1991. It was succeeded by the 'Commonwealth of Independent States,' created four days earlier. Russia itself became a presidential democracy known as the Russian Federation. The Warsaw Pact ended. One of the two post-war hegemonies was no more. The conflict between the free West and the totalitarian East was over.

Eastern Europe had been liberated from the Soviet yoke. Much of the credit for this belonged to Reagan. Margaret Thatcher said in 1991, 'Ronald Reagan won the Cold War without firing a shot.'[9] Reagan himself was loath to claim a victor's credit. When Gorbachev came to Washington in December 1987 and was wildly popular for his role in the changes, Reagan's friend Ben Wattenberg asked Reagan, 'Have we won the Cold War?' When Reagan hedged, Wattenberg asked again 'Well, have we?' Reagan finally said, 'Yes.' I can recall seeing Reagan saying modestly and matter-of-factly on a TV interview, I believe in a snippet filmed by Fox News, 'We won the Cold War.' Bush presided over the disintegration of the Soviet empire but Reagan's presidency had proved the turning-point.

The US view of what had happened is that the American hegemony had been too strong for the Soviet hegemony by forcing it into bankruptcy through an ever-escalating arms race. The American economy had been able to cope, the Soviet economy had collapsed due to its expenditure on arms.

A more independent view is that the Cold War ended due to Gorbachev's reforms and his championing of liberalization. Had Gorbachev embarked on a cosmetic PR exercise that had got out of control? Or did he intend to shut down the Soviet empire? Was he even a Western agent? It is likely that he was a staunch Soviet Communist trying to give communism a more human face in a changing world, perhaps seeking to achieve old Communist aims by deception. It has, however, been suggested that he was implementing a Western agenda. (See pp.124–5 for further details.)

Whatever the reason for the collapse of the Soviet hegemony in 1991, the American hegemony was supreme and was absorbing as allies some of the Soviet hegemony's 'confederate states,' particularly the ex-Soviet republics in the Caspian region. For the third time in the 20th century the United States had prevailed in a world war – for the Cold War was in effect a Third World War that lasted from 1945 until 1991. Reagan had been a Churchill. His vision and leadership had won the Cold War.[10]

The American hegemony had become a superpower. Liberty's empire was poised to dominate the world. It was even more powerful, in relative terms, than the rising Roman Empire after Rome's defeats of Carthage.

The Cold War had defined the world role of the United States after 1945. Its posture was that it was defending and protecting the liberty of the Free World against Soviet hegemony. Beneath the *façade* of this posture, it was driven by an expansionist imperialism to spread its own hegemony into the sphere of influence of its rival. By 1989 the United States had military alliances with 50 countries and 1.5 million troops posted in 117 countries.[11] It is estimated to have spent $8 trillion on military expenditure during the Cold-War years, and 100,000 Americans were killed in the Korean and Vietnam Wars.[12] Millions died in the two hegemonies' local proxy wars, especially in South-East Asia.

The received view is that Liberty's hegemony had defended the Free World against the tyrannical Soviet Union; and that it was therefore firmly based on the anti-imperialist libertarianism of the Declaration of Independence.

However, there is another influence behind Liberty's hegemony and empire. This had long been a force behind the scenes and it became even more influential after the collapse of the Soviet hegemony in 1991. To understand it we must go back before 1898 to when Liberty's empire *really* began.

# PART TWO

# When Liberty's Empire *Really* Began: The Rise of the United States

CHAPTER 4

# LIBERTY'S FEDERAL UNIFICATION

Liberty's empire really began when the Thirteen Colonies grouped themselves into a federal state after achieving independence from Britain. That was the true beginning of the force behind the expansionism that has shaped America's present and may determine its immediate future.

## The Planting of Colonies

I have told the story of the early planting of American settlements in some detail elsewhere.[1] However, we need to understand how 13 colonies emerged from these settlements in the 18th century, and review the disparate settling of America that gave rise to them.

### Spanish Catholics in Florida

The first Europeans to plant a settlement in the New World were the Spanish. Ponce de Léon landed in the New World in 1513 on the day of the Catholic Feast of Flowers, *Pascua Florida*, and named the region *La Florida* because of its luxuriant foliage. There was another Spanish landing in Florida in 1528. Between 1540 and 1542 Hernando de Soto explored Florida and the south of what would later become the United States.

In 1562 the Frenchman Jean Ribaut led an expedition of five ships to what is now St. Augustine, Florida, and left a garrison there. Three more French ships returned in 1564 and reinforced the garrison. In September 1565 five Spanish ships under Menéndez de Avilés chased off the French and cleared out the French garrison, executing Ribaut. In 1565 Avilés established the first settlement (as opposed to garrison) in the New World in Florida's St. Augustine. The first real settlers were therefore Spanish Catholics.

## English Anglicans in Jamestown

The first English-speaking settlement was at Jamestown, Virginia, in 1607. The voyage of three ships seems to have been organized by Captain Bartholomew Gosnold, who is thought to have used his uncle's house, Otley Hall in Suffolk, as a recruiting base for crew and settlers.

Gosnold was well known in mariners' circles. He had made an earlier voyage to the New World in 1602, when he had named Martha's Vineyard after his infant daughter Martha who had died aged one; he also named Cape Cod. His wife's cousin, Sir Thomas Smythe, funded the voyage, and the Virginia Company of London, created by royal charter, gave the orders.

Shortly before the voyage, the leadership was taken away from Gosnold and given to Admiral Newport, probably for political reasons: Newport was closer than Gosnold to the political faction of Sir Robert Cecil, the Secretary of State (chief minister) of Queen Elizabeth I and her successor King James I, who came to the throne in 1603. Gosnold's family had supported the 2nd Earl of Essex, the leader of another faction, who had been executed after leading a rebellion against the Queen.

The Virginia settlement was established in a swampy area visited by native Americans and named Jamestown after James I. As the settlers built a wooden stockade, the first Council was sworn in by the Anglican cleric who had accompanied the voyage, the Rev. Robert Hunt. A lean-to church was erected, made of sail and wood. In August 1607, 13 settlers including Gosnold died of swamp fever, dysentery, and starvation.

There were fierce quarrels among the settlers, and the leadership passed to John Ratcliffe and then to Captain John Smith, a swaggering fellow who had been confined to the hold for complaining about Newport's handling of the voyage even before the ships had left the English Channel. Smith later wrote an account of the voyage in which he admitted that Gosnold was its 'prime mover' but inflated his own role so successfully that *his* statue now stands at Jamestown, not Gosnold's.

Smith explored Chesapeake Bay and founded another settlement. In 1587 Sir Walter Raleigh had sent a ship there, but it never arrived as it had put in at the ill-fated Roanoke settlement and gone no further. Smith consolidated the Chesapeake settlement, but after many adventures returned to England under something of a cloud in 1609. Discipline then collapsed and Jamestown came under attack from the native Americans.

In 1610 a new church was built in Jamestown and under Governor Thomas Gates a strict religious regime was put in place. The settlers were compelled to pray twice a day and attend three church services a week: the bell for prayers rang at 10 a.m. and 4 p.m., and there were services every Thursday and twice on Sundays. The Church became an instrument of the State. In fact, in Virginia at this time the Church *was* the State, providing the new colony's principal structure of government. In the words of William Strachey in 1612, the Virginian colony of Chesapeake was a 'Christian colonie.'

When Gates left for England in 1616, Jamestown had crumbled. Tobacco, the main means of commerce, was growing in all open spaces and many native Americans were in the streets as the local Chickahominy Indians had been forcibly persuaded (having witnessed many burning villages) to accept James I as their king. In 1622 an epidemic and a massacre by Indians killed half the colonists, and the Jamestown colony collapsed. In 1624 Virginia was financially bankrupt and placed under royal control.

## Puritan Separatists in Massachusetts Bay

Meanwhile, in England there had been a clamp-down on Separatists, Christians who wished to separate from the Church of England and form independent local churches of Christian believers. Some had had enough of England. In 1620 English Separatists traveling on the *Mayflower* had settled at New Plymouth in Massachusetts Bay. These 'pilgrims' were followed in 1629 by 400 Puritans, reformers who wanted further 'purification' of the Church of England from remnants of Roman-Catholic 'popery,' and then in 1630 by 700 more Puritans on the *Arbella*.

All the Puritan settlers were led by John Winthrop, who established a civil commonwealth modeled on the Church. As in Virginia, the Church *was* the State, and Winthrop composed a lay sermon, *A Modell of Christian Charitie*, on the notion of the 'Christian commonwealth,' in which Church and State would be one. From 1633 to 1635 some settlers left to plant a similar Christian commonwealth in Connecticut. There were settlements in Hartford, Wethersfield, and Windsor, and in 1638 New Haven. The commonwealth's Fundamental Orders (or basic constitution) based the civil government on divine authority.

During the 17th century, organizational groupings changed as settlements were taken over by royal charter. The colony of Massachusetts Bay accepted the surrender of the Plymouth colony in 1640, and of the province of New Hampshire in 1641. In 1643 it joined the colonies of Plymouth, Connecticut, and New Haven in the Confederation of New England.

The Dutch established a number of trading posts in the New World to buy pelts from native Americans, including Fort Amsterdam, which in 1625 developed into the town of New Amsterdam. This became part of the Dutch colony of New Netherland, which the English captured in 1664. New Amsterdam was renamed New York after Charles II's brother and heir presumptive, James, Duke of York, the future James II, who became its proprietor. In 1686 James, now King, created the Dominion of New England out of Massachusetts Bay and the other New-England colonies and two years later added New York, East Jersey, and West Jersey.

In 1691–2 Massachusetts Bay was unified with the Plymouth colony, Martha's Vineyard, Nantucket, Maine, and Nova Scotia to form the province of Massachusetts Bay.

## English Quakers in Pennsylvania

In 1682 the Quaker William Penn left England to found what came to be known as Pennsylvania. He had secured a charter for land on the Delaware River in 1681 which made him ruler of the new colony. He wrote: 'There may be room there, though not here [England], for such an holy experiment.'[2] Of the 'holy experiment,' Penn had written: 'God will plant America and it shall have its day in the Kingdom.'[3]

Penn returned to England in 1684 to sort out a boundary dispute with Maryland arising from a poor map. The Catholic James II ruled from 1685 until the 'Glorious Revolution' of 1688–9 replaced him with the Protestant William III. In 1692–4 William placed Pennsylvania under royal rule as Quakers opposed the colonial war with France which had begun in 1689 and continued to 1697. Penn was back in Pennsylvania from 1699–1701 to effect a sale of the province. The 'holy experiment' collapsed and Penn died in 1718 before he could sell Pennsylvania. Penn's family continued to own the province until 1776.

# The Thirteen Colonies

The early settlements had passed, higgledy-piggledy, into a system of embryonic colonies. Prior to 1730 the following colonial divisions were in force:

- The Dominion of New England, created in 1685 by James II, which consolidated Maine, New Hampshire, Massachusetts Bay colony and the former Plymouth colony, Rhode Island, Connecticut, the province of New York, East Jersey, and West Jersey into a single larger colony until the nine former colonies re-established their separate identities in 1689 after William III's revolution;
- The province of Maine, merged with the Massachusetts-Bay colony briefly during the 1650s and again from 1691 to 1820;
- Plymouth colony, absorbed by Massachusetts-Bay colony in 1691;
- Saybrook colony, founded in 1635 and merged with Connecticut colony in 1644;
- New Haven, settled in 1637 and absorbed by Connecticut colony in 1662;
- East and West Jersey, created when New Jersey was divided into two separate colonies in 1674 and reunited in 1702;
- The province of Carolina, founded in 1663 and then divided into two colonies, North Carolina and South Carolina, in 1712, both colonies becoming royal colonies in 1729.

By 1760, 13 English colonies had emerged on the East Coast. They were founded between 1607 and 1733, and included land that had been wrested from the Dutch. From north to south there were four New-England colonies, four Middle colonies, and five Southern colonies. They were:

*New-England colonies*
1 Province of New Hampshire (later New Hampshire);
2 Province of Massachusetts Bay (later Massachusetts and Maine);
3 Colony of Rhode Island and Providence plantations (later Rhode Island and Providence plantations);
4 Connecticut colony (later Connecticut);

*Middle colonies*

  5 Province of New York (later New York and Vermont);

  6 Province of New Jersey (later New Jersey);

  7 Province of Pennsylvania (later Pennsylvania);

  8 Delaware colony (before 1776 the Lower Counties on Delaware and later Delaware);

*Southern colonies*

  9 Province of Maryland (later Maryland);

  10 Colony and Dominion of Virginia (later Virginia, Kentucky, and West Virginia);

  11 Province of North Carolina (later North Carolina and Tennessee);

  12 Province of South Carolina (later South Carolina);

  13 Province of Georgia (later Georgia).

The independence of the Thirteen Colonies (also known as 'British America,' which from 1763 included Canada) was recognized by the Treaty of Paris in 1783. They gave rise to 18 present-day states: the original 13 listed above plus Vermont (an independent republic from 1777–91), Kentucky (part of Virginia until 1792), Tennessee (part of North Carolina until 1790 and then the federally-administered Southwest Territory until 1796), Maine (part of Massachusetts until 1820) and West Virginia (part of Virginia until 1863).

Much of the North-American territory outside the Thirteen Colonies had been won from the French by Britain during the Seven Years' War, which ended in 1763. In 1760 the map of North America showed a band of British control extending 100–200 miles (160–320km) inland from Maine down to Georgia; then a native-American-controlled buffer zone separating the British from the French interior; and in the south, Spanish Florida. The local Americans had looked to the British to protect them against the French, who had been fighting wars in America since 1689. In 1763, under the Paris peace settlement, Britain acquired Canada, Florida, and all of the continent east of the Mississippi. British supremacy in America seemed unchallengeable.

However, provincial American power grew due to the distance separating England and America, America's pressure on royal officials, and the inefficiency of the large English bureaucracy. By the 18th century, colonial legislators gained control over their parliamentary prerogative and assumed responsibility for legislation involving taxation and defense, and eventually for the salaries paid to royal officials. Provincial American leaders made recommendations for appointments, which the royal governors accepted. In the same way, governors' councils came to be dominated by local leaders' interests rather than the interests of the royal government in London. By the mid-18th century political power in America was mostly in the hands of local leaders rather than royal officials.

By now the economic resources of America were controlled by a small American *élite*: by planters and their merchants and lawyers in Virginia and Maryland; by rice- and indigo-planters in the Carolinas; and by town merchants, lawyers, and clergymen in New England.

The increasing political and economic autonomy of the American colonies was matched by an increase in their population from an estimated 52,000 in 1650 to 1.7 million by 1760. The growth of the population was partly due to the influx of African slaves. From around 2,000 in 1670, the population of slaves increased to around 150,000 in 1770, more than half of whom were in South Carolina, where blacks outnumbered whites by two to one.

## Freemasonry Unites the Thirteen Colonies

The origins of the move to unite the Thirteen Colonies into one federal state can be found within the institutions of Freemasonry. An occult, philosophical secret society that guards the secret knowledge of the ages (including architectural knowledge that may go back to 15th-century-BCE Egypt), Freemasonry has two main branches, both of which look back to the building of the Temple of Solomon in the tenth century BCE.

English Freemasonry may have started with the stonemasons who built the medieval Gothic cathedrals and may have been overhauled in 1579 by the philosopher-statesman Sir Francis Bacon, who absorbed symbolism from Kabbalistic Jews in Navarre, which he visited while living in Paris with the English Ambassador to France while still a teenager. Navarre, an independent Protestant-ruled kingdom in the western Pyrenees between Spain and France, was home to a secret society run by Bacon's brother Anthony.

French Freemasonry was based on the crusading Order of the Knights Templar (Templars), founded in 1118 by St. Bernard to guide and protect pilgrims in the

Holy Land. In 1307 the Templars were banned in France and many fled to Scotland. There, Templars became Freemasons and Templarism thus became Freemasonic and was followed by the Stuart royal line. When the Stuart James VI of Scotland became King James I of England in 1603, he brought Templar-Freemasonry to London and in due course it was taken to France via the Jacobite descendants of James II (James I's grandson) as the Scottish Rite of French Templar Freemasonry. (Henceforward in this book, the term 'Templar' in a post-14th-century context means 'Templar-Freemasonic.')

## English Freemasonry in Jamestown

As I have shown in some detail elsewhere,[4] English Freemasonry may have arrived in the New World as early as 1607, with the voyage to Jamestown.

The man who planned the voyage, Bartholomew Gosnold, was Bacon's cousin and would have met him when Bacon was MP for Ipswich from 1597 to 1610. Ipswich was only seven miles (11km) from Otley Hall. Moreover, Captain John Smith may have had links with Bacon via Gosnold before 1607. A pamphlet by George Tudhope, *Freemasonry Came to America with Captain John Smith in 1607* (1959), cites Smith's later links with Bacon.

Bacon, whom many regard as the founder of English Freemasonry, was listed as a shareholder of the Virginia Company in 1609 and was one of the 52 members of the Virginia Council (the Company's board of directors).[5] He threw the weight of his secret society of Freemasons behind American colonization. The society helped with the printing of a number of publications that promoted Protestantism and imperialism against Catholic Spain, particularly in relation to the New World.

Tudhope draws attention to similar colophons (ornamental decorations at the tops of pages) found in publications of Bacon's society and on other works that promoted Protestantism and imperialism between 1575 and 1640. These included light-dark scrolls and an 'AA' design, short for 'AthenA,' that were linked to a secret society Bacon had founded in 1586, the Order of the Knights of the Helmet, for which Athena, or Pallas Athene, the helmeted Greek goddess of wisdom, was iconic.

Colophon designs from the Bacon stable connect:

- prints of illustrations of Sir Francis Drake's voyages (1590), which challenged Spanish maritime supremacy;

- the Authorized King James Version of the Bible (1611), which spread Protestantism;
- Sir Walter Raleigh's map of Virginia (1585) and *History of the World* (1614), a history written by a colonizer of America;
- Shakespeare's First Folio (1623), which championed English sovereignty against Spain and referred to a 'brave' New World;
- John Smith's *The Generall Historie* (1624), which described the New World; and
- Bacon's *New Atlantis* (1626), which stood for an 'English Israelite' New World rather than a Spanish one.[6]

On the evidence of colophons in Smith's 1624 book, by the mid-1620s he was being secretly helped by Bacon, and it may be that the connection pre-dated the 1607 voyage, since the colophon evidence suggests that Bacon and his circle had a deep interest in New World exploration from at least 1585.

There may have also been a Templar influence on the 1607 voyage. 'Jamestown' means 'James's Town.' As James I brought Templarism to London, the choice of the name 'Jamestown' for the 1607 settlement may have drawn covert attention to a Templar influence there.

### The Federal System of English Rosicrucian Freemasonry

English Baconian Freemasonry gave birth to a new secret Freemasonic brother-hood claiming to possess wisdom handed down from ancient times, which came to be known as Rosicrucianism. By 1586 Bacon's Order of the Knights of the Helmet had spawned the Fra Rosi Crosse Society, which became a degree, or rank, in the Knights of the Helmet.[7] The Rosi Crosse was also a reorganization of the old Knights Templar, an organization which Bacon seems to have encountered in Navarre in the late 1570s. He appears to have met the descendants of Templars who had fled France in 1312 and had reacted to the burning of the Templar leader, Jacques de Molay, by forming a secret society in the French part of Navarre. Bacon revisited France between 1580 and 1582 when, as a result of the Rosi Crosse, Bacon's system of lodges – local groups of Knights of the Helmet and members of the Rosi Crosse – was already so established that it could easily be transplanted from England to France and Germany.

Bacon had written a series of pamphlets on Freemasonry and Rosicrucianism, and some hold that he took with him to the Continent the first of the controversial 'Rosicrucian Manifestos' (see below), which were eventually published anonymously in German.

The Rosicrucians were invisible, in the sense that they operated secretly, until 1613, when the 17-year-old Frederick V, Elector Palatine of the Rhine and leader of the German Protestants, married the 17-year-old Elizabeth Stuart, daughter of the Templar James I of England in London. Bacon composed a masque, *The Marriage of the Thames and the Rhine*,[8] in honor of the marriage and there were performances of Shakespeare's *Othello* and *The Tempest*. The couple then returned to Heidelberg in the Palatinate, escorted by the 3rd Earl of Southampton, thought to be Shakespeare's patron.[9] They built a replica of the Globe theatre, where Shakespeare's later plays were performed, in Heidelberg Castle, where the surrounding wall of the theatre can still be seen.

The Palatinate now became a Rosicrucian state, and in 1614 the 'Rosicrucian Manifestos' appeared in Heidelberg: *Fama Fraternitatis* and *Confessio*. A third book appeared in 1616: *The Chemical Wedding of Christian Rosenkreutz*. All three were later attributed to, and acknowledged by, a pastor named Johann Valentin Andreae. They emanated from Heidelberg and there are references to the Elector Palatine and to Heidelberg Castle. But it is held by many that the real author of the Manifestos was Bacon, the 'invisible' Rosicrucian.

It is very important to grasp that English Rosicrucian Freemasonry developed the federal system of 'Grand Lodges.' In 1717 English Freemasonry, which in 1688 had supported the Rosicrucian William of Orange[10] against the Catholic James II, appealed for an increase in Rosicrucian Freemasonry's English membership. (Henceforward, any reference to 'Rosicrucianism' after the early 17th century refers to Rosicrucian Freemasonry; compare note on 'Templars' on p.53.) As a result, a 'Grand Lodge' was formed at a meeting in the Apple Tree tavern in Covent Garden, London.

One of the seven men present was Dr James Anderson, a Presbyterian minister in London who was chosen to draw up a constitution that would dechristianize the Grand Lodge and turn Freemasonry into a universal religion.

The Grand-Lodge system of English Freemasonry was set down in writing in Anderson's *Constitutions* of 1723, the printed version of which had the same Baconian signs and emblems reviewed earlier (see pp.53–4), suggesting that Bacon's secret society fed Anderson's material into the lodges of Freemasons nearly 100 years after Bacon's death. Anderson's work turned Freemasonry into an open organization behind which secret organizations could hide. Anderson wrote: 'A lodge is a place where Masons assemble and work...and is under the regulations of the General or the Grand Lodge.'[11]

The Grand Lodge was federally above all individual lodges, which were internally independent but linked to the Grand Lodge, to which they could appeal. Dr Anderson based his regulations on the regulations of the Society of Jesus (the society founded by Jesuits), even to the extent of plagiarizing their title. In the 16th century the Jesuits' founder, St. Ignatius of Loyola, had written his *Constitutions* to lay down ground rules as to how Jesuits should pray, dress, and be punished. When he died in 1556, there were 1,000 Jesuits in 12 adminis- trative units called provinces. To Anderson, lodges were like these provincial units, independent but under a federal Grand Lodge similar to the Order of the Society of Jesus. (In 1776 Adam Weishaupt also based the structure of his secret society, the Order of the Illuminati, on the Jesuit structure, and in doing so he was following Anderson's example.)

The lodge system was formalized in America in the 1720s, the first decade in which there are reports of American lodges. The first American Grand Lodge appeared in 1723, the year of Anderson's *Constitutions*. In 1733 Rosicrucian Freemasonry formally entered America when St. John's Lodge was established in Boston. It became the Masonic capital of Britain's American colonies. By 1737 there were lodges in Massachusetts, New York, Pennsylvania, and South Carolina.[12] The Founding Father Benjamin Franklin had become a Rosicrucian Mason in February 1731 and a Provincial Grand Master in the Grand Lodge of Pennsylvania in 1734.

### Freemasonic Federalism Behind the US Constitution

Since Bacon's time Freemasons had dreamt of a united world in which all men would be brothers and all nations would be linked in a federal union like Grand Lodges. Franklin's Freemasonic experience led him to apply the Freemasonic Grand- Lodge model to the British colonies to further Freemasonry's one-world agenda.

In 1744 Franklin attended a native-American-treaty council meeting at which representatives of Maryland, Virginia, and Pennsylvania met the chiefs of the Iroquois League. The native-American spokesman Canassatego recommended that the British colonies unite as the Iroquois had done.

In 1751 Franklin urged that the colonies should unite and, at a time when the French were encroaching into British colonial territory, he drew up a Plan of Union, which was confirmed by the Albany Congress in 1754. Convened at the request of the British Board of Trade to cement the loyalty of the Iroquois League against the French, the Congress confirmed the Anglo-Iroquois alliance and Franklin's Plan of Union.

Under the Albany Plan of Union,[13] a 'President-General' would lead the 11 English colonies taking part (excluding Delaware and Georgia, who for reasons that are still subject to speculation did not feel able to join a colonial union for mutual defense and security). The opening paragraph of the Albany Plan of Union states: 'One general government may be formed in America, including all the said colonies, within and under which government each colony may retain its present constitution.' The 'general government' would have a 'general constitution.' There would be a single 'Grand Council' with 48 members drawn from the 11 colonies, similar to the Iroquois Great Council. The Grand Council would meet once a year. Each state would retain its internal sovereignty. A careful study of the Albany Plan of Union and of Anderson's *Constitutions* shows that the Grand Council would have been based on the concept of a Grand Lodge.

The British rejected the proposal, but it would resurface 20 years later when the colonies united in opposition to the Stamp Act of 1765. Franklin's Albany Plan of Union eventually resulted in the Articles of Confederation of 1777 (see p.59).

In 1757 Franklin had traveled to London to represent Pennsylvania in a dispute, and while there he was initiated as a Rosicrucian.[14] He stayed in England from 1764 to 1775 and was introduced to English Baconian Freemasonry's 'Secret Doctrine' to create a 'philosophical Atlantis' in America, a Masonic blueprint Bacon had concealed in his *New Atlantis*. Franklin sought the federal unification of the English American colonies as an implementation of the Freemasonic 'philosophical Atlantis.' This concept held up a restored version of the drowned Golden-Age Atlantis referred to by Plato as a better, non-Spanish-Catholic world. The concept was behind Bacon's *New Atlantis* (1626).

Meanwhile, America had undergone a Christian revival during the Great Awakening of the 1740s. This was a surge of evangelical fervor that tilted American Christianity from its planting origins in Catholicism, Anglicanism, and Puritanism toward evangelical Protestantism. The development coincided with the arrival of French Freemasonry in America.

French Templarism reached America by 1746,[15] when many Irish and Scottish Templar Jacobites (pro-Stuarts) fled to America in the wake of the failed attempt to restore the Stuarts to the British throne. Those who fled took the Scottish Rite with them. In 1756 Jacobite Templarism reached Boston. Its American headquarters were at St. Andrew's Lodge. After 1769 another branch of Templarism, the Grand Lodge of York, set up lodges in Virginia for the York Rite. Templars were well established by the time of the Boston Tea Party of 1773, when 200 Templar Masons disguised as Mohawk Indians threw tea into Boston harbor in protest at British Government policy in the colonies.

By 1775 disputes between Britain and its colonies had escalated into an armed conflict that rapidly became a war for American independence. The American statecraft of the 1770s and 1780s, during the War of Independence, or Revolutionary War, and its aftermath, drew heavily on the Freemasonic federal model. On July 2, 1776, the Continental Congress, established to give the colonies a unified voice in opposition to the British Government, voted for independence. Two days later, on July 4, 1776, Congress published the Declaration of Independence, which had been written by Thomas Jefferson of Virginia. Of the 56 signatories of the Declaration, who were drawn from all 13 colonies, 53 may have been Master Masons.[16]

On the very same day, Franklin, Jefferson, and John Adams were appointed to design the Great Seal of the United States, as the Thirteen Colonies now called themselves. In December 1776 Franklin was sent to Paris to seek help for the colonies. There he met Illuminatists, and perhaps Adam Weishaupt himself, who, as we have seen, followed Anderson's Jesuit structure. As I have explained elsewhere,[17] Franklin returned from Paris with the idea of using the seal Adam Weishaupt had devised for the Order of the Illuminati in May 1776 as the basis of the US Seal. It had a 13-layered pyramid with the capstone missing and the Freemasonic All-Seeing Eye of Osiris and Sion, and a 13-letter inscription: *Annuit Coeptis*. (The Latin, taken from Virgil's *Aeneid*, book 9, line 625, should read *Adnuit Coeptis*, 'He (Jupiter) has approved our beginning.') At one level, this suggested that God was approving the beginning of the United States from the Thirteen Colonies. At another level, however, it suggested that God was approving the beginning of the Freemasonic New Atlantis and recalled the 13th day of October 1307, when Templarism was suppressed. The Illuminati Seal was eventually adopted as America's Great Seal in 1782.

In 1777 a Continental Congress met and drew up the Articles of Confederation, which were approved on 15 November that year after the Battle of Saratoga, when Templar Freemasonic American military leaders captured the British commander, General Burgoyne. The American victory drew the French into the War of Independence. There was now a prospect of an American–French alliance and it was important for America to speak with one voice. The Articles were based on Franklin's Albany Plan of Union. By approving them, the Constitutional Congress agreed a new system that would be a federation of states, and the confederacy was to be called a 'perpetual union.' The states' ratification of the Articles of Confederation took until 1781.

The Articles of Confederation proposed a 'firm league of friendship' (Article 3) rather than a strong national government. The Articles and the state constitutions they created saw America through to victory in the war, which formally ended with the Treaty of Paris in 1783. However, the United States was muddling through, and by May 1787 it was clear that a new arrangement was needed that would be more effective as a system of national government.

A Constitutional Convention of 1787 drew up a Constitution of the United States that would replace the Articles of Confederation. Those who drafted the Constitution took three principles from Freemasonry: the investment of power in a man's office, not in the man; the adoption of a system of checks and balances between executive, legislative, and judicial branches of government; and the adoption of the Masonic federal system of organization. The 1787 federal constitution was based on Anderson's 1723 federal *Constitutions*, as Henry C. Clausen has emphasized:

> 'Since the Masonic federal system of organizations was the only pattern for effective organization operating in each of the original Thirteen Colonies, it was natural that patriotic Brethren should turn to the organizational base of the Craft for a model. Regardless of the other forces that affected the formation of the Constitution during the Constitutional Convention in 1787, the fact remains that the federalism created is identical to the federalism of the Grand Lodge system of Masonic government created in Anderson's *Constitutions* of 1723.'[18]

The President of the Constitutional Convention, George Washington, who had become a Rosicrucian Mason in 1752 and a Templar Mason in 1768, was behind the scrapping of the Articles. The new Constitution said nothing about religion. By implication it reversed the Planting Fathers' view of the State and the Church as one, and put in its place a separation of Church and State so that all religious sects operated in a marketplace of free choice within a secular State.

At the convention, George Washington sat in a chair on top of which was a half-sun with two eyes and a nose and 13 rays like hairs, which in this instance represented the 13 former colonies. Benjamin Franklin declared that the sun on the chair was rising, not setting, on the new nation.[19] The rising sun marked the beginning of the rising of the United States to empire.

Freemasonic federalism had become the principle behind the US Constitution, and the United States had therefore become a Freemasonic State. Was this deliberate on the part of Freemasonry?

George Washington was Grand Master of the Templar Alexandria Lodge no. 22 in Virginia by the time he was elected President of the convention. Had Freemasonry instructed first Franklin in his Albany Plan of Union and then Washington (under Franklin's gaze in his rising-sun chair) to impose Freemasonic federalism on America, in order to achieve the 'philosophical Atlantis' and spread a universal religion? Had there been a Freemasonic *coup* in the Thirteen Colonies?

In February 1789, Washington became the first President of the United States. Was he a reluctant president, much like Lucius Quinctius Cincinnatus, who in 458BCE reluctantly gave up his plow to lead the Romans to victory over the Aequi, and then immediately renounced power and returned to his farm? Or was Washington carrying out the instructions of Freemasonry's secret headquarters all along via his lodge, Alexandria Lodge no. 22?

The answer may lie in the Freemasonic architectural symbolism of Washington, DC. As the site of the new US capital, George Washington chose a marshy swamp in 1790 and asked Pierre Charles L'Enfant, a Templar Mason,[20] to design a city for 800,000 inhabitants at a time when there were only three million people in the United States. There was a vision of expansion behind George Washington's plan for the new city. It was laid out round Freemasonic symbols: compass, square, rule, pentagram, pentagon, octagon.[21] In 1793, Washington laid the foundation stone of the Capitol in a Masonic ceremony, and he eventually had a Masonic funeral.

In conclusion, it could well be that Washington was acting on instructions from Freemasonry's hierarchy when he brought Franklin's Freemasonic federalism into the Constitution of the United States.

The unification of the Thirteen Colonies into the United States was a political unification that began Liberty's expansion into empire. The widening of Freemasonic federalism now continued in a continental expansion.

# CHAPTER 5

# LIBERTY'S WESTERN EMPIRE: Continental Expansion Westward

Liberty's empire continued with a new bout of expansion westward to fill the unoccupied territory across the Mississippi.

Drawn by the vast, rich, empty land to the west, in the 1770s the population had begun to expand across the Allegheny Mountains (the eastern part of the Allegheny Plateau in the Appalachian Mountains extending south-westward from central Pennsylvania to south-western Virginia). After independence many went west to seek their fortune as new settlers, traveling from eastern to central North America in the same spirit in which immigrants traveled from Europe to the East Coast.

## 'Empire of Liberty'

In 1780 Thomas Jefferson, the writer of the Declaration of Independence and future President, was looking westward when he wrote of America as an 'empire of liberty.'[1] He meant that an American empire to the west did not have to be imperialistic and oppressive, like the perverted British Empire in America, but rather a kind of commonwealth, a free association of like-minded communities, a union of free states.

Jefferson had a vision of a United States of America stretching westward, and in 1784 he was appointed by Congress to chair two committees to deal with the West. With settlers advancing across the Appalachian Mountains into Indian territory, he set out a framework for the government of western lands until the population to the west had increased enough for new states to be formed. He also mapped 14 new states and named ten of them, including 'Michigania' and 'Illinoia.' His proposals formed the basis of two major laws: the Land Ordinance of 1785 and the Northwest Ordinance of 1787.

## New States

The 1783 Treaty of Paris with Britain defined the original borders of the United States. In 1788 nearly a thousand boats took 18,000 settlers down the Ohio River. Emigrants from New England turned 'the Western Reserve' into a second New England, with its own town meetings and New-England lifestyle. Other settlers trekked through the mountain passes to the south. By 1790 there were 170,000 settlers in the Western country.[2] Kentucky was admitted as a state in 1791 and Tennessee in 1796, when diplomat and future sixth President John Quincy Adams was a supporter of continental expansion and urged his father, John Adams, who was then Vice-President, to pursue an expansionist policy.

Whereas the seaboard colonists had preserved their links with British imperial rule – through charters, royal governors and a strong attachment to their mother country – the new colonists who built towns over the mountains devised their own governments. Some had built Jamestown-style stockaded villages in clearings and were beyond the reach of any government. By 1800 a million Americans were living west of the mountains. Some settlers wanted to join the United States to their east, others were content to start afresh and make up their own rules. By 1800 the Ohio Territory was growing crops for export worth $700,000 and building ships to be used on the Mississippi and its tributaries. Ohio entered the United States in 1803.

During the American Revolution, the United States established relations with France, Spain, and the Netherlands, urging them to intervene in its war against Britain, their mutual enemy. Following the Revolution, the United States restored peace with Britain in its 'Olive Branch Policy.' But after the French Revolution it maintained a special relationship with France.

The United States was generally isolationist until attacks against US shipping by Barbary corsairs, or pirates, spurred the young republic into strengthening its naval capability.

### First Barbary War

The Barbary 'pirate states' of North Africa had long been a threat to passing ships when, in 1783, the United States became responsible for the safety of its own commercial shipping and citizens. Not having a naval force, it elected to pay tribute to the Barbary states of Algiers, Tripoli, and Tunis to protect US ships from attack. The Americans paid Algiers $1 million a year for 15 years during a time when the total US annual income was only $10 million.

After Jefferson's inauguration as President in 1801, Yusef Caramanli, Pasha of Tripoli, demanded $225,000 as tribute from the US in return for not attacking American ships in the Mediterranean. Jefferson, who had opposed paying tribute in the first place, refused and the Pasha declared war on the United States by chopping down the flagpole outside the US Consulate in Tripoli.

While the United States was developing westward, it undertook a naval expedition against the Barbary pirates. Taking advantage of a law allowing for the creation of a US Navy, Jefferson sent a group of frigates to defend US interests and though Congress did not formally declare war, the American ships attacked the ships of the pirate corsairs in 1801.

The American fleet was reinforced next year, but in October 1803 Tripoli pirates captured the USS *Philadelphia* when it ran aground in Tripoli harbor. The ship's captain, William Bainbridge, and all officers and crew were taken ashore and locked up in Tripoli Castle as hostages.

In February 1804, in a dramatic rescue, Stephen Decatur in the USS *Intrepid* stormed the *Philadelphia* and set it on fire to deny it to the enemy. Later the *Intrepid* was destroyed when, packed with explosives, it attempted to sink the pirates' fleet.

In April–May 1805 William Eaton and First Lieutenant Presley O'Bannon led a force of eight US Marines across the desert from Egypt and captured Derna, the first time the US flag was raised in a victory overseas, an exploit commemorated in the *Marines' Hymn*: 'From the Halls of Montezuma, / To the shores of Tripoli; / We fight our country's battles / In the air, on land, and sea.' In June 1805 Yusef Caramanli signed a peace treaty.

The First Barbary War of 1801–5 had established America's naval reputation throughout the world. American ships probed the Pacific and in 1813 Commodore

David Porter seized the South Pacific island of Nukahiva for the United States. (The US Congress never ratified the claim and eventually France took possession of the island.) Meanwhile the attention of the United States had switched to its deteriorating relationship with Britain. An escalating series of disputes eventually led to the United States declaring war on the British in 1812. The United States launched a couple of incursions into Canada, which US leaders hoped to annex.

## Louisiana Purchase

The westward expansion of the United States into empire was not by conquest but by purchase of government bonds. While the American fleet fought off Barbary shores, in 1803 the United States under Jefferson acquired a vast swathe of territory covering 800,000 square miles (2.1 million sq. km) that doubled the size of the United States and included all or parts of 14 future states.

Known as 'Louisiana across the Mississippi,' it had been part of a vast swathe of land claimed by France in 1682 and named for King Louis XIV. In 1763, following the French defeat in the Seven Years' War, 'the French interior' was ceded to Britain (east of the Mississippi) and Spain (west of the Mississippi), but in 1800 Napoleon secured the return of Spanish Louisiana, the portion west of the Mississippi, including New Orleans. Excluded from North America since 1763, France once more had a presence there, but it regarded the land as unusable and Napoleon was pleased to offload Louisiana for some badly needed income. British naval power had confined Napoleon's fleet to Europe, and the French accepted Jefferson's offer of $11.25 million in US Government bonds. The United States had effectively bought Louisiana on a mortgage brokered by the London bank Barings.[3]

(It is fascinating to reflect that US history might have been very different but for Napoleon's fateful decision to sell – a decision he made in his bathtub. Had Napoleon not sold up, Louisiana would probably have passed to Britain in 1815 when Napoleon was defeated by the British at Waterloo and France was forced to surrender some of its possessions.)

Jefferson's 'empire of liberty' had envisioned the United States and other republics in association. The 1803 Louisiana Purchase began the process of continental expansion. The 14 future states it encompassed were: all present-day Arkansas, Missouri, Iowa, Oklahoma, Kansas, and Nebraska; parts of Minnesota west of the Mississippi; most of North Dakota; nearly all South Dakota and north-eastern New Mexico; portions of Montana, Wyoming, and Colorado east of the Continental Divide; and Louisiana (including New Orleans), which entered the United States in 1812.

The Oklahoma Panhandle and south-western portions of Kansas and Louisiana were still claimed by Spain in 1803, but in addition the Purchase included portions of land that would eventually become part of the Canadian provinces of Alberta and Saskatchewan.

The Purchase amounted to 23 percent of current US territory. A small portion of the Purchase was ceded to Britain in 1818 in exchange for the Red River Basin. Some land was ceded to Spain in 1819 but was recovered in the 1840s.

### Second Barbary War

The War of 1812 between the United States and Britain lasted until 1815. Then America was again forced to turn its attention to North Africa. Despite the actions of Bainbridge and Decatur, the United States was still paying tribute to the Barbary states. In June 1815 Decatur captured the Algerian flagship *Meshuda* and brig *Estedio* and released them in return for some ten American captives and the cancellation of all tributes. The shipping rights of the United States were confirmed.

However, Tunis revoked this agreement and in early 1816 Britain sent a squadron of ships to Tunis, Tripoli, and Algiers to convince them to stop all piracy. The Algiers troops massacred 200 Corsican, Sicilian, and Sardinian fishermen who were under British protection, and the British fleet bombarded Algiers for nine hours. A treaty was signed in September 1816 and the Second Barbary War was over.

### Six More States

The wars of the United States against the British and Barbary pirates had caused a surge of pro-US feeling across the mountains, and four more states joined the Union: Indiana in 1816, Mississippi in 1817, Illinois in 1818, and Alabama in 1819.

The war against the British had caused Spanish authority in Florida to disintegrate, and when residents around Baton Rouge proclaimed a Republic of West Florida, President Madison ordered it to be annexed. A treaty of 1818 with Britain agreed a northern US boundary, the 49th parallel, separating British possessions in what became Canada from the unorganized territory to the south, and agreed that Britain would give up aspirations for what would become North Dakota. Under an 1819 treaty with Spain, Spain ceded East Florida and the 'Sabine Free State,' the neutral strip between Louisiana and Spanish Texas which had been disputed by the United States and Spain, and recognized a western boundary along the border of what would become Oklahoma.

Missouri lay north of the line (36°, 30′) which in 1820 would mark the northern limits of slavery. Slavery serviced the Southern plantations as fundamentally as machines serviced the Northern factories. Nevertheless in 1819 Missouri was admitted to the Union as a slave state and Maine was admitted as a sop to the outraged North in 1820.

With newly-independent Spanish colonies finding their feet in Latin America, in 1823 the United States established the Monroe Doctrine, which declared opposition to European interference in the Americas. US expansion westward would lead to local wars with Indians and Mexico, but generally the United States was now unchallenged abroad as it pushed westward.

The frontier was being advanced further and further westward as more and more eastern settlers spilled over the Mississippi Valley in wagons filled with bedding, utensils, and provisions, drawn by small horses or oxen. They were in search of land and the 19th-century version of the American Dream: the good life in which there was the prospect of prosperity and liberty for all Americans.

The westward migrants entered into lands of Indians whose rights were insufficiently protected. White invaders occupied the prairies and hardwood forests of Wisconsin.

In 1820 the western frontier was the Mississippi. By the 1840s it had reached the 100th meridian, which bisects modern North Dakota and Texas.

For a while the westward push stopped. The Great Plains to the west had too little rainfall for farming. However, from the 1840s on, wagon trains set out from states such as Missouri and Illinois to cross the Rocky Mountains through native-American territory and settle near the Pacific coast. There were two routes: the Oregon Trail and, diverging from it at its junction with Snake River, the California Trail.

It took the migrants six months to reach the Far West in their ox-drawn, canvas-clad wagons. They were often attacked by Indians and suffered infectious disease. Some turned back, but most continued, lured by the prospect of cheap land. Professional people – lawyers, doctors – moved west to boom towns which, like Chicago, a small town on the shore of Lake Michigan in 1837, grew into great cities. Michigan's population was 31,000 in 1830, 212,000 in 1840.[4]

Pioneer settlers wielding axes cut down parts of forests and built log cabins from which a succession of 19th-century presidents would claim to have originated, and tamed the wilderness with their horse-drawn plows. The westward expansion probed south, west and north of the Louisiana territory into land held by Mexico or Britain, and this led to conflict between these governments and the United States.

## Texas

With the permission of the newly-independent Mexican Government, Texas had been colonized from 1821. By 1835 the American settlers outnumbered Mexicans. They took up arms and established an independent Republic of Texas, defeating the Mexican Army at the Battle of San Jacinto in 1836. That year, the republic voted to be annexed by the United States. However, there was resistance in Congress and years dragged by.

Although Mexico still claimed Texas and the Mexican leader Antonio Lopez de Santa Anna warned that joining the Union would be 'equivalent to a declaration of war against the Mexican Republic,' US President John Tyler signed a treaty of annexation with Texas in April 1844. Congress approved the annexation on February 28, 1845, just before President James K. Polk, a supporter of territorial expansion and a Freemason, took office. On December 29, 1845, Texas became the 28th state.

The settlers' cause had been enthusiastically championed by Presidents Andrew Jackson (1829–37), Tyler, and now Polk, who all sought to enlarge the 'empire of liberty.' Jackson (Harmony Lodge no. 1, Tennessee) and Polk (Colombia Lodge no. 31, Tennessee) were both Freemasons.

## Free and Slave States

Now new states came into the Union in pairs, to balance slave states and free states in a fair way: slave Arkansas in 1836 and free Michigan in 1837; slave Florida in 1845 and free Iowa in 1846; slave Texas in 1845 and free Wisconsin in 1848. Meanwhile, in the 1840s Mormons headed west and began to congregate in Utah.

## New Mexico and Upper California

In 1846 the Freemason President Polk persuaded the British to negotiate a treaty under which the Oregon Territory south of the 49th parallel, including practically all of the Colombia River, would revert to the United States. No payment was made by the United States. The agreement extended the 49th-parallel boundary to the west coast. Under the compromise British North America received territory north of the 49th parallel.

Polk was intent on securing the Mexican territories of New Mexico and Upper California, and in 1846 he used a border incident to start a war with Mexico, which was incensed at Congress's high-handed approach over Texas. Congress did not declare war and many Congressmen privately opposed the war.

In March 1846 Polk ordered General Zachary Taylor to march from the Nueces River to the Rio Grande. The United States won a series of victories and in February 1847 crushed the Mexican General Santa Anna's large force at Buena Vista. Another US army under General Winfield Scott landed at Veracruz and captured Mexico City in September 1847.

Under the Treaty of Guadalupe Hidalgo of February 1848, the United States and Mexico drew their boundary at the Rio Grande and Gila Rivers, and for a payment of $15 million the United States acquired the provinces of New Mexico and Upper California, what is now most of New Mexico, Arizona, California (where gold had been discovered a few months before), western Colorado, Texas, Utah, and Nevada.

In return the United States agreed to settle more than $3 million in claims made by US citizens against Mexico, leaving Mexico free from such claims. The United States now had access to California, and the Californian Gold Rush of 1849 was inspired by what had motivated the American Dream: the promise of a quick profit from a new economic opportunity. California was admitted to the Union in 1850.

# Manifest Destiny

The new term 'manifest destiny' had justified American expansion into both Texas and Oregon. This phrase suggested that America was destined, even divinely ordained, to expand across the North-American continent from the Atlantic seaboard to the Pacific Ocean. To some, it meant the eventual absorption of all North America within the United States, including Canada, Mexico, Cuba, and

THE SECRET AMERICAN DREAM

Central America. To advocates of manifest destiny, expansion was ethical, readily apparent ('manifest') and inexorable ('destiny').

The concept of manifest destiny was first aired by a journalist, John L. O'Sullivan, in 1839. He predicted a 'divine destiny' for the United States, which would be one of a 'Union of many Republics' sharing the common values of equality, conscience, and personal enfranchisement.

In 1845 O'Sullivan wrote an article entitled 'Annexation' for the *United States Magazine and Democratic Review*[5] in which he urged the United States to annex the Republic of Texas not only because Texas deserved it but because it was 'our manifest destiny to overspread the continent allotted by Providence for the free development of our yearly multiplying millions.'[6]

On December 27, 1845, O'Sullivan expanded on the term 'free development' when he wrote in the *New York Morning News* that the United States had the right to claim 'the whole of Oregon':

'And that claim is by the right of our manifest destiny to overspread and to possess the whole of the continent which Providence has given us for the development of the great experiment of liberty and federated self-government entrusted to us.'[7]

In this wording, O'Sullivan shifts the emphasis of America's 'manifest destiny' from the practical aim of greater 'living space' for a free people to the ideological aim of spreading liberty itself. In other words Providence had given the United States a mission to spread republican democracy ('the great experiment of liberty') throughout North America. British claims to Oregon could be overruled because Britain would not spread democracy throughout Oregon.

To O'Sullivan there would be no territorial expansion by force or involvement of the US Government or military. He disapproved of the Mexican–American war of 1846. Settlers would emigrate to new regions where they would set up democratic governments and seek admission to the United States, as Texas had done. O'Sullivan predicted that California would be next, then Canada.

The concept of manifest destiny tapped into the idea of the virtue of the American people and their institutions, later known as 'American Exceptionalism.' The term goes back to the French historian Alexis de Tocqueville,[8] who claimed that the United States, when 50 years old, held a special place among nations because it was a country of immigrants and the first modern democracy. However, the concept can be tracked back to John Winthrop's 1630 'City upon a Hill' sermon in which he called for a virtuous community that would be a shining example to the Old World.

Manifest destiny also tapped into Tom Paine's 1776 pamphlet, *Common Sense*, which argued that the American Revolution was an opportunity to create a better society: 'We have it in our power to begin the world over again. A situation, similar to the present hath not happened since the days of Noah until now. The birthday of a new world is at hand.' In other words, the United States had embarked on a special experiment in freedom and democracy, rejecting Old-World monarchy for republicanism. President Lincoln echoed this concept in his message to Congress on December 1, 1862, when he spoke of the United States as being 'the last, best hope of Earth.'

However, Whig opponents of the Polk Administration criticized the concept of 'manifest destiny.' On January 3, 1846, representative Robert Winthrop said in Congress: 'I suppose the right of a manifest destiny to spread will not be admitted to exist in any nation except the universal Yankee nation.' He claimed that advocates of Manifest Destiny were justifying expansion by citing 'Divine Providence' whereas the expansion was really motivated by self-interest and chauvinism.

Whigs argued that America's mission was to serve as a virtuous example to the rest of the world so other countries would establish their own democratic republics.

## Purchased Expansion into Native Americans' Land

Continental expansion meant occupying native-American land. The United States continued the European colonial practice of limited recognition of indigenous peoples' land rights. George Washington's Secretary of War, Henry Knox, formulated a policy of expanding westward through the legal purchase of native Americans' land in treaties. Indians should sell their tribal lands, abandon hunting, become farmers, and be 'civilized.' This would liberate land for white Americans to 'homestead' (settle and farm). Some Indians who signed treaties were not aware of the consent they were giving.

Jefferson at first held that whites and native Americans were intellectually equal and would merge to create a single nation. Later he came to believe that native

Americans should cross the Mississippi River and live separately in the Louisiana Purchase territory, an early form of *apartheid* known as 'Indian Removal.'

Many Americans regarded native Americans as savages who were in the way of American expansion and believed they would melt away into the remoter areas of the wilderness as the United States expanded. The historian Francis Parkman wrote in 1851 that Indians were 'destined to melt and vanish before the advancing waves of Anglo-American power, which now rolled westward unchecked and unopposed.'[9]

The US Government's policy toward the native Americans was ambivalent. Tracts of land in the West had been set aside for specified Indian tribes, but the outbreak of Indian wars and the pressure on the frontier led some Westerners and military officers to connive in removing Indian tribes from areas unofficially and illegally requisitioned by whites.

There was pressure on such areas after the 1862 Homestead Act, which offered 160 acres of land free to anyone who settled and farmed it. Steps were taken from 1869 to assimilate Indians into American society. In 1889 Congress enacted the Dawes Act, which empowered the President to grant 160 acres to the head of each Indian family, with small allotments to members of each tribe. Such measures attempted to absorb native Americans, rather than preserve aspects of their culture.

There had already been numerous conflicts between the colonial or federal government and native Americans, starting with the Pequot War of 1637. East of the Mississippi, the Revolutionary War was the most extreme and destructive Indian war in US history. This continued with the Chickamauga Wars and with wars in the Northwest Territory, US-occupied lands bordering the Great Lakes northwest of the Ohio River. The Indian leader Tecumseh had allied with the British shortly before the 1812 war and encouraged the Creek Indians to attack the US forces.

Andrew Jackson signed the Indian Removal Act in 1830 under which tribal land in the east could be exchanged for western lands acquired under the Louisiana Purchase. Some Indians were resentful and this resulted in the Black-Hawk War of 1832, the Creek War of 1836, and the Second Seminole War in Florida of 1835–42. West of the Mississippi, Plains Indians and Comanches fought the Texans on and off from 1836 to 1870. There were wars in the Great Basin and on the Plains. The Dakota War (or Sioux Uprising) of 1862, the Sand

Creek Massacre, the Sioux Indian War of 1865 in Colorado, and the Black-Hills War of 1876–7 were all very bitter, and there was also fighting in the southwest. The last of the Indian wars was the Wounded Knee Massacre of 1890, which ended in the closing of the American frontier.

The result of the American–Indian wars was a general opening of native-American lands to further colonization, the conquest and assimilation of native Americans, and sometimes their forced relocation to Indian reservations. It has been estimated that 45,000 Indians and 19,000 white Americans were killed in these wars.[10]

America's westward expansion opened up the possibility of dominating sea trade to the West Coast. In a speech to the Senate in 1850, William Henry Seward welcomed California into the Union: 'The world contains no seat of empire so magnificent as this, which…offers supplies on the Atlantic shores to the overcrowded nations of Europe, while on the Pacific coast it intercepts the commerce of the Indies. The nation thus situated must command…the empire of the seas, which alone is real empire.'[11]

But in fact the United States continued to purchase its westward expansion. In 1851 it secured the limits of the Oregon Territory by agreeing that the border with the British, the 49th parallel, should be extended to the Pacific. In 1853 under the Gadsden Purchase – James Gadsden was the American Ambassador to Mexico at the time – the United States bought more territory from Mexico for $10 million: southern Arizona and the New-Mexican border area.

In 1867 Seward, now US Secretary of State, acquired Alaska from the Russian Tsar for $7.2 million as a discreet way of settling Russia's bill for putting the Russian fleet at Lincoln's disposal in 1863.[12] Alaska was regarded as useless land and the transaction was known as 'Seward's Folly.'

The American purchase of Alaska concentrated British minds and in 1867 Britain created the self-governing Dominion of Canada, which by 1871 extended from the Atlantic to the Pacific. The northern border of the United States ran for 4,000 miles (6,400km) from coast to coast, for the most part following the 49th parallel west of the Great Lakes.

# Railroads and New States

As the West was opened up by settlers, communications between the West and the East improved. In 1851 a stagecoach service began between Independence, Missouri, and Salt Lake City, in the newly-created Utah Territory. In 1851 the overland mail was introduced between St. Louis and San Francisco. The telegraph service linking Kansas and California began in 1861.

Railroad building began in the mid-1850s. In 1862 Congress authorized the construction of two railroads that together would link the Mississippi Valley and the Pacific Coast: Union Pacific was to run westward from Council Bluffs, Iowa, and Central Pacific was to run eastward from Sacramento, California. To speed up the construction, Congress provided subsidies: land grants and loans. The two lines eventually met in May 1869 at Promontory Summit, Utah.

In 1869 the first transcontinental railroad was completed. In the 1870s railroads carried farmers onto the Great Plains and with new technology in the form of steel plows they turned the Plains into wheatfields to create the breadbasket of America.

The pioneer settlers, ranchers, and homesteaders who braved the dangers of the 'Wild West,' including attacks from native Americans who had been constantly driven from their hunting-grounds by white men's westward probings, had now been joined by railroad builders who opened up the West for the coming generations.

Railroad-building slowed down during the depression of 1873–7, but then speeded up again. By 1865, 35,000 miles (56,000km) of track were in operation, and 122,000 miles (196,000km) more had been added by 1887. Four years earlier, in 1883, three more connections had been established between the Mississippi Valley and the West Coast: the Northern Pacific from St. Paul, Minneapolis to Portland, Oregon; the Santa Fe from Chicago, Illinois to Los Angeles, California; and the Southern Pacific from New Orleans, Louisiana to Los Angeles.

The West developed along the railroads, which brought vitality to regions. The railroad owners fixed prices and sought to impose a transportation monopoly where they operated. In the 30 years after gold was discovered in California in 1848, gold or silver was found in every territory in the Far West. In western Nevada, the Comstock Lode of silver was found in 1859 and then developed, and gold was discovered in the Black Hills of South Dakota in 1874 and in Cripple Creek,

Colorado, in 1891. Mining towns quickly grew near these sites, but when the prospectors left with their silver or gold they became deserted ghost towns.

The railroad development of the West had continued to add new states to the Union even though the issue of slavery proved even more divisive in the 1850s and 1860s than in the 1830s and 1840s. Decisions on whether to have slavery were left to the territories of Utah and New Mexico on their creation in 1850, and likewise to Nebraska Territory and Kansas Territory in 1854. Now Oregon entered the Union in 1859, Kansas in 1861, Nevada in 1864, Nebraska in 1867, and Colorado in 1876. North and South Dakota, Montana, and Washington all achieved statehood in 1889, Wyoming and Idaho in 1890.

The last few states would join the Union in dribs and drabs: Utah in 1896, Oklahoma in 1907, New Mexico and Arizona in 1912. Alaska and Hawaii were late entrants in 1959. With the admission of Hawaii in March that year the expansion of the federal United States was complete.

In 1880 the US population was just above 50 million. In 1900 it was just under 76 million, 9 million of whom were new immigrants, mostly from Europe, a 50-percent increase in 20 years. In 1880, 22 percent of Americans lived west of the Mississippi. By 1900 the figure was 27 percent.

By now the population of the United States and of the Far West was increasing rapidly. In 1890, 21 years after the opening of the first transcontinental railroad, the US Census Bureau announced that there was no continuous free land left for settlement in the West. The frontier line had ceased to exist, and the westward expansion of America had ended. Now the United States was looking overseas.

★

The impulse behind the westward expansion was different from the impulse behind federal unification. Westward expansion was a thrusting outward into the unknown in the hope of a better life, a primitive version of the American Dream, taming the wilderness. It was different from exporting Liberty's values to the colonial empire at the end of the 1890s. It was a fulfilling of Liberty's Manifest Destiny, not conquering the West but taking it over from the native Americans in order to make it better – to fulfill the American destiny to improve.

The federal Government was very pleased to receive new states into the federal Union, and different Presidents – Freemasons like Jefferson, Jackson, and

Polk – encouraged the spread of federalism out into the world, imperialistically. The individual settlers had the energy and godliness of a civilization that was at its start, of a thrusting, young civilization. The Freemasonic federal center harnessed this raw energy and carried on adding to the expanding Freemasonic State that had begun with the unification of the Thirteen Colonies. And this Freemasonic impulse to add to federal expansion would continue overseas in the spreading of a colonial empire, as we saw at the beginning of Part One.

We are now in a position to see that Freemasonry has been a strand that co-existed with Christianity from early on, and that besides being behind Franklin, Washington, Jefferson, Jackson, and Polk, it was behind the bouts of expansion we encountered in Part One. For three figures who were key to establishing the US colonial empire of 1898 – President William McKinley (Hiram Lodge no. 21, Virginia) and future Presidents Theodore Roosevelt (Matinecock Lodge no. 806, Oyster Bay), and William Howard Taft (Kilwinning Lodge no. 356, Ohio) – were Freemasons, which brings a new angle to the expansion into empire at that time.

Woodrow Wilson's adviser, Colonel House – who was behind the Fourteen Points and the setting-up of the League of Nations, so much so that he gave Wilson the idea[13] – was a 33rd-Degree Grand-Lodge Freemason. And also Freemasons were Franklin D. Roosevelt, Truman (Belton Lodge no. 450, 33rd Degree and Grand Master), and Johnson (entered Apprentice), who presided over America's inter-vention in the Second World War, in the post-war involvement in Europe and in the Pacific, and in the escalation of the Vietnam War.

The impulse we have detected of ever-increasing American expansion into the outside world backed by a hidden Freemasonry continued after 1989 with American superpowerdom, and its expression in the economic–political phenomenon known as globalization.

# PART THREE

# What Liberty's Empire Turned Into:
# The Rise of American Supremacy

## CHAPTER 6

# LIBERTY'S SUPREMACY:
## Superpowerdom and
## World Empire

T he accepted view of the role of the United States since 1989 is that when the Soviet hegemony collapsed, Liberty's empire was left as the sole superpower. There seems to have been more to it than that, but before we pass on to the force behind the scenes (see p.44) we need to focus on American superpowerdom.

## American Superpowerdom and Its Challenges

What is a superpower? A superpower has a leading position in the international system and is able to influence world events and its own interests. It projects dominating power and influence everywhere in the world and appears to be a global hegemon, the leader or possessor of a hegemony (see p.30).

America clearly was now a superpower within this definition. The United States was a strong political republic with ties to Western Europe, Latin America, the (originally-British) Commonwealth, and East-Asian countries. Geographically it was the third-largest country in the world (after the Russian Federation and Canada, disregarding the EU) with the fourth-largest population (after China, India, and the EU). It had the most advanced military and now has the highest military expenditure.[1] It had the world's largest navy, which now surpasses the combined force of the next 13 navies.[2] It had between 700 and 800 military bases all over the world,[3] which ringed the Warsaw-Pact countries and now ring Iran and China. It had powerful military allies in NATO, and a global-intelligence network in the CIA. It had ties with paramilitary and guerrilla groups in the developing world and huge armaments production levels. It had the biggest economy in the world[4] and was home to many large global corporations. It was very influential in music, TV, films, art, and fashion.

In short, as Samuel P. Huntington has said: 'The United States, of course, is the sole state with pre-eminence in every domain of power – economic, military, diplomatic, ideological, technological, and cultural – with the reach and capabilities to promote its interests in virtually every part of the world.'[5]

Huntington adds that although there was only one superpower there were several major powers among the many other lesser powers.

American supremacy and world domination now allowed America to throw its weight around and expand American influence. Lady Liberty was now in charge of leading the world to liberty, and though UN approval was desirable it was not essential.

American superpowerdom was swiftly challenged by the outbreak of ethnic, nationalist, and separatist conflicts. The first involved Iraq, which had long laid claim to neighboring Kuwait.

## Iraq: Gulf War

The American superpower was now challenged by Saddam Hussein, who wanted to annex Kuwait. Like Iraq, Kuwait had been part of the Ottoman Empire's Mesopotamian provinces for 400 years. In 1880, the British Government appointed the Emir of Kuwait, Abdullah al-Salem al-Sabah, its representative outside Iraq's southern border near the recently-discovered Iraqi Rumaila oilfields. In 1899 Kuwait became a British protectorate and al-Sabah ceded land inside Iraq, including the Rumaila oilfields, to the British and British Petroleum – which he had no right to do. Two years earlier Ottoman Turkey had demanded that Britain should not interfere with its empire, but then backed down. Now the Ottomans resented al-Sabah's transaction but did not block it.

During the First World War, the pro-German Ottoman Empire began to dis-integrate. In 1915, the British set up a mandate in North Iraq and a puppet regime under King Faisal of Syria in South Iraq. The British agreed to grant Iraq independence in 1923 and it became independent in 1932.

In 1961 the Iraqi leader, General Abdul Karim Kassem, who had overthrown the monarchy in 1958, claimed that Kuwait was Iraqi territory. Britain granted Kuwait independence in 1965, which meant that Kuwait could not be given back to Iraq and that Iraq's claims could be ignored. The British continued to rule Kuwait unofficially through the al-Sabah family.

Saddam Hussein, an ex-criminal, had been recruited by the CIA to assassinate Kassem in 1959, an attempt that left Kassem wounded. Saddam subsequently rose to prominence following the Ba'ath Party's US-backed *coup* of 1968 and took supreme power in 1979, again with American backing. By the end of the 1980s, Saddam had milked Iraq for his family and wanted to recover part of the Rumaila oilfields taken by Kuwait during the Iran–Iraq War of 1980–8. (Kuwait had illegally acquired 900 square miles (2,230 sq. km) of Iraqi territory by moving its borders northward. This had been presented to Iraq as a *fait accompli* and gave Kuwait access to the oilfields.) Saddam also wanted the al-Burqan oilfields in Kuwait, the second largest in the world.

Having been armed by America to fight the eight-year war against Iran, Saddam was now reported to be on the verge of making Iraq a nuclear power. In 1989 the US Department of Energy reported to general consternation that Iraq had begun to build an atomic bomb, using US technology.[6]

In November 1989, the month in which the Berlin Wall was opened, America responded to a reported Iraqi nuclear test by resolving to effect 'regime change' in Iraq. The CIA Director met the head of Kuwaiti State Security and promised US support if Kuwait pressed Iraq on its border dispute.[7] A memo of this meeting, seized by Iraq, was later shown to an Arab Summit meeting in mid-August 1990.[8]

Saddam's animosity toward Kuwait began when the Iran–Iraq War left him broke. He had borrowed from Kuwait and, claiming to have defended Kuwait and other Arab states from the Iranian threat, he asked the emirate to pay its share by canceling the $17 billion that Iraq owed to Kuwait as a result of the war. Kuwait refused. Outraged, Saddam accused Kuwait of stealing oil worth $10–14 billion by slant-drilling (that is, illegally drilling into Iraqi oilfields from the Kuwaiti side of the border) in the 1980s. In February 1990 he condemned the US military presence in the Persian Gulf. In April he called for a pan-Arab troop build-up to expel Israel from the Occupied Territories.

In April 1990, President George H.W. Bush held a meeting of advisers at the White House at which it was agreed that the United States should change its favorable attitude to Iraq.[9] Robert Gates, the head of the Committee of the National Security Council and later Secretary of Defense, was crucial to carrying through the change.[10] In May the US National Security Agency blocked a $500 million loan due to be made to Iraq by the US Department of Agriculture.[11]

The sole superpower used cunning to rebuff Saddam's challenge. On July 25, 1990, on Bush's instructions, the US Ambassador to Iraq, April Glaspie, met Saddam Hussein and assured him that America had no quarrel with him and would not intervene in any inter-Arab border disputes.[12] She said the United States had no opinion about such disputes.[12]

Saddam took this as US consent that he could invade Kuwait and take the ten percent of the Rumaila oilfields illegally occupied by Kuwait. Four days later Saddam began moving troops. Glaspie now denied making her earlier assurances and resigned from the State Department. Her involvement had had the effect of luring Saddam into Kuwait and of setting the trap for him.

On August 2, 1990, Saddam's forces invaded Kuwait and annexed it as Iraq's 19th province. The same day the UN Security Council demanded that Iraq should withdraw from Kuwait.

Now the United States laid the foundations for regime change. Secretary of State James Baker and Secretary of Defense Dick Cheney flew to Saudi Arabia and convinced King Fahd that Saddam was about to invade Saudi Arabia and threaten Saudi oil, even though the CIA had told George H.W. Bush that Iraq had no such invasion plans.[13] They persuaded Fahd to base American troops in his Kingdom even though their presence would defile holy territory. (Saudi Arabia is home to Islam's most sacred sites, Mecca and Medina.) Saudi Arabia and Kuwait agreed to pay most of the costs of a war with Iraq, and Japan and Germany would contribute.

The sole superpower used its influence to set up a war that would not cost the United States a dollar. (In the event, the total cost of the war came to $61 billion and there was a shortfall of $7 billion, which the United States met.)

On August 7, US troops were joined by troops from Egypt, Morocco, and Syria in an alliance between the United States, Saudi Arabia and other Arab countries. The Americans ignored Iraqi proposals to withdraw from Kuwait in exchange for Israel's evacuation of the West Bank and Gaza; Syria's evacuation of the Lebanon; Iraqi control of the Rumaila oilfields; and the replacement of US forces by UN troops.

It is alleged that the United States launched its war by bribing other members of the UN Security Council: the ailing Soviet Union with $6 billion; Colombia, Ethiopia, and Zaire with new aid and loans from the World Bank and IMF; and China with the release of frozen World-Bank credits, ending Chinese isolation after the Tiananmen-Square massacre of 1989. Through these countries' votes on November 29, the United States secured authorization for a war against Iraq.[14] Yemen voted against and found that $70 million in US aid had been canceled.

As a result of US manipulation, the UN set a deadline for Iraq to accept UN demands to withdraw from Kuwait or be attacked under a resolution that permitted the use of 'all appropriate measures.' The US-led Coalition, known as 'Desert Shield,' was swelled to 550,000 men.

*Operation Desert Storm* began on January 17, 1991, with an aerial bombardment. In a display of awesome superpowerdom US fighter bombers used precision bombing to demonstrate US military superiority and control of the skies. 'Smart' bombs attacked Saddam's main palace, Baghdad airport, nuclear reactors, oil refineries, and electrical plants in Baghdad. The Iraqi Republican Guard, sitting in trenches along the Kuwait–Saudi border, were bombed by B-52s. More than 100 Tomahawk cruise missiles were launched from the sea.

In retaliation Saddam fired Scud missiles at Israel and one Scud (which was destroyed in the air) at the US base in Dhahran, Saudi Arabia. He also created the largest oil slick in history, 35 miles long by 10 miles wide (56km by 16km), in the Persian Gulf. However, on the same day, 80 Iraqi pilots flew their planes to Iran and gave themselves up.

For six weeks America's superior technology destroyed Saddam's air force, disabled his infrastructure, and battered and culled his army. Saddam sent his Foreign Minister, Tariq Aziz, to speak to Soviet President Gorbachev, but the ensuing peace plan was not implemented.

The United States launched a ground attack on February 24, having warned Saddam to withdraw his troops from Kuwait by February 23, a deadline Saddam ignored. On February 25, Saddam's troops belatedly withdrew and as they retreated set fire to 100 Kuwaiti oil wells in the Rumaila oilfields, all the property of British Petroleum.

On February 27, George H.W. Bush declared in a live address to the nation: 'Iraq's army is defeated and Kuwait is liberated. Our military objectives are met.'[15] The Coalition ceased hostilities, claiming that the UN mandate to expel

Iraqi troops from Kuwait had been fulfilled. The decision came as a shock as the road to Baghdad was wide open and Saddam could have been captured and a pro-Western regime installed.

The sole superpower had been at pains to adhere to its UN brief. The United States was not going to risk the lives of its troops in taking Baghdad or risk fracturing the international alliance by deposing the Sunni regime. Bush counted on Iraqis to overthrow Saddam. In spite of the Gulf War's abrupt end, the United States had laid to rest the Vietnam defeat, and there was a feeling of pride and unity throughout the country that had not been felt since 1945.

Saddam, however, remained in place, and continued to rule with Russian support. However, he had failed in his attempt to take back the illegally-occupied part of the Rumaila oilfields.

UN sanctions imposed on Iraq in August 1990 remained in force until 2003. They were tied to Iraq's compliance with Security Council Resolution 687, which required the demolition of Iraq's weapons of mass destruction (WMDs) and compliance inspections at 60-day intervals. The sanctions could only be lifted when there was unanimity between the Security Council's Permanent Members, but the United States and Britain were opposed to lifting them.

When Saddam suppressed uprisings by Iraqi Shias and Kurds soon after the end of the Gulf War, America did not intervene but tightened sanctions. Saddam avoided implementing the next 12 UN resolutions, which demanded reparations and reinforced the imposition of UN inspection teams to hunt for weapons of mass destruction. Saddam seemed to have destroyed most of these, but this is not certain. He certainly encouraged the belief that he still had WMDs in order to discourage Israel and Iran from attacking Iraq – a deliberate misrepresentation that would come back to haunt him in 2003.

### The Balkans
American superpowerdom was further challenged by ethnic, nationalist, and separatist conflicts in the Balkans.

Following the death in 1980 of Marshal Josip Broz Tito, Yugoslavia's leader since the Second World War, there was a growth in separatist feeling in some of the constituent republics of the Yugoslav Federation. By the early 1990s it appeared clear that Slovenia and Croatia intended to declare independence. Serbia, which dominated the Federation, was vehemently opposed to a break-up and its

President, Slobodan Milosevic, began calling for a 'Greater Serbia' that would restore the pre-1915 Serbian borders and include Croatia. Until the 1990s a third of ethnic Serbs had been living outside Serbia's borders. Seeing that the United States was preoccupied with the aftermath of the Gulf War and was happy to leave the Balkans to the European Community, Serbia then removed the autonomy of Kosovo, a Serbian province with a mainly ethnic-Albanian population, and opposed independence in Slovenia and Croatia.

Serbia's aim was to seize as much territory as possible by driving Croatians and Muslims from 'Greater Serbia,' a process that came to be known as 'ethnic cleansing.' The Serbs thought that the UN would be called in to adjudicate and would duly award all Serb-held land to Serbia.

The Serb-dominated Government of the Yugoslav Federation acted alongside the Serbian Government to resist the break-up. In June 1991 the federal forces of the Yugoslav People's Army (JNA), supported by Serbia, moved into Slovenia. The JNA soon abandoned this tiny Alpine republic in the far west of Yugoslavia to its own devices. Breakaway Croatia, with its large Serb minority, was another matter and in July fighting spread across Croatia.

At first Croatian police forces attacked ethnic Serbs living in Croatia. The Croatian Government then attacked the Yugoslav People's Army (JNA) and forces of the newly-proclaimed Republic of Serbian Krajina (RSK) within Croatia. By August, Serb forces occupied a third of Croatian territory.

In 1992 the war spread to Bosnia-Herzegovina, a largely Muslim republic that had also declared independence. The move was opposed by its substantial Serb and Croat minorities, who proclaimed two rival statelets within Bosnia-Herzegovina, the Republika Srpska (Serb Republic) and the Croatian Republic of Herzeg-Bosnia.

Croatia supported the forces of Herzeg-Bosnia while Serbia gave military and financial support to the largely-Serb JNA; the army of Republika Srpska; the Serbian Ministry of the Interior; the Ministry of the Interior of Republika Srpska; and the Serb Territorial Defense Forces. Bosnian Serbs fought both Croats and Bosnian Muslims, and the Serbs set up concentration camps to service their policy of 'ethnic cleansing.'

Under Bill Clinton, George H.W. Bush's successor as President, the United States played the role of a sole superpower in keeping the peace in the Balkans. From 1992 to 1996, US planes provided humanitarian relief in Bosnia and Herzegovina.

In July 1993, President Bill Clinton deployed 350 US soldiers to the Republic of Macedonia, another breakaway Yugoslav republic, to participate in the UN Protection Force to maintain stability in former Yugoslavia.

In 1994, the United States supported Bosnian Muslims and NATO air strikes against the Bosnian Serbs. On February 28, NATO jets shot down four Serb aircraft over central Bosnia. In April 1994, Clinton sent 200 more troops to Macedonia.

European-Community diplomats negotiated truces, cease-fires, peace plans, and agreements, and the UN passed numerous resolutions, but neither the EC nor the UN could persuade the Serb leader, Slobodan Milosevic, to accept that the new republics had the right to self-determination. Eventually, the 1995 Dayton Agreement (based on talks held in Dayton, Ohio) ended the Croatian and Bosnian wars.

But peace did not come to the Balkans, for now the Albanians of Kosovo became active. The Kosovo Liberation Army (KLA), an ethnic Albanian group, offered armed resistance to Serbian and Yugoslav forces.

Again, the sole superpower oversaw the fighting. In March 1997, US military forces evacuated US Government employees and US citizens from Tirana, Albania. Many Albanians were displaced and after a cease-fire war broke out again in 1998. Between March and June 1999, NATO intervened again by bombing Serbia to force the withdrawal of its forces from Kosovo. The military action was not authorized by the UN Security Council and was therefore contrary to the UN Charter.

UN administration of Kosovo began in June 1999. In February 2008, the Assembly of Kosovo approved a declaration of independence, which was recognized by the United States. In all, 64 UN states recognized Kosovo, but Russia did not. Meanwhile Montenegro had been the last constituent Yugoslav republic to declare independence, in 2006.

## Africa and Asia

During the 1990s, the sole superpower imposed a new *Pax Americana* on the world. US planes evacuated Westerners from Zaire (1991), Sierra Leone (1992), the Central African Republic (1996), Liberia (1996 and 1998), Congo and Gabon (1997), and Sierra Leone again (1997 and 2000). US armed forces were in Somalia from 1992 to 1995 for humanitarian support, and were sent to Cambodia (1997), Guinea-Bissau (1998), and Kenya and Tanzania (1998–9). There were US air strikes on Afghanistan and Sudan (1999), East Timor (1999–2001), and Yemen (2000 and 2002).

America's role as sole superpower changed under Bill Clinton's successor, George W. Bush. Having seen itself as one of the family of nations with ideals that are universally applicable and desirable, the United States was now influenced by the 'neoconservative' ideology in the 1997 mission statement of the Project for the New American Century (PNAC), a think-tank whose stated goal was 'to promote American global leadership' and which became influential by the turn of the century. Bush championed American supremacy, and his administration threatened to block all UN peacekeeping missions as they came up for renewal unless American peacekeepers were granted immunity from prosecution by the International Criminal Court. In other words, American soldiers were subject only to American law, not international law.

## 9/11

The change in America's role as sole superpower was evident following '9/11' – the attacks of September 11, 2001, when two hijacked planes flew into the Twin Towers of the World Trade Center, seemingly causing them – and WTC7, another building on the same site – to collapse. A third hijacked plane crashed into the Pentagon and a fourth plane crashed, perhaps on its way to the Capitol's Rotunda. In all, more than 3,000 lost their lives. The symbols of American financial and military superiority had come crashing down on the anniversary of September 11, 1683, when the conquering armies of Islam were thrown back from the gates of Vienna, allowing Christian powers to dominate the Muslim world for the next three centuries.

America's leadership of the world was suddenly questioned, and a quick response was essential to demonstrate that American supremacy was unscathed and not vulnerable. Many of the reported hijackers were linked with Osama bin Laden, whose father had emigrated from South Yemen to Saudi Arabia and founded a construction business that had made a fortune renovating royal palaces, improving the mosques of Mecca and Medina, and rebuilding the al-Aqsa mosque in Jerusalem, part of the Haram as-Sharif, Islam's third-holiest site.[16]

Between 1979 and 1989, bin Laden helped drive the Russians from Afghanistan as part of the Western-backed *mujahideen*. Having subsequently fled to Sudan and then been expelled from there, in 1996 he was invited to Afghanistan by Mullah

Omar, the leader of the fanatical Islamic Taliban movement that was fighting the Communist Afghan regime. Between 1996, when the Taliban came to power, and the end of 2001, bin Laden allegedly gave Omar £68 million[17]

After the Taliban's victory, bin Laden established training camps in Afghanistan for 2,000 terrorists and allegedly made $1 billion from heroin deals.[18] He persuaded Mullah Omar to rename his country 'The Islamic Emirate of Afghanistan.'

Historically, 'Emirs' were regional rulers owing loyalty to the Caliph (Arabic *Khalifa*, 'Successor'), the political leader of the Ummah, the entire community of Islam, in succession to the Prophet Muhammad. After Muhammad's death in 632, the title of Caliph was claimed by rulers of successive Muslim empires, for example the Umayyads, who ruled from Damascus (661–750); the Abbasids, who ruled from Baghdad (754–1258) and Cairo (1261–1517); and finally the Ottomans, who ruled from Istanbul (1517–1924).

The Ottoman Caliphate was abolished in 1924, since when the title of Caliph has remained in abeyance. In 1989 bin Laden founded al-Qaeda, literally 'the Base' for the establishment of a new Caliphate, which would unify the Muslim world from Morocco to Pakistan, with himself as Caliph. It was to be based in Baghdad, like the Abbasid Caliphate that lasted from 750 to 1258.[19] On August 23, 1996,[20] and several times subsequently, bin Laden called for Holy War (*jihad*) against the Americans, whom he saw as al-Qaeda's chief enemy. He was associated with attacks on Americans in both Kenya and Tanzania in 1998.

Between 1992 and 9/11 bin Laden had made 32 separate attempts to acquire nuclear material (see pp.242–50) – the tally would reach 69 attempts by April 2005[21] – and there was some evidence that he had purchased 48 nuclear-suitcase bombs from the Chechen Mafia before October 1997 and certainly by October 1998.[22] These had been stolen from the Russian stockpile of nuclear weapons (12,987 in 2009 out of 23,574 in the world),[23] and al-Qaeda had planned to detonate ten of them, one in each of ten American cities.[24]

For four years leading up to 9/11, the CIA followed bin Laden via a surveillance team of Afghans,[25] and Israeli Mossad intelligence agents also followed him until a few days before 9/11. Mossad had acquired evidence that al-Qaeda were planning an attack on America, though the details were not clear.

After 9/11 the Americans quickly pinned the attacks on bin Laden and demanded that the Taliban should surrender him. Mullah Omar refused. American public opinion, appalled at the collapse of the Twin Towers, which now served as a Pearl-Harbor-style incident to stir America to war, swung behind Bush. The United States declared war on world terrorism and put together a Coalition of nations[26] that would implement the will of the UN and its resolutions.

## Afghanistan

On October 7, 2001, American and British forces struck al-Qaeda training camps and Taliban military installations in Afghanistan.

In a pre-recorded videotape shown on the Arab satellite channel *Al-Jazeera* on the same day, bin Laden spoke as if he were a new Saladin, the 12th-century Muslim leader against the Western Crusaders, who was trying to widen the war: 'I envision Salah ad-Din [Saladin] coming out of the clouds carrying his sword, with the blood of unbelievers dripping from it.'

In a scornful demonstration of American supremacy, the sole superpower proclaimed a 'self-defense' war. The United States' allies, the Afghan Northern Alliance, swept through Afghanistan. Mazar-i-Sharif fell, Kabul was evacuated. Jalalabad fell, and pockets of Taliban were mopped up at Kunduz, where 10,000 Taliban were surrounded along with 600 fanatical al-Qaeda fighters including Chechens, Arabs, Pakistanis, and Chinese Muslims. Al-Qaeda fanatics executed 470 Taliban for planning to defect.

In early December Kandahar fell and Mullah Omar fled into the mountains near Baghran with a fighting force of around 2,000 Taliban and al-Qaeda troops. When this force was surrounded he escaped by motorbike. On the run, he telephoned the BBC World Service and warned that America faced extinction – seemingly a reference to al-Qaeda's ex-Soviet nuclear-suitcase bombs.

The United States received word that bin Laden and the remnants of his army were in a cave system – perhaps a vast multistory complex – in the White Mountains at Tora Bora, 13,000 feet (3,962m) above sea level. It had been rein-forced to withstand Russian onslaughts in the 1980s, allegedly by bin Laden's family construction business, and the fugitives were reported to be sheltering in a network of tunnels. The American sole superpower's B-52s carpet-bombed the Tora-Bora mountainside with daisy-cutters that wiped out everything within 600 yards (550m).

The battle lasted a fortnight. Many al-Qaeda fighters were killed. Some were captured, the rest were dispersed. There were several reports that bin Laden himself had escaped across the border to Pakistan with his deputy, Ayman al-Zawahiri.

There they disappeared. Bush claimed victory – 'America has prevailed' – as if the United States would hear no more from the Taliban or bin Laden.

What happened to bin Laden? He apparently made his way to Balochistan in West Pakistan, which borders Iran. From there came Ramzi Yousef, the mastermind of the 1993 World Trade Center bombing, and his uncle Khalid Shaikh Mohammed, who planned the 9/11 attacks.

According to a former Iranian intelligence officer, bin Laden sent an audio tape by courier to the Supreme Leader of Iran, Ayatollah Ali Khamenei, in early July 2002, in which he requested asylum in return for handing over the leadership of al-Qaeda to Iran. Khamenei apparently agreed, and bin Laden's four wives and his eldest son Saad entered Iran. On July 26, 2002, bin Laden arrived in Iran from the Afghanistan border near Zabol and traveled to Mashad.[27]

Bin Laden reportedly spent the next year in safe houses west of Tehran, between Quazvin and Karaj, guarded by the Iranian Revolutionary Guard. He was seen by two Iranian intelligence officers near Najmabad, Iran on October 23, 2003, in the company of his deputy, al-Zawahiri, and wearing an Iranian cleric's turban above dark glasses. He had dyed his beard. He no longer resembled the FBI's wanted posters.[28] (The former Bosnian-Serb president, Radovan Karadzic, also disguised himself – as a New Age hippy – when on the run.) Both bin Laden and al-Zawahiri were passing themselves off as Iranians.

## Iraq: the Bush Doctrine of Pre-emption

Now the sole superpower turned its attention to Iraq. There had been irritation that Saddam had survived since the Gulf War and had defied a dozen UN resolutions, and that he was less than transparent about his known desire to possess nuclear weapons.

It was suspected that Saddam was behind an attempt to wipe out George H.W. Bush – as well as his wife Barbara, two of his daughters-in-law (including Laura, wife of the future president), and his son Neil – with a car bomb in Kuwait in 1993.[29] During a speech to the United Nations on September 12, 2002, George W. Bush said, 'In 1993, Iraq attempted to assassinate the Emir of Kuwait and a former American President.' And at a fundraising dinner in Houston, Texas on September 26, 2002, Bush said of Saddam, 'There's no doubt his hatred is mainly directed at us. There's no doubt he can't stand us. After all, this is the guy that tried to kill my dad.' Whether or not Saddam was involved in the murky event of 1993, George W. Bush clearly believed that he was and was full of resentment. In his mind there was a score to settle between the Bushes and Saddam.

(The FBI at first implicated the Iraqi Intelligence Service in the assassination attempt after interviewing suspects and examining the wiring of the bomb, and the Kuwaiti authorities made 17 arrests. However, the FBI later came to the conclusion that the attempt was staged by Kuwait so that it could pretend to foil the 'plot,' ingratiate itself with the Bushes, and put pressure on the current President, Bill Clinton, to retaliate against Iraq by attacking Baghdad with 23 cruise missiles.)[30]

It had also been alleged that Saddam had paid $2 billion to stop the Gulf War,[31] and that the US Administration were bent on obliterating this transaction.

The United States had to import half the oil it needed and Saddam had 11 percent of the world's known oil reserves. We have seen that bin Laden sought to revive the Caliphate and unify Islam from Morocco to Pakistan from a 'base' – 'al-Qaeda' meaning 'the Base' – in Baghdad, where the Abbasid Caliphate had been based (see p.87). The US Administration wanted to deny al-Qaeda Baghdad.

For all these reasons the Bush Administration had decided on regime change in Iraq at least as early as March 2002. Indeed, Bush had referred to the possible involvement of Saddam in the events of 9/11 on September 12, 2001, when he asked Richard Clarke, his adviser on counter-terrorism, 'See if Saddam did this. See if he's linked in any way.'[32] PNAC (Project for the New American Century) neoconservatives had tried to connect Saddam and al-Qaeda. One connection *was* made: Iraq's explosives expert Brigadier Salim al-Ahmed had met bin Laden on the latter's Khartoum farm in September and October 1995 and in July 1996 to discuss technical assistance in making bombs.[33] There was some evidence that al-Qaeda operatives had been trained by the Iraqi military and treated in a Baghdad hospital reserved for Saddam's *élite*.

The Iraqi denial of these links may have been connected with the official Iraqi silence regarding bin Laden's ambition to revive the Caliphate in Baghdad, and regarding his purchase of nuclear-suitcase bombs from the Chechen Mafia.

Bush challenged this silence. On March 11, 2002, he had made a speech suggesting that Saddam might supply al-Qaeda with nuclear or biological weapons which could threaten America. On September 12, 2002, Bush went to the UN General Assembly and called Saddam's regime 'a grave and gathering danger.'

The sole superpower again leaned on Saudi Arabia, whose leadership remembered Saddam's firing of a Scud against it during the Gulf War. Saudi Arabia decided to allow US and British planes to launch air strikes on Iraq from its soil if they received UN authority. On September 16, Iraq sent a letter to the UN agreeing to admit the UN's weapons inspectors, who had been expelled four years previously. Iraq thus technically complied with all UN resolutions, but had made no mention of disarming or destroying weapons stocks.

On September 20, 2002, Bush's Administration announced a new foreign-policy doctrine that put pressure on Iraq. The new foreign policy was contained in a document, *The National Security Strategy of the United States*,[34] which stated what came to be known as the Bush Doctrine:

> 'The security environment confronting the United States today is radically different from what we have faced before. Yet the first duty of the United States Government remains what it always has been: to protect the American people and American interests. It is an enduring American principle that this duty obligates the government to anticipate and counter threats, using all elements of national power, before the threats can do grave damage. The greater the threat, the greater is the risk of inaction – and the more compelling the case for taking anticipatory action to defend ourselves, even if uncertainty remains as to the time and place of the enemy's attack. There are few greater threats than a terrorist attack with WMD.
>
> 'To forestall or prevent such hostile acts by our adversaries, the United States will, if necessary, act pre-emptively in exercising our inherent right of self-defense. The United States will not resort to force in all cases to pre-empt emerging threats. Our preference is that non-military actions succeed. And no country should ever use pre-emption as a pretext for aggression.'

The sole superpower was telling the world in this document that it could conduct aggressive attacks to defend itself, but that the rest of the world should not do the same. The Bush Administration claimed that the United States was in a global war in which its enemies had a common ideology, a common loathing of democracy. In his State-of-the-Union address of 2003 Bush listed three of these enemies who formed an 'Axis of Evil': Iraq, Iran and North Korea.[35]

The Bush Doctrine stated that the United States had the right to secure itself from countries that harbor or give aid to terrorist groups, and that it should depose foreign regimes that represented a potential or perceived threat to the United States. The doctrine was summarized in an address to a Joint Session of Congress and the American People,[36] in which Bush said:

> 'We will pursue nations that provide aid or safe haven to terrorism. Every nation, in every region, now has a decision to make. Either you are with us, or you are with the terrorists. From this day forward any nation that continues to harbor or support terrorism will be regarded by the United States as a hostile regime.'

The Bush Doctrine, then, advocated unilaterally pursuing US military interests, striking pre-emptively against terrorists and spreading democracy. It grew out of a number of US foreign-policy strategies and decisions, which were influenced by the PNAC outlook of the neoconservatives and by Natan Sharansky's book, *The Case for Democracy*, on which Bush would base his 2005 State-of-the-Union address.

With one eye on Iraq, the Bush Doctrine emphasized pre-emptive action against 'hostile states' and terrorist groups alleged to be developing weapons of mass destruction. It advocated defending American interests rather than using deterrence and containment. It held that the United States would never allow its military supremacy to be challenged as it was during the Cold War. The new doctrine put the US in conflict with the internationalism of the UN, and it asserted that the UN would only have an international role if it passed a tough resolution on Iraq.

The UN obliged by doing what was expected of it. On November 8, 2002, the UN Security Council unanimously (by 15 votes to nil) approved Resolution 1441 'bringing the civilized world together to disarm Saddam Hussein.' It authorized the use of force without the need for another resolution and gave Iraq until November 18 to comply and until December 11 to provide a complete declaration of all its weapons of mass destruction. The inspectors, led by a Swedish diplomat, Hans Blix, would start work in Iraq by December 26 and would report to the Security Council by February 24, 2003.

The UN's unanimity confirmed the world's view of the United States as a 'hyperpower' – a word used by Russians after it had first been made current by the French Foreign Minister, Hubert Védrine, in 1998 – or sole hegemon with an unprecedented mastery of sea, land, and air and with a global reach.

Iraq's response was less than transparent. Saddam presented the UN with a declaration in Arabic exceeding 11,000 pages and denied possessing any weapons of mass destruction. His tome did not reveal what had happened to 8,500 liters (2,245 gallons) of anthrax (allegedly destroyed without record in 1991), 50 warheads (allegedly destroyed), 550 mustard-gas-filled artillery shells (declared lost), and 400 biological weapon-capable aerial bombs. Some 6,000 chemical gas bombs and 26,000 liters (6,900 gallons) of anthrax were not accounted for, together with 1,200 liters (317 gallons) of botulinum toxin and 5,500 liters (1,453 gallons) of *Clostridium perfringens*. Also undeclared were nearly 30,000 empty munitions that could be filled with chemical agents; MiG-21 remote-piloted vehicles that could carry a biological weapon spray system, which Iraq admitted possessing in 1995; quantities of VX nerve gas; and parts of nuclear bombs.

The West thought it knew Saddam had these weapons because the United States had financed and supplied them. None other than US Secretary of Defense Donald Rumsfeld, then Reagan's envoy, had met Saddam in 1983 and given him billions of dollars in loans so that he could buy weapons for Iraq's war with Iran. A month before Rumsfeld's visit, on November 1, 1983, the CIA informed Secretary of State George Shultz that Iraqis were making 'almost daily use of chemical weapons' against Iran. In the mid-1980s dozens of biological agents, including anthrax, were shipped to Iraq under license from the US Commerce Department.

Saddam's 11,000-page declaration was alleged on Western television to contain a laconic section listing all the American companies that supplied these biological agents. This section was missing from the 5,000-page reduced version which the United States had circulated, having volunteered to effect the copying and distribution of the declaration. US intelligence claimed that Saddam's weapons of mass destruction had been moved to a secret underground bunker in the desert north of Baghdad.

In his New-Year message for 2003, British Prime Minister Tony Blair parroted the new US foreign policy of pre-emption. He said that Iraq posed a threat that demanded 'defensive aggression.' In other words, the West should attack Saddam to defend itself. Even though the British people had had years of experience of Blair's 'spin,' they were bemused by the assertion that aggression is self-defense, the plea of every playground bully.

And this was the difficulty Westerners had with the Bush Doctrine. For 65 years, Westerners, including Americans, had been on the 'good side,' defending the world against Hitler and then, in alliance with NATO, against communist aggression in South Korea, Hungary, Czechoslovakia, and South Vietnam. They were now being told that they should be on the side of the aggressors, that (in Blair's Orwellian newspeak) aggression was defense, and many Western intellectuals felt uncomfortable at the implications of this position. It put them in the position Soviet intellectuals had been in during the Cold War.

Weapons searches in Iraq were inconclusive. On January 16, 2003, the UN weapons inspectors found 12 empty chemical 122mm chemical warheads. On January 28, Blix reported that Saddam had still not accounted for 6,500 chemical bombs, 'several thousand' chemical rocket warheads, 550 shells filled with mustard gas, chemicals used to make VX nerve gas, and 8,500 liters of anthrax virus, all of which were known to exist in 1998. Moreover 380 rocket engines illegally smuggled into Iraq were missing. Blix was told to report to the Security Council by February 14.

In his State-of-the-Union address, Bush declared that thousands of Iraqis were moving the missing chemical weapons, missiles, and mobile germ-warfare units ahead of the UN inspectors' visits, and that Saddam was deceiving the West. Only war could disarm him.

On February 5, US Secretary of State Colin Powell, Chairman of the Joint Chiefs of Staff during the Gulf War, presented 'evidence' to the UN (which it later turned out was based on a subsequently discredited British dossier) of Iraq's chemical weapons programs, claiming that the Iraqi officer responsible for liaising with the UN was the main concealer of weapons of mass destruction in Iraq. He said that al-Qaeda were operating freely from Baghdad, including the leader of Al-Qaeda in Iraq, Abu Mousab al-Zarqawi. He spoke of 18 biological-weapons laboratories hidden in lorries or train carriages, of 500 tons of chemical weapons agents and of Iraq's attempts to obtain nuclear weapons components and to develop missiles and planes that could act as warheads for chemicals or germs. Powell failed to persuade the UN Security Council to back military action against Iraq.

In February 2003 the UN weapons inspectors found a banned Samoud-2 missile system which could fly beyond the permitted 150km- (93-mile-) range and threaten Israel. Iraq was given until the end of February to destroy 100–120 missiles but in March had only destroyed 30 of them.

On March 7, Blix presented a balanced report, praising Saddam for co-operating with the UN and glossing over the missing weapons. The UN Secretary-General, Kofi Annan, then warned that military action against Iraq without international backing from the UN would be illegal. Perhaps sensing the moral ambivalence of pre-emption, the UN had failed to act.

When the British asked for a second UN resolution to supplement UN Resolution 1441 of November 8, 2002, Rumsfeld said that America was ready to launch a war without the UK. A second resolution was abandoned and US military action was based on Resolution 1441 alone, which many interpreted as permitting an attack without further UN approval.

To Rumsfeld, United States superpowerdom was the main reality in world power and the UN had marginalized itself by failing to support the sole superpower. Small countries that held influential positions within the UN expected bribes in return for their votes. To the US superpower in the person of Rumsfeld, democracies acting through the UN were powerless to enforce the will of the free democratic world against anti-American tyrannies such as Iraq, Iran, and North Korea, which were bent on developing their own weapons of mass destruction, and the UN had lost its credibility.

The United States gave Saddam and his two sons a 48-hour deadline to leave Iraq. At 2:30 a.m. on March 20, 2003, before the expiry of the deadline, it launched an attack intended to 'decapitate' the regime. Saddam appeared to survive. A figure purporting to be him appeared on television wearing battledress, a beret, and horn-rimmed spectacles and looking disheveled. He denounced a 'criminal raid.'

The sole superpower now demonstrated its military supremacy to the world. On March 21, as American and British forces, part of a Coalition that included Australia and Spain, advanced to Umm Qasr, Basra, and Nasiriyah, US B-52s launched 1,000 missiles at Baghdad in *Operation Shock and Awe*, striking Saddam's palace complex and intelligence headquarters and creating fireballs, mushroom clouds, and a firestorm in central Baghdad. At the same time, Mosul and Kirkuk were bombed.

*Shock and Awe* was designed to shock the world and leave it in awe of American superpower and supremacy. Its codename was taken from a study of Gulf-War strategy by Harlan Ullman that had been published by Washington's National Defense University in 1996. It recommended intimidating an adversary into losing the will to fight. Originally planned to last eight days, it in fact lasted just a few hours. Even so its intensity did damage requiring reconstruction that would cost between $100 billion and $500 billion.

The sole superpower swept up through Iraq, capturing two bridges intact at Nasiriyah, crossing the Euphrates, and reaching Kerbala. A 100-mile- (160km-) long line of tanks moved in to attack Baghdad.

From April 5 to 8, US tanks pushed into first western, then eastern Baghdad. The 20-foot- (6m-) high statue of Saddam on a plinth in Firdos Square was toppled. A figure in battledress and beret purporting to be Saddam made a final appearance in a street in Baghdad as he fled. Baghdad had fallen.

US tanks entered Tikrit, Saddam's hometown, on April 13. The next day US troops captured the main palace in Tikrit. There was no sign of Saddam.

On May 1, 2003, Bush appeared on the USS *Abraham Lincoln* and spoke to troops. Behind him a banner announced 'Mission Accomplished.' In fact, the sole superpower would be preoccupied with Iraq for the next seven years or more as Sunnis, financed by funds that Saddam had embezzled over the years and hoarded in secret bank accounts, attacked the US occupiers and Iraq's large Shia majority. The American post-war Administration found Iraq difficult to pacify and round the world people questioned whether America really was the superpower that *Shock and Awe* had suggested.

Iraq technically became a democracy with the general election of December 2005, when Nouri al-Maliki became Prime Minister, but it had swiftly disintegrated into a Sunni–Shia civil war and into a guerrilla war between Al-Qaeda in Iraq and the occupiers, with many car bombs and suicide bombs causing daily mayhem. The leader of Al-Qaeda in Iraq, al-Zarqawi, operated out of Iran as part of a Sunni–Shia alliance within Iran.

Amid the mayhem, little reconstruction took place, and electricity and water services were not fully restored. The British were as good as defeated by pro-Iranian Shia militias in the south. Zarqawi was tracked down by Jordanian intelligence and killed by Americans in June 2006. Saddam Hussein, who had finally been captured in December 2003, was executed in December 2006, by which time his two sons had been hunted down and killed.

Saddam's death, and that of his sons, knocked the stuffing out of the Sunni-led campaign. The US 'surge' of 2007, which introduced 30,000 new US troops into Iraq, and the tenacity of US commander General Petraeus in buying off Sunni sheikhs and moving the newly-arrived troops into Muslim communities brought some semblance of order to the newly-democratic Iraq. By the end of the surge in July 2008 Iraq had been pacified to a considerable extent.

## Afghanistan Again, Iran

US superpowerdom was further challenged in Afghanistan. The regrouped Taliban and al-Qaeda had returned and occupied the wild mountainous areas the Coalition forces could not hold.

US and Allied troops in Afghanistan were hard pressed. Roadside IEDs (Improvised Explosive Devices) took their toll and were the major cause of Allied deaths. By the spring of 2006 Coalition forces had traced IEDs back to one factory in Iran through specific welding designs and materials. The same was true of EFPs (Explosively Formed Projectiles) which penetrated tank armor. The munitions factory complex was in north Tehran: within the Ordnance Factories Complex, a subdivision of Iran's Defense Industries Organization, a company named Sattari specialized in making different types of anti-tank mines, including EFPs.[37] These were smuggled into Iraq and Afghanistan.

Iran is situated between Iraq and Afghanistan, and the concept of roadside bombs was exported to the anti-American forces in those two countries. Richard Clarke, former White House counter-terrorism expert, said in March 2006: 'I think it's very hard to escape the conclusion that, in all probability, the Iranian Government is knowingly killing US troops.'[38] Tehran was clearly behind the roadside bomb attacks.

We saw (on p.89) that bin Laden was reported to be living in Iran. The Americans did not think this was the case. In 2009 American advisers were convinced that bin Laden was being sheltered by the Haqqanis, a powerful Taliban group who controlled territory on both sides of the Afghanistan–Pakistan border near Khost, where seven CIA officials specializing in hunting bin Laden were killed by a suicide-bomber on December 30, 2009. Were they looking in the wrong country?

In January 2010 bin Laden's former aide, Abu al-Fida, revealed from the Yemen that bin Laden, whose father was a Yemeni, had married a fifth wife, Amal al-Sadah, a Yemeni girl, in Kandahar, Afghanistan shortly before 9/11. Hala Jaber had driven Amal to Kandahar for her wedding. He reported that bin Laden was alive and well in 2010 and living with Amal, who had not returned to the Yemen.

The rest of bin Laden's family were scattered in Syria, Iran and Saudi Arabia.[39]

In March 2010 a supply of Iranian-made IEDs with inscriptions in Persian was impounded in Herat Province on Afghanistan's northernmost border with Iran.[40] This haul appeared to confirm long-held US and British military suspicions that Iran had supplied insurgents in both Iraq and Afghanistan with IEDs and EFPs that had killed so many of their troops, and that Iran had trained insurgents to use them.[41]

In the same month, the pro-Iranian Prime Minister, Nouri al-Maliki, was defeated in Iraqi elections. Iran tried to put together a new coalition of Shia parties, with a view to Maliki's heading a new Iraqi government despite having come second in the election. The victor in the election, former-Prime Minister Ayad Allawi, a non-sectarian Shia, said, 'Iran is interfering quite heavily and this is worrying. They have invited everybody – but they haven't invited us – to Tehran.'[42] Iran was situated strategically between Iraq and Afghanistan.

Was bin Laden living with Amal in Iran and orchestrating the supply of these weapons to insurgents? Was he living near Tehran among his nuclear-suitcase bombs and in cahoots with Iranian President Mahmoud Ahmadinejad's anti-American drive for nuclear weapons at Natanz and other nuclear sites, including one hidden from the UN weapons inspectors near Qom? If this was the case, it was completely understandable, from bin Laden's viewpoint, that Ahmadinejad had to be re-elected in 2009 and that all opposition to his stealing of the election had to be crushed, even though it meant that Iran would develop into a tyranny.

### Lebanon, Gaza, Georgia, Pakistan

The United States' pre-emptive War on Terror also involved the sole superpower in overseeing Israel's invasions of Lebanon in 2007 and Gaza in 2008–9, and in the war between Georgia and Russian forces in South Ossetia and Abkhazia in 2008. US Predator pilotless drones struck targets in Pakistan (2006) and US forces missiled an insurgent encampment in the northern mountains of Pakistan and supported a Pakistani attack on al-Qaeda there (2009).

### Other Challenges

In the course of the War on Terror after 9/11, US military personnel mounted operations in Côte d'Ivoire (2002), Liberia (2003), Georgia and Djibouti (2003), Haiti (2003 and 2004), Kenya, Ethiopia, and Eritrea (2004) and Somalia (2007).

Regime change, a feature of the Bush Doctrine, had long preceded 2002. As we saw on p.41 the United States was accused of attempting covert regime change during the Cold War. It has been accused of attempting regime change in the following countries since the Cold War: Iraq (1992–5), Guatemala (1993), Zimbabwe, Serbia, and Venezuela (2000), Iran (2001–present), Georgia (2003), Ukraine and Equatorial Guinea (2004), Lebanon (2005), the Palestinian Authority (2006–present), Somalia (2006–7), Venezuela again (2007), and Myanmar (Burma, 2007). The Bush Doctrine had made regime change overt rather than covert.

## The American Superpower's Global Spread

The outlook contained in the Bush Doctrine persisted until Bush stepped down as President in early 2009.

The Bush Doctrine must be seen in relation to the Pentagon's wider strategy. After the fall of the Berlin Wall in November 1989, it pursued a step-by-step military strategy to dominate the Earth. The Pentagon called this strategy 'Full-Spectrum Dominance,' the 'full spectrum' implying dominance of everything everywhere: the seas, land, air, and space. Full-Spectrum Dominance is a military concept in which a joint military structure controls all battlespace. It was the key term in *Joint Vision 2020, America's Military – Preparing for Tomorrow*, which was signed by the chairman of the US joint chiefs of staff and released by the US Department of Defense on May 30, 2000.[43]

The document states: 'The overall goal of the transformation described in this document is the creation of a force that is dominant across the full spectrum of military operations – persuasive in peace, decisive in war, pre-eminent in any form of conflict.' This newly-developed US strategy sought to surround with bases in Central Asia, and destroy by deception, the only power capable of resisting American dominance: Russia.[44]

The global spread of the sole superpower could then be judged by the spread of its bases. We have seen on pp.78–9 that in 2009 America had between 700 and 800 military bases round the world. Some have held that by 2007 there were more than 1,000.[45]

Earlier estimates were somewhat contradictory. According to 2005 official Pentagon data the United States had 737 bases in foreign lands in 2005.[46] Another estimate in 2003 stated that the US military had 752 military installations in more than 130 countries.[47] Significant numbers of American troops were stationed in 65 of these.[48] In 2002 it was estimated that US military personnel were in 156 countries[49] (of the UN's 192 countries at the time of writing).

In 2007 it was estimated that the US military had bases in 63 countries, and brand-new bases have been built in seven countries since September 11, 2001.[50] Since then the US has built or expanded bases in Afghanistan, Kyrgyzstan, Pakistan, Tajikistan, Uzbekistan, Bulgaria, Georgia, Hungary, Poland, Romania, the Philippines, Djibouti, Oman, Qatar, and Iraq.[51] One estimate in 2009 put the total active US military personnel deployed worldwide at 1.445 million, the second-largest in the world after China. The breakdown was: 548,000 in the Army, 203,095 in the Marine Corps, 332,000 in the Navy, and 323,000 in the Air Force.[52] In 2007 there were more than 6,000 military bases and/or military warehouses within the US.[53]

Bush said in a speech on February 26, 2003, 'After defeating enemies [in 1945], we did not leave behind occupying armies.'[54] Yet in 2000 there were 70,000 US troops in Germany, 40,000 in Japan, and 36,500 in South Korea.[55] Camp Bondsteel in Kosovo was acquired during the 1999 war. In January 2010 there were 70,000 US troops in Afghanistan and an additional 30,000 troops were scheduled to be deployed by summer 2010[56] and the US Bishkek Air Base in Kyrgyzstan serviced flights directed against the Taliban. There were some 142,000 US troops in Iraq, all of whom were scheduled to be withdrawn by December 2011.[57] The Bush Administration planned to keep and maintain four permanent bases in Iraq: at the International Airport outside Baghdad; at Tallil near Nasiriyah; at H1, an airstrip in the western desert near Jordan; and at the Bashur airfield in the Kurdish-held north. These bases would ring Iran. In the US there are 6,000 military bases.[58]

The military technology on these bases was awesome. On land the US had 9,000 M1 Abrams tanks; at sea 9 'supercarrier' battle groups; in the air three kinds of undetectable Stealth aircraft. The rest of the world could not compete with the tanks and had no supercarriers or Stealth aircraft. The United States was ahead in smart missiles and pilotless high-altitude drones that could missile-attack terrorists.[59] The Pentagon's budget equaled 'the combined military budgets of the next 12 or 15 nations.'[60]

American superpowerdom manifested itself in the Unified Combatant Command (UCC), a joint military council composed of forces from two or more services, co-ordinating the US Army, Navy, Air Force, Marine Corps, and Coast

Guard and other federal agencies. Six of the ten competent commands were organized on a geographical basis: US Northern Command, US Southern Command, US European Command (based in Germany), US Central Command, US Pacific Command (based in Hawaii), and US African Command (based in Germany, established in 2007). The other four were organized on a functional basis: US Joint Forces Command, US Special Operations Command, US Strategic Command, and US Transportation Command. Together, these ten commands covered the world, carrying forward and fulfilling a principle begun in December 1946 by President Truman, who co-ordinated earlier forces. Southern Command, for example, originated in 1903 with the US Marines who arrived in Panama.

The superpowerdom of the United States could be measured by its dominance over the rest of the world. But there was unease at the use to which its dominance was being put. Critics of the Bush Doctrine found it a *carte blanche* for foreign interventionism and believed that such a radical departure from former US foreign policies would alienate the goodwill to America in the regions of the world where minds and hearts had to be won. They believed that it contradicted the universal values Liberty had always striven for. It replaced Liberty's struggle for freedom from colonialism with a vitriolic and unfeeling form of American supremacy.

# Globalization

A consequence of America's being a hegemon and then sole superpower has been globalization. This is a process in which regional economies, societies and cultures become integrated in a network which stretches round the globe.

## Economic Globalization

When used in an economic context globalization 'refers to the reduction and removal of barriers between national borders in order to facilitate the flow of goods, capital, services, and labor.' (The United Nations Economic and Social Commission for Western Asia, or UN ESCWA.)[61]

Globalization is not a new phenomenon. All the large empires removed barriers between national borders in the interests of free trade. The Mesopotamian civilization had trade links with the Indus Valley under the Sumerians in the third millennium BCE. The Roman Empire had links with the Parthian Empire and the Chinese Han Dynasty which led to the development of the Silk Road. The

Mongol Empire also had trade links along the Silk Road. The Islamic Golden Age promoted the Hajj pilgrimage to Mecca, which involved cross-border trade links. The Portuguese and Spanish Empires colonized the Americas. The British Empire colonized India via the British East India Company (founded in 1600), just as the Dutch Empire colonized the Dutch East Indies via the Dutch East India Company (founded in 1602). The Portuguese Empire followed suit via the Portuguese East India Company (founded in 1628). The British Empire's Industrial Revolution produced a 19th-century form of globalization.

Politicians have long planned to break down borders that hamper trade, in order to increase prosperity. This process led to the Bretton Woods conference, which set out a framework for international commerce and finance and created the World Bank (or International Bank for Reconstruction and Development) and the IMF (International Monetary Fund) as international institutions that would oversee the process of globalization.

Since the Second World War, international trade agreements such as GATT (General Agreement on Tariffs and Trade, 1947) and the WTO (World Trade Organization, which replaced GATT in 1995 following the Uruguay Round of 1986–94) have promoted free trade. They have done so by eliminating tariffs; creating free-trade zones; reducing transportation costs by the use of containers; eliminating capital controls; equalizing subsidies for local businesses by scrapping them or harmonizing them; creating subsidies for global corporations; and harmonizing the recognition of patents worldwide. The European Maastricht Treaty and the North American Free Trade Agreement (NAFTA) contributed massively to this process.

Cultural globalization involved the worldwide marketing of Western culture by communications technology. Culture includes what people eat, how they dress, what they believe, and other activities they engage in. American superpowerdom led to American culture's dominating world culture and challenging the persisting diversity of local regional cultures.

Economic globalization can be measured in terms of the flow of goods and services, of labor and migrants, of capital and technology. Indicators of globalization include exports, imports and capital as a proportion of national income, net migration rates, and the proportion of populations using telephones, cars, and broadband Internet.

The Swiss think-tank KOF measures economic, social, and political globalization in terms of an index that takes account of economic restrictions, personal contact, the flow of information and cultural proximity. It has found that the world's most globalized country in 2009 was Belgium. The next most globalized countries were Ireland, the Netherlands, Switzerland, and Austria.[62] According to another index jointly published by A.T. Kearney and *Foreign Policy Magazine*, the most globalized countries in 2007 were Singapore, Ireland, Switzerland, the Netherlands, Canada, and Denmark.[63]

However, such indices do not acknowledge that the sole superpower has the most globalizing impact on the world.

## How Globalization is Experienced

Globalization has impacted on the world in a number of different ways:

- Industrially, worldwide production markets have emerged, giving consumers and companies access to foreign companies so that material and goods can move between national boundaries. The American-developed Internet has led the world in such industrial globalization.
- Financially, worldwide financial markets have emerged that give borrowers better access to financing. Again, the American-developed Internet has led to a global financial infrastructure which is outside transnational regulation. It has proved unstable, as the 2008 financial crisis has shown.
- Economically, a worldwide common market has emerged. It is based on the freedom of exchange of goods and capital between national markets. Again, the US-developed Internet has led to such interconnected markets. However, economic collapse in one market or country cannot be contained within that market or country, but affects the whole, as the 2008 financial crisis illustrated.
- Politically, a potential world government has emerged which regulates the relationships between governments through institutions of global governance, and guarantees rights between governments. The United States has led such political globalization because of its strong and wealthy economy. It is the world's fourth-biggest exporter (behind the EU, Germany, and China).[64] The United States has helped the rapid growth of the People's Republic of China to extend its influence among world powers, and America can be seen as being behind the rise of China.

- Informationally, an increase in information flow has emerged between geographically remote locations. The United States has led this with technological innovation, much of which came from America's NASA-driven space program. The new technology includes fiber-optic communications, satellites, and increased availability of cellphones and the Internet. Linguistically, a global language has emerged. It is English, which first emerged as a result of the British Empire. The role of English as a global language has been extended by American superpowerdom. About 35 percent of the world's mail, telexes, and cables and about 40 percent of the world's radio programs are in English, while about 50 percent of all Internet traffic is in English.[65]
- Competitively, a new global business market has created increased productivity and competition; as the market has become worldwide, companies have upgraded their products and improved their technology to cope with increased competition. The United States has led the world in such movements.
- Ecologically, environmental solutions to challenges such as climate change, water and air pollution, and over-fishing are being sought by international co-operation. However, developing countries have competed globally and their factories have increased pollution. Until recently the United States has been a polluter rather than a solver of pollution. This is now changing.
- Culturally, local regions participating in world culture have imported American culture such as Hollywood films. Such imports have increased multiculturalism and cultural diversity, but have often supplanted local culture. The United States has led the world in cultural domination.
- Socially, global political policy has been led by non-governmental organizations, especially those linked to the UN. The United States has led the way in creating these.
- Technically, global telecommunications and trans-border data have improved. The United States has led the world in creating the Internet, communication satellites, submarine fiber-optic cable, and wireless telephones.
- Legally, an international criminal court and international justice movements have emerged to cope with global crime-fighting, and a

global administrative law has emerged. The United States has led
the world in such developments although, out of American self-
interest and in the interests of American superiority, it has resisted
subordinating US troops to the International Criminal Court.

There is therefore overwhelming evidence for seeing the globalization we
experience as owing most to the world domination of the sole superpower: the
United States. Globalization in the 20th century has been driven by the global
expansion of multinational corporations based in the United States, and by the
export of American culture to all countries in the world through film, television,
and recorded music.

The future of globalization is in some doubt. The likelihood is that it will
continue along with some form of American dominance. However, the 2008 world
recession wiped 45 percent off global wealth,[66] and some have said that the
world is in fact deglobalizing.[67]

Would a reaction against US superpowerdom result in a reaction against
globalization?

We have followed the public trail of American superpowerdom. Outwardly
American superpowerdom appeared to be an expression of the US military's global
spread, and globalization appeared to be a consequence of it. A look behind the
scenes tells a different story, and the events we have been considering then take
on a different meaning.

# CHAPTER 7

# LIBERTY'S COMMERCIAL *ÉLITES* BEFORE 1989: The Birth of the New World Order

Behind the accepted view of America's superpowerdom which I have just set out is a less well-known scenario: that a relatively small number of *élites*, a secretive network of dynastic families and interests, pushed America into superpowerdom to achieve a New World Order that would run the world to boost their own commercial interests. This was the 'force behind the scenes' I referred to on p.44.

## Two Family Hegemonies

This network is nearly 250 years old and is the story of two families whose ambitions became intertwined.

### The Rothschilds

The dynastic network began with the Rothschilds, and in particular the first of the Rothschild financial dynasty, Mayer Amschel, a Frankfurt Jew.[1] He made his money after becoming court agent in 1776 to the Elector William IX, Landgrave of Hesse-Kassel, who buried the equivalent of $3 million[2] in his garden when Napoleon invaded Germany and then fled, having given a power of attorney to his finance officer. The finance officer made Mayer Amschel his banker to collect the interest on William's royal loans and to guard his buried wealth. Mayer Amschel was known as Rothschild after the red (*rot* or *roth*) shield (*Schild*)[3] that hung over the door of the family's Frankfurt house. (It is likely that Mayer Amschel came to be known as 'Mayer Amschel *zum rot(h)en Schild*,' – 'Mayer Amschel at the sign of the red shield,' the appellation being shortened over time to 'Roth-Schild(t).')

Mayer Amschel Rothschild's influence increased after he financed Adam Weishaupt's Order of the Illuminati, which in 1779 passed into Freemasonry and influenced the birth of the French Revolution.[4] By 1782 Rothschild controlled the Frankfurt headquarters of the new Order, which the Luciferian-Satanist Weishaupt hid within Templar Grand-Orient Freemasonry in December 1781. The Illuminati were banned by the Bavarian Elector in March 1785, but the Illuminati agenda and its following survived within Grand-Orient Freemasonry. This was the branch of Freemasonry founded by the Duke of Orléans, who organized the French Revolution of 1789.[5]

Through Weishaupt, Rothschild had financed the introduction of a Luciferian-Satanistic strain into Freemasonry which was responsible for promoting the French Revolution of 1789 behind the closed doors of Freemasonic lodges. This marked the beginning of the Rothschild family's use of Freemasonry to achieve its political ends.

Mayer Amschel Rothschild had five sons, who opened banks in London, Paris, Frankfurt, Vienna, and Naples. By the time of his death in 1812 Mayer was the richest man ever,[6] with a fortune worth $3.5 million.[7] By speculating on the outcome of the Battle of Waterloo in 1815,[8] his eldest son Nathan bought the market after a price collapse and became effectively the owner of the Bank of England. By 1820 Nathan had increased the fortune to $7.5 billion, and further increased it to around $100 billion by 1840. In 1875, Nathan's son Lionel bought the Suez Canal on behalf of the British at the instigation of Prime Minister Benjamin Disraeli.[9]

The Rothschilds were now the richest family ever. Their wealth was more than that of all the crowned heads of Europe put together and they owned 42 great country houses throughout Europe. They financed the new US railroads, and, having failed to establish an American Central Bank during the Civil War, in 1914 created the US Federal Reserve System, a Rothschild-controlled central-banking system for the United States. They had already gone into oil, exchanging their entire lucrative Russian oil trade in 1911 for shares in the potentially even more profitable Royal Dutch Shell.[10]

### The Rockefellers

The Rothschilds' *protégé* in the late 1860s was John D. Rockefeller, an American of German descent. His ancestor, a man named Roggenfelder (which means 'rye fields' in German)[11] was a Hessian mercenary with Turkish ancestry who fought for the British army during the American Revolutionary War. He deserted, settled on land in New Jersey, and changed his name to Rockefeller.[12]

In 1870 his descendant, John D. Rockefeller, became an oil magnate when he incorporated Standard Oil of Ohio with Rothschilds' financial help. By the end of the decade he controlled 90 percent of all refined oil sold in the United States. He owned 20,000 oil wells and had 100,000 employees, with branches in Western Europe and China. By 1911 he was worth £1 billion (equivalent to well over $13 billion in today's money),[13] and he doubled – in some cases trebled – his shares and wealth by shedding 37 subsidiaries and creating 34 separate companies to exploit the new US anti-trust laws.[14] John D. Rockefeller's son, John II, had five sons including Nelson and David.

The Rockefellers took pride in their German and Turkish links. They gave the German Kaiser $300 million[15] to finance the First World War, and also supplied the Germans with oil. In 1914 Standard Oil loaned Germany's Turkish allies $35 million, and were permitted to drill for oil in Ottoman territory.

The Rockefellers very swiftly gained control of the Soviet Union. Aware that the Rothschilds were behind the first 1917 Russian Revolution of Kerensky (to achieve which Rothschilds had mobilized Lord Milner, the most influential member of British Prime Minister David Lloyd George's War Cabinet and a 33rd-degree Mason[16]), the Rockefellers backed Lenin's October 1917 Bolshevik Revolution and later threw their weight behind Stalin.[17] By then Freemasonry had turned the Soviet Union into a Masonic state by setting up Grand-Orient lodges in Paris that would become the Supreme Council of the Scottish Rite in Russia, or the Supreme Council of Elders on which the 'Supreme Soviet' (or Council) would be based.[18]

In 1925 the Rockefellers made a deal with Stalin, a Martinist Rosicrucian Freemason,[19] whereby they received half the oil produced in the Soviet Union in return for funding Stalin's Five-Year Plans.[20]

The Rockefellers continued to support Germany and they supplied Hitler with oil via Standard Oil of New Jersey, through Spain. They funded part of Hitler's war effort and in 1939 gave the Nazis $25 million.[21] In anticipation of Germany's post-war role as master of the world, Hitler constructed the vast buildings that can today be visited in Nuremberg, including a Colosseum, an open Congress Hall to accommodate 50,000 representatives, and the foundations for a stadium to accommodate 350,000 to 450,000 people.[22] It is fascinating to wonder whether some of the Rockefellers' $25 million was applied to the rebuilding of Nuremberg as a world center and therefore funded Hitler's architectural base to project himself as master of the world after the war.

At the beginning of the Second World War, Rockefellers supported Hitler and Stalin at the same time, wanting a ruler who would dominate the world and make possible all their commercial aspirations. However, in the course of the war they transferred their allegiance from Hitler to Stalin. The turning-point seems to have been Hitler's misconceived invasion of the Soviet Union. This led them to conclude that Hitler would not conquer the world, whereas Stalin might. They wanted to back a leader who would bring in a 'New World Order.'

In the United States, meanwhile, the Rockefellers had funded a sub-Masonic offshoot of Freemasonry called the Council on Foreign Relations (CFR), which had taken over the State Department by 1939.[23] It was underwritten by the Rockefeller Foundation[24] and urged world government. It received $500,000 from both the Rockefeller Foundation and the Carnegie Endowment after the war.[25] The CFR had nominated most of the officials in every President's administration since the 1920s.[26] Through the CFR, half Roosevelt's Cabinet were Rockefellerites, including Henry Stimson, Secretary of War.

Rockefellers had turned Roosevelt into their puppet ever since Colonel House had intrigued to secure his presidency on the basis that Roosevelt followed a Rockefellerite agenda.[27] In 1929 the CFR had bought new headquarters at 45 East 65th Street, New York City, literally next door to the house Roosevelt was living in, underlining the Rockefellerites' control of Roosevelt.[28]

It seems that General George C. Marshall, US Chief of Staff and Eisenhower's boss during the Second World War, was leaned on to bar the British commander, General Bernard Montgomery, from capturing Berlin. The rise of Stalin's East-European empire began with Eisenhower's decision, on General Marshall's instructions, to prevent Montgomery from taking Berlin, ostensibly on the grounds that fighting for Berlin would cost 100,000 American lives and that it was better to let Stalin make the sacrifice.[29]

Through Roosevelt, Marshall, and Eisenhower, the Rockefellers left the way clear for Stalin to reach Berlin before the British and Americans. Stalin grasped that the way to Berlin was open, and he moved in, establishing an East-European empire of satellites that would become the Soviet hegemony. Having backed both Stalin and Hitler on the principle that in a two-horse race it is best to back both runners, the Rockefellers now intensified their backing for Stalin.

The CFR now reconstructed Europe. Jean Monnet, a young French socialist sent to Canada in 1910, had met associates of US President Woodrow Wilson's special adviser, Colonel House, and had been made deputy secretary-general of the League of Nations in 1919. He had developed the idea of a United States of Europe in conjunction with the CFR, and had become personal adviser on Europe to President F.D. Roosevelt.

The CFR and Monnet devised 'the Marshall Plan' for European recovery after the Second World War. It was originally to be called 'the Truman Plan' but it was named the Marshall Plan because General Marshall, now Secretary of State, could attract bipartisan congressional support as he had been much-admired as Chief of Staff during the war.[30] From 1946 to 1947 David Rockefeller, one of John D. Rockefeller's grandsons, acted as secretary to a CFR study group on European reconstruction.[31]

The Marshall Plan was largely funded by the Rockefellers, for whom General Marshall acted as a proxy.[32] The Plan implemented Rockefellers' intention to re-establish capitalism and also implemented the Truman Doctrine of blocking Communism globally. It poured $13 billion into Europe initially ($72.5 billion by 1959) to combat Soviet moves. Besides planning the recovery of Europe, CFR study groups planned the reconstruction of Germany (toward which Rockefellers felt warmly) and Japan, and the creation of the International Monetary Fund and World Bank.[33]

While Stalin established his East-European bloc and General Marshall established a West-European bloc through Marshall Aid, a fund largely put up by the Rockefellers,[34] the Rockefellers were setting up the UN. The idea was proposed at the 1944 Dumbarton Oaks conference, where the draft of the UN Charter was written by the Soviet foreign minister Molotov and Alger Hiss, the Rockefellers' employee and later Nelson Rockefeller's personal representative at the UN.

In 1950 Hiss, a former State-Department official, was convicted of perjury and exposed as a Soviet spy.[35] Hiss was therefore acting on the Soviet side when, in February 1945, he and Molotov wrote the final version of the UN Charter at Yalta,[36] where Roosevelt, Churchill, and Stalin agreed that the UN should be established.[37]

The American delegation to the UN conference at San Francisco in 1945 contained at least 47 CFR members.[38] Hiss was the founding conference's Secretary-General. Under his guidance the UN was formally established and the US Senate approved the idea in days.

In December 1946 the Rockefeller Foundation donated a check to buy 18 acres (7.3ha) of land in Manhattan on which the UN building was to be built. John D. Rockefeller III, David's brother, contributed $8.5 million, and New York City contributed a further $4.25 million.[39] The $65 million to build the UN building on the land was raised as an interest-free 'loan' from the American taxpayer. (From 1970 to 1985 David Rockefeller was the chairman of the CFR, again underlining the close connection between the Rockefellers and that organization.)[40]

At the Dumbarton Oaks conference, Stalin had demanded 16 votes for the USSR in the UN General Assembly, one for each republic. Shocked, and at Hiss's urging, Roosevelt conceded that the USSR should have three votes to America's one. The five Permanent Members of the Security Council each had a veto, which Stalin used frequently to stir up decolonizing wars.

Against this background, Nelson Rockefeller, John III's brother, agreed with Stalin that the UN would not interfere in Russian affairs.[41] In return Stalin would continue to supply Soviet oil to Rockefeller's companies and keep the Bolsheviks out of Saudi Arabia and Iran.

NATO was founded in April 1949. It was funded for five years by the Marshall Fund (i.e. by the Rockefellers). The USSR retaliated by forming Comecon, an aid program for Eastern Europe to promote trade between Iron-Curtain countries. Western Europe countered with economic treaties: the economic union of Belgium, the Netherlands, and Luxembourg ('Benelux') in 1948, which France, Italy, and West Germany joined in 1951 to form the union of Western Europe's coal and steel industries; and the Western-European economic treaty of 1951, which signaled the beginning of a common market for all goods and services.

The latter scheme was known as the 'Schuman Plan' after French Foreign Minister Robert Schuman, but it was really the work of Jean Monnet, who as we have seen had links with the Rockefellerite CFR. However, the idea originally came from Stalin's 1912 essay, 'Marxism and the National Question,' in which he called for 'regional autonomy' to bring about the 'eradication' of nationalism. Stalin followed this essay up with his 1926 address to the Soviet Politburo: 'There should be a Federated State of Europe, to which the USSR would adhere and in which ... Great Britain would be included. Once Great Britain had been absorbed the USSR would ... become the dominant power.'[42]

General Marshall had been sent to China in December 1945 to broker a peace settlement between the Nationalists under Chiang Kai-shek and the Communists under Mao Tse-tung (Mao Zedong). As well as controlling half Russian oil, the Rockefellers owned substantial reserves of Chinese oil. Through General Marshall, the Rockefellers can be presumed to have secured a promise by Mao to preserve the Rockefellers' oil interests. In all other respects the peace effort failed, and Marshall returned to the United States in January 1947 to be made Secretary of State.

In 1950 a Soviet–Chinese treaty was concluded. Emboldened by this, North Korea invaded South Korea, which appealed for assistance to the Americans. Marshall was made Secretary of Defense in September 1950 and ordered General Douglas MacArthur to escalate the war in Korea: 'We want you to feel unhampered tactically and strategically to proceed north of the 38th parallel.'[43] North Korea received oil from Rockefellers, supplied by Caltex Co. at US taxpayers' expense.[44]

Truman dismissed MacArthur in April 1951 for insubordination: the previous month MacArthur had called for an attack on China unless Communist forces laid down their arms in Korea.[45] Attacking China, where the Rockefellers had oil interests, was not an option the Rockefellers were prepared to consider.

## Syndicate Oil during the Cold War

It is now convenient to refer to the secretive network of dynastic families as 'the Syndicate.' According to the *Concise Oxford Dictionary*, a 'syndicate' is 'a combination of individuals or commercial firms to promote some common interest.' The families of the commercial *élites* had a common purpose, of unifying the world under their leadership for their own commercial gain.

I shall now start placing inverted commas round the family names 'Rothschilds' and 'Rockefellers.' By doing so I seek to make it clear that I am not referring to particular individuals but to a particular emphasis of a commercial pattern: in the case of 'Rothschilds,' a commercial drive associated with their 19th-century financial dominance and imperialism; and in the case of 'Rockefellers,' a commercial drive associated with their 20th-century acquisition of oil and shaping events through revolutions.

In the 1950s, the Rothschilds and Rockefellers were the two wealthiest – and most secretive – families in the world. By the time of the death of John D. Rockefeller in 1937, the Rockefellers owned a known fortune of at least $5 billion[46] and owned 20 percent of American industry. In 1940 the Rothschilds were estimated as being worth $500 billion.[47] The common purpose of both families was to continue their dynastic policy of working for global governance and a world government so that they could continue to corner the Earth's natural resources and then sell them, thereby advancing their own financial interests.

## Bilderberg Group

In 1954 'Rothschilds' and 'Rockefellers' co-founded the secretive Bilderberg Group, another sub-Masonic group which was named after the Hotel de Bilderberg in Oosterbeek, Holland, where the Group first met. The Group represented a *rapprochement* between the two family hegemonies and at the same time an attempt to create a kind of permanent, ongoing latter-day Yalta Conference involving the two families that would divide the world between them into spheres of influence, particularly regarding the world's oil. The two families worked together to unify Europe and were responsible for the 1957 Treaty of Rome that created the Common Market, a forerunner of today's European Union.

The Bilderberg Group have met annually ever since 1954, bringing together the most powerful political and industrial figures in the world to establish a consensus on forthcoming policy. Meetings take place in great secrecy under the 'Chatham House Rule,' under which participants may use information they receive but are not at liberty to reveal the identity of the speakers or the location of the forum. Since 1954 the most prominent attendee has been David Rockefeller, who in the early 1970s created the Trilateral Commission to bring together about 250 political and industrial leaders from the United States, Europe, and Pacific nations (especially Japan).

The dynastic *élites* represent around 6,000 sympathizers who covertly run the world by deciding what course of action governments should take in the forthcoming year, influencing the lot of a world population that exceeds six billion.

During the Cold War, local wars prospered under the nuclear umbrellas of both military hegemonies. As both the United States and the Soviet Union were building up stocks of nuclear weapons, it was safer to confine wars to local regions, fight them with conventional weapons and keep them 'cold.' It was essential that they should avoid any direct US–Soviet confrontation – such a 'hot' scenario would precipitate nuclear confrontation.

Soviet-backed insurgency challenged all the West-European empires: the British, French, German, Dutch, Belgian, Italian, Spanish, and Portuguese. All these empires held territories under a colonialism that was opposed by the Soviet Union.

Some of these territories made tempting prizes for the 'Rockefellerite' Syndicate. In 1948 anti-European insurgency destabilized India, Burma, Malaya, Indonesia, and the Philippines. The anti-French Indo-China War destabilized the French Empire. Riots in West Africa led to the British promising independence to the Gold Coast. In 1952 the anti-British Mau Mau insurgency began in Kenya, and there was fighting in British-held Cyprus.

In the context of the Cold War there was a power struggle within the alliance between 'Rothschilds' and 'Rockefellers' as they co-operated to bring in a New World Order that controlled the world's oil. Like a squabbling couple who appear publicly in harmony, 'Rothschildite' countries came into conflict with 'Rockefellerite' countries under the umbrella of the Cold War.

*Suez*

'Rothschilds' and 'Rockefellers' came into collision over the 1956 Suez Crisis. 'Rothschilds' had long focused on the Middle East. In 1917, Lionel Walter, 2nd Baron Rothschild, Nathan's eldest son and the head of the British branch of the dynasty, had received a letter from the British Foreign Secretary, Lord Balfour, promising a permanent settlement for the Jews in what was then called Palestine, a former Ottoman province which the British held under a 30-year League of Nations mandate. In 1948 the concept of a permanent settlement was translated into the State of Israel, with 'Rothschild' funding.

The Suez Crisis was precipitated by a partner of 'Rockefellers,' John Foster Dulles, who withdrew American financial support for the Aswan Dam. Colonel Nasser, the pro-Soviet Egyptian leader, announced that he was nationalizing the Suez Canal Zone, which was controlled jointly by Britain and France. In 1875 the

British Government's share in the canal had been bought for £3.67 million by Nathan Rothschild's London bank, N. M. Rothschild & Sons, from Egypt's Khedive. Nasser's move would give Egypt control over the vital Suez Canal, along which 'Rothschildite' oil was sent by tanker to the Far East.

The three 'Rothschildite' countries, Israel, France, and Britain, colluded to attack Egypt in October 1956. President Eisenhower, a 'Rockefellers' man, instructed Dulles to block the Israelis.[48] Dulles went to the UN and said: 'The Israeli–French–British invasion is a grave error inconsistent with the principles and purpose of this Charter.'[49] He exerted great pressure on the British and French, who withdrew their troops.

The 'Rockefeller' faction of the developing New World Order had thus blocked the 'Rothschild' faction and forced them to pull back. At the same time, 'Rockefellers'' Soviet Union gained Hungary after Soviet tanks invaded.

The Suez *débâcle* accelerated a British retreat from empire and in 1957 the Earl of Gosford, joint Parliamentary Under-Secretary of State for Foreign Affairs, saw this retreat in terms of the world government that the Syndicate hoped to bring about: 'Her Majesty's Government are fully in agreement with world government. We agree that this must be the goal, and that every step that is humanly possible must be taken to reach that goal.'[50]

That same year, Egypt hosted a Solidarity Conference of the people of Africa and Asia, with Soviet backing. Many independence movements destabilized all corners of the Earth. In Iraq, General Kassem overthrew King Faisal in 1958 and set up an anti-Western regime. There was a communist revolution in Cuba, after President Eisenhower asked President Batista to resign in October 1958, and Fidel Castro came to power in 1959.

## Arms Sales

The US military and arms industry now dominated American life. By the mid-1950s 40,000 defense contractors worked for the Federal Government. With many people depending on companies supported by the Department of Defense, at the beginning of the 1956 economic recession President Eisenhower allocated money to defense rather than to public works. Funded by Syndicate banks and endorsed by Congress, the US military led the arms industry into a massively-escalating arms race with the Soviet Union.

President Eisenhower was deeply worried about the consequences, for it made nuclear war more rather than less likely. In 1961, at the end of his presidency, he warned:

> 'We have been compelled to create a permanent armaments industry of vast proportions.... Three and a half million men and women are directly engaged in the defense establishment. We annually spend on military security more than the net income of all the United States corporations. This conjunction of an immense military establish-ment and a large arms industry is new in the American experience.... We must guard against the acquisition of unwarranted influence, whether sought or unsought, by the military-industrial complex.'[51]

In an early draft, Eisenhower spoke of the 'military-industrial-congressional complex.'[52] He was referring to the Syndicate's dynastic *élites*.

In fact, the Syndicate was selling arms to both sides during Eisenhower's presidency, as it had done in the 1930s: 'Rockefellers' were financing the Soviet Union's purchase of missiles (with some input from 'Rothschilds'), 'Rothschilds' the American purchase of missiles (with some input from 'Rockefellers').

During the Cold War, the Syndicate made a fortune out of servicing the Soviet and US stockpiling of nuclear weapons. From a high of 69,401 nuclear weapons in 1985, in 2009 there were 23,574 nuclear warheads in the world (see p.87). Of these, Russia had 12,987 and the United States 9,552. Many of these weapons of mass destruction were bought with money borrowed from the two dynastic *élites*.

## Decolonization

Meanwhile, the ignominious ending of the three 'Rothschildite' powers' invasion of Egypt marked the end of British imperialism, which had become identified with 'Rothschilds.' 'Rothschilds' went along with the plan to offload the British Empire and encouraged Macmillan's 'winds-of-change' speech of February 1960, which spoke of the coming rapid decolonization of Africa. This process had begun in 1957 with the independence of the Gold Coast (as Ghana).

A nation-state trying to retain its colonies would have suppressed such sentiments. The feeling among imperialists was that hard-up Western governments would no longer be responsible for financing colonies and feeding their starving populations. However, the Syndicate would still want to control their oil.

In Africa's Guinea, Mali, the Central African Republic, Algeria, the Republic of the Congo, Ghana, Sudan, Tanzania, Uganda, the People's Democratic Republic of Yemen, and Somalia, the installation of pro-Soviet regimes made it look as if the Cold War was being won by the Soviet Union.

Within the Syndicate 'Rothschilds' had weakened and 'Rockefellers,' funders of the Soviet Union, seemed to be increasing their influence.

## *Vietnam, Cuba*
'Rockefellers' were behind the North Vietnamese during the Vietnam War.

The Vietnamese Communists are thought to have been armed at the end of the Second World War by Laurance Rockefeller, General MacArthur's assistant and David Rockefeller's brother, who sold weapons and munitions from the US stockpile on Okinawa to Ho Chi Minh,[53] the Vietnamese Communist leader.

In the early 1950s, 'Rockefellers' calculated that Ho would drive out the French and allow Standard Oil to develop Vietnam's newly-discovered offshore oilfields. The whole of Indo-China stands on an oil basin. In 1950 'Rockefellers' had found huge oilfields off the Vietnam coast. During a seismic survey of the seabed that lasted until 1960, 'Rockefellers' located vast oil reserves. For this reason they wanted a unified Vietnamese government to negotiate with, one that would divide the seabed into oil lots, and bid for the ones which 'Rockefellers' knew to have the most oil.

'Rockefellers' saw Ho as offering the best prospect of a unified Vietnamese Government. However, following the defeat of the French in 1954, Vietnam had been split at the 17th parallel into North and South Vietnam. To effect unity there would have to be another war which would ideally result in a reunified Vietnam. Realistically, this would be most likely to happen as a result of a North-Vietnamese victory as South Vietnam was unstable. Needing a stable government throughout the whole of a reunified Vietnam to extract the Vietnamese oil, through their links with the Soviet Union 'Rockefellers' backed North Vietnam to reunify Vietnam – while also backing pro-American South Vietnam to be on the safe side, or at least appearing to back it to win the approval of US public opinion.

The Vietnam War began in 1961 when President Kennedy sent 400 Special Operations Forces to teach the South Vietnamese how to fight a counter-insurgency war against Communist guerillas.[54] US public opinion had to be thrown behind resisting the Soviet Union in Asia, and it is likely that 'Rockefellers' intrigued to bring about the Cuban Missile Crisis to swing US public opinion against the Soviet Union.

The Cuban Missile Crisis of 1962 was a watershed. After Cuba had been expelled from the Organization of American States, the 'Rockefellerite' Soviet Union poured arms into the island, including 42 Soviet medium-range ballistic missiles. President Kennedy faced down the Soviet premier Nikita Khrushchev and made him withdraw the missiles (see p.36).

It is likely that a Cuban nuclear threat was intended to serve as a new Pearl-Harbor incident, manipulate US public opinion and panic America into supporting 'Rockefellers'' forthcoming policy of escalating the Vietnam conflict. Nelson Rockefeller had unsuccessfully sought the Republican presidential nomination against Kennedy in 1960 and was probably angered by Kennedy's stated desire to withdraw from Vietnam by 1965. It is also likely that 'Rockefellers' encouraged Khrushchev to send the missiles to Cuba in order to spur the US Administration into spending more on arms.

It is likely that Khrushchev, leader of one of the two hegemonies, was secretly a proxy of 'Rockefellers' and was urged to create the Cuban Missile Crisis by planting medium-range ballistic missiles on America's doorstep, suggesting a new bout of Soviet expansionism that had to be resisted.

Kennedy could have been assassinated for a number of reasons. Some of these have been given above (see p.37), but there are other possible motives, and in the light of what we have learned in this chapter it is useful to present here a fuller list. The assassination has been linked to:

- Kennedy's signing of Executive Order no. 11110 on June 4, 1963, which gave the US Government the power to issue currency against silver bullion held in the US Treasury's vault and would have put the Syndicate's Federal Bank of New York out of business;
- Cubans paying Kennedy back for the 1961 Bay of Pigs invasion;
- the CIA's opposition to the plan to withdraw from Vietnam by 1965, during a second Kennedy term;
- Soviet revenge for their humiliation in 1962;
- the Mafia, which Kennedy was attempting to clean up;

- friends of Marilyn Monroe with whom Kennedy had had an affair, the end of which may have caused her suicide or murder; and
- Freemasons who had lost influence under Kennedy and wanted to restore it under his successor-presumptive, Vice-President Lyndon B. Johnson (who was an Entered Apprentice Freemason).

But the assassination may have been linked to:

- the 'Rockefellerite' Syndicate's attempt to eliminate a leader who wanted to withdraw from Vietnam and thereby jeopardize their extraction of Vietnamese oil.

The level to which the Syndicate had controlled Khrushchev via David Rockefeller can be gleaned from the sacking of Khrushchev. Being partners with the Soviet Union in cash-for-oil, 'Rockefellers' expected Khrushchev to advance their commercial interests in Asia.[55] However, Khrushchev's anti-Maoist policy had caused Soviet–Chinese trade to break down. David Rockefeller was President of Chase Manhattan Bank, which now had the rights to all oil exported from China. 'Rockefellers' had defended their Chinese oil interests against the Japanese during the 1930s and had influenced the decision to drop the first atomic bomb on Hiroshima in order to protect their Chinese interests from a new invasion by Japan. Chinese trade was important to David Rockefeller.

When the United States bombed North Vietnam for the first time on August 5, 1964, after a naval incident in the Gulf of Tonkin, David Rockefeller was attending a Bilderberg conference in Leningrad (now St. Petersburg) to urge the export of 'Rockefellers'' oil from the USSR to China. The export of the oil could be handled by his new Hong-Kong branch of Chase Manhattan Bank, which he had personally opened six months previously.[56] Khrushchev phoned Rockefeller and pleaded with him to go to Moscow immediately to discuss the matter in the Kremlin.

It was a difficult meeting. While David Rockefeller's daughter Neva took notes,[57] her father criticized Khrushchev's failure to advance 'Rockefellers'' oil interests. In October 1964, Khrushchev was ousted by the Council of the Elders[58] (the Supreme Council of the Scottish Rite in Russia, which came to be known as the 'Supreme Soviet') to protect 'Rockefellers'' Chinese oil interests.

David Rockefeller seems to have been able to go to Moscow, demand the replacement of the Soviet leader, and secure it two months later. The Soviet Union was now a 'Rockefeller' satellite and David Rockefeller came to be known as the 'Czar of the New World Order.'[59]

Whereas Kennedy had been set to withdraw from Vietnam (and had possibly been killed as a consequence), his successor, President Johnson, increased US involvement in Vietnam. He ordered the bombing of North Vietnam for the first time on August 5, 1964, following the naval incident in the Gulf of Tonkin. The 'Rockefellerite' Soviet Union promised to help North Vietnam on November 26, 1964, and the Soviet premier Kosygin visited Hanoi in February 1965. In the same week Johnson again gave orders to bomb North Vietnam.

From then on US planes regularly bombed North Vietnam. From 16,000 American 'advisers' in 1963, Johnson sent an additional 3,500 troops there in March 1965. The number of US troops had risen to 75,000 by July 1965 and to 510,000 by early 1968. Together with 600,000 South Vietnamese they fought 230,000 Viet Cong guerrillas and 50,000 regular North-Vietnamese troops.

'Rockefellers' supplied the Viet Cong with arms.[60] They went into arms production within the Soviet Union before January 1967. Through the International Basic Economy Corporation, which had been founded by Nelson Rockefeller in 1947 and was controlled by the Rockefeller brothers, they had joined with Tower International Inc., which was headed by Cyrus Eaton, once John D. Rockefeller I's secretary.[61] His son Cyrus Eaton Jr. was a close acquaintance of Kosygin and Brezhnev. 'Rockefellers' and Eaton Jr. teamed up to build arms production plants, and in particular a $50 million aluminum plant in Russia.[62] 'Rockefellers' invested in Soviet industry and owned a massive oil refinery in North Vietnam that was not bombed by US planes.

In April 1967 Ché Guevara, an Argentine-born Cuban citizen close to Fidel Castro, was fighting a guerrilla war to overthrow the government of oil-rich Bolivia. Ché called for new revolutionary fronts: 'Two, three…many Vietnams.'[63] Besides the revolutionary front in Bolivia, a new revolutionary front had opened in South Vietnam following 'Rockefellers'' pumping in of arms.

In South Vietnam the turning-point in the Vietnam War was the Tet Offensive in early 1968, when the Viet Cong and North Vietnamese attacked more than 100 cities and military bases with 'Rockefeller'-produced weapons.

Deciding that a military victory was no longer possible, Washington declined to send another 206,000 troops, thereby in effect admitting that there would have to be a withdrawal. On March 31, 1968, President Johnson announced that he would negotiate a settlement with Hanoi and restrict the bombing of North Vietnam.

I visited Saigon from October 24 to 26, 1967, shortly before this offensive and vividly remember how Saigon was then under siege. Enemy guns thumped on the fringes of the city at night, the 'Coliseum' in the suburb of Cholon was heavily barricaded with sandbags and defended by sentries, and a journey in a single-decker bus with grenade-mesh over the windows through Viet-Cong-held territory to the American base at Bien Hoa was very tense. The road through palm fronds and slums on stilts had often been ambushed, and the GIs I was with expected the bus to be grenade-attacked or bombed at any moment. It was clear to me that it was now only a matter of time before the Viet Cong triumphed.

Bien Hoa was where the US Air Force entered the Vietnam War, and where the last battle of the war took place on January 31, 1968, the first day of the Tet Offensive.

### Six-Day War

Meanwhile, a third revolutionary front had been opened in the Middle East. In one sense, 'Rockefellers' precipitated the 1967 Arab–Israeli Six-Day War as they had armed Colonel Nasser, the leader of Egypt.[64] However, Nasser subsequently plotted to take over Saudi Arabia and other nearby states to persuade them to break their oil contracts, demand an increased share in oil profits, and attack Israel.

'Rockefellers'' oil firms Caltex and Aramco gave the King of Saudi Arabia 50 percent of their profits. Nasser pressed him and other Arab rulers to demand 75 percent.[65] Nasser had now upset both 'Rothschildite' Israel (over Suez) and 'Rockefellers' – both sides of the Syndicate.

In the ensuing dispute, the 'Rockefellerite' Soviet Union supported Nasser when he blocked the Red Sea and the Gulf of Aqaba to Israeli shipping. The Soviets sent much of their Black-Sea fleet to the Mediterranean. 'Rockefellers,' not wanting to pay Arab leaders an additional 25 percent of their oil profits, stepped back to allow 'Rothschilds' to teach Nasser a lesson.

Alarmed at Nasser's blockade and at the arrival of the Soviet fleet, 'Rothschildite' Israel launched a pre-emptive strike against its neighbors on June 5, 1967. Israel defeated Egypt, Syria, and Jordan and captured the Golan Heights from Syria, Gaza from Egypt, and the West Bank and East Jerusalem from Jordan. (Jordan had initially occupied East Jerusalem in 1948, in the brief war accompanying the creation of Israel, and annexed it in 1950. Until 1967 Israel's capital was in West Jerusalem. The city was reunited by the Six-Day War.)

## Defeat in Vietnam and Détente

'Rockefellers'' seismic survey of the Vietnamese oilfields had finally been concluded in 1970. It had lasted 20 years. (US planes dumping unsafe or unused bombs before returning to their carriers were guided to drop zones that would not interfere with the seismic survey.) When the survey was completed there was no need for the Vietnam War to continue.

The Syndicate wanted to bring Vietnam, and the world, together to establish an eventual world government for its own benefit. Following the military difficulties in South Vietnam from 1968, US policy favored *détente*. This was a 'Rockefellerite' policy, for 'Rockefellers'' ultimate aim was always to bring the two sides together and unite Vietnam under a unifying government.

*Détente*'s architect was Dr Henry Kissinger, a 'Rockefellerite.' Kissinger left Nelson Rockefeller's employ as chief adviser on foreign affairs after working for him for 15 years. Nelson Rockefeller gave him $50,000 in January 1969 before he joined the White House as national security adviser.[66]

At the same time, on cue, the 'Rockefellerite' Soviet leader Leonid Brezhnev welcomed *détente*. In the spring of 1968 a fourth revolutionary front had been opened, in Europe. Soviet tanks had rolled into Czechoslovakia and crushed Alexander Dubček's 'Prague-Spring' liberalization movement, thereby strengthening the Soviet bloc's control of its own oil. It is likely that these Soviet tanks were from the 'Rockefellers'–Eaton production line. Now Brezhnev tried to repair the damage to the USSR's image after the repression of Czechoslovakia's Prague Spring. There were US–Soviet talks to limit nuclear weapons.

In this spirit of *détente*, during his visit to China in 1972 President Richard Nixon, Johnson's successor, announced that Asia must be defended by Asians, with America providing logistical and economic support. Besides making possible a settlement in Vietnam, this visit opened up trade, including Chinese trade with the Soviet Union which had been an objective of David Rockefeller's in 1964.

In 1972 Nixon, in China, agreed to withdraw from Vietnam. A cease-fire was signed in Paris in 1973 and the United States withdrew, abandoning equipment worth $5 billion. The North Vietnamese invaded and Saigon fell to the Communists in April 1975.

With Vietnam once more under a single, relatively stable regime, 'Rockefellers' could at last have access to Vietnamese offshore oil. As 'Rockefellers' had wanted back in 1960, the new unified Vietnamese Government lost little time in dividing the offshore coastal area into lots, and invited bids for the right to drill for oil. BP, Royal Dutch Shell, Norway's Statoil, Russia, Germany, and Australia won bids, but found no oil. However, the lots that 'Rockefellers'' Standard Oil bid on and won were carefully chosen – identified as a result of their 20-year survey, they contained huge oil reserves.[67]

Standard Oil had gained access to Vietnamese oil in return for helping the Soviet Union win victory in South Vietnam through its arms production. One of the two commercial *élites* had put commercial advantage above patriotism.

## Cold War Intensifies

In spite of *détente*, there was in fact little real thawing between the two imperialistic hegemonies, the United States and the USSR; indeed the Cold War even intensified beneath the veneer of *rapprochement*.

Whereas no new Soviet satellites were created between the Communization of China in 1949 and the converting of Cuba into a Soviet satellite in 1967–70 following 'Rockefellers'' military partnership with Soviet imperialism, from 1967 many new satellites or pliant states emerged in territory that had once belonged to the European empires: India and Bangladesh (1971), Egypt (which in 1967–70, had 17,000 Soviet 'advisers' who were expelled in 1972) and Iraq (1972); the Yemen, Somalia, and Afghanistan (1974); Guinea-Bissau, Mozambique, and Angola (by the USSR Friendship Treaty of 1976 after a Cuban-led conquest); and Libya (following a $12-billion Soviet arms deal in 1976, although Libya was already pro-Soviet and therefore pro-'Rockefeller' from the time of Gaddafi's 1969 revolution).

The new revolutionary front in the Middle East intensified, for following the Six-Day War terrorism began to spread – an Arab response to Israel's expansion. Palestinian terrorists trained in 223 Soviet-backed training camps in the USSR and were responsible for 50,000 acts of terror between 1970 and 1985.[68] The Palestinians co-ordinated 50 terrorist groups for the Soviet Union and its satellites.[69]

Terrorist groups could exert pressure on events that assisted the Soviet Union and their 'Rockefeller' partners. For example, in 1975 the terrorist known as

'Carlos the Jackal' kidnapped Sheikh Yamani, Saudi Arabia's oil minister and the most powerful figure in OPEC (the Organization of Petroleum Exporting Countries). This was an act calculated to influence Saudi Arabia's and OPEC's oil policy. In 1973 the OPEC oil-producing countries of the Middle East had rebelled against Western-owned oil companies and quadrupled the price of crude oil – a defiant Arab continuation, during the aftermath of the 1967 Six-Day War, of Nasser's pre-War outlook. Saudi Arabia continued to push for price reductions from the $11.65 per barrel level, which were opposed by other OPEC members. The kidnapping of Yamani did not change Saudi-Arabian policy, for at an OPEC meeting in May 1976 in Bali, Saudi Arabia upheld a six-month price freeze even though Iran and seven other OPEC members wanted a 20-percent increase in oil prices to match inflation.

It now suited the 'Rockefellerite' Soviet Union and its Libyan partner to drive up the price of Arab oil. Carlos's controller was Soviet and most of the inside information was supplied by Gaddafi, but the international hit team had all been trained in the Popular Front for the Liberation of Palestine's Socotra camp in South Yemen.[70] The Palestinians had acted as Soviet proxies.

A true coming-together of the two imperialistic hegemonies did not occur until the collapse of communism, the end of the Soviet Union, and the dismantling of the Berlin Wall, which ended East–West confrontation.

We saw earlier that Gorbachev urged East Germany to open the Berlin Wall in November 1989 (see p.42). In fact, the initial impetus leading to the eventual communist collapse involved Poland and seems to have come from the Bilderberg Group.[71] David Rockefeller and Henry Kissinger told Gorbachev that they could arrange US financial aid to Poland only if Americans could observe a 'free election.' The Polish regime agreed that one-third of the seats in the Polish lower house would be reserved for the ruling communist Polish United Workers' Party and another third for its pro-communist allies. One-third of the seats would be 'freely elected,' as would all the seats in a new upper house, the Senate.

In the ensuing, partially-free election of June 1989, the anti-communist opposition, led by the Solidarity trade union, won almost every seat it contested. In the lower house, 'young Turks' among the ruling party's former allies voted with the opposition to throw out the communists and elect a Solidarity-led government with veteran anti-communist Tadeusz Mazowiecki as Prime Minister.

A yearning for freedom then swept through the 'Captive Nations' of the

Soviet bloc and in November 1989 Gorbachev was forced to urge East Germany to tear down the Iron Curtain. The Bilderberg Group had not intended this result when requesting a partially-free election in Poland, but they were pleased at the outcome.

The collapse of Soviet Communism and the end of the USSR swiftly followed. 'Rockefellers' could now implement their true aim of uniting the world on the basis of extended *détente*.

CHAPTER 8

# LIBERTY'S COMMERCIAL *ÉLITES* AFTER 1989:

## The Rise of the New World Order

The Syndicate continued to manipulate the US Government and military after the East–West confrontation ended when the Berlin Wall was breached in November 1989 and the Soviet Communist Party surrendered its monopoly of state power in February 1990. There was now a *Pax Americana*, which was tellingly reinforced when Saddam Hussein was crushed in February 1991.

## 'Rockefellers' Struggle for Oil and Gas

We have seen (on pp.80–1) that Saddam Hussein was lured into invading Kuwait, which gave the Americans an excuse to crush him and demonstrate American power to the world. What we have not seen is that the Gulf War, or First Iraq War, was really about oil.

*Gulf War*

The Syndicate's fingerprints were all over the Gulf War as they endeavored to protect Kuwaiti oil; to make their multinational oil companies less dependent on Saudi Arabia by giving those companies a share of Iraqi oil; and to help Israel by cutting Saddam down to size.

The pro-Israeli US Secretary of Defense, Dick Cheney, and Under Secretary of Defense, Paul Wolfowitz, stated that the United States was committed to defending Kuwait. The Interagency Deputies Committee of the National Security Council – the crucial White-House meeting of advisers in April 1990 that reversed the favorable US attitude toward Iraq (see pp.80–1) – was headed by Robert Gates, later US Secretary of Defense, who was instrumental in carrying through the change in the United States' attitude.[1]

Some time between April and July 25, April Glaspie, the US Ambassador to Iraq, was seemingly sent to lure Saddam to invade Kuwait in accordance with Gates' recommendation. The two Secretaries who persuaded King Fahd of Saudi Arabia to host US troops, James Baker and Dick Cheney, were both 'Rockefellerites.' When Saddam held West-European hostages as a 'human shield' against American attack, former British Prime Minister Edward Heath, a 'Rothschildite,' traveled to Baghdad to speak to him.

In February 1991 the retreating Iraqis set fire to 100 Kuwaiti oil wells in the Rumaila oilfields. These were all the property of British Petroleum, which was under the 'Rockefeller' umbrella after the British Government sold its stock in BP in 1987. The terms of the settlement confirmed Kuwait's – and therefore the Syndicate's – disputed ownership of 900 square miles (2,230 sq. km) of the Rumaila oilfields (see p.80).

## New World Order

Under the new *Pax Americana* the Syndicate had increased its access to Iraq's oil. American superpowerdom now spread the concept of a New World Order under which all countries should live at peace and any that broke international law such as Iraq would be subjugated.

The concept of a 'new world' had first been used in modern times by US President Woodrow Wilson in an address to Congress on January 8, 1918: 'We wish her [Germany] only to accept a place of equality among the peoples of the world – the new world in which we now live – instead of a place of mastery.'[2] The phrase 'New World Order' was also used by Hitler: 'National Socialism will use its own revolution for the establishing of a new world order.'[3]

Nelson Rockefeller claimed in 1962 that events demanded 'a new world order' as the old order was crumbling.[4] Richard Nixon took up the phrase in 1967 when he wrote of the evolution of a 'new world order.'[5] Nelson Rockefeller returned to the phrase during the 1968 presidential campaign, being quoted by Associated Press on July 26 as promising that 'as President he would work toward international creation of a "new world order."'

On January 30, 1976, a new 'Rockefellerite' document, *The Declaration of Interdependence*, signed by 32 Senators and 92 Representatives, stated the Syndicate's ambition:

> 'We must join with others to bring forth a New World Order.... To establish a New World Order of compassion, peace, justice, and security, it is essential that mankind free itself from the limitations of national prejudice, and acknowledge that...all people are part of one global community.'[6]

President George H.W. Bush made much use of the phrase 'New World Order' during the Gulf War (First Iraq War). On September 11, 1990, he said that 'a New World Order can emerge' that could 'shape the future for generations to come.' Secretary of State James Baker echoed the phrase: 'There's an opportunity here for a New World Order.'

Bush made numerous references to the New World Order in the early months of 1991. On January 7, he said, 'What's at stake here is the New World Order.' This was followed on January 9 by the statement that: '[The Gulf crisis] has to do with a New World Order. And that New World Order is only going to be enhanced if this newly activated peace-keeping function of the United Nations proves to be effective.' A week later, on January 16, he said: 'When we are successful, and we will be, we have a real chance at this New World Order.'

On 6 February, asked by a reporter for his definition of a New World Order, Bush said: 'My vision of a New World Order foresees a United Nations with a revitalized peace-keeping function.' And several months after the Gulf War had ended, in August 1991, Bush wrote: 'I hope history will record that the Gulf crisis was the crucible of the New World Order.'[7]

The term 'New World Order,' in the sense that Bush used it, meant that American superpowerdom would underpin a peace enforced by the UN, and would police it. During the 1990s the term came to have a second meaning: a world government imposed by the Syndicate, led by 'Rothschilds' and 'Rockefellers,' which would corner all the world's natural resources including gas and oil, convey them through pipelines to ports, and sell them round the world. Piping would replace arms sales as the principal way of raising revenue for Syndicate multinationals.

## 'Rockefellers' Asset-Strip the Collapsed USSR

The New World Order, in this last sense, soon benefited from the collapse of Soviet Communism. It was reported in 1996 that Russian President Boris Yeltsin's Prime Minister, Viktor Chernomyrdin, was in partnership with David Rockefeller. Chernomyrdin privatized and then stripped off all the energy assets of the new Commonwealth of Independent States (CIS) – the loose association of independent ex-Soviet republics that replaced the USSR in 1991 – and sold them to 'Rockefellers' for knock-down prices.[8]

Russia's state-owned gas company, Gazprom, privatized in February 1993, was sold in Moscow via Moscow banks that seemed to have acted as fronts for 'Rockefellers' for $228 million though it was valued at $3.4 billion according to a 1993 World Bank study. Lukoil, Russia's largest petroleum conglomerate, was sold for $294 million though it was valued at $3.4 billion.

United Energy Systems, the Soviet bloc's main power and utility generator, was sold for $467 million when it was said to be worth $3 billion. 'Rockefellers' picked up the new Russia's energy for one tenth of what it was worth. Earlier, in 1991, 85 percent of the world's diamond output, including Russia's diamond exports, was sold to Chase Manhattan, a bank with strong 'Rockefellerite' links.

But that was not the only reason why the USSR was broken up into independent republics. 'Rockefellers' were also after oil and gas under the Caspian Sea, and the break-up of the USSR meant that pipelines could be run from the newly-independent states. Geologists have estimated that there are 200 billion barrels of oil under the Caspian.

It could be said, therefore, that the end of the Cold War was precipitated so that the USSR could be dismantled, opening the way for 'Rockefellers' to gain access to Caspian oil and gas.

In view of Chernomyrdin's partnership with David Rockefeller, it is reasonable to conclude that Yeltsin, the first President of post-Soviet Russia, was 'Rockefellers'' man. Gorbachev, the last Soviet leader, had also been linked with 'Rockefellers.' After he left office in December 1991, his links with 'Rockefellers' became overt, for the Gorbachev Foundation was capitalized in the US with $3 million from the

Carnegie Endowment for International Peace, the Ford Foundation, the Pew and Mellon Funds – and the Rockefeller Brothers Fund. [9]

This connection suggests that 'Rockefellers" backing for Stalin from 1925, for Khrushchev over Cuba (which culminated in David Rockefeller's alleged sacking of Khrushchev), and for Kosygin over North Vietnam was extended to Gorbachev, whose role was to loosen the union of the USSR to make possible a New World Order's world government, under which oil could be piped westward.

### 'Rockefellers" Oil Pipelines from Baku

'Rockefellers' had plans for the westward flow of oil from Baku in the ex-Soviet republic of Azerbaijan.

Two pipelines pump oil from Baku to the Black Sea, both controlled by the British-led Azerbaijan International Oil Co. (AIOC), which is headed by the BP Group. British Petroleum merged with Amoco, formerly the 'Rockefellerite' Standard Oil of Indiana, in December 1998 and formally renamed itself BP in 2001. An American pipeline opened in April 1999. It runs from Baku through neighboring Georgia to Supsa on the Black Sea. The other, Russian, pipeline runs through Chechnya – a republic of the Russian Federation that has oilfields – to Novorossiysk on the Black Sea.

Although officially controlled by AIOC, both pipelines were in effect controlled by Moscow as one passed through Georgia's pro-Russian rebel parts and the other passed through rebel parts of Chechnya. The AIOC consortium therefore proposed an alternative new $2.4 billion pipeline branching off Georgia to Ceyhan in Turkey. It would still have to pass through pro-Russian rebel parts of Georgia but an exit port in Turkey rather than Georgia would remove Moscow's control over the flow of oil to the West at the Black Sea. A treaty had been signed by Turkey, Georgia, Azerbaijan, and the United States.[10]

In the summer of 1999 Chechen nationalists closed the Baku–Chechnya–Novorossiysk pipeline. Outraged, Russia proposed a new pipeline well north of Chechnya which would branch off a pipeline from the Tengiz oilfield in Kazakhstan and run to Novorossiysk. In November 1999 'Rockefellerite' Yeltsin ordered Russian forces to attack Grozny, the capital of Chechnya, retake the oilfields and oil refineries and control the Baku–Chechnya–Novorossiysk pipeline.

Russian control over the pipeline was restored, giving Russia, and therefore 'Rockefellers,' control over all oil flowing to the West once again.

Oil was an issue in the break-up of Yugoslavia and the Balkan Wars of the 1990s, as can be seen from the implementation of the Trans-Balkan oil pipeline. In October 2008 work began on this 575-mile- (920km-) long pipeline, which was due to be in operation in 2013.[11]

Oil was to be piped from Baku on the Caspian to Ceyhan on the Black Sea, conveyed by tanker across the Black Sea, and then piped from Burgas in Bulgaria across the Balkans and the ex-Yugoslav republic of Macedonia to the Adriatic port of Vlore in Albania.[12] The Trans-Balkan pipeline was built by the US-owned Albanian-Macedonian-Bulgarian Company (AMBO). Oil companies working under AMBO included Texaco, Chevron, Exxon, Mobil, BP, Amoco, Agip, and Total Fina Elf.

To sum up, the five planned oil pipelines were:

- the US Baku–Georgia–Supsa pipeline;
- the Russian Baku–Chechnya–Novorossiysk pipeline;
- the US Baku–Georgia–Ceyhan pipeline;
- the Russian Tengiz (Kazakhstan)–Novorossiysk pipeline.
- the US Trans-Balkan pipeline (Baku–Ceyhan–Burgas–Alexandroupoli/Vlore).

Camp Bondsteel in Kosovo, the largest overseas US military base since Vietnam, was built by Halliburton (a company whose Chief Executive had been Dick Cheney). Halliburton was serving US troops in the Balkans and their British subsidiary, Brown & Root Ltd of London, had made a feasibility study for the AMBO pipeline.

There has been a tussle between the United States and EU for control of the territory along the pipeline. Three former communist states, Macedonia, Bulgaria, and Albania, were set to be absorbed into the EU, but the United States wanted to distance these three countries from Germany and the EU by cocooning them in US protectorates.

As the AMBO line branches into Greece, the United States had promised a 'Greater Albania' which would include part of Greece. There are also ethnic Albanian populations in Kosovo and Macedonia, and between 1999 and 2001 the ethnic-Albanian KLA and NLA terrorists attacked non-Albanians and sought to spread 'Greater Albania.'

# War for the Trans-Afghan Pipelines

The 2001 invasion of Afghanistan can now be seen as partly motivated by an attempt to implement the Trans-Afghan pipelines. To the extent that this was so, 9/11 looked in part – but only in part – a Syndicate operation.

### Was 9/11 an Inside Job?

There is a weird connection between the Bushes, 'Rockefellers' and the bin Ladens involving Syndicate oil. Osama bin Laden's eldest brother Salem, who was ten years older than Osama, was a business partner of George W. Bush in the 1970s. He was co-founder with him of the Arbusto Energy oil company in Texas, Bush's home state.[13] (*Arbusto* means 'bush' in Spanish.)

They were put in touch with each other by Bush's neighbor and friend from the Texas Air National Guard, James R. Bath of Houston. Bath channeled $50,000 via the Bank of Credit and Commerce International put up by two Saudi sheikhs, Khalid bin Mahfouz and Salem bin Laden, and received a five-percent interest in Arbusto'79 and Arbusto'80, limited partnerships controled by George W. Bush.

Arbusto was bought by Spectrum 7, which in 1986 was bought by Harken Energy Corporation. Harken put Bath on the board as a representative of Salem bin Laden.[14] The White House later made an unsourced denial of these links.

Salem was killed in 1988 when his ultra-light plane inexplicably turned right instead of left during take-off and crashed into power lines in San Antonio, Texas.

It is not clear to what extent Salem was an active partner of Bush. It is likely that he invested in oil via Bath and was a sleeping rather than an active partner in Bush's enterprise. On the other hand, he *was* killed in Texas, suggesting that he actively worked with Bush.

It seems that Osama bin Laden was a CIA asset during the war to liberate Afghanistan from Soviet occupation from 1979 to 1989. In spring 1986 he had been brought to the United States by the CIA under the name 'Tim Osman.'[15] It is weird that during Osama bin Laden's commercial activities in 1991 he allegedly shared a joint bank account with Sharon Rockefeller, the wife of Senator John D. ('Jay') Rockefeller IV at the Bank of Chicago.[16] It is a measure of the high commercial respectability and standing in which bin Laden was then held that such an arrangement can be alleged when with hindsight it seems so obviously incredible.

Bin Laden's companies in the Sudan at this time were: the Wadi al-Aqiq Trading Company; Ladin (*sic*) International Company; Al-Hijra Construction, which built roads and bridges in conjunction with the Sudanese Government; Al-Themar Agricultural Company, which had 4,000 employees working on a million-acre farm; Taba Investment Ltd, which exported gum, corn, sunflower and sesame; The Blessed Fruits Company, which grew fruit and vegetables; Al-Ikhlas, which produced sweets and honey; Al-Qudurat Trucking Company; Khartoum Tannery; a bakery; a furniture-maker's; and Al-Shamal Islamic bank in Khartoum, which held $50 million of bin Laden's own money.[17]

Bush's first act after 9/11 was to ban all flights out of America. However, at a time when flights were banned all over America, it is bizarre that he then rounded up and repatriated to Saudi Arabia some 140 Saudis, including all bin Laden's family and colleagues in the United States, in a succession of flights between September 14 and 24:[18]

- on September 14, a flight carrying bin Laden's sister left Los Angeles for Orlando, picked up his brother Khalil, and flew on to Washington;
- on September 16, one flight left Las Vegas for Geneva and another left Lexington for Newfoundland and London;
- on September 17 a flight left Dallas for Newark;
- on September 18 and 19 two more flights left Boston; and
- on September 22 and 24 more flights left New York and Las Vegas.

It was a very thorough program, rounding up Saudis and bin Ladens from different parts of America and flying them back to Saudi Arabia.

It is also strange that the financial assets of bin Laden's family company, the Saudi Binladen Group (SBG), whose chairman was another of Osama's brothers, Bakr, were run by the Carlyle Group: the 11th-largest American armaments company, worth $12 billion, which was represented abroad by George H.W. Bush and ex-British Prime Minister John Major, the two men who conducted the (First) Gulf War and were now being rewarded by the Syndicate with jobs.[19]

So Osama bin Laden, younger brother of George W. Bush's business partner, alleged sharer of a joint account with Senator Rockefeller's wife, and an ex-CIA asset, who was thus allegedly tied into the American Establishment three times over, became US Public Enemy Number One after 9/11, acquired nuclear-suitcase bombs allegedly for use against ten American cities, projected himself as a new Saladin and reviver of the Caliphate, and apparently disappeared without trace off the face of the Earth, beyond the reach of American superpowerdom – allegedly into Iran. Meanwhile, intersecting flights took bin Laden's family and leading Saudis back to Saudi Arabia. They were repatriated in two waves – one collecting them from all over the United States and depositing them at a central collecting point, another taking them to Saudi Arabia. This detailed and complex operation took place when there was no flying over America.

Donald Rumsfeld said on October 25, 2001, that bin Laden might never be caught,[20] but had to retract this observation later. Had bin Laden been doing the CIA's bidding in the run-up to 9/11?

It has been suggested that 9/11 was an 'inside job,' and that bin Laden, acting in conjunction with the CIA, provided the United States and the Syndicate with the excuse to occupy Afghanistan and reactivate the Trans-Afghan pipeline. If this was so, then the post-9/11 vilification of bin Laden by the United States – claims about suitcase bombs, his grandiose aims, and asylum in Iran – are suspect and were possibly fabricated; and the CIA, Rumsfeld, and the Syndicate probably knew exactly where he was – somewhere safe. However, as we shall see on p.135, it is more likely that while 9/11 was to some extent an inside job, bin Laden was indeed a new Saladin; that he had organized a genuine attack on 9/11; perhaps even that the CIA knew of the attack before it occurred but allowed it to happen to give the United States a Pearl-Harbor-like pretext to invade Afghanistan; and that bin Laden did subsequently find shelter in Iran.

PROMIS (Prosecutor's Management Information System) was a highly secret computer software program that enabled its operators to keep track of case management, including tracking people down. It was used in the American legal system in the 1980s and 1990s. The FBI had installed PROMIS software in its headquarters to track terrorists. Robert Hansen, FBI computer specialist and Soviet mole, handed a copy of his German BND PROMIS software to his KGB controllers for $2 million. The USSR then used it for computer-based espionage against the United States.

According to the *American Free Press*, after the collapse of the USSR, a redundant KGB officer approached one of bin Laden's representatives and sold him the PROMIS software for $4 million. The PROMIS software helped bin Laden to escape capture.[21]

There were many suspicious features about 9/11 that linked the operation with the Syndicate. It seems that Mossad (and also perhaps French intelligence) had wind of an impending attack and told the CIA about it in confidence, in general rather than specific terms.[22] The CIA did nothing but, wanting a pretext to attack Afghanistan and bin Laden, made sure that on September 10 there was a plan in place to topple bin Laden.

The Syndicate's man, Dick Cheney, took charge and chose to conduct an air exercise on 9/11.[23] A US intelligence agency, the National Reconnaissance Office in Chantilly, Virginia, about four miles (6km) from Dulles Airport's runways, which operates US reconnaissance satellites, scheduled a simulated security exercise for September 11, in which a plane would crash into one of the four towers of the agency's headquarters.[24] The Pentagon and CIA were aware of the planned 'category response,' which is why at least three of the four planes were not intercepted by fighters. (The fourth plane may have been shot down over Pennsylvania.)

As regards the fighters that could have been used, three US squadrons had 54 'primary assigned' F-15C fighter jets that could have intercepted the hijacked airliners. On 9/11 the F-15s of the 94th Fighter Squadron, which was stationed at Langley Air Force base in Virginia, were in Saudi Arabia, where the squadron had been sent to reinforce the no-fly zones over southern Iraq. The F-15s of the 27th Fighter Squadron, also based at Langley, had returned from identical no-fly-zone duties two days before. There was a Red-Flag exercise in Nevada which took most of the F-15s of 71st Fighter Squadron away from Virginia. It was against this background that the Chantilly exercise took place.[25]

The effect of all this was that officials close to Cheney shut down American air space, and that Cheney sent his boss Bush to meet Republican donors and visit a primary school in Sarasota, Florida. When intruding aircraft were reported in American air space, American air defenses took no action, believing the intruders were part of the exercise.

Mossad and perhaps the CIA arranged for the two hijacked planes to be filmed live from all sides – just as 60 years earlier the attack on Pearl Harbor was caught on camera because of foreknowledge. Five Mossad agents were arrested for dancing and clapping near the collapsed Twin Towers. They said they were recording what was happening, having been tipped off that it would happen. It seems that they were observing the impacts for Mossad.

The Twin Towers could not have been destroyed by aircraft impact. Rather,

THE SECRET AMERICAN DREAM

according to an experienced structural architect, they were taken down by explosives, specifically nano-thermite.[26] It crossed people's minds that small tactical-nuclear-suitcase bombs may have been on board the hijacked planes – hence the diagnosis of cancer years later in a number of passers-by and members of auxiliary services who rushed into the Twin Towers to help.

In an interview with *American Free Press* ("Were 'Mini-Nukes' Used to Bring Down WTC?", September 20 and 27, 2010) aerospace and chemical engineer T. Mark Hightower said: 'If nukes were used to disintegrate the World Trade Center's immense inner core, only a small percentage actually reacted when these devices were detonated. The leftover materials subsequently continued to react, and therefore kept producing tremendous amounts of heat. This continual source of energy explains the molten steel discovered beneath ground level weeks after 9/11.' It took 100 days to extinguish all the fires at ground zero, and many contractors saw trapped molten metal beams melted by heat. Molten steel was found after the meltdown at Chernobyl.

While nano-thermites could explain the pulverization in mid-air of the Twin Towers, which turned to dust before they hit the ground, vaporization (as opposed to mere melting) of the internal metal columns required something more intense than nano-thermites, on the level of a nuclear reaction. Reports from NASA (National Aeronautics and Space Administration) described 'hot spots' exceeding 1,300 degrees Fahrenheit on ground zero in the weeks and months after 9/11. Hightower said, 'The heat signature images recorded from space couldn't be produced by simple detonations.' He theorized, 'Regular detonators and nano-thermites were potentially used as incendiary devices to cut through metal on the WTC's exterior sections. But if mini-nukes were located at the buildings' core and shielded from view, no one would have seen their extremely bright flashes and superheated explosions. The release was so energetic that it may have momentarily reached millions of degrees.' Were some tactical-nuclear-suitcase bombs – perhaps identical to some of those bin Laden is said to have acquired – planted in the World Trade Center prior to the explosions?

At 5:20p.m. on September 11, WTC7 (the 47-story Salomon Brothers Building in the same complex as the Twin Towers), which housed a CIA area on the top floor, smokestacked neatly to the ground many hours after the first impact, apparently without explanation. It was too far from the Twin Towers to be affected structurally by the earlier impacts.

It later transpired that there were other coincidences involving Israel. Larry Silverstein, who had strong links with Israeli Prime Ministers Ariel Sharon, Ehud Barak, and Benjamin Netanyahu, bought the lease for the three WTC buildings on July 23. He insured the Twin Towers for $3.5 billion, which was more than the $3.2 billion of the lease. Silverstein Properties' insurance compensation was staggering. In December 2004 they were awarded $2.2 billion and later $4.6 billion, as they collected twice for the two impacts on the Twin Towers. They received $861 million against their insured investment of $386 million for WTC7.[27]

Furthermore, an Israeli company, Zim American Israeli Shipping Co., whose parent company Zim Israel Navigation Co. was nearly half-owned by the State of Israel, broke its lease of rented offices on the 16th and 17th floors of the North Tower at the beginning of September, and lost $50,000.[28] It was suggested that the company had been tipped off, another case of Israel's advance knowledge.

The US Government later said that it was a 'bizarre coincidence' that the security exercise had been scheduled for 9/11, but in view of what we have just seen it is likely that Syndicate agents set up a simulated crash and then substituted actual crashes, which is why no planes from the ground intercepted the hijacked planes. If this was not the case, it has to be asked how a man living in an Afghan mountain cave without even a cellphone could achieve the collapse of the Twin Towers and flatten part of the Pentagon without getting American superpower-dom's super-technological defensive fighters off the ground.

In short, it seemed that Mossad alerted Syndicate contacts within the American administration about al-Qaeda's operation, that Bush was kept in the dark by Cheney and that the United States did nothing to prevent the attack and indeed helped it forward by closing its air space for an exercise. The resulting Pearl-Harbor-style clamor swung public opinion behind a revenge war on Afghanistan and the hunting down of Bush's ex-business partner who had allegedly shared a bank account with Sharon Rockefeller and had, until 1989, been in the CIA.

A US plan to topple bin Laden had been approved by Bush the day before 9/11. The text had been placed on National Security Adviser Condoleezza Rice's desk on September 10 for Bush to review. It recommended thwarting bin Laden 'through work within the Northern Alliance to dismantle al-Qaeda and the Taliban,' making use of a $140-million CIA program to arm Afghanistan's Northern Alliance and anti-Taliban forces.

On the same day, September 10, Lieutenant-General Mahmoud Ahmad, head of Pakistan's Inter-Services Security Agency (ISI), which had long been linked to the CIA, was involved in wiring $100,000 from banks in Pakistan via Ahmad Sheikh to hijacker Mohammed Atta's accounts in two banks in Florida.[29]

On the morning of 9/11, Lieutenant-General Ahmad met the co-chairmen of the Joint Intelligence Committee, Bob Graham and Porter Goss, for breakfast in Washington while the attacks which Ahmad had co-financed were in progress. Three days later Ahmad met Secretary of State Colin Powell, other American politicians and CIA Director George Tenet. Lieutenant-General Ahmad was subsequently dismissed. Do the wiring and these meetings suggest that the CIA financed 9/11 via the Pakistani ISI?

A former research minister in the German Government, Andreas von Bülow, wrote in *The CIA and September 11* that the 9/11 attacks could only have happened with the support of the CIA, and that they were staged to justify the subsequent wars in Afghanistan and Iraq. Al-Qaeda saw these wars as hegemonistic manifestations of superpowerdom masquerading as self-defense, but they also brought commercial gain to Syndicate companies via pipelines, and cheaper oil to the United States.

It later came to light that the Twin Towers had been jokingly nicknamed after David and Nelson Rockefeller for they had been built by the Port Authority of New York and New Jersey with 'Rockefeller' assistance at a time when David Rockefeller was a prominent banker and Nelson Rockefeller was Governor of New York. The Twin Towers were a symbol of American financial dominance. They were the highest towers in the world until their main structures were surpassed by Chicago's Sears Towers and Kuala Lumpur's Petrona Towers (and more recently by the Burj Khalifa, Dubai, which was opened in January 2010). The Twin Towers remain technically the tallest structures ever built as the North Tower had a 347 foot (106m) radio mast. Even though they had been leased to Silverstein they had the image of being 'Rockefellers" buildings.

## The Syndicate's Oil and Gas Interests in Afghanistan

It now became apparent that the war in Afghanistan had much to do with the Syndicate's oil and gas interests.

Many of Bush's inner circle had oil interests, like Bush himself: Vice-President Dick Cheney had previously served as Chairman and Chief Executive of Halliburton Co., the world's largest oilfield services company, which had operations in

Azerbaijan; both Cheney and Commerce Secretary Donald Evans ran energy-related companies; National Security Adviser Condoleezza Rice had been a director with Chevron from 1991 until January 2001; her adviser Brent Scowcroft was a director of Pennzoil-Quaker State Co. and Enron Global Power & Pipelines, a unit of Enron Corp.; Defense Secretary Donald Rumsfeld had between $3.5 million and $15.5 million invested in energy-related companies; and Deputy Secretary of State Richard Armitage was a co-chairman of the US-Azerbaijan Chamber of Commerce.[30]

For decades a 762-mile- (1,226km-) long gas pipeline had been planned to run from the Turkmen Dauletabad fields through Afghanistan to Multan in Pakistan, and then on to India. The project was known as TAPI: Turkmenistan–Afghanistan–Pakistan–India. It was also known as the Trans-Afghan Pipeline (TAP).

There had long been rumors that the Taliban were created in 1994 by the CIA and Pakistan's ISI (Inter-Services Intelligence Agency) to guard pipelines that would carry oil and gas from ex-Soviet republics across Afghanistan to Pakistan.

In May 1997, Unocal, the spearhead for 'Rockefellers'' Standard-Oil interests, secured a $2.5 billion pipeline deal with the Taliban, Turkmenistan, and Pakistan. The pipeline would run from Turkmenistan's Chardzhou oil refinery through Afghanistan to Pakistan and eventually India. Unocal offered to pay the Taliban $100 million a year as rent for oil and gas pipelines. However, Unocal withdrew from its involvement in August 1998 following the attacks against the US Embassies in Kenya and Tanzania, and withdrew from the consortium in December 1998 following the US cruise-missile attack against an unstable Afghanistan. The pipeline was not constructed at that time.

In February 2001, Bush began to negotiate with the Taliban to get the pipeline project resumed. US officials met the Taliban in Berlin in July and pressed them to form a government of national unity in return for aid.

Now Unocal planned to build a 1,030-mile- (1,660km-) long Central-Asian oil pipeline from Chardzhou in Turkmenistan to Pakistan's Arabian coast.[31] Following 9/11, bin Laden was reported to have ordered al-Qaeda to attack 'US oil and gas pipelines' if either he or Mullah Omar were captured or killed. As a result, locations were removed from websites.

Unocal's top adviser during negotiations with the Taliban was none other than Hamid Karzai, who was later installed by the Bush Administration as the new ruler of Afghanistan. Zalmay Khalizal worked for Unocal and liaised between Unocal and the Taliban. He had drawn up the risk analysis for the pipeline in 1997 and had lobbied the Taliban. He was made George W. Bush's Special National Security Assistant and Special Envoy for Afghanistan. He worked on risk analyses in connection with the pipeline for US National Security Adviser Condoleezza Rice.

The United States now had a permanent base in Afghanistan, Shamsi Air Base, from which it launched Predator drones that observed and attacked al-Qaeda militants in the Afghanistan–Pakistan border area. At the time of writing this pipeline is being built by the US company General Electric in conjunction with Bechtel, and is guarded by US soldiers.

To sum up, the planned Unocal pipelines crossing Afghanistan were:

- the Trans-Afghan gas pipeline (Turkmenistan [Dauletabad]– Afghanistan–Pakistan [Multan]–India);
- the Trans-Afghan oil pipeline (Turkmenistan [Chardzhou]– Afghanistan– Pakistan–India), built by General Electric in conjunction with Bechtel.

In view of the new Afghan leadership's and the US military's links to the Trans-Afghan pipeline, it looks as if the war in Afghanistan was primarily fought to get the projects involving oil and gas pipelines back on track and to create a secure environment for them.

Iran made an attempt to snatch away the Trans-Afghan pipeline. The IPI, the Iran–Pakistan–India gas pipeline, was a plan conceived by India and Iran in 1989. It had Pakistani and Indian consumption in mind, but at the time of writing, construction has not yet begun. This Iranian pipeline would avoid Afghanistan by running from Iran's South-Pars gas field through Balochistan (where the Baloch Liberation Front have mounted attacks) to Multan and then Delhi – and ultimately to China.

Concerned at the deteriorating situation in south-west Afghanistan and in Balochistan, in April 2007 India and Pakistan signed an accord for the IPI gas pipeline with Iran, and this accord has delayed the Unocal project, to the dismay of the United States. The Americans had opposed the Iranian plan in March 2006 because of Iran's nuclear activities, support for terrorism, and poor human rights record. Washington wanted Hamid Karzai, now Afghanistan's President, to sign an accord with India and Pakistan before Iran became involved.

However, Iran's plan has stalled. Differences between Iran on the one hand and Pakistan and India on the other hand were not resolved, and in August 2008 Turkey's energy minister visited Tehran to propose an Iran–Turkey oil pipeline.

To sum up, the planned pipelines involving Iran were:

- the Iran/South Pars–Pakistan–India gas pipeline;
- the Iran–Turkey oil pipeline.

## Second Iraq War and Oil

The 2003 Second Iraq War, too, now looks like an oil war. It had Syndicate fingerprints all over it, but those of 'Rothschilds' rather than 'Rockefellers.'

Had both factions been involved in the planning of the war, the war would have been firmly on the Bilderberg Group's agenda for its 2002 meeting in Chantilly, Virginia. But it was not on the agenda. In fact, Donald Rumsfeld told the meeting (held between May 30 and June 2) that an invasion of Iraq would not take place until the following year.[32] Discussion focused on the idea of a world tax on oil as an alternative to a UN tax on all world citizens, which it was thought would be resisted. Had the Iraq War been a joint venture it would surely have been the main item on the Bilderberg agenda, although such openness could be expected to have alerted Saddam.

With hindsight one can see that George W. Bush was converted to attacking Iraq some time between the PNAC's (see p.90) Statement of Principles of June 3, 1997, and September 12, 2001, when he said to his counter-terrorism 'czar,' Richard Clarke, 'See if Saddam did this.'[33]

Cheney, Rumsfeld, and Wolfowitz were all linked to 'Rothschildite' Israel, as was the British Prime Minister, Tony Blair, who was later rewarded with a job with the 'Rothschildite' J.P. Morgan. Bush was a front man for Cheney and found himself surrounded by 'Rothschildite' proxies while not being one himself, though he too had strong links with Israel.

Despite their manipulating proxies, 'Rothschilds' were officially aghast at Bush's American-supremacist stance which cut across their plans for a New World Order, as their associate George Soros made clear in *The Bubble of American Supremacy*: 'I consider the Bush Doctrine of pre-emptive military action pernicious, and so do many others around the world.'[34]

Interestingly, 'Rockefellers' were equally officially aghast. Senator Jay Rockefeller, the Senate Intelligence Committee's senior Democrat, appeared on television to call for televised hearings into the 'accuracy' of intelligence used by Bush to justify war. He conveyed 'Rockefellers'' view that no weapons of mass destruction had been found: 'We have found nothing of significance. We went into the war based on the fact that Saddam's ties to al-Qaeda and weapons of mass destruction were posing an imminent threat to our country. We need to know if this was accurate.' He suggested that Cheney's many visits to the CIA during the previous year were to put pressure on CIA officials to make their assessments fit the Administration's policy aims. Senator Rockefeller asked, 'What was he doing there?'

In July 2004, Rockefeller introduced the Senate's report into the 'flawed' intelligence of the CIA and said that Congress would not have voted to go to war had it known of the intelligence shortcomings. There may have been an element of double-talking in these remarks as 'Rockefellers,' who had benefited from many oil deals since their 1925 arrangement with Stalin, also benefited from Iraqi oil.

Not just 'Rockefellers' but the Syndicate collectively stood to benefit from Iraqi oil. After the involvement of Saudi Arabians in 9/11, Saudi Arabia was considered to be unstable and the PNAC group wanted to be less dependent on Saudi oil by drawing on Iraqi oil. The oil companies had eyed Iraq, which then held eleven percent of the world's known oil reserves. If Saddam were toppled, the Western oil companies would have access to Iraq's oil reserves and become less dependent on Saudi oilfields. It mattered more to these companies that Iraqi oil was an opportunity to be grasped than that Saddam was a threat.

In January 2010 in London, the Chilcot Inquiry into the Iraq War shed light on PNAC's oil ambitions when it heard that Bush and Blair had made a pact 'signed in blood' at Camp David in April 2002, and that Blair had written a number of letters to Bush that have never been published. The suggestion was that they had agreed to topple Saddam. George W. Bush resented an attempt to wipe out his family in 1993, for which he blamed Saddam, as we saw on pp.89–90. Israel wanted the toppling of Saddam, and the Bush–Blair collusion to invade Iraq may suggest that they were implementing a 'Rothschildite' PNAC agenda.

The Syndicate benefited from the invasion of Iraq. The contract to put out the wellhead oil fires, worth about $50 million, was given to Kellogg, Brown & Root, a subsidiary of Halliburton, the oil company of which Cheney had been Chief Executive. But by far the greatest potential benefit involved the plan to reconstruct the Kirkuk–Haifa pipeline (see p.263).

This pipeline had first been built by British Petroleum in 1935. It had been inactive since the end of the British mandate in Palestine in 1948 when the flow from Iraq's northern oilfields to Palestine was redirected to Syria. The reactivating of this pipeline would give a source of cheap Iraqi oil to the United States and Israel, cutting Israel's energy bill by 25 percent. The contract to reconstruct this pipeline was given to Bechtel Company, to which the Bush Administration also awarded a $680 million contract for the reconstruction of Iraq in mid-April 2003.

The beginning of the reconstruction of the pipeline was delayed by the instability in Iraq, and it is not certain whether President Obama would persevere with the plan. The pipeline would run from Iraq through Jordan, another ex-British mandate territory, to Israel. It is not clear how, given Arab public opinion, Jordanians could be persuaded to give Bechtel transit rights for oil to flow from Iraq to Israel across its territory. The concept of reconstructing this pipeline belonged to the era of US supremacy and hegemony, when the United States could impose its will by force, rather than to the more multipolar world that Obama ushered in.

The concept may already have been secretly implemented. It was claimed by the American author and filmmaker Texe Marrs, in an interview carried by the *American Free Press* of August 23, 2010, that 'after US troops invaded Iraq, they began rebuilding a pipeline from Iraq through Israel to ports on the Lebanese border.' (Haifa is near the Lebanese border.) 'There the oil is loaded onto tankers and transported to China, where it is refined.... The Chinese refineries are, in actuality, privatized front companies owned by the Rothschilds.... Why do we still have 50,000 troops in Iraq, 13 permanent military bases, and the world's largest embassy? The plan is to establish a Greater Israeli prosperity sphere, with our embassy serving as grand central for Middle-East oil distribution.... Goldman Sachs – a Rothschild front company – has financed thousands of warehouses in China to stockpile billions in natural resources.... Why does Israel continue its assault on Lebanon? It's to ensure they retain control of the ports in that area so their oil can be laundered to China.... When you talk about Israel, you're really talking about the Rothschilds. They founded Tel Aviv, nicknamed the "White City", in 1909 and turned Israel into their own personal theocratic super-state.' If this claim is true, and it must be said that it has not been verified, then the arrangement is a left-over from the era of US supremacy and hegemony.

Both 'Rothschilds' and 'Rockefellers' benefited in other ways. In 2000 'Rothschilds' controlled every central bank in the UN except for seven: Cuba, Libya, North Korea, Sudan, Iran, Afghanistan, and Iraq.[35] After the Iraq War they took control of the latter two, and as a result now controlled 187 out of 192 UN nation-states' central banks.

'Rockefellers' benefited via Lukoil. In 1997 Lukoil, the Russian firm which they had acquired during Chernomyrdin's privatization and sell-off of Russian energy, had signed a $3.7 billion contract to refurbish the huge West-Qurna oilfield in Iraq. In a deal worth $20 billion to Lukoil, 'Rockefellers' would receive half of the field's 667 million tons of crude oil, while Iraq and Russian-government agencies would receive a quarter each. In February 2003 Saddam had canceled the deal, but in December 2003, Russian President Vladimir Putin managed to achieve its reinstatement, to the benefit of Lukoil.

To sum up, the planned pipelines from Iraq were:

- the US Kirkuk–Haifa oil pipeline;
- the Russian West-Qurna (Lukoil) pipeline.

There was a further oil-related benefit. In August 2003 it emerged that America planned to mortgage Iraq's future oil supplies to pay for expensive post-war reconstruction work. Loans of $30 billion over ten years would be made on the security of Iraq's oil reserves, which were then the second largest in the world. Indirectly the Syndicate had begun to siphon off Iraqi oil.

'Rockefellers' seem to have manipulated Saddam through Russia. The Russian ex-premier, Yevgeny Primakov, visited Saddam in Baghdad on Putin's orders on February 23, 2003. Primakov arranged the transfer of Iraq's secret-service files to Moscow in the event of Saddam's defeat. It later turned out that, at the time, Primakov was an employee of the US Total Information Awareness (TIA) office,[36] and so the Syndicate were presumably able to monitor Iraq's secret-service files.

After the US-led invasion of Iraq, Saddam was able to evade capture for six months until December 13, 2003. According to an *American Free Press* article of 2003 there is evidence that George H.W. Bush provided Saddam with the PROMIS software – which allowed him to escape capture, and which Osama bin Laden also later acquired – during the Iraq–Iran War in the 1980s. George W. Bush brought America's top spy-catcher, Paul Redmond, out of retirement to investigate how Saddam obtained PROMIS. When Redmond eventually told Bush that it had been supplied by his father, George W. Bush sacked Redmond and the next day placed a $25 million bounty on Saddam's head, and $15 million on the heads of his sons – in order to terminate their use of PROMIS, which enabled them to keep one step ahead of their pursuers.[37] The plan worked, for Saddam's two sons were betrayed for their bounties in July 2003.

It is strange that both the anti-American figureheads of the Afghan and Iraq wars were able to use the American superpower's most advanced technology to avoid being tracked down.

If we approach the Second Iraq War with an open mind, in a spirit of honest enquiry, and lay out the evidence, we have to conclude that at face value it was an attempt by skeptical Western leaders – who genuinely believed that Saddam had WMDs, which he was hiding – to compel Iraq to comply with UN Resolution 1441. But behind this overt action was the hidden agenda of the Syndicate.

We have seen that the Syndicate's New World Order is a complex mosaic of conflicting family and corporate interests, and that it works through proxies who ensure that their policies conform to a global plan that would benefit the Syndicate: a plan that would enforce a *Pax Americana*, using the US military as a global army. There is circumstantial rather than incontrovertible evidence that some of these proxies used their access to push for war in Iraq, and that they operated within a culture that sought to introduce the New World Order by deception.

## US–Russian Oil and Gas Pipeline Conflict and the Syndicate

Meanwhile the Caspian pipelines (see pp.130–1) have progressed.

### US Baku–Tbilisi–Ceyhan Oil Pipeline

The way was cleared for the United States to build the 1,100-mile- (1,760km-) long Baku–Tbilisi–Ceyhan oil pipeline. It would run through Azerbaijan, where in December 2003 the son of the pro-American President, Aleyda Aliyeva, inherited the leadership on the death of his father. Rumsfeld visited Azerbaijan that same month and proposed that NATO troops should guard the pipeline.

The pipeline would then pass through Georgia. Also in December 2003, the pro-Russian leader of Georgia (and ex-Soviet Foreign Minister), Eduard

Shevardnadze, was replaced by the pro-American Mikhail Saakashvili. In January 2004 it was announced[38] that the United States would implement the oil pipeline to Ceyhan. BP Group,[39] led the consortium that would build it. The pipeline was built between 2003 and 2005.[40] The first oil left the Baku end of the pipeline on May 10, 2005, and reached Ceyhan on May 28, 2006.[41]

In 2008 Russia invaded Georgia in support of two breakaway pro-Russian provinces, South Ossetia and Abkhazia, expelling Georgian forces and recognizing the independence of the two provinces. The Russians' presence in those territories meant that they could, if they so wished, disrupt the flow of oil in this pipeline when it was built. It seemed that 'Rockefellers' were seeking a stranglehold over a 'Rothschildite' project. Azerbaijan and Georgia were ruled by 'Rothschildites' but 'Rockefellerite' Russia was set to cut the flow of oil if it suited its self-interest.

### Russian Baku–Chechnya–Novorossiysk Oil Pipeline

The Baku–Chechnya–Novorossiysk oil pipeline was also implemented.[42] The first oil flowed through on October 25, 1997, but in 2007–8 a dispute between Azerbaijan and Russia reduced the supply and the whole operation was disrupted and delayed.

### US Trans-Caspian Gas Pipeline

The Trans-Caspian gas pipeline remains unconstructed. If built, it would transport gas from Kazakhstan and Turkmenistan to Baku in Azerbaijan, and thence via Tbilisi in Georgia and Ceyhan in Turkey to Central Europe, circumventing both Russia and Iran.[43] It would run under the Caspian Sea and in Baku it would link to the South-Caucasus pipeline (the Baku–Tbilisi–Erzurum pipeline) and through this with the planned Nabucco pipeline.

### US Nabucco Gas Pipeline

The Nabucco pipeline was scheduled to be constructed from 2010 to 2014 and run from Erzurum in Turkey to Baumgarten an der March in Austria. It would flow from Turkey through Bulgaria, Romania, and Hungary to Austria and rival the planned Russian South-Stream natural-gas pipeline through Bulgaria, Serbia, and Hungary to Austria. It would therefore lessen Europe's dependence on Russian energy. The name Nabucco was taken from Verdi's opera of that name, which representatives of the five partners (Austria, Hungary, Bulgaria, Romania and Turkey) attended at the Vienna State Opera after formalizing their agreement in 2002.

### Russian Trans-Ukraine Gas Pipeline

Now US access to the Caspian was undermined by Russia. Following the 2008 'pipeline war' in Georgia, the United States found itself in a pipeline conflict with Russia over the Ukraine. Ukraine's 'Orange Revolution' of 2004 had transformed independent Ukraine from a pro-Russian ex-Soviet republic into a pro-NATO US satellite and potential member of the EU. However, the 'Orange Revolution' came to an end on February 14, 2010, when Ukraine's Electoral Commission (in circumstances suggesting a degree of fraud) declared the pro-Russian Viktor Yanukovych the winner of new presidential elections, rolling back Washington's hold over the Ukraine.

The neutralization of Ukraine knocked a hole in the US strategy of encircling Russia, which now once more had access to the Black Sea. (The 'Orange' government had ended Russia's lease on its Crimean naval bases – a decision quickly reversed by Yanukovych.) Russia's 'Rockefellerite' Gazprom now had a transit contract to reach the Black Sea through Ukraine, which had failed to join 'Rothschildite' Europe. Russia was using its energy (oil and gas) as a geopolitical lever.[44]

### Russian Nord-Stream Gas Pipeline

Russia had been building up to this confrontation for some while. From 2004 Russia had bypassed Ukraine and Poland by constructing an underwater gas pipeline, Nord Stream, westward under the Baltic waters off Sweden, Finland, and Denmark that ran from the Russian port Vyborg to northern Germany's Greifswald. Deliveries were scheduled to begin in 2011.

### Russian South-Stream Gas Pipeline

The United States had retaliated by building the Nabucco pipeline (see p.146) to southern and south-eastern Europe. Russia now promoted the South-Stream gas pipeline, which would run southward under the Black Sea from the Russian coast to the Bulgarian coast where it would fork, one arm proceeding to Bulgaria, Serbia, Hungary, and Austria (see p.146), and the other arm to southern Italy. This pipeline was scheduled to be operational by 2013.

## Russian Eastern Siberia–Pacific Ocean Oil Pipeline

At the end of 2009, Russia moved eastward by opening the Eastern Siberia–Pacific Ocean (ESPO) oil pipeline that would allow it to export oil from its East-Siberian oilfields to China, South Korea, and Japan. The final link of pipeline was scheduled to be completed by 2014.

## More Pipeline Conflicts

Russia now began its first deliveries of LNG (liquefied natural gas) from the Gazprom-led Sakhalin-2 pipeline.

At the same time, in late 2009 China completed the first stage of the Central Asia–China (or Turkmenistan–China) gas pipeline. This would take natural gas from Turkmenistan across Uzbekistan to southern Kazakhstan, and would connect with the West–East gas pipeline that crosses China. This was the first pipeline to take Central-Asian natural gas to China.

Russia then moved northward in the direction above the Arctic Circle. In August 2007 two Russian submarines had planted the Russian flag at a depth of 2.5 miles (4km) on the floor of the Arctic Ocean, laying claim to the seabed's natural resources of oil and gas. In 2008 the US Geological Survey came to the conclusion that there were huge amounts of oil and gas just north of the Arctic Circle.

## Civil War within the Élites?

Following the collapse of Communism in 1991 the Russian economy had been stripped by Western companies acting in conjunction with new Russian oligarchs, but now Russia was re-emerging as an economic power, its 'Rockefellerite' investment shaping its challenge to Western Europe and the 'Rothschildite' EU.

It now looks as if there is a civil war within the commercial *élites* for global control of the world's pipelines. Russia has been 'Rockefellerite' since 'Rockefellers'' oil deal with Stalin in 1925, and 'Rockefellers' seem to be behind the Russian pipeline activity to the west, south, east, and north. Europe has long been 'Rothschildite,' and the EU is under 'Rothschildite' commercial tutelage. 'Rothschilds' also seem to have been behind the Saakashvili regime in Georgia, perhaps because of possible historical links between the Khazars, a people of ancient Georgia who apparently converted to Judaism in the eighth century CE, and some of the Jewish communities of medieval Europe, who may have included the ancestors of Mayer Amschel Rothschild.[45]

The US–Russian pipeline conflict may be an expression of a conflict within the *élites* for global control of all pipelines: a global élitist civil war for world commercial mastery in which regimes and administrations (including those of Russia and the United States) have been caught up.

## Iranian Oil, Iran–Pakistan–India Gas Pipeline

This pipeline conflict has extended to Iranian oil, which the Syndicate covets. According to an exclusive report in the *Sunday Herald Scotland*[46] hundreds of US bunker-busting bombs were being shipped from Concord, California, to the American base on the British island of Diego Garcia in the Indian Ocean to prepare for an attack on Iran, which is 1,000 miles (1,600km) from Diego Garcia and within range of the American base there. The US Government signed a contract with Superior Maritime Services, Florida for $699,500 in January 2010 to transport ten ammunition containers to the island. According to a cargo manifest from the US Navy the containers included 195 smart, guided 1,000-pound (453kg) Blu-110 bombs and 192 massive 2,000-pound (907kg) Blu-117 bombs used for blasting hardened or underground structures. Dan Plesch, director of the Centre for International Studies and Diplomacy at the University of London, was quoted as saying, 'They are gearing up totally for the destruction of Iran.... US bombers are ready today to destroy 10,000 targets in Iran in a few hours.'

Iran is oil-rich. It looked as if there were pipeline considerations behind this shipment. It looked as if the Syndicate had given up hope that US troops could pacify Afghanistan sufficiently for the Trans-Afghan pipeline to be implemented and had decided to run with the Iran–Pakistan–India pipeline (see pp.139–40). It looked as if they had calculated that an attack on Iran's nuclear sites and getting on for another 10,000 targets in Iran could bring about regime change, prevent Iran from supplying roadside bombs to Afghanistan and Iraq and install a pro-Western, post-Islamic democratic government that would permit the piping of oil from Iran – without the instability and disrupted flow that could be expected to continue if the Trans-Afghan pipeline was implemented in Afghanistan.

Political developments involving Afghanistan suggested that this might be the scenario. The new American President, Barack Obama, opted for a surge of troops in Afghanistan of the kind he had opposed when it was applied to Iraq, and accompanied it by a statement that troop withdrawals from Afghanistan would begin in 2011. In June 2010 he accepted the resignation of General Stanley

McChrystal, Commander of NATO forces in Afghanistan, who, frustrated at realizing that he could not achieve the success that could justify serious troop withdrawals in 2011 and that his approach diverged from Obama's, had been openly contemptuous of his civilian bosses in a magazine interview in which an aide spoke of 'the real enemy' as 'the wimps in the White House.' (As President, Obama was the Commander-in-Chief of the US armed forces, and there was a degree of insubordination in the aide's remarks.) Obama replaced McChrystal with General David Petraeus, strategist of the Iraq 'surge' (see pp.96–7).

In 2010 the leader of the new British coalition government, David Cameron, grasping that the Iraq and Afghan wars had cost Britain £20 billion and, seeking to eliminate the war as a cost, said that he would like to see all British troops withdrawn from Afghanistan by 2015. The G8 group of leading economies, including the United States, supported this ambition.

Western politicians were seeking a political rather than an exclusively military solution in Afghanistan and an exit strategy, and were looking to turn a military operation into a training operation in order to leave Afghanistan able to defend itself from al-Qaeda and its Taliban allies. If it was implemented, the Trans-Afghan pipeline would be guarded by Afghan troops. However, if Afghanistan continued to be turbulent after 2015, the way would be clear to proceed with the Iran–Pakistan–India pipeline.

### Syndicate Self-Interest

Given all this, there was a case for concluding that the 'War on Terror' was a fraud, and that the Bush Administration's concealed agenda was to create the conditions in which the Syndicate could loot the oil and gas reserves in former Soviet territories in the Caspian basin – the biggest untapped source of fossil fuel on Earth – and siphon it off to the west, south and east.

Oil and gas pipelines are good for humankind. They spread access to gas and oil round the world. The capitalist system delivers them and multinationals make a profit from installing them. That is as it should be. They are being laid with a view to eventual world government. Again, that is as it should be.

What is less good, indeed deplorable, is that the ownership of the oil and gas the pipelines convey is claimed by self-interested *élites* who are cornering the Earth's natural resources with a view to bringing in a deceptive New World Order that will benefit them before it benefits the rest of humankind.

America has been making the world a better place for everyone, and that is good. Behind this veneer, however, is a group of people who place their own interests above the best interests of humankind. The Syndicate have been driving American superpowerdom for their own commercial gain, in the hope that they can bring in a world government of a kind that would suit their commercial self-interest.

## The Financial Crisis and the Syndicate

The Syndicate have found another way to make money: by persuading the governments of North America, Europe and Asia to hand over trillions of dollars to Syndicate-controlled banks to tackle the credit crunch and so-called 'toxic assets.'

The problem was compounded on September 11, 2008, the seventh anniversary of 9/11, when there was a massive withdrawal from the American banking system. Between 9 a.m. and 11 a.m. $550 billion was withdrawn, and the US Treasury spent another $105 billion in propping the currency up. The loss in two hours totaled a staggering $655 billion.

At that point the Treasury stopped trading for the day. If it had not done so there would have been a cascade and $5.5 trillion would have hemorrhaged by the end of the day, the US economy would have collapsed and the world economy would have followed the next day.[47] The Treasury, Federal Reserve, and President Bush agreed that the withdrawal should be kept secret and should be plugged as soon as possible.

Congress agreed to make available $700 billion on September 23, 2008. The amount was to buy 'toxic assets from many banks.' In fact this money was replacing the $655 billion that had hemorrhaged. As panicking governments propped up unstable banks, $3 trillion were transmitted from Western and Eastern governments to Syndicate banks.

One does not have to look far to see who was doing the withdrawing. One *élite*, 'Rothschilds,' owned or controlled 187 central banks[48] in the 192 UN nations as we saw on p.144. A group of rabbis connected with the Holy Temple and the Temple Mount movements, Jerusalem, had warned Bush in a formal scroll known as the Megillat Bush Scroll that there would be consequences if he did not change his policy towards Israel.[49] The warning was delivered when Bush attended Israel's 60th-anniversary celebrations in May 2008, and the 'consequences' may have followed on September 11, 2008 – fatally damaging the Republican cause just before the November-2008 election.

The huge withdrawal seems to have been a multi-purpose operation. Besides creating world panic and thereby extracting $3 trillion from governments, its knock-on effects caused a collapse in confidence in the Republican Party and influenced the American presidential election of November 2008. It perhaps also served as a warning to the American presidency that it should not force a two-state solution on Israel, and that it should abandon handing over East Jerusalem (which includes the Temple Mount or Haram as-Sharif, a site sacred to both Jews and Muslims) to a new Palestinian state. The sheer power of the New World Order to influence world leaders and events is graphically illustrated by the events of those two hours on September 11, 2008.

The withdrawal may have also been linked to the meeting in spring 2009 of the Bilderberg Group, which agreed to create a global 'Department of the Treasury' and as a first step propelled an internationally little-known ex-Prime Minister of Belgium, Herman van Rompuy, into the role of President of the European Union. Van Rompuy promptly distributed an unpublished paper to EU governments calling for a new regime of 'economic governance.' He proposed that the EU should set economic targets for all member states and that these should be monitored by EU bureaucrats.[50] The EU would be in firm control of the member-states' economies.

It was reported that the Bilderberg Group, set to meet in Sitges, Spain in June 2010, planned to keep the global recession going for at least a year as persuasive pressure to get this global 'Department of the Treasury' implemented.[51] At the same time the spreading of the pandemic H1N1 'swine flu' across national borders led to calls for a global 'Department of Health.'

The Syndicate's financial dealings were also linked to the offshore-drilling disaster that occurred in the Gulf of Mexico on April 20, 2010: the world's worst oil disaster. This resulted in a moratorium on offshore drilling.

It seems that what happened was far more serious than was officially announced. BP-commissioned drilling from Deepwater Horizon's oil rig tapped into a high-pressure subterranean oil vein. Senior researchers reported that BP drilling had hit an 'oil-migration channel,' a deep fault on which hydrocarbons generated in the depth of the earth migrate to the crust and are accumulated in rocks, and that leakage could therefore continue for years if not successfully capped. The oil spill was near the origin of the Gulf-Stream current, and there was a prospect that the oil could spread up the US Atlantic coast to North Carolina and then be carried by the Gulf Stream to the North Sea and Iceland, and eventually to the shores of the UK and Northern Europe. It was claimed that the Obama Administration and BP conspired to hide the true extent of the ecological disaster.[52]

It was further alleged in the *American Free Press*[53] that the oil leak was not caused by incompetence but was deliberately engineered. The cement used by Halliburton (the US company formerly associated with ex-Vice President Cheney) to plug the wellhead had been contaminated with heavy-drilling mud, and though the cement had not had time to set, an order was given – perhaps on the instructions of a saboteur – that the mud, which was now the primary key to maintaining safety, should be removed.

As could have been predicted, once the mud was removed gases and fluids under tremendous pressure, estimated at 30,000 to 70,000 pounds per square inch (2,109–4,921kg per sq. cm), burst upward from 32,000 feet (9,750m) below the surface of the Gulf of Mexico, causing a massive explosion and the loss of eleven lives on the oil rig.

According to this view, the displacing of oil beneath the seabed would create an enormous cavity which could cause tectonic plates to contract and shift. Earthquakes and perhaps a tsunami could be expected. The costs arising from the ensuing devastation would bankrupt BP, described by the *American Free Press* as a 'Rothschild' subsidiary, and cause a global economic and financial collapse. A 'Rothschild' bank, it was claimed, would then step in and pick up the pieces, including the remnants of its own subsidiaries.

In 1987 Edmund de Rothschild created the World Conservation Bank (renamed the Global Environment Facility in 1991). This institution was designed to pick up pieces after a collapse of all the major banks – a process that began with the financial crisis of 2008, which took several banks to the brink of ruin. To secure loans from 'Rothschild'-controlled central banks, countries use land as collateral. If their banks fail, the 'Rothschild'-controlled 'superbank' would be in a position to seize, and legally own, this collateral: the world's national parks, natural resources, farmland, and forests. It could assume ownership of 30 percent of the globe's prime real estate and effectively control the world.

It sounds like something out of a James Bond film, and one can be forgiven for being skeptical. Nevertheless, this scenario is being alleged. Is it believable that the 'Rothschildite' Syndicate orchestrated the Gulf of Mexico cataclysm in order to bring about a collapse in the global economic system and to drive forward a plan to seize a third of the world's land?

And did 'Rockefellers'' 'Big-Oil' faction of the Syndicate decide that the wellhead should be capped to conserve the enormous amount of oil in the Gulf of Mexico for their own eventual use? If so, 'Rockefellers'' strategy was to stop the oil leak and keep the Gulf open for (their own) deepwater drilling. Stopping the oil leak meant turning against – indeed, sacrificing – their 'Rothschildite' junior partner BP. Keeping the Gulf open for drilling meant using the courts. On June 22, 2010, Obama had imposed a ban on deep-sea drilling below 500 feet (152m), which would have appalled 'Rockefellers.' On July 9 the US court of appeal in New Orleans rejected Obama's federal ban, which would have delighted 'Rockefellers.' Were 'Rockefellers' trying to keep as much oil under the seabed as possible for themselves while preserving their access to it? Did 'Rockefellers' block 'Rothschilds'' attempt to profit from the Gulf of Mexico via BP? And was Obama, caught between the two, buffeted by both 'Rothschilds' (seeking to profit from the Gulf) and 'Rockefellers' (blocking him in the New-Orleans court)?

A look back over the years since 1989 suggests that there is considerable evidence to indicate that President George W. Bush was an independent figure who stood apart from the maneuverings of the Syndicate and the Bilderberg Group. Influenced by PNAC from 1997 and driven by Cheney of the Syndicate, he was a front man for imperialist-supremacist policies that favored Israel – with the image of being his oilman father's son who appealed to the Syndicate as he could draw in men who served his father such as Dick Cheney and Donald Rumsfeld. Under extreme pressure from the Syndicate he allowed the New World Order to expand into Afghanistan and Iraq, and brought democracy to both countries, for which he should be applauded.

In the course of treading a fine line between extending democracy and backing pipelines with troops, Bush Jr. resisted bin Laden's nuclear-suitcase threat and ambition to revive and restore the Caliphate in Baghdad. He presided over plans to construct new pipelines in Afghanistan and Iraq, which could one day be used for the benefit of humankind – if a new President were able to extract America from the influence and commercial self-interest of the Syndicate.

# PART FOUR

# What Will Become of Liberty's Empire: The Rise of Liberty's World State

# CHAPTER 9

# THE SECRET
# AMERICAN DREAM:
## America's Philanthropic Mission

It is now time to return to the seven bands of a rainbow. On p.xv we saw that they are in fact a unified spectrum whose separate colours are only distinguishable through the refraction of light in raindrops. Similarly, we saw that the seven bouts of expansion in American history are a unified spectrum that can be distinguished only by the refractive consciousness of a discerning historian. The seven bouts of expansion, in chronological order, were:

- federal unification;
- westward expansion;
- colonial empire ca.1898;
- isolationism with interventions in two world wars;
- imperial hegemony;
- world empire based on American supremacy; and
- the New World Order of the commercial *élites* before and after 1989.

We look back at these seven bands from the stage that the North-American civilization has now reached. I can say with some confidence that the first four bands of the above list cannot come again. They were stages in America's past growth, phases in the growth of the American Empire. The fifth band ended with the collapse of the Berlin Wall and of Soviet Communism in 1989–91. The sixth band is the one we have recently been in, Bush's world empire based on American supremacy. This band is shadowed by a seventh band, the world order planned by the commercial *élites*.

## American Prospects

What are the prospects of America's world empire of the sixth band? Can it be enlarged more than it already is?

The United States already has a massive influence on world events. It has established control over the 192 countries of the UN. It has 700–800, perhaps even 1,000, bases in 130 of these countries. It has 26 in Germany, nine in Japan, eight in Great Britain and eight in Italy.[1] The United States is behind NATO, which has 30 bases.[2] All this amounts to an extensive empire which could intensify if further bases are established in the remaining countries. The US empire could develop from extensive control to absolute domination.

### America Perpetually Supremacist?

There is an idea abroad that America took over the mantle of empire that it deposed, and conceptualized itself in terms of a nation and empire that is perennially and perpetually supremacist and universal; that America is different, exceptional, and above international law at all times.

This view of the world has recently been advanced by American thinkers such as Michael Ignatieff in an article, 'The American Empire: The Burden'; Robert Kagan in an article, 'The Benevolent Empire'; and Philip Bobbitt in *The Shield of Achilles*.[3] The skeptical side of this view is that America represents a perennial danger to the world. Hence a book with the title *American Dream, Global Nightmare*, which sees American benevolence as a 'cultural delusion.'[4]

However, as we have seen, the seven bouts of American expansion all have individual characteristics, and the latest, 'supremacist' phase of pre-emptive action and the contemporaneous pressure from commercial *élites* are not typical of America's universal, and Universalist, benevolent outlook on the world, which sees all humankind as being one political entity. This is Liberty's most fundamental and true cultural principle.

The United States makes much of defending the Free World against terrorism. *The Global 2000 Report to the President*[5] of 1980 outlined 'the state of the world' in terms of the level of threats which might undermine US interests. This concept has been perpetuated in the global 'War on Terror.'[6] One such terrorist threat took the form of bin Laden's attempt to restore the Caliphate and base its capital in Baghdad, as we saw on p.87. The United States defends the Free World against the threat that bin Laden will explode ten nuclear-suitcase bombs, one in each of ten American cities, as we saw on p.87. The reality of Afghanistan may be that the West is searching for the missing nuclear-suitcase bombs that fell into the hands of the Chechen Mafia and thence, via bin Laden, into the hands of al-Qaeda, ally of the Taliban.

## America Hegemonistic?

However, America's posture of defending the world has been greeted with skepticism. Skeptics say that the military interventions that amount to the global War on Terror are a smokescreen for a war against all who oppose the US hegemony formed during the Cold War. Certainly the War on Terror has had the effect of enabling the commercial *élites* of the Syndicate to criss-cross the world with oil and gas pipelines. (See Chapter 8 and Appendix V.) It is possible that the US Government is being driven by the commercial Syndicate. Some skeptics assert that it is in fact a front for the Syndicate, in which Syndicate political puppets implement Syndicate policies in the public sector.

Even the Haiti earthquake of January 12, 2010, can now be seen to have a link with oil. Haiti may have twenty times the offshore oil of Venezuela, and it has been suggested by one human rights attorney that 'hydraulic fracturing' caused by drillers searching for oil caused the earthquake.[7] Haiti may be, in oil terms, a new Saudi Arabia, and so the US rescue mission in Haiti may in fact be a disguised invasion to secure the oil resources for the commercial *élites*.[8]

The sway of America's world empire has been blunted by the financial crisis of 2008, which was in part a natural slowdown in the economic cycle caused by excessive borrowing and debt. The slowdown was hugely compounded by the rapid withdrawal of $550 billion from US banks on September 11, 2008 (see p.150). America's financial prospects looked more fragile than before, and the level of the United States' borrowing from China was worrying.

## *America in Decline and Breaking Up?*

It has been argued for some time that America has begun to decline. Paul Kennedy, in *The Rise and Fall of the Great Powers*, maintained as much, blaming 'imperial over-stretch.'[9] According to Kennedy, as more and more US money and manpower are assigned to protect increasing wealth and expanding territory, less money and fewer men are available to perpetuate progress, and decline sets in. Since his book came out in 1988 America has fought three wars, so far successfully.

It has also been argued that America is facing a period of post-American dominance, which will impact on the lives of Americans as if they had been plunged into a modern 'Dark Ages.'[10] It has been asserted by Igor Panarin[11] that the US will break into six parts: the Pacific coast, which has a substantial Chinese population; the South, which is largely Hispanic; Texas, where there are already independence movements; the Atlantic Coast, which has a separate mentality; five poorer central states, where native Americans are a force; and the northern states, which are linked to Canada.

Quite apart from the fact that Panarin predicted that the United States would break up in 2010, I disagree with both these arguments. In my study of 25 civilizations[12] I show that all civilizations, both dead and living, pass through 61 stages, and that at present the North-American civilization is in stage 15 of its life. This is the same stage that the Roman civilization was at from 341BCE to 218BCE. Anyone predicting the demise or break-up of Roman civilization after the First and Second Punic Wars against Carthage (264–241BCE and 218–201BCE) would have been proved wrong by the expansion of 30BCE–270CE (stage 29). The American empire's stage 29 lies some way ahead.

Furthermore, the EU's potential break-up of the UK into 12 regions can be seen as part of a Syndicate-influenced attempt to break up all the nation-states in the EU into 'European regions.' The involvement of the Syndicate, an alliance of the commercial *élites*, surfaced from behind the scenes with the founding of the Bilderberg Group in 1954.

The Syndicate may well want to break America up in preparation for a coming New World Order which would similarly break all nation-states in the world into world regions, but the North-American civilization is too young for such a plan to succeed. A stage-15 civilization is far more resilient in protecting its independence than a stage-43 civilization such as the European civilization that includes the UK.

## *America in a Clash of Civilizations, Imposing Universalism by Force?*

Samuel Huntington has argued that America can expect to be caught up in a clash of civilizations.[13] I agree with this view. There has been a prolonged clash between the North-American and Arab-Islamic civilizations in our time: Muslim jihadists, wanting to revive the Islamic Caliphate, have clashed with American troops preserving the *Pax Americana*. However, Western politicians have sought to present the conflict not as one between the North-American and Arab civilizations or between Christendom and Islam, but as one between forces of law and order and a motley group of extremists, opium traders, and lawbreakers who must be crushed.

Such a view obscures the truth. Huntington was right to see the conflicts as cultural rather than ideological or economic, as being between Muslims on the one hand and, on the other hand, Orthodox Serbs (in the Balkans), Jews (in Israel), Hindus (in India), Buddhists (in Burma), and Catholics (in the Philippines). As Huntington says, 'Islam has bloody borders.'[14]

We have seen that the sixth band was a world empire based on American supremacy. This was the way of George W. Bush, asserting American military supremacy in intercivilizational conflicts in Afghanistan and Iraq. Huntington, writing a few years before George W. Bush became President, rejected this supremacist way as it is imposed by violence :

'The belief that non-Western peoples should adopt Western values, institutions and culture is immoral because of what would be necessary to bring it about. The almost-universal reach of European power in the late nineteenth century and the global dominance of the United States in the late twentieth century spread much of Western civilization across the world. European globalism, however, is no more. American hegemony is receding if only because it is no longer needed to protect the United States against a Cold War-style Soviet military threat. Culture, as we have argued, follows power. If non-Western societies are once again to be shaped by Western culture, it will happen only as a result of the expansion, deployment and impact of Western power. Imperialism is the necessary logical consequence of universalism.'[15]

Huntington objects to Western universalism being imposed by violence, by force. He anticipated America's drive for supremacy in the early 21st century, which had already begun with the collapse of Soviet Communism in 1991 and the prosecution of the Gulf War.

### America Spreading Universalist Liberal Democracy by Consent?

But there is another way to arrive at universalism – the way of consent rather than of violence. It is at least theoretically possible that all the civilizations and nation-states in the world could consent to adopt universalism, that they should opt for liberal values and put aside their cultural clashes.

Such was Francis Fukuyama's view in *The End of History and the Last Man*. Fukuyama saw a coming universalization of Western liberal democracy as the final form of human government. Liberal democracy would spread throughout the world and represent the end of humankind's ideological evolution, what Hegel called 'the end of history.'[16]

In fact, if such a consensual universal liberal democracy were to be adopted in every civilization and nation-state in the world, this would represent a stage in the development of one of the civilizations: the North-American civilization, which is the youngest and most dominant. All the other living civilizations are much older and are in stages which suggest that they may soon be conquered and occupied. It is therefore possible, within my view of history, that there can be a consensual embracing of liberal democracy throughout the world *for a time* – not forever, but for a few decades.

In 2006 Fukuyama recanted on Iraq in *After the Neocons: Where the Right Went Wrong* and by doing so admitted that America had not won the global argument. There would not be permanent American hegemony and liberal democracy. Fukuyama may now agree with my view that global liberal democracy can only last for a while.

## Obama Jettisons American Supremacy and Implements the Secret American Dream

On the face of it, on assuming office in January 2009, President Obama found himself faced with a choice: to continue American supremacy (band 6) or to move toward universal liberal democracy, possibly as front man for the commercial *élites* (band 7). However, Obama's presidency has brought a review of America's world empire.

## America Not to Dominate Other Nations

Obama has set a new agenda. As President his main principle has been that America should not dominate other nations but should be their equal. In Berlin on July 24, 2008, he had already spoken of the 'burdens of global citizenship' – not of global leadership – and had promised to 'remake the world.' He was encouraged in his reappraisal of American aims by the award of the Nobel Peace Prize, which was decided less than a month into his presidency.

On September 24, 2009, when speaking to the UN General Assembly, Obama said: 'No one nation can or should try to dominate another nation. No world order that elevates one nation or group of people over another will succeed.'

Obama implemented his new concept by seeking *rapprochement* with the Islamic world. At his inauguration on January 20, 2009, he appealed to Iran: 'We will extend a hand if you are willing to unclench your fist.' On June 4, 2009, he went to Egypt and extended a hand of friendship to all Muslims. He applied the new concept of American equality with other nations to Russia, saying he wanted to abolish nuclear weapons.

What did Obama mean by these approaches? What kind of world did he have in mind? It was clear that Bush's world empire based on American supremacy (band 6) was now dead, but what did he seek to put in its place?

## America Bringing in the Syndicate's New World Order?

To some, Obama had turned to the Syndicate's New World Order. Their New World Order was to be a federal union of all the nation-states of the world, who should all be equal. In promoting a new American posture of equality, was Obama acting as an instrument of the Syndicate?

At first sight it may seem that he was. He came from nowhere to snatch the Democratic candidacy from Hillary Clinton and to win the presidential election in November 2008. It has been suggested on the Internet that the Bilderberg Group gave the go-ahead for Obama to become President.[17] It has also been suggested (on a dubious website no longer active) that David Rockefeller gave Obama the phrase 'spread the wealth,'[18] and that he advised Obama to be a redistributive President and to emphasize socialist-style redistribution during his campaign. The source for this view is highly questionable, but it can be argued that Obama's health-care program was an aspect of this.

He could be seen as being within the 'Rockefellerite' fold. He was a member of the Council on Foreign Relations (CFR)[19] and set out his ambitious geopolit-ical plans in a magazine published by the CFR, *Foreign Affairs*.[20] He was allegedly also a 32nd-degree Prince Hall Freemason[21] and a member of Royal Arch Masons, and Knights Templary.[22]

Amazingly, according to the *Chicago Sun-Times*, Obama was related to the top two members of the Republican Administration he ousted. Obama and George W. Bush were allegedly tenth cousins once removed, linked through a 17th-century Massachusetts couple, Samuel Hinckley and Sarah Soole.[23] Obama and Dick Cheney were allegedly 11th cousins – eighth cousins, according to Dick Cheney's wife Lynne Cheney – through 17th-century immigrants from France, Mareen and Susannah Duvall.[24]

All this may suggest that he had been welcomed into the Syndicate to do a job that would be easier for an African-American to do rather than a traditional, white, Republican American: to bring the Syndicate's New World Order formally into being. Furthermore it is interesting that, despite having accepted the Nobel Peace Prize, Obama adopted the principle of the 'surge' – a rapid injection of huge numbers of troops – that General David Petraeus had used so successfully in Iraq (see pp.96–7). As a Senator, Obama was very critical of the surge in Iraq, but nev-ertheless he sent 30,000 additional troops to Afghanistan in a very similar move. While this may suggest a continuation of Bush's policy that would continue to benefit the Syndicate's development of the Trans-Afghan pipeline, Obama's intention was clearly to bring about an improvement to the Western position in Afghanistan in order to pave the way for a prompt hand-over to Afghan forces and a speedy American withdrawal.

We saw earlier that the oil leak in the Gulf of Mexico might have been caused by the Syndicate (see p.152). If this was so, the Syndicate would probably have looked to Obama to hide the long-term implications of the disaster behind boisterous criticism of BP's 'recklessness.'

In short, it might appear that Obama had jettisoned American supremacy to work toward the commercial *élites'* New World Order of equal nation-states: a United States of the World.

### *America to be Benevolent to Humankind*

However, there is evidence that Obama had another course of action in mind. Let us look at some passages from Obama's speech in Cairo on June 4, 2009:[25]

'Just as Muslims do not fit a crude stereotype, America is not the crude stereotype of a self-interested empire. The United States has been one of the greatest sources of progress that the world has ever known. We were born out of revolution against an empire. We were founded upon the ideal that all are created equal.... We are shaped by every culture, drawn from every end of the Earth, and dedicated to a simple concept: *E pluribus unum* – "Out of many, one."'

'The dream of opportunity for all people has not come true for everyone in America, but its promise exists for all who come to our shores – that includes nearly 7 million American Muslims in our country today who enjoy incomes and education far higher than average.'

'I believe that America holds within her the truth that regardless of race, religion, or station in life, all of us share common aspirations – to live in peace and security; to get an education and to work with dignity; to love our families, our communities, and our God. These things we share. This is the hope of all humanity.'

'Human history has often been a record of nations and tribes subjugating one another to serve their own interests. In this new age, such attitudes are self-defeating. Given our interdependence, any world order that elevates one nation or group of people over another will inevitably fail.'

'We do not want to keep our troops in Afghanistan. We seek no military bases.'

'Today America has a dual responsibility: to help Iraq forge a better future – and to leave Iraq to Iraqis. I have made it clear to the Iraqi people that we pursue no bases, and no claim on their territory or resources. Iraq's sovereignty is its own.'

All these excerpts are making the same point: America does not seek 'a self-interested empire' but seeks to work for peace, disarmament, and the unity of humankind ('Out of many, one'). The 'promise' of the American Dream exists for all immigrants to America. The new 'world order' should not have any one nation elevated over the rest. Contrary to the practice of America's world empire based on American supremacy, there should be no bases in Iraq or Afghanistan.

Obama did say that the American Dream 'has not come true for everyone in America' but the fact that 'its promise exists for all who come to our shores' means, by implication, that the promise of the American Dream exists for all humankind, since by implication all are potential immigrants to America. The new 'world order' that Obama had in mind seems to be one in which the American Dream is applied to all humankind.

As we have seen on pp.9–13 America has always seen itself as acting benevolently toward the rest of humankind: exporting the values of Liberty not to dominate or be imperialistic by conquest and military intervention, but to improve the lot of humankind so that all people are free and living in peace and prosperity under the values set out in the 1776 Declaration of Independence: the values of 'Life, Liberty, and the pursuit of Happiness.' The dream is that all nation-states will have liberty from colonialism and imperialism, and will be free so that their peoples will enjoy liberal-democratic government.

Many would say that Liberty's true mission is philanthropic, and would lament the charge that America has become imperialist and supremacist, which have been leveled by Muslim extremists, among others. Quite simply, many Americans have long secretly felt that it is Liberty's mission to hand liberty to all humankind as a philanthropic act, not out of self-interested imperialistic conquests or commercial-industrial self-interest.

## The Secret American Dream in Obama's Speeches

What is the secret American Dream? It is an American leadership acting altruistically and philanthropically with the whole of humankind in mind, not acting just to promote the self-interest of America or the Syndicate. It is:

- bringing peace and disarmament to the world;
- having a policy to share the world's natural energy resources so that all humankind can raise its standard of living, not just to divide them up among US multinational corporations or the Syndicate;
- solving environmental problems from humankind's perspective, not solely America's;
- ending disease, despite the interests of American pharmaceutical companies that benefit from the continuation of disease;
- ending famine by advancing humankind's ability to feed itself, not making American food exporters the first consideration;
- solving the world's financial crisis so that humankind, not American banks, benefits;
- working to end poverty for the world's oppressed and downtrodden, not just restricting poor relief to America.

The secret American Dream puts all humanity at the center of its focus, not just America.

The historian Arnold Toynbee summed up the secret American Dream when he stated: 'Our age is the first generation since the dawn of history in which mankind dares to believe it practical to make the benefits of civilization available to the whole human race.'[26]

Many Americans have long secretly felt that Liberty's mission is to rearrange the world so that all nation-states are unified and can live in peace. This is Liberty's secret American Dream.

Obama's early speeches have covered all these points and there were global initiatives to implement them. It is worth laying out the evidence for this.

### Peace

Peace reverberates through Obama's early major speeches. He concluded his Cairo speech (June 4, 2009):[27] 'The people of the world can live together in peace. We know that is God's vision. Now that must be our work here on Earth. Thank you. And may God's peace be upon you.'

In his speech to the United Nations General Assembly (September 24, 2009),[28] Obama spoke of the second pillar for the future: 'the pursuit of peace'. He said:

'We can recognize that the yearning for peace is universal, and reassert our resolve to end conflicts around the world.... Our efforts to promote peace, however, cannot be limited to defeating violent extremists.... We will work with the UN and other partners to support an enduring peace.... I will not waver in my pursuit of peace.'

In his speech accepting the Nobel Peace Prize (December 10, 2009),[29] he said:

'I do not bring with me today a definitive solution to the problems of war.... Let us reach for the world that ought to be – that spark of the design that still stirs within each of our souls. Somewhere today, in the here and now, a soldier sees he's outgunned but stands firm to keep the peace.... We can understand that there will still be war, and still strive for peace.'

### Disarmament
Nuclear disarmament was central to Obama's Prague speech (5 April, 2009):[30]

'The existence of thousands of nuclear weapons is the most dangerous legacy of the Cold War.... The Cold War has disappeared but thousands of those weapons have not. In a strange turn of history, the threat of global nuclear war has gone down, but the risk of a nuclear attack has gone up. More nations have acquired these weapons. Testing has continued. Black market trade in nuclear secrets and nuclear materials abound. The technology to build a bomb has spread. Terrorists are determined to buy, build, or steal one.... One nuclear weapon exploded in one city – be it in New York or Moscow, Islamabad or Mumbai, Tokyo or Tel Aviv, Paris or Prague – could kill hundreds of thousands of people.... So today, I state clearly and with conviction America's commitment to seek the peace and security of a world without nuclear weapons.... We will reduce the role of nuclear weapons in our national security strategy, and urge others to do the same.... To reduce our warheads and stockpiles, we will negotiate a new Strategic Arms Reduction Treaty with the Russians this year…. This will set the stage for further cuts, and we will seek to include all nuclear weapons states in this endeavor.'

In one passage in his Prague speech,[31] Obama seemed to refer by implication to bin Laden's acquisition of nuclear-suitcase bombs (see pp.242–50):

'All nations must come together to build a stronger, global regime….We must ensure that terrorists never acquire a nuclear weapon. This is the most immediate and extreme threat to global security. One terrorist with one nuclear weapon could unleash massive destruction. Al-Qaeda has said it seeks a bomb and that it would have no problem with using it. And we know that there is unsecured nuclear material across the globe. To protect our people, we must act with a sense of purpose without delay. So today I am announcing a new international effort to secure all vulnerable nuclear material around the world within four years. We will set new standards, expand our co-operation with Russia, pursue new partnerships to lock down these sensitive materials. We must also build on our efforts to break up black markets, detect and intercept materials in transit, and use financial tools to disrupt this dangerous trade. Because this threat will be lasting, we should come together to turn efforts such as the Proliferation Security Initiative and the Global Initiative to Combat Nuclear Terrorism into durable international institutions. And we should start by having a Global Summit on Nuclear Security that the United States will host within the next year.'

Obama gave a later indication of this view when he spoke to the US Military Academy at West Point on December 1, 2009:

'We will have to take away the tools of mass destruction. That is why I have made it a central pillar of my foreign policy to secure loose nuclear materials from terrorists; to stop the spread of nuclear weapons; and to pursue the goal of a world without them.'[32]

The 'loose' 'tools' could be a reference to nuclear-suitcase bombs. He told the cadets that the additional troops for Afghanistan 'will allow us to accelerate handing over responsibility to Afghan forces, and allow us to begin the transfer of our forces out of Afghanistan in July of 2011.' It seemed that his intention was to seize al-Qaeda's nuclear material, expel al-Qaeda from Afghanistan, hand over to the Afghan security forces, and then leave.

Speaking at Bagram air base in Afghanistan on March 28, 2010, Obama went out of his way to tell US troops that they were in Afghanistan to prevent al-Qaeda 'and its extremist allies' from re-emerging in Afghanistan and Pakistan.[33] It was clear that he regarded al-Qaeda as the main enemy, a perception that appeared to be linked to its nuclear-suitcase bombs, and that the Taliban were a subordinate enemy who must not be allowed to re-establish al-Qaeda.

Welcoming the leaders of 46 nations to the Global Summit on Nuclear Security in Washington on April 12, 2010, Obama said:

> 'The single biggest threat to US security, both short-term, medium-term, and long-term, would be the possibility of a terrorist organisation obtaining a nuclear weapon. This is something that could change the security landscape in this country and around the world for years to come. If there was ever a detonation in New York City, or London, or Johannesburg, the ramifications economically, politically and from a security perspective would be devastating. We know that organizations like al-Qaeda are in the process of trying to secure nuclear weapons or other weapons of mass destruction and would have no compunction in using them.'[34]

He spoke of al-Qaeda's 'trying to secure nuclear weapons'. In other words, the process set out in Appendix III (see pp.242–50) was continuing, and New York and London were at risk from al-Qaeda nuclear-suitcase bombs.

The next day Obama told the Summit:

> 'The risk of nuclear confrontation between nations has gone down, but the risk of nuclear attacks has gone up. Nuclear materials that could be sold or stolen and fashioned into a nuclear weapon exist in dozens of nations. Just the smallest amount of plutonium – about the size of an apple – could kill and injure hundreds of thousands of innocent

people. Terrorist networks such as al-Qaeda have tried to acquire the material for a nuclear weapon, and if they ever succeeded, they would surely use it. Were they to do so, it would be a catastrophe for the world – causing extraordinary loss of life, and striking a major blow to global peace and stability. In short, it is increasingly clear that the danger of nuclear terrorism is one of the greatest threats to global security – to our collective security. And that's why, one year ago in Prague, I called for a new international effort to secure all vulnerable nuclear materials around the world in four years.'[35]

## Energy and the Environment

As regards energy, Obama asserted US leadership in combating climate change. He announced a Global Energy Plan to make America a global-energy leader, and the creation of a Global Energy Forum based on the G8 + 5 (all the G8 – the world's eight leading economies – plus Brazil, China, India, Mexico, and South Africa; see p.188) to focus exclusively on global energy and environmental issues. The 13 members represented the largest greenhouse gas emitters.

Obama also re-engaged with the UN Framework Convention on Climate Change (UNFCCC). He has created a Technology Transfer Program within the Department of Energy to transfer American technology to the developing world to fight climate change. Obama announced that the United States would urge oil importers to reduce demand and developing countries to reduce carbon and global greenhouse gas emissions, and confront deforestation. Obama's plan would invest $150 billion over ten years to develop and deploy climate-friendly energy supplies.[36]

The environment and energy are interlocked, as clean energy is thought to have a beneficial effect on climate change. In addition to Obama's energy measures, which also apply to the environment, there was an initiative as a result of the disappointing 2009 Copenhagen Summit to create a $100-billion-a-year Global Climate Fund from 2020 to shield poor countries from the ravages of global warming.[37] In this connection Obama researched a Council-on-Foreign-Relations plan to undertake geo-engineering: 'seeding' and cooling clouds by shooting pollution particles into the upper atmosphere to reflect the sun's rays.[38]

## Disease

Obama tackled global disease in a massive Global Health Initiative, announced on May 5, 2009. He asked Congress for $63 billion over six years to help the poorest regions of the world fight health challenges, including tropical diseases, that kill people who could otherwise be saved with improved health care. The $8.645 billion spent in the first year included $7.4 billion to refinance both the Bush Administration's President's Emergency Plan for AIDS Relief (PEPFAR) and the President's Malaria Initiative[39] (which had been launched by Bush on June 30, 2005).

## Famine

Obama lost no time in investing in agricultural development to reduce global hunger. In 2008 the G8 financially assisted the Global Partnership for Agriculture and Food Security (GPAFS).[40] At the G20 Summit in London (for the G20 see p.188) Obama announced that he would ask Congress to double US agricultural development assistance to more than $1 billion in 2010 and provide at least $3.5 billion over three years. In all, G20 leaders meeting at L'Aquila, Italy, in July 2009 promised $20 billion over three years under the Global Partnership's umbrella.

The Global Partnership also channeled funds to the Comprehensive Africa Agriculture Development Program (CAADP).[41]

The Global Hunger and Food Security Initiative document of September 29, 2009, called for a global hunger co-ordinator to work with President Obama. The concept was a key part of the Roadmap to End Global Hunger and Promote Food Security Act that was introduced to Congress on June 11, 2009. This developed a comprehensive global hunger and food strategy that included emergency food assistance, nutrition, safety nets, and agricultural development programs.

The Global Food Security Act of 2009 focused more on long-term agricultural development, and also had a White-House Co-ordinator for Global Food Security.[42] The Obama Administration worked closely with the UN World Food Programme.

At the G20 meeting on June 27, 2010, Obama announced that all G20 countries would at least halve their deficits by 2013. Despite the fact that the US and some European countries had enormous deficits, the G20 countries promised to invest more than $20 billion to reduce hunger and promote agricultural development.[43]

## Financial Crisis

Obama supported Bush's bail-out of banks to counter the financial crisis: $700 billion announced on September 23, 2008. There were a number of measures to combat the global recession. For example, under Obama's encouragement the G20 undertook to give $1 trillion to the IMF and World Bank to help struggling nations around the world.[44]

## Poverty

Obama tackled global poverty in 2008, before he became President. Poverty is defined by the UN as living on less than $2 a day, extreme poverty as living on less than $1 a day.

Obama's desire to switch funds from American wealth to the world's poor, one aspect of the secret American Dream that would ensure that all humankind could benefit from America's wealth, can be gleaned from the abortive Global Poverty Act,[45] which he co-sponsored and introduced on behalf of his co-sponsors. The bill passed the Foreign Affairs Committee in July 2008 but was never scheduled for a vote in the Senate and died at the end of the session.

The bill had aimed to reduce global poverty and eliminate extreme poverty in fulfillment of the United Nations' Millennium Development Goal of halving by 2015 the number of people living on less than $1 a day. It would have added 0.7 percent of the US gross national product to the United States' overall spending on humanitarian aid. This 0.7 percent was fixed by a UN General-Assembly resolution in the early 1970s. It would cost $65 billion a year, and would amount to $845 billion over a 13-year period from 2002 (when the UN's Financing for Development Conference was held) to the target year of 2015.[46]

The Global Poverty Act was a fulfillment of Principle 12 of the 2000 Charter for Global Democracy, which held that all debt owed by the poorest nations should be canceled and that there should be 'equitable sharing' of global resources on the basis of allocations by the United Nations. The '12 principles' of the Charter for Global Democracy were turned into 'eight goals' at the UN's Millennium Summit. Goal One was to 'eradicate extreme poverty and hunger.' The Obama-sponsored Global Poverty Act was an attempt to address this goal.

The figures for global poverty are deeply shocking. The World Bank estimated in 2007 that 'in 2001, 1.1 billion people had consumption levels below $1 a day and 2.7 billion lived on less than $2 a day.'[47] Over a third of humankind lived on less than $2 per day at the beginning of the 21st century.

*Obama's Global Initiatives to Implement the Secret American Dream*
It is now clear that Obama began to implement the secret American Dream in his first year of office. This can be seen if I tabulate the components of the secret American Dream I have just identified, together with Obama's initiatives to implement them on a worldwide scale:

## Table 9.1: Global Initiatives to Implement Components of the Secret American Dream

| Components | Initiatives |
|---|---|
| **Peace** | Cairo speech, June 4, 2009;[48] UN General Assembly speech, September 24, 2009;[49] Obama's Nobel Peace Prize speech, December 10, 2009.[50] |
| **Disarmament** | Prague speech, April 5, 2009, which put nuclear disarmament at the center of US foreign policy; continued the Proliferation Security Initiative,[51] launched by Bush on May 31, 2003; and the Global Initiative to combat Nuclear Terrorism,[52] launched by Bush on October 30–31, 2006; a Global Summit on Nuclear Security, announced on July 8, 2009, was scheduled for April 12–13, 2010.[53] |
| **Energy** | Global Energy Plan, to make America a global-energy leader; Global Energy Forum; re-engagement with UN Framework Convention on Climate Change (UNFCCC); Technology Transfer program, April 27, 2009.[54] |
| **Environment** | See Energy above; Copenhagen Summit initiative, $100 billion-a-year global climate fund from 2020;[55] geo-engineering to 'seed' and cool clouds.[56] |
| **Disease** | Global Health Initiative, May 5, 2009 (six years, $63 billion); continued Bush's President's Emergency Plan for AIDS Relief (PEPFAR), as announced November 25, 2009.[57] |
| **Famine** | Global Partnership for Agriculture and Food Security (GPAFS); the Comprehensive Africa Agriculture Development Program (CAADP);[58] the Global Hunger and Food Security Initiative, announced on September 29, 2009, whose document calls for a global hunger co-ordinator to work with Obama; the Roadmap to End Global Hunger and Promote Food Security Act, 2009; the Global Food Security Act, 2009;[59] G20 promise to invest $20 billion to reduce hunger and promote agricultural development, announced on June 27, 2010 (see p.171). |
| **Financial crisis** | Supported Bush's bail-out of banks, $700 billion, September 23, 2008; $1 trillion from G20 to IMF/World Bank to help struggling nations, announced on April 2, 2009.[60] |
| **Poverty** | Global Poverty Act, July 2008 (abortive, see p.172).[61] |

# Obama's American Initiatives to Implement the Secret American Dream within the US

While Obama made his global plans in these areas, he made sure that there was an American dimension within each, as we can see from his speeches and initiatives.

## Peace and Disarmament

In his State-of-the-Union speech of January 27, 2010, Obama was careful to present peace and disarmament within an American context:

> 'This war [in Iraq], is ending and all of our troops are coming home.... We are also confronting perhaps the greatest danger to the American people: the threat of nuclear weapons. I have embraced the vision of John F. Kennedy and Ronald Reagan through a strategy that reverses the spread of these weapons, and seeks a world without them.... We are working through the G20 to sustain a lasting global recovery.... We are helping developing countries to feed themselves, and continuing the fight against HIV/AIDS. And we are launching a new initiative that will give us the capacity to respond faster and more effectively to bio-terrorism or an infectious disease, a plan that will counter threats at home, and strengthen public health abroad. As we have over sixty years, America takes these actions because our destiny is connected to those beyond our shores.'[62]

## Energy and Environment

Clean-energy grants totaling $2 billion were awarded between September 2009 and March 2010, 79 percent of which went to foreign companies. A $1.5-billion project for Chinese-made wind-turbines to be sited in west Texas occasioned a protest from Democratic Senators Schumer, Casey, Brown, and Tester at the clean-energy funds going overseas rather than staying within the United States to finance American jobs.[63] This transaction was further evidence that the global thinking of the secret American Dream was behind Obama's New Energy for America plan.

Obama announced a New Energy for America plan on January 21, 2009. This focused on America within global climate change and announced $150 billion over ten years for Americans to build a clean-energy future. By 2010, ten percent of American electricity would come from renewable sources, and 25 percent by 2025. Greenhouse gas emissions would be reduced by 80 percent by 2050. There were many domestic incentives and initiatives in this comprehensive plan.[64]

### Famine, Financial Crisis, Poverty

Obama tackled domestic environment, food and poverty issues in the all-embracing American Recovery and Reinvestment Act (ARRA), which was unveiled on February 17, 2009. Its 500 pages included sections on agriculture, rural development, food and drug administration; energy and water development; interior environment and related agencies; and health information technology. It also announced a state fiscal stabilization fund.[65] There was also a Financial Stability Plan that focused on Americans.[66]

### Disease

Obama addressed American health issues in his Health Care Reform which lowered insurance costs and widened health-care coverage to all Americans, 45 million of whom had been uninsured because of rising costs or pre-existing medical conditions their insurance company would not cover. Some 80 percent of the uninsured were in working families. The Obama–Biden plan was to provide affordable, accessible health care to all.[67]

To make clear that Obama's initiatives implemented the secret American Dream within America as well as globally, Table 9.2 sets out the American dimension of the global table (Table 9.1) that appears on p.173:

## Table 9.2: National Initiatives to Implement Components of the Secret American Dream

| Components | Initiatives |
| --- | --- |
| Peace | State-of-the-Union speech, January 27, 2010;[68] Cairo speech, June 4, 2009;[69] UN General Assembly speech, September 24, 2009;[70] Obama's Nobel Peace Prize speech, December 10, 2009.[71] |
| Disarmament | State-of-the-Union speech, January 27, 2010;[72] Prague speech, April 5, 2009, which put nuclear disarmament at the center of US foreign policy.[73] |
| Energy | New Energy for America plan, January 21, 2009.[74] |
| Environment | The American Recovery and Reinvestment Act, February 17, 2009.[75] |
| Disease | Health Care Reform, 2010.[76] |
| Famine | The American Recovery and Reinvestment Act.[77] |
| Financial crisis | Supported Bush's $700-billion bail-out of banks on September 23, 2008, and ran the 2010/2011 budgets at a combined record deficit of $2.9 trillion; the American Recovery and Reinvestment Act;[78] Financial Stability Plan.[79] |
| Poverty | The American Recovery and Reinvestment Act.[80] |

## Obama Continues the Tradition of American Benevolence toward Humankind

In laying out the evidence for Obama's focus on the issues of the secret American Dream, I have just demonstrated that in his first year of office he continued the altruistic tradition of the Americans who mentally turned away from colonizing the Philippines ca.1900 and sought to act benevolently toward all humankind.

There is further evidence that Obama was inspired by this secret American Dream to improve the lot of humankind. Again let us look at passages from his speeches, beginning with his Inaugural Address of January 20, 2009:[81]

'The time has come to reaffirm our enduring spirit; to choose our better history; to carry forward that precious gift, that noble idea, passed on from generation to generation; the God-given promise that all are equal, all are free, and all deserve a chance to pursue their full measure of happiness.'

Let us look again at Obama's Cairo speech of June 4, 2009:[82]

> 'America does not presume to know what is best for everyone, just as
> we would not presume to pick the outcome of a peaceful election.
> But I do have an unyielding belief that all people yearn for certain
> things: the ability to speak your mind and have a say in how you are
> governed; confidence in the rule of law and the equal administration
> of justice; government that is transparent and doesn't steal from the
> people; the freedom to live as you choose. Those are not just American
> ideas, they are human rights, and that is why we will support them
> everywhere.'

And here are some points Obama made in his speech to the United Nations
General Assembly of September 24; 2009:[83]

> 'It is my deeply held belief that in the year 2009 – more than at any
> time in human history – the interests of nations and peoples are
> shared.'

> 'The time has come for the world to move in a new direction.'

> 'I have outlined a comprehensive agenda to seek the goal of a world
> without nuclear weapons. In Moscow, the United States and Russia
> announced that we would pursue substantial reductions in our
> strategic warheads and launchers. At the Conference on Disarmament,
> we agreed on a work plan to negotiate an end to the production of
> fissile materials for nuclear weapons.'

> 'No one nation can or should try to dominate another nation. No
> world order that elevates one nation or group of people over another
> will succeed. No balance of power among nations will hold. The tra-
> ditional divisions between nations of the South and the North make
> no sense in an interconnected world; nor do alignments of nations
> rooted in the cleavages of a long-gone Cold War.'

'The choice is ours. We can be remembered as a generation that chose to track the arguments of the 20th century into the 21st; that put off hard choices, refused to look ahead, failed to keep pace because we defined ourselves by what we were against instead of what we were for. Or we can be a generation that chooses to see the shoreline beyond the rough waters ahead; that comes together to serve the common interests of human beings, and finally gives meaning to the promise imbedded in the name given to this institution: the United Nations. That is the future America wants – a future of peace and prosperity that we can only reach if we recognize that all nations have rights, that all nations have responsibilities as well.'

'Today, let me put forward four pillars that I believe are fundamental to the future that we want for our children: non-proliferation and disarmament; the promotion of peace and security; the preservation of our planet; and a global economy that advances opportunity for all people.'

'This Assembly's Charter commits each of us – and I quote – "to reaffirm faith in fundamental human rights, in the dignity and worth of the human person, in the equal rights of men and women." Among those rights is the freedom to speak your mind and worship as you please; the promise of equality of the races, and the opportunity for women and girls to pursue their own potential; the ability of citizens to have a say in how you are governed, and to have confidence in the administration of justice. For just as no nation should be forced to accept the tyranny of another nation, no individual should be forced to accept the tyranny of their own people.'

'The United Nations can either be a place where we bicker about outdated grievances, or forge common ground; a place where we focus on what drives us apart, or what brings us together; a place where we indulge tyranny, or a source of moral authority. In short, the United Nations can be an institution that is disconnected from what matters in the lives of our citizens, or it can be an indispensable factor in advancing the interests of the people we serve. We have reached a pivotal moment. The United States stands ready to begin a new chapter of international co-operation – one that recognizes the rights and responsibilities of all nations.'

Obama referred to 'a global economy that advances opportunities for all people' – meaning all humankind. In his Beijing speech of November 16, 2009, he reinforced this view. It rejected the old US policy of containing China and emphasized the interconnectedness of humankind:

'I've said many times that I believe that our world is now fundamentally interconnected. The jobs we do, the prosperity we build, the environment we protect, the security that we seek – all of these things are shared. And given that interconnection, power in the 21st century is no longer a zero-sum game; one country's success need not come at the expense of another. And that is why the United States insists we do not seek to contain China's rise. On the contrary, we welcome China as a strong and prosperous and successful member of the community of nations.'

In these excerpts Obama set out – in a necessarily covert way – the secret American Dream that all humankind should have access to the 'promise' of the 'dream of opportunity.'

## Funding of the Secret American Dream
The 'dream of opportunity' will cost money. To accommodate these and other initiatives, Obama earmarked unprecedented funds for 2010 and 2011. His budgets for 2010 and 2011 projected a combined deficit of $2.9 trillion, a deficit more massive than has ever been experienced on Earth.[84]

It was hard to see how such a deficit could be funded unless the US Federal Reserve System bought the US Treasury's bonds with printed money ('quantitative easing'), or arranged for banks to buy the Treasury's bonds. The banks could only buy the bonds if the Federal Reserve System bought their toxic financial instruments, thereby providing banks with the cash for bond-buying. The deficit could also be partly funded if there were a collapse in equity values that encouraged investors to buy 'safe' Treasury bonds.

At the time of writing, it remained to be seen how much of this deficit was intended to fund a transfer of wealth from rich America to the world's poor, or whether such a transfer would take place.

### End of America's Imposing Democracy by Force

It is clear from studying Obama's speeches that the old foreign policy of George W. Bush (band 6) has passed. 'American exceptionalism,' which placed the United States above the rest of the world as a unique beacon of democracy, has been rejected.[85]

Bush's vision of American power and supremacy was combative and aggressive: the vision that the United States would 'seek and support the growth of democratic movements and institutions in every nation and culture' which would result 'in the eventual triumph of freedom.' Bush said in his 2005 Inaugural Address:[86]

> 'The survival of liberty in our land increasingly depends on the success of liberty in other lands.... It is the policy of the United States to seek and support the growth of democratic movements and institutions in every nation and culture, with the ultimate goal of ending tyranny in the world.'

America's crusade to end tyranny has been wound down.

### Influence of the Syndicate

Some wonder whether, in his first year of office, Obama began to lead the world's greatest power along a path of decline. However, Henry Kissinger, 'Rockefellers'' longstanding right-hand man, said on January 20, 2009:[87] 'The alternative to a new international order is chaos.' And, 'The extraordinary impact of the President-elect on the imagination of humanity is an important element in shaping a new world order.' Obama's new way clearly had the support of Kissinger and therefore of the Syndicate. It was clearly a considered strategy.

To the dismay of environmentalists, Obama announced in March 2010 that he was opening up huge areas of American offshore waters to oil and gas drilling. There would be new platforms along the Atlantic coastline, the Gulf of Mexico, and off parts of Alaska.[88] The new policy appeared to reflect the United States' thirst for energy and the need to produce jobs and keep US businesses competitive, and seemed to favor the Syndicate. In fact, the drilling was part of a trade-off strategy with the major energy companies in order to get his climate-change legislation through Congress: at the time, a new energy and climate bill was on its way to the Senate.

Could Obama break away from the commercial *élites* that Kissinger has represented? Could the philanthropic secret American Dream of exporting liberty peacefully to all nation-states free itself from entanglement with the self-interested aims of the Syndicate? Having rejected band 6, could Obama also reject band 7 and unveil the secret American Dream for all humankind, a unified spectrum of American history that incorporates all the separate bands – an eighth way?

### The Eighth Path

To return to the image of the eight-pathed star encountered on p.xiii, at his Inaugural Address[89] Obama was standing at a double crossroads. Behind him, and on either side, were the seven paths of the past, including imperial hegemony, world empire based on American supremacy, and the New World Order of the commercial *élites*.

He could either stand still in the center of the star and take no new direction. Or he could travel back along any one of these paths which have led to America's present choice. He could:

- follow federalism and form a federal association of many states in central America and in the Caribbean;
- expand further westward into Pacific islands;
- build a benevolent empire in the Caribbean and Pacific;
- be isolationist from the Middle East and succumb to the clamor for American decline and withdrawal;
- continue imperial hegemony by continuing Marshall Aid and protect free nations from a new Russian expansionism;
- demonstrate American supremacy in an even wider world empire with more bases; or
- create a new political network to enact American commercial pipeline interests.

There was scope to continue the last three as new paths. Obama could:

- extend America's imperialist hegemony to every country;
- pursue American supremacy by conquest of tyrannies and extend its sway; and
- deliver a New World Order to the Syndicate, for 'Rothschilds'' and 'Rockefellers'' commercial interests.

Alternatively, Obama could break with the past and follow a new, eighth path, benevolently sharing the benefits acquired on the previous seven paths with all humankind.

It is now clear that in the course of his first year of office, Obama had already quietly chosen the eighth way. He said as much in his Prague speech of April 5, 2009:

> 'We know where that road leads. When nations and peoples allow themselves to be defined by their differences, the gulf between them widens. When we fail to pursue peace, then it stays forever beyond our grasp. We know the path when we choose fear over hope. To denounce or shrug off a call for co-operation is an easy but also a cowardly thing to do. That's how wars begin. That's where human progress ends.'[90]

He ended the same speech by asserting, 'Human destiny will be what we make of it.' In other words, he would shape the destiny of the world by his will – bringing peace and disarmament to a warring world and solving humankind's problems.

To many, Obama's first year in office was disappointing. He was perceived to have done too little. He had attempted to look west from his native Hawaii and be a Pacific president focusing on China, India, and Japan, rather than look east to old Europe and new Europe. His approaches to both Iran and the Arab world had been rejected, and there was no prospect of a peace between Israel and the Arabs. His receipt of the Nobel Peace Prize had signaled an ambition to achieve world peace, but he had sent 30,000 additional troops to Afghanistan to prevent al-Qaeda from re-emerging. By February 2010 there had been no concrete movement in the reduction of nuclear weapons or disarmament. It was reported that the US National Security Council did not share his view that a nuclear-weapons-free world was an achievable objective, and that the US Department of Defense was also resisting the new policy.[91]

But this disappointing impression was deceptive.

## Benevolence in Action

Then suddenly, Obama was heading down the eighth path – the path of the secret American Dream – and working energetically to bring the universal values of 'Life, Liberty, and the pursuit of Happiness' to all humankind. Within one week from March 22 to 26, 2010, his health-care program was passed by the House of Representatives and he had reached a nuclear agreement with Russian President Dmitry Medvedev.

The nuclear agreement was for a 30-percent reduction of deployed nuclear weapons by 2015 to 1,550 on each side; of missile-launchers to 800 on each side; and of nuclear-armed land- and sea-based missiles and strategic bombers to 700 on each side.[92] Stockpiles of nuclear weapons were unaffected. The reduction was welcomed by the Russians, who would not now need to replace their deteriorating stockpile of nuclear weapons, thus saving huge amounts in the immediate future.

This reduction was regarded by both sides as the gateway to a world free from nuclear weapons. The US–Russian pipeline conflict which involved conflicting branches of the commercial *élites* (see pp.145–8) was now dwarfed by this general context of US–Russian agreement and massive and rapid disarmament, and the prospects for world peace looked good. For nuclear weapons were now perceived to be a liability. No government would contemplate exploding hundreds of nuclear weapons from its stockpile, and as the weapons deteriorated they would become unstable and unsafe and need to be replaced at huge cost. Getting rid of them before they had to be renewed would benefit all nuclear powers' budgets.

As we saw on p.148 it seemed that the United States was preparing for an attack on Iran if diplomacy failed to persuade Iran to cancel its nuclear program. Obama apparently felt it would be better for the United States, rather than Israel, to act against Iran. Pipeline considerations had muddied the waters, but it was clear that although Obama wanted a world at peace and disarmed there had to be some disarming, regime-changing missions to achieve that objective. If the United States bombed Iran, Obama would not be motivated by a supremacist ideology but by a desire to 'bring in' a regime that the Americans could have benevolent dealings with, for the good of humankind.

Obama had said when accepting his Nobel Peace Prize, 'I do not bring with me today a definitive solution to the problems of war.'[93] The definitive solution was to bring in a limited supranational World State that is above the UN and has the legal power to abolish war.[94]

If it was always Obama's intention to take the eighth path rather than the seventh path – the path of bringing the prospect of the American Dream to all humankind rather than handing the world to commercial *élites* for their own gain – then he would have to bring in a World State that, although technically (semantically) a new world order, would be very different from the Syndicate's New World Order. What this World State would be like we can now see.

# CHAPTER 10

# HOW THE WORLD STATE MIGHT LOOK AND HOW IT COULD BE FUNDED

T he imminent rise of the World State can be traced back to the First World War and the destruction of Europe, which gave rise to the League of Nations. The concept of a World State has emerged from the attempts to create a New World Order by the Syndicate, the commercial *élites* dominated by 'Rothschilds' and 'Rockefellers.'

We saw in chapters 7 and 8 that after Woodrow Wilson set up the League of Nations, 'Rockefellers' backed both Stalin and Hitler to bring in a state that would dominate the world and were then instrumental in setting up the United Nations; that the Bilderberg Group were behind the Treaty of Rome that came into force in 1959 and that led to the EU, a regional grouping in a projected World State; that the world has been criss-crossed with pipelines as a preparation for a World State; and that 'Rothschilds' control 187 out of 192 central banks.

These developments have been accompanied by numerous Cold-War revo-lutions[1] and war – such as the Chinese, Vietnamese, Cuban, Egyptian, Iraqi, Libyan, Cambodian, and Iranian revolutions and local Arab–Israeli, Korean, and Vietnamese wars – which have had the effect of 'leveling down' nation-states in preparation for a coming World State. At the same time there have been attempts to create the institutions of global governance.

# The Institutions of Global Governance

The question of world governance did not exist during the Cold War when there was a balance of hegemonies. It arose in the early 1990s, when the previous 'interdependence' was felt to be inadequate. Economic globalization had weakened nation-states and global regulation was felt to be more effective than regulation at national or regional levels.

Growing environmental concerns were aired at the Rio Earth Summit of 1992. There were conflicts over the impact of trade on the environment, social rights, and public health, and there was a move toward global regulation of standards. As there was no world government to implement such regulations, existing institutions of global governance filled the vacuum. Global governance has been defined as 'the management of global processes in the absence of global government.'[2]

## UN, World Bank, IMF

The main international institution was of course the United Nations. The creation of the UN, which we have seen had much to do with 'Rockefellers,' was a landmark in the growth of global governance. Two other key institutions were also brought into being toward the end of the Second World War: the World Bank and the International Monetary Fund (IMF), both established at the 1944 Bretton Woods conference. The World Bank promoted loans to poor countries for capital programs perceived as reducing poverty. The IMF promoted global monetary co-operation and worked for financial stability, the expansion of international trade, high employment, and economic growth.

After the Second World War, the UN's International Court of Justice was established to adjudicate in disputes between nation-states.

## Global Organizations

A number of UN organizations established an early network of global governance: the UN Food and Agricultural Organization; the World Health Organization; the International Labour Organization; the World Meteorological Organization; the UN Environment Programme; and the UN Development Program. In addition, the International Bank for Reconstruction and Development was created by the World Bank in 1945 as its principal lending arm to countries in need. All these organizations had supranational authority of a limited kind.

## Secretive Agencies

There was also a network of global agencies advanced by the Syndicate.

The first of these was the Round Table, which originated in a secret group established in 1891 in South Africa by Cecil Rhodes, the architect of British colonialism in southern Africa. It was based on the legend of King Arthur and his Knights.[3] Funded out of the diamond fortune of 'Rothschilds'' *protégé* Cecil Rhodes, its aim was 'the extension of British rule throughout the world.' It consisted of an 'Inner Circle of Initiates' established in 1891, which included Rhodes, and an 'Outer Circle,' 'the Association of Helpers,' established between 1909 and 1913, that was known as 'the Round Table' after King Arthur's table of the same name.

The Royal Institute of International Affairs (RIIA) was set up in 1919 as a front[4] for the Round Table by one of its members, Lionel Curtis. Its declared aim was to fulfill the plans of the Round Table. Its first paid official was the world-government historian Arnold Toynbee, a member of Rhodes' Inner Circle who knew John D. Rockefeller. Rockefeller made a contribution of £8,000 per annum from 1932.[5] The RIIA has since received millions of dollars from the Rockefeller Foundation and Carnegie Corporation.

The Council on Foreign Relations (CFR) was a separate version of the RIIA in the United States. It was founded in 1921 and funded by 'Rockefellers,' and sought to influence the US Government's agenda by infiltrating it.

The Institute of Pacific Relations was established by Lionel Curtis in 1925 and funded by 'Rockefellers.'

The Bilderberg Group was founded in 1954, allegedly by the Chairman of the RIIA, Alistair Buchan, son of John Buchan (Lord Tweedsmuir), the author, director of information for the British Government, assistant director of the British international news agency Reuters, and also ex-Governor General of Canada, with input from Arnold Toynbee.[6] The Group has met each year since 1954, and power is shared between 'Rockefellers' and 'Rothschilds.'

The Club of Rome first met in 1968 at David Rockefeller's private estate in Bellagio, Italy.[7] It studied depopulation and is believed to have formulated NATO's post-1968 policies.[8]

The Trilateral Commission was proposed by David Rockefeller in 1971 following the American retreat from Vietnam.[9] It focused on North America, Western Europe, and Japan, and out of it came a new policy toward China that allowed US trade with China, where 'Rockefellers' owned oil.

The later Syndicate agencies strengthened the institutions of global governance. Most significantly, the Bilderberg Group planned to turn the UN into a world government in which an 'American Union' (eventually comprising the entire western hemisphere including Cuba) and an 'Asia-Pacific Union' would become single political entities like the European Union, with their own common currencies.[10] The noble vision of a world government was undermined by the evident self-interest of the Syndicate *élites* which sought to intrigue it.

### G6, G7, G4, G8, G20

The G6 (Group of Six), G7 (Group of Seven), G8, and G20 meetings of ministers added to the network of global governance.

The G6 began as a forum for the world's main industrial democracies after the 1973 oil crisis. In 1974 the United States brought together Britain, West Germany, France, and Japan at a summit to discuss the global economy. In 1975 the French President invited the heads of government of West Germany, Italy, Britain, the United States, and Japan, and from then on this 'Group of Six' held annual meetings under a rotating presidency.

In 1976 Canada joined, and the G6 became the G7, to which were added the President of the European Commission and the leader of whichever country held the annually-rotating presidency of the Council of the EU. The EU took part in G7 meetings after 1981 but could not host or chair.

In 1987 a parallel G4 was established by Brazil, Germany, India, and Japan to support each other's bid for permanent seats on the UN Security Council, against opposition from the United States.

In 1994 Russian officials held separate meetings with G7 leaders, and in 1997 Russia was invited to join and the G7 became the G8. The European Union continued to be represented within the G8 but still could not host or chair. After 2005 the finance and energy ministers of the G8 and Brazil, China, India, Mexico, and South Africa met as the 'G8 + 5.'

Meanwhile the G20, a group of finance ministers and central-bank governors, had been formed in June 1999. It superseded a short-lived G33 group, which in turn had superseded a short-lived G22 group in that same year. The G20 comprised the EU and 19 nation-states: Argentina, Australia, Brazil, Canada, China, France, Germany, India, Indonesia, Italy, Japan, Mexico, Russia, Saudi Arabia, South Africa, South Korea, Turkey, Britain, and the United States.

Following the 2008 Washington summit, its leaders announced on September 25, 2009, that the G20 would replace the G8 as the main economic council of wealthy nations, and that G20 heads of government would meet biannually.

## Regional Groupings

Since the end of the Cold War in 1989–91, the world has been covered by a network of regional groupings which have strengthened the notion of a world community. This can be seen as the spreading of the federal template which began with the Freemasonic federalism of Anderson's *Constitutions* of 1723 (see pp.55–6), and developed into the federal union of the United States as expressed in the Constitution of 1787.

We have seen that the federal idea was behind the spreading of the federal union westward (see chapter 5) and into Central America (see pp.13–16). After 1991 the federal principle was extended throughout North America, Latin America, Europe, Africa, and Asia in regional trade groupings that await federal linkage in a New World Order. There were now:

- the 1994, 34-state Free Trade Area for the Americas (FTAA), which is an extension of NAFTA (the North American Free Trade Agreement), CAFTA (the Central American Free Trade Agreement), and LAFTA (the Latin American Free Trade Association, created in 1960 and replaced in 1980 by LAIA, the Latin American Integration Association), and was set to pass into an American Union;
- the 2008 Union of South American Nations, which replaced the South American Community of Nations (created in 2004) and was also set to pass into an American Union;
- the CARICOM (the Caribbean Community), which grew out of CARIFTA (the Caribbean Free Trade Association) in 1973;
- the EU (European Union, with a legal personality that overrides its 27 member nation-states), which grew out of the EC (European Community), whose roots were in the EEC (European Economic Community) and before that the ECSC (the European Coal and Steel Community);
- the AU (African Union), which grew out of the OAU (the Organization of African Unity);

- the APEC (the Asia-Pacific Economic Co-operation), a forum for 21 Pacific Rim Countries that was growing into an AEC (Asian Economic Community) and was set to pass into an Asia-Pacific Union;
- the SAFTA (South Asian Free Trade Area), which was also growing into an AEC (Asian Economic Community).

Each of these unions and free-trade associations was based on regional links, geographical proximity, and common history and culture.

All these instruments of global governance were developed by the Syndicate, notably 'Rothschilds' and 'Rockefellers,' as stepping-stones toward a New World Order that would create a world in which the Syndicate would control the natural resources in accordance with the planning in the 1980 *Global 2000 Report to the President* and the 1981 *Global Future, Time to Act: Report to the President*.

### Ineffectiveness of the Inter-National UN

Elsewhere[11] I have argued that the existing institutions of global governance do not have as full a supranational authority as is required to abolish war and maintain world peace. The UN, for example, has not been able to abolish war. In fact, there have been wars or civil wars in 123 countries since 1945.[12]

This is because the UN is an *inter*national and not a *supra*national body. As an international (or 'inter-national') body, it is one in which nation-states negotiate with each other on the same level, without collective legal authority to impose solutions. Both the General Assembly and the Security Council are filled with representatives of nation-states who bring their own national interests to the UN building and endeavor to reach solutions while preserving these interests.

## Need for a New Supranational Authority

It has become increasingly clear that there needs to be a supranational authority with legal power to declare war illegal. President Harry S. Truman said in April 1945:

'It will be just as easy for nations to get along in a republic of the world as it is for you to get along in the republic of the United States.

When Kansas and Colorado have a quarrel over the water in the Arkansas River, they don't call out the National Guard in each state and declare war over it. They bring a suit in the Supreme Court of the United States and abide by the decision. There isn't a reason in the world why we can't do that internationally.'[13]

However, it is also increasingly clear that a new supranational authority should confine itself to limited federal goals and leave the day-to-day activities of civilizations and nation-states as they are.

## Seven Federal Goals of a Supranational Authority

There are seven federal goals that a supranational authority should pursue, wherever possible:

- bringing peace between nation-states, and disarmament;
- sharing natural resources and energy so that all humankind can have a raised standard of living;
- solving environmental problems such as global warming, which seem to be beyond self-interested nation-states;
- ending disease;
- ending famine;
- solving the world's financial crisis; and
- redistributing wealth to eliminate poverty.

These federal goals are the core principles and tenets of the secret American Dream which I identified on p.166. If incorporated into a limited World State they would provide a new context for humankind.

The supranational authority would secure peace; provide access to the Earth's natural resources and energy without Syndicate manipulation; have a unified approach toward environmental problems; work to end disease and famine; provide financial stability without Syndicate manipulation; and eliminate poverty in an affordable way. I shall have more to say about how these last two goals can be afforded out of a 'peace dividend' that would accrue with the abolition of war.

Outside the areas of these seven goals, civilizations and nation-states would continue as they are.

## Seven Models for a Supranational Authority

Over the years a number of models have been put forward for such a supranational authority that could abolish war. These proposals range from tinkering with the *status quo* to fundamental, radical reform. Beginning with the tinkering end of the spectrum, they are:

- nation-states should work through existing institutions of global governance to introduce world law;
- nation-states should persevere with the UN and strengthen great-power agreement, while using international treaties to resolve disputes (a variation on the first proposal);
- a World Constitutional Convention should draft a World Constitution that nation-states would accept;
- the UN Charter should be revised to give the UN power to resolve disputes (a proposal put forward by Clark and Sohn in their *World Peace Through World Law* (1958, amended 1960 and 1966));[14]
- a new UN-related organization should be created to exist alongside the UN to strengthen its practice of international law in areas not covered by UN Charter (a proposal also put forward by Clark and Sohn as an alternative to the previous model);
- a supranational authority should be approached through the *élites'* exclusive groups, such as the Bilderberg Group and Trilateral Commission;
- the UN should be democratized to make global governance more accountable.

Abolishing the UN and putting nothing in its place is not an option as it would leave the world at the mercy of warring, disputatious nation-states. The UN may not have been effective in abolishing war, but it is better than nothing.

The trouble with all the seven proposed models is that they represent more of the same. In each, the proposed authority is inter-national, not supranational. It involves a negotiation between nation-states, not a legally enforceable abolition of war. The sixth proposal is worrying: leaving it to the *élites* to create a World State that would suit the Syndicate and not humankind is not a desirable option.

The seven proposed models contain some good ideas: the World Constitutional Convention and the democratizing of the UN. But there will have to be a different model of a supranational authority if the seven goals I have identified are to be attained.

## Structure of an Ideal World State

Bearing in mind that a supranational authority should restrict itself to seven federal goals and leave local civilizations and nation-states free to continue their progress outside these areas, I can put forward a structure for a World State that would spread the secret American Dream of liberty for all within a peaceful context. At the inter-national level:

1   The UN General Assembly could be converted into an elected **World Parliamentary Assembly** of 850 seats.[15] This would be a lower house at the inter-national level. It would legislate supranationally in conjunction with the **World Senate** (see p.194), acting as a global legislature in some sessions, as well as representing individual nation-states' parliaments.

2   All the offshoots of the UN General Assembly would continue to operate: the Economic and Social Council, the International Criminal Court, the International Court of Justice, and the UN organs (UNDP, UNHCR, UNICEF and UNEP) and specialized agencies (FAO, UNESCO, WHO, and WTO).

3   All members of the new Assembly would belong to one of the world political parties: a World Center/Left or Social Democratic Party, a World Center/Right Party, a World Socialist Party, a Liberal-Centrist Party, a World Green Party, a Far-Left Party, a Far-Right Party, and a Party for World Skeptics.

4   The UN Security Council would be converted into a vetoless UN Executive Council of five Permanent and 12 Non-Permanent Members.

At the supranational level:

1   A **World Commission** of 27 Members drawn from all regions of the world[16] could be established.

2 A **World Senate** of 92 Senators,[17] could be set up. This would be an
  elected upper house like the US Senate. Senators would belong to
  World Parties. The Senate would work with the World
  Parliamentary Assembly in the same way that the upper and lower
  houses work together in the US Congress. The **World President** (see
  p.195) would have a power of veto similar to that of the US
  president.

3 There would be **World Senatorial Committees** to monitor the
  implementation of the seven federal goals.

4 A **World Openness Committee**, a World Senate committee, would
  control the agencies of the *élites*. The Committee would scrutinize
  all candidates for world officialdom in terms of their possible links to
  the Syndicate ('Rockefellers' and 'Rothschilds'). The Committee
  would receive advance copies of all agendas of meetings of
  Syndicate agencies such as the Bilderberg Group and Trilateral
  Commission, and would receive all minutes of their meetings. Two
  members of the Committee would attend all meetings of these
  agencies and report back to the Commission. Thus, the Syndicate
  would be allowed to go on functioning but its activities would be
  controlled and members would be excluded from secret decision-
  making and subject to investigation by the civil police and to law
  enforcement.

5 A **World Council of Ministers** could represent 29 **World
  Departments**, each of which would work closely with Senatorial
  committees covering its field:
  • World Finance;
  • World Treasury;
  • World Peace;
  • World Disarmament;
  • World Resources;
  • World Environment;
  • World Climate Change;
  • World Health (ending disease);
  • World Food (ending famine; crop-growing programs);
  • World Regions, Communities, and Families;

- World Labor (or World Work and Pensions)
- World Housing;
- World Economic Development;
- World Regional Aid and International Development (ending financial crises);
- World Poverty (eliminating poverty by introducing a minimum entitlement of $10 per day for all world citizens);
- World Population Containment (as opposed to reduction);
- World Energy Regulation;
- World Transportation (world aviation, roads, shipping, and rail);
- World Law;
- World Oceans;
- World Space;
- World Education;
- World Citizenship (law and order);
- World Culture and History;
- World Sport;
- World Unity in Diversity;
- World Dependent Territories;
- World Foreign Policies (liaising with nation-states' Foreign Ministers); and
- World Human Rights and Freedom (guaranteeing individual freedoms, including freedom from population reduction under the new system).

6 A **World President** would be elected every four years like the President of the United States. Candidates for World President would each be nominated by one of the world political parties. There would be several candidates and each would be vetted by the World Commission and the Senatorial World Openness Committee. The President would lead the **World Cabinet** of the World Council of Ministers and be responsible for achieving the seven federal goals.

7 There could be a **World Guidance Council** of elder statesmen and distinguished world figures. They would meet every three months to advise the World Commission, World Senators, and World Council of Ministers.

8   There would be **World Leaders' Meetings** for heads of nation-states or their foreign ministers. There would be a **Regional Leaders' Meeting** for the leaders of the 13 main regions: North America; Europe; Japan; Oceania; China; Tibet; the Russian Federation; South America; Islam (representing Muslims in West, Central, South and South-East Asia and North and North-East Africa, and focusing on Indonesia and India which have the world's largest Muslim populations); Africa; India; South-East Asia; and Central Asia.

9   The **World Bank** and **World Investment Bank** would be overhauled to operate at a supranational level. The World Bank would continue to make loans to poorer countries for capital programs to reduce poverty.

10  An executive of international lawyers would help the World Commission, World Senate, and World Parliamentary Assembly (the world lower house based on an elected UN General Assembly, see p.193) turn the World Commission's proposals into international laws. It would liaise with the **World Peace Enforcement Committee** and the World Court of Justice.

11  The **World Court of Justice** would have 25 judges and would hear acts brought by the World Commission against nation-states for breaking a directive. It would rule on legal disputes between nation-states. A **World Court of First Instance** would exist alongside it to hear actions against the World Commission for deeds or failure to act. **World Judicial Tribunals** would hear cases in which world law needed to be enforced, and would enforce international laws.

12  The **World Armed Force** or **World Rapid Reaction Force** of 200,000-400,000 troops would serve the World Commission, the World President, the World Senate, and the World Court of Justice. There would be a reserve force of 300,000-600,000.

The supranational tier would be above the inter-national tier, in which associations of nation-states try to keep peace between nation-states. From the perspective of nation-states, life under the UN and under the supranational institutions would be little different from now. Civilizations would go on rising and falling, nation-states would continue with their progress.

The structure of such a World State can be found in the diagram/flow chart on p.199.

# Practical Consequences

The above scheme would have practical consequences:

1 **Implementation**. The US President would propose the above scheme to the UN General Assembly, which would hold a vote for a World Constitutional Convention to draw up a world constitution that would establish these new institutions. All nation-states would vote to grant federal powers in the areas of the seven goals to a new World Commission and the other supranational bodies. Nation-states would voluntarily opt to create a supranational authority that would abolish war and release funds thus saved, a 'peace dividend.'

2 **Sovereignty**. At the inter-national level nation-states would accept the authority of the World Commission and the new supranational structure. They would give up a small amount of sovereignty in the areas of the seven federal, supranational goals together with their right to fight wars and stockpile nuclear warheads. Otherwise, civilizations and nation-states would continue as before with a great amount of sovereignty intact.

3 **Universalism**. A political Universalism would now have come into being. Having renounced the right to fight wars and stockpile nuclear weapons, nation-states opting for the new supranational structure would in effect unite humankind – provided that the vote in the UN General Assembly had backing from the majority of nation-states.

4 **Location of the Supranational Assembly**. The UN General Assembly would continue to meet while the World Parliamentary Assembly was being set up and elected. The World Parliamentary Assembly would then meet in the same UN chamber as the UN General Assembly on different days. For a while there would be an overlap of the two bodies until the World Parliamentary Assembly

was ready to succeed the UN General Assembly. The UN chamber in which the UN General Assembly meet can accommodate 1,898 persons in all and so could easily accommodate the 850 seats of the World Parliamentary Assembly and attendant staff. A chamber could be found somewhere within the UN where the 92-seat World Senate could meet. Conference Room Two on the fourth floor of the UN building in Vienna could be adapted to provide temporary accommodations. Office accommodations within or near the UN in New York would initially be provided for the World Commission of 27 Commissioners. In due course the World Commission could be more centrally located between East and West. It could be located in London, which is on the 0 meridian, perhaps eventually making use of the 2012 Olympic site.

5 **Funding**. The funding of the supranational authority would partly be afforded out of the existing budget of the UN. Funding for the UN General Assembly would be switched to the World Parliamentary Assembly that would replace it. At the same time the 18 separate budgets of the 18 agencies under the UN Economic and Social Council would be converted into a centralized UN budget that would cover the entire UN. This would be funded from nation-states' taxation revenues, which would no longer have to go toward military expenditure.

Of these five consequences, the implications for funding may be the most significant, for all nation-states' budgets would be transformed by the creation of a supranational authority. All nation-states would be able to cut their defense budgets as the World Commission would have abolished war and would enforce their abolition legally. The enforcement would be backed by the World Armed Force. Each nation-state would pay toward maintaining this global peace-keeping force but would no longer need to budget for expenditure on arms or armies of their own. The supranational budget would be hypothecated so that every nation-state would know how its contribution was being divided up among the various agencies of the supranational authority.

# The Structure of the World State

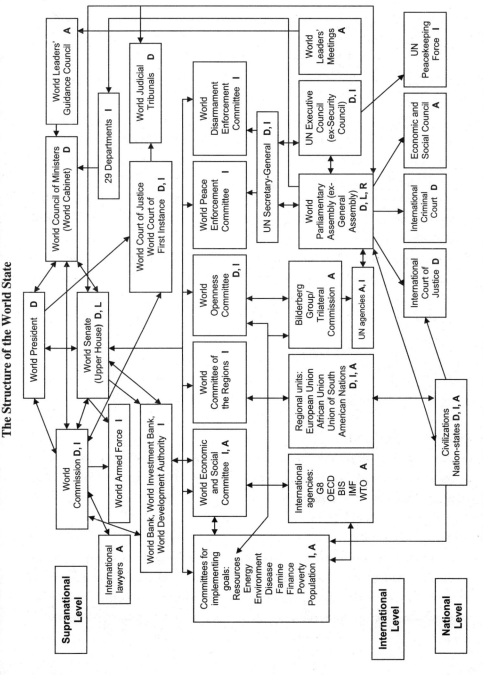

**Abbreviations:**    D = Decision-making    I = Implementation    A = Advisory    L = Law-passing    R = Recommendations

## Peace Dividend

The 'peace dividend' would be colossal. In 2008 global military spending by nation-states totaled $1,472.7 billion, of which some 70 percent – $1,049.8 billion[18] – was spent by NATO alone. There would also be a massive saving from not having to replace deteriorating nuclear weapons following a world disarmament agreement.

Nearly $1.5 trillion per annum, minus the cost of financing the World Armed Force but plus the saving from not having to replace nuclear weapons, would be available to raise the standard of living for the benefit of all humankind, and there would be further savings which would fund the supranational authority's structure and seven goals.

The immediate creation of a supranational authority would make savings that would release funds for all nation-states and would arrest some nation-states' economic decline.

The way to spread the American Dream is to set up a partial World State of the kind I have proposed. It would have a worldwide liberal democracy for which all nation-states would vote in the UN General Assembly. This democracy would not be imposed by force or conquest, but would be accepted by consensus. Those nation-states (such as North Korea and Iran) that voted against bringing in a supranational authority would be isolated – prevented from participating in international relations, not militarily occupied – by the World Armed Force and prevented from sharing the global 'peace dividend.' Their refusal to abolish war and disarm would be illegal in relation to the majority decision taken by the UN General Assembly.

If war were abolished by international law following a substantial vote in favor in the UN General Assembly, Huntington's clashing civilizations would be able to live in harmony for a while as the World State would last for a while rather than for ever (see p.161), and enjoy universal liberty within a peaceful World State while retaining their local diversity and identity.

Pacifying rejectionist nation-states would fall to the World Commission and the supranational structure of the World Senate and World Parliamentary Assembly, the World Court of Justice, and its enforcer, the World Armed Force. The populations of the rejectionist states would soon grasp that they were missing out on the improved lifestyle of other states that qualified to share the 'peace dividend' and would take steps to overthrow the tyrannies that ruled them. In the case of rejectionist nation-states such as North Korea (whose people have long missed out on a better lifestyle yet have taken no such steps to overthrow their regime), the World Commission would use all technological means to inform the population of the better lifestyle they would have if they qualified for the peace dividend.

If the US President were to ask the UN General Assembly to take the first steps to set up such a supranational authority that would abolish war, enforce peace, control the Syndicate, and use the 'peace dividend' to realize his – and Liberty's – secret Dream, what would life be like in Liberty's World State? What would it be like living in universal peace?

# CHAPTER 11

# LIBERTY'S WORLD STATE:
## Life Under Universal Peace

The English Romantic poet Coleridge believed in the 'esemplastic' power of the imagination. 'Esemplastic' comes from the Greek *eis hen plattein*, 'to shape into one,' to perceive unity. To Coleridge the imagination is the faculty that perceives unity. It is the opposite of rational analysis which distinguishes differences and reduces the One into disparate parts.

Using the esemplastic power of our imagination, therefore, let us project ourselves into the future and imagine that the *Pax Universalis* has arrived and that the world is one – a united whole.

## Life in the World State

A World State with limited supranational authority has been set up following a vote in the UN General Assembly and a World Constitutional Conference that recommended the scheme shown in the diagram on p.199.

### The Seven Federal Goals Achieved
As a result of a Washington-inspired initiative, war has been abolished by law across the world, and peace is enforced by the World Court of Justice and the World Armed Force, which has bases in the United States, Latin America, Europe, the Middle East, the Russian Federation, Africa, Central and East Asia, India, China, and Australia/Oceania.

The World Commission oversees a world government that moves between several locations: New York, London, Strasbourg (occupying the EU Parliament building there), Jerusalem, Dubai (a regional Arab center), Johannesburg, Moscow, New Delhi, Beijing, Tokyo, and Sydney. Reports on the World Commission, World Senate, and World Parliamentary Assembly are carried on television each day.

There are no national armies. The only military force in the world, the World Armed Force, patrols Afghanistan and Iraq to ensure that the peace is kept. Many ex-al-Qaeda and ex-Taliban fighters have downed arms and returned to civilian life.

Gas and oil pipelines supply gas and oil to all nation-states at cheaper-than-ever prices which are regulated in accordance with global standards. Prices are not manipulated upward by the Syndicate. A network of nuclear power stations across the Earth supplies electricity to all humankind. These are guarded by World Armed Force troops. Wind and solar sources have lessened humankind's dependence on diminishing oil in regions such as the Middle East.

The World Cabinet (the World President and the Council of Ministers) acts effectively to regulate man-made pollution of the Earth, including carbon emissions widely believed to contribute to global warming.[1]

Throughout the world there are programs to control disease. AIDS and malaria are completely under control. The 'peace dividend' has funded programs to turn deserts green, and starvation is already a phenomenon of the past.

Millions of families have moved from conditions of squalor to conditions of sanitary living. All the world's citizens have been guaranteed access to pure water and medical care.

The world is in a period of financial stability and plenty as money switched from military expenditure has boosted economic growth and public spending in every region. There is one global currency, and speculation against national currencies and hedge-fund betting are features of the past.

The world's central bank, 'Rothschilds,' is allowed to operate in all 209 nation-states (the 192 that were in the UN in 2010, plus 16 then-disputed territories and Taiwan, not then in the UN). However, all movements between central banks of funds beyond a certain amount are scrutinized by the Senatorial World Openness Committee.

All world citizens have access to a mortgage if their income permits. Job-creation programs round the world mean that all people have an opportunity to achieve an income which can fund a mortgage.

No one exists on less than $10 a day – a minimum entitlement for every world citizen that has been funded from savings made by the achievement of the seven goals. The seven goals have been fully implemented.

There are no borders and migration is free, although each region has quotas. When the limits of these are reached it is deemed that the region is full, that there are no schools and hospitals to cope with new arrivals, and migration to that region is then strictly regulated.

## World Regions

The main world regions are the American Union, the European Union, the West-Asian (or Middle-Eastern) Union, the Central-Asian Union, and the East-Asian-Pacific Union, which has developed from the Asia-Pacific Union. Each of these is divided into sub-regions and zones. These regions differ from the 13 regions mentioned on p.196, which are based on historical civilizations, each of which sends a regional leader to the Regional Leaders' Meeting.

## World Parliamentary Assembly Representation

The World Parliamentary Assembly has 850 seats, of which 816 are based on nation-states within the UN in 2010, 26 on dependent territories then outside the UN, and eight on formerly disputed territories.

Seats were allocated according to the size of populations but world influences were taken into account – in particular Permanent Membership of the UN Security Council. The four largest countries by population in 2010 (China, India, the EU, and the United States) have 30 seats each, while the three Permanent Members that are not among these four largest countries (Russia, France, UK) have 15 seats each. The ten largest countries after the largest four have 12 seats each and thereafter representation diminishes as populations get smaller.

Population percentages were based on the July 1, 2009, estimates by the UN Department of Economic and Social Affairs – Population Division.[2] (See the Appendix on pp.232–8 for this list.) In the following list each group of nation-states is assigned a letter. (Also see the same pages of the Appendix for the letter of each nation-state.)

# Table 11.1: World Parliamentary Assembly (WPA) Representation

| Group* | Countries | WPA seats each per country | Total no. of seats |
|---|---|---|---|
| A. | The 4 largest: China, India, the EU (on the basis of 27 members including Bulgaria and Romania, excluding the UK and France, see B), the United States | 30 | 120 |
| B. | 3 Permanent Members of the UN Security Council: the Russian Federation, UK, France | 15 | 45 |
| C. | The 10 largest countries after the largest 4: Indonesia, Brazil, Pakistan, Bangladesh, Nigeria, Japan, Mexico, Philippines, Vietnam, Ethiopia | 12 | 120 |
| D. | The 15 next-largest countries: Egypt, Iran, Turkey, the Democratic Republic of Congo, Thailand, Myanmar (Burma), South Africa, South Korea, Ukraine, Colombia, Tanzania, Argentina, Kenya, Sudan, Algeria | 8 | 120 |
| E. | The 20 next-largest countries: Canada, Uganda, Morocco, Iraq, Nepal, Peru, Venezuela, Malaysia, Afghanistan, Uzbekistan, Saudi Arabia, North Korea, Ghana, Yemen, Taiwan, Mozambique, Australia, Syria, Côte d'Ivoire, Sri Lanka | 6 | 120 |
| F. | The 30 next-largest countries: Madagascar, Cameroon, Angola, Chile, Kazakhstan, Burkina Faso, Niger, Malawi, Cambodia, Ecuador, Guatemala, Mali, Zambia, Senegal, Zimbabwe, Chad, Cuba, Tunisia, the Dominican Republic, Guinea, Haiti, Rwanda, Bolivia, Serbia, Belarus, Somalia, Benin, Azerbaijan, Burundi, Switzerland | 4 | 120 |
| G. | The 40 next-largest countries: Honduras, Israel, Tajikistan, Papua New Guinea, Togo, Libya, Paraguay, Laos, Jordan, El Salvador, Nicaragua, Sierra Leone, Kyrgyzstan, Turkmenistan, Eritrea, Singapore, Norway, United Arab Emirates, Costa Rica, Croatia, Central African Republic, Georgia, New Zealand, Lebanon, Bosnia and Herzegovina, Republic of the Congo, Moldova, Liberia, Panama, Uruguay, Lithuania, Mauritania, Armenia, Albania, Kuwait, Oman, Jamaica, Mongolia, Namibia, Lesotho | 3 | 120 |
| H. | The 49 next-largest countries: Republic of Macedonia, Botswana, Gambia, Guinea-Bissau, Gabon, Qatar, Trinidad and Tobago, Mauritius, Swaziland, East Timor, Djibouti, Fiji, Bahrain, Guyana, Bhutan, Comoros, Equatorial Guinea, Montenegro, Solomon Islands, Suriname, Cape Verde, Brunei, Bahamas, Belize, Iceland, Maldives, Barbados, Vanuatu, Samoa, St. Lucia, São Tomé and Principe, Federated States of Micronesia, St. Vincent and the Grenadines, Grenada, Tonga, Kiribati, Antigua and Barbuda, Andorra, Seychelles, Dominica, Marshall Islands, St. Kitts and Nevis, Liechtenstein, Monaco, San Marino, Palau, Tuvalu, Nauru, Vatican City | 1 | 49 |

* See pp.232–8, and also pp.206–8.

| Group | Countries | WPA seats each per country | Total no. of seats |
|-------|-----------|---------------------------|---------------------|
| I. | 2 non-UN-members with largest populations: Puerto Rico, Palestine | 1 | 2 |
| | **Initial total of seats** | | **816** |
| J. | 26 dependent territories outside the UN with associate status, and seats held in reserve, until they become independent: Macau (a Special Administrative Region of the People's Republic of China from 1999 to at least 2049 with the potential to be dependent after 2049), Western Sahara, Netherlands Antilles, Guam, US Virgin Islands, Aruba, Jersey, Northern Mariana Islands, Isle of Man, American Samoa, Bermuda, Guernsey, Greenland, Cayman Islands, Faroe Islands, Turks and Caicos Islands, Gibraltar, British Virgin Islands, Cook Islands, Anguilla, Montserrat, St. Helena, Falkland Islands, Niue, Tokelau, Pitcairn Islands. | 1 | 26 |
| K. | 8 disputed territories not on the UN-based list: Kashmir, Abkhazia, Nagorno-Karabakh, Kosovo, Transnistria, South Ossetia, Chechnya, Tibet | 1 | 8 |
| | **Eventual total of seats** | | **850** |

## World Senate Representation

Within the World Regions are sub-regions or zones that form the basis of 46 con-stituencies, each of which elects two World Senators, making a total of 92 Senate seats. These zones are based on the table in the Appendix, pp.239–41.

The allocations of seats are based on population, topographical size and political significance – hence the making of Israel and Iran zonal regions. In the table on p.207 (and the table on pp.208–9) WPP means World Population Percentage (given to justify the problematic allocation of seats in China, India, and South-East Asia); PM means Permanent Member of the UN; N means nuclear/dis-armament considerations for the representation (in the sense that a country possessing nuclear weapons needs to be represented so that it can participate in world disarmament negotiations); and R means regional considerations for the representation (in the sense that representation is partly determined by the country's regional importance).

## Table 11.2: World Senate Representation

| World Senate Constituency | Seats |
| --- | --- |
| China: East, West, North (including Mongolia), South (PM, N, WPP 19.5%) | 4 |
| USA: East, West, North, South, including dependent territories (PM, N) | 4 |
| Europe: 2 North-Western (including Scandinavia, Germany), 1 Eastern, 1 Southern (i.e. Northern Mediterranean – Spain, Italy, Greece / Aegean) | 4 |
| Africa: North, East, West (including Atlantic Ocean), South (N.B. Middle Africa distributed among these 4) | 4 |
| Russian Federation: East, Central, West (PM, N) | 3 |
| Canada: East, West, North (including Greenland and Arctic) | 3 |
| South America: North-East (Brazil, Bolivia, Paraguay), South (Argentina, Chile, Uruguay, Antarctica), North-West (Peru, Ecuador, Colombia, Venezuela, North Coast) | 3 |
| India: North (including Nepal), Central, South (including Sri Lanka, Maldives and Indian Ocean) | 3 |
| Middle East: Northern (including Turkey, Iraq, Palestinian Authority), Southern (including Egypt, Saudi Arabia) | 2 |
| Central Asia: North-Central (including Kazakhstan), South-Central (including Pakistan) | 2 |
| East-Central Asia (Bangladesh, Myanmar / Burma, Thailand, Laos, Vietnam, Cambodia) | 2 |
| East Asia (Japan, North / South Korea, Philippines) | 2 |
| Australia: East, West | 2 |
| UK (PM, N) | 1 |
| France (PM, N) | 1 |
| Central America, including Mexico | 1 |
| Caribbean | 1 |
| Israel | 1 |
| Iran | 1 |
| South-East Asia (Malaysia, Indonesia, WPP 3.39%) | 1 |
| Oceania (New Zealand, islands and dependent territories) | 1 |
| **Total** | **46** |

## World Commission Representation

The World Commission of 27 Commissioners is drawn from wider regions than the World Senate, taking into account population, topographical size and political significance – hence, again, Israel and Iran each have Commissioners even though they are too small to warrant this in terms of their populations and topographical size. However, no nation-state may have more than one Commissioner. There is one World Commissioner per region (which is sometimes a nation-state).

The 27 World Commissioners represent the following regions:

1. China (PM, N, WPP 19.5%)
2. China's Communist/ex-Communist neighbors (Mongolia, North Korea [N], Laos, Vietnam)
3. Russian Federation (PM, N, topographically largest country in world)
4. Central Asia (ex-Soviet)
5. Canada (seat justified by topographical size of country regardless of world influence) and Greenland
6. USA (PM, N)
7. UK (PM, N)
8. France (PM, N)
9. Western Europe including Germany (R)
10. Eastern Europe (R)
11. Central America and Caribbean (R)
12. North-East South America (including Brazil [N, R])
13. South-West South America (including Argentina [R])
14. Northern Africa (R)
15. Southern Africa (R)
16. Arab Middle East (R)
17. Israel (N)
18. Iran (N?)
19. Pakistan (N)/Afghanistan (R)
20. India (N, WPP 17.23%)
21. West-Central and South-East Asia (Bangladesh to Cambodia [R])
22. East Asia (Japan, South/North Korea, Philippines [R])
23. Indonesia (WPP 3.39%)/Malaysia

24   Australia/Oceania ([R], WPP 0.5%)

25   UN (secondment of executive expert)

26   World Bank (secondment of expert)

27   Agencies of global government (secondment of expert)


## Life in a Sample of Regions and Nation-States

What is it like to live under a global government? Let us consider how people might
live in some of the regions and nation-states of the World State, taking account
of how they will be represented. (See table on pp.205–6 for individual nation-states'
representation in the World Parliamentary Assembly.) The picture is as follows:

- **North America**. The United States has 30 World Representatives in
  the World Parliamentary Assembly and eight World Senators (two
  per zone in four zones). As the World State was US-inspired and
  created as the result of a US initiative, many Americans are in the
  World Commission's bureaucracy and World Armed Force. There is
  no stockpile of nuclear weapons, all have been destroyed. Poverty
  within the United States was abolished soon after the advent of
  universal health care. All Americans are entitled to a minimum
  standard of living (dollars per day/housing). Canada has six World
  Representatives in the World Parliamentary Assembly, six World
  Senators and one World Commissioner. Canada has moved closer to
  North America in lifestyle and outlook.
- **Central America/Caribbean**. The region has four World Senators
  and one World Commissioner. There is no poverty.
- **South America**. There are six World Senators and two World
  Commissioners. All South-American citizens are entitled to a
  minimum of $10 per day.
- **China** has 30 World Representatives in the World Parliamentary
  Assembly, eight World Senators and one World Commissioner.
  Communism is officially dead and China is now a liberal democracy.
  The death penalty has been abolished. There is a minimum
  entitlement of $10 per day for all Chinese citizens.
- **India** has 30 World Representatives in the World Parliamentary
  Assembly, six World Senators and one World Commissioner. There
  is no famine.

- **Africa** has eight World Senators and two World Commissioners. AIDS and malaria have been eliminated.
- **Europe** has 30 World Representatives, 12 World Senators and four World Commissioners. All European citizens have a minimum entitlement per day/housing.
- **The Russian Federation** has 15 World Representatives in the World Parliamentary Assembly, six World Senators and one World Commissioner. There is no stockpile of nuclear weapons, all have been destroyed.
- **Afghanistan** is within the South-Central Asia region. It has six World Representatives in the World Parliamentary Assembly, shares four World Senators with Central Asia, and shares one World Commissioner with Pakistan. There is a minimum entitlement of $10 per day for all Afghans. Minimum-standard housing has replaced mud huts. All Afghan citizens receive full education.
- **The Middle East**. The region has eight World Senators (if Israel and Iran are included) and three World Commissioners. There are no local wars.
- **Central Asia** has four World Senators and one World Commissioner.
- **South-East Asia/Asia** has seven World Senators (one for South-East Asia, two for Central Asia, two for East-Central Asia and two for East Asia) and access to three World Commissioners (for West-Central/South-East Asia, East Asia, and Indonesia).

All of the world's citizens live under conditions of liberty. There are no tyrannies under the World State. There is no Syndicate tyranny of any kind. The New World Order's dream of federal tyranny has been controlled. There is a Universalism (which focuses on all humankind) of minimum standards of living and a context of peace.

## A Golden Age of Universalism

A new Golden Age has dawned, and with it Obama's secret American Dream. The benefits of living under Liberty have now been spread from the United States to all the world's citizens.

It is a Golden Age of peace, promise, and prosperity. State persecution is unknown – it is of the past. All the bad things of history – plunder, pillage, rapine, air raids, invasion, missile attacks, barbaric hordes, poverty, squalor, disease, blighted crops – have been abolished.

True political Universalism, which sees all humankind as belonging to one political entity, has arrived. No one in the world falls below a minimum standard of living and housing, and there are no avoidable diseases caused by poor environmental conditions. In the past, wars created refugees living in tented squalor that bred diseases. Such conditions no longer apply.

With political Universalism linking all the Earth's regions into a World State, all religions are drawing together. There will be a religious Universalism, uniting within diversity the essence of Christianity, Islam, Buddhism, Hinduism, Taoism, and other world religions. There will be a spiritual revival.

### Restoration of Spiritual Values

In 1966 I visited China during the Cultural Revolution and a few months later Moscow. In Moscow's Cathedral of the Archangel I had a vision of an end to the division of Europe and of the Cold War, and of a future paradise ruled by a 'World-Lord.' I wrote it into my poem on Communism, *Archangel* (1966), which is in my *Collected Poems*:

> 'As I stared at the murals' centre
> In this Cathedral-tomb,
> The Archangel became a Shadow
> With a sword and wings outstretched,
> And I saw in the second icon
> The future of the West,
> From the Atlantic to the Urals:
> Into the People's Square
> From the Cathedral gates,
> File in the morning rush-hour
> An *élite* of self-made Saints
> Each still on the last hour's quest.
> They reach the central banner
> In the forum of statues and graves,
> The great mazed mandala
> Under which the suppliants wait;

> Decades of contemplation
> Show in their white-haired peace
> As, trusting to perfect feelings,
> They value each equal they greet;
> Until, whispering on silence,
> They glide to the Leaders' Hall,
> Their hearts, with a World-Lord's wholeness,
> At the centre of life, of all,
> Their hearts where all past and future meet.'[3]

In this future paradise that I glimpsed, spiritual values have been restored and are practiced by leaders. It is conceivable that the World State of the secret American Dream will not merely be a materialist paradise of near-perfect living conditions for all humankind, but also a spiritually meaningful paradise in which the human soul and spirit are nourished along with the human body.

## How Long the World State will Last

The secret American Dream that has been implemented through a World State and supranational authority offers an optimistic prospect for the future. It is quite unlike the more pessimistic vision of a continuation of the world order we know, with its wars, financial instability, and other shortcomings.

### Optimistic Prospect of an American-Controlled World State
The optimistic prospect is quite different from the pessimistic views of Aldous Huxley's *Brave New World* and George Orwell's *1984*.

It foresees a utopia rather than a dystopia, one in which the poor and downtrodden in Central and South America, in Africa, Asia, and remotest China could all find their children's lives transformed through the new opportunities presented by the secret American Dream. Peace would come to war-torn Sudan and Palestine, relief from poverty to the slums of Rio and Mumbai and to peasants scratching a living on the Chinese–Mongolian border.

If the World State comes into being – if the US President has indeed chosen the eighth path to make it happen – how long will the World State last?

The likelihood is that the World State will be American-controlled just as the

Roman Empire was Roman-controlled. America will have set it up and it will have to be seen as a development within the North-American civilization.

In my Universalist study of history[4] I have followed the progress of 25 civilizations as they have risen and fallen during the last 5,000 years of recorded history. Each of these civilizations passes through 61 similar stages. When a civilization ends it passes into another civilization and overnight adopts that civilization's main god. Thus in 642 the Egyptian civilization passed into the Arab civilization and Allah was worshipped in place of Ra and the Egyptian gods.

## America in Stage 15 of 61 Stages
In my study of history I show the North-American civilization to be the youngest. It was founded by the Jamestown settlers of 1607, who were actually preceded by Spanish settlers, as we saw on pp.xiv and 46–7, and is currently in stage 15 of its 61 stages, a similar stage to the Roman civilization's stage 15 which ran from 341 to 218BCE, ending after the First Punic War against Carthage and just before the Second Punic War (see p.159) – the equivalent of America's involvement in the First and Second World Wars. The United States passed into stage 15 ca.1913, with Woodrow Wilson's inauguration.

## Other Living Civilizations in Stage 43 or 46
It is significant that all the other living civilizations have either reached stage 43, the stage in which 'a civilization loses its national sovereignty to a secularizing conglomerate,' or stage 46, the stage in which there is 'a further attempt at counter-thrust under foreign federalist influence.'

The stage-43 civilizations that are now within a 'secularizing conglomerate' are the European civilization (which has entered stage 43 with the advent of the European Union), the Japanese civilization, the Oceanian civilization, the Chinese civilization (which entered stage 43 in 1949), and the Tibetan civilization.

The stage-46 civilizations that are in a foreign-influenced federation are the Byzantine-Russian civilization (which passed into stage 46, the Russian Federation, in 1991), the Andean and Meso-American civilizations, the Arab civilization, the African civilization (which entered stage 46 with the advent of the African Union), the Indian civilization (a federation since 1947), the South-East-Asian civilization and the Central-Asian civilization. (See also Table 11.4 on p.216.)

## New Civilizations Conquer Older Ones

The older a civilization is, the more likely it is to be occupied. Stage 49 is a stage in which 'foreign invaders occupy a civilization.' As stage-46 civilizations pass into stage 49, there is an increasing likelihood that they will be conquered.

I have revealed a rule within the pattern of rising and falling civilizations. Their history has shown that new civilizations always conquer older ones – that is, until the production of the nuclear bomb gave older civilizations (such as the Arab civilization) a chance to turn the tables on new ones (such as the North-American civilization).

## Comparison of Stage-15 Expansions

My prediction has been that the North-American civilization's stage 15 will last until ca.2250. This estimate, or projection, takes into account the length of time that the other 24 civilizations spent in stage 15 while taking into account the accelerating effect of modern communications.[5] The dates of stage-15 expansion of each of my 25 civilizations can be found in Table 11.3 on p.215.

## Comparison of Living Civilizations' Stage-46 Federations

During the time-span of the North-American civilization's stage 15 (ca.1913–ca.2250), I have seen several living civilizations passing into federations in their stage 46 that could be under the influence of the North-American civilization and a North-American-inspired World State. In stage 49, all of these federations will be under foreign occupation: they will be regions or provinces of the North-American-inspired World State.

In Table 11.4 on p.216 are the living civilizations in question, together with the projected dates that they can be expected to be (a) within federations (stage 46) and (b) under foreign occupation (stage 49).[6]

According to the pattern revealed by my study of 25 civilizations, the momentum of history is in favor of an American-dominated world of federations (passing from stage 43 to stage 46 and stage 49). This will last as long as America remains in stage 15, i.e. until ca.2250.

The World State we have just imagined is therefore a World State within the American civilization, just as the Roman Empire which covered the world known to the Mediterranean peoples was within the Roman civilization.

## Table 11.3: Stage-15 Expansion of 25 Civilizations

| Civilization | Date of expansion | Expansion |
|---|---|---|
| 1. Indo-European Kurgan | ca.2550–2200BCE | Funnel-Neck Beaker Folk |
| 2. Mesopotamian | ca.1950–1750BCE | Old Babylonian Empire |
| 3. Egyptian | 2110–1786BCE | Empire of Middle Kingdom |
| 4. Aegean-Greek | ca.1650–1450BCE | Minoan Empire on mainland Greece |
| 5. Roman | ca.341–218BCE | Roman Empire in Italy |
| 6. Anatolian | ca.1471–1300BCE | Hittite Empire in Syria/Canaan |
| 7. Syrian | ca.1471–1360BCE | Ugaritic hegemony in Canaan |
| 8. Israelite | ca.1140–960BCE | Israelite Empire to David |
| 9. Celtic | ca.337–250BCE | Celtic La Tène expansion |
| 10. Iranian | ca.280BCE –10CE | Parthian Empire |
| 11. European | ca.951–1244 | Europe's expansion into Mediterranean |
| 12. North-American | ca.1913–ca.2250? | America's world expansion |
| 13. Byzantine-Russian | ca.677–1071 | Byzantine Empire (including Balkans) |
| 14. Germanic-Scandinavian | ca.38–170 | Expansion of Germanic tribes |
| 15. Andean | ca.350BCE–300CE | Expansion of Mazca/Moche |
| 16. Meso-American | ca.350BCE–100CE | Post-Olmec expansion |
| 17. Arab | 790–1055 | Abbasid Caliphate expansion |
| 18. African | ca.370–540 | Aksum Empire |
| 19. Indian | ca.120 or ca.290–750 | Gupta Empire |
| 20. South-East Asian | ca.850–1100 | 7 South-East Asian Empires |
| 21. Japanese | ca.710–1000 | Imperial state ruled from Nara/Kyoto |
| 22. Oceanian | ca.850–950 | Polynesian expansion |
| 23. Chinese | ca.354–907 | Sui/Tang Empires |
| 24. Tibetan | ca.1247–1481 | Tibetan expansion |
| 25. Central-Asian | ca.1–950 | Expansion under Xiongnu (Hsiung-nu) etc. |

## Comparison of Stage-26 New Peoples and Stage-29 Expansions

After the Punic wars, Rome progressed to its expansion in stage 29, which began in 30BCE and lasted until 270CE: a new people's renewal in terms of a new Universalism under the Caesarian Principate (imperial rule) which replaced the Roman Republic.

## Table 11.4: Living Civilizations Passing into Federations and Occupations

| Civilization | Date | Stage 46:<br>Foreign federalist influence | Date | Stage 49:<br>Foreign occupiers |
|---|---|---|---|---|
| 11. European | ca.2150–2250? | Federation of European nation-states? | ca.2250–2325? | Non-Americans? |
| 12. North-American | — | The North-American civilization is in stage 15 and has many stages to pass through before it reaches stage 46. | — | The North-American civilization is in stage 15 and has many stages to pass through before it reaches stage 49. |
| 13. Byzantine-Russian | ca.1990/2050–2150? | Federalist post-Communist Russia linked to coming United States of Europe. | ca.2150–2225? | Americans? |
| 15. Andean | ca.1810–ca.2015/2020? | Pan-American federalism in Latin America under US (now through OAS). | ca.2050–2125? | Americans? |
| 16. Meso-American | ca.1810–ca.2015/2020? | Pan-American federalism in Latin America under US (now through OAS). | ca.2050–2125? | Americans? |
| 17. Arab | ca.1980/ca.2015?–2100? | Coming Federation of Arab and Islamic states through Arab League? | ca.2100–2175? | Europeans, Americans? |
| 18. African | from ca. 1980/2015 | Coming Federation of African states (starting with OAU)? | ca.2100–2175? | Americans? |
| 19. Indian | ca.1947–ca.2015/2020? | Independent federal India under West? | ca.2050–2125? | US, Europeans or Japanese? |
| 20. South-East-Asian | ca.1950–ca.2015/ca.2020? | Coming Federation of S.-E. Asian states (eventually Pacific Community)? | ca.2050–2125? | Japanese Pacific Community? |
| 21. Japanese | from ca. 2015/2020? | Coming Federation of Japanese Pacific territories | ca.2150–2225? | Americans |
| 22. Oceanian | from ca. 2015/2020? | Coming Federation of Oceanian states? | ca.2100–2175? | Japanese Pacific Community? |
| 23. Chinese | from ca. 2020 | Federalist post-Communist China linked to coming Federation of S.-E. Asian states? | ca.2150–2250? | Americans |
| 24. Tibetan | from ca.2020 | Coming Federation of S.-E. Asian states (eventually Asia-Pacific Community)? | ca.2150–2225? | Americans |
| 25. Central-Asian | ca.1911–ca.2015?/2020? | Federalism under Russia and China, and coming Federation of Arab and Islamic states? | ca.2050–2125? | Europeans, US, or Pacific Community? |

The United States still has its stage 29 ahead. Its 'new people' are likely to be Universalists (who see all humankind as belonging to one unified political entity regardless of nation-states), and their heretical reality – the 'new god' that characteristically adopted in stage 29 – is likely to be the Universalist 'Light' that is common to all religions.

In Table 11.5 on p.218 I show for comparison all the dead and living civilizations; the new people of stage 26; the date of their expansion in stage 29; and their heretical new god which made the new universalism possible in their stages 27 and 28.[7] I have included a projected entry for these future stages in the North-American civilization, which is at present in stage 15.

### The US-Inspired World State Can Spread the Secret American Dream
The World State, then, will absorb America's superpowerdom and all the dwindling living civilizations, which dovetail neatly into it. This American-inspired World State can spread the secret American Dream across the world just as the Roman Empire, the Roman equivalent of a World State, spread the benefits of Roman citizenship across the known Roman world.

We have seen that if the World State happens, the prospects for the world will be optimistic in view of the removal of the threat presented by bin Laden's nuclear-suitcase bombs, and of the 'peace dividend' –the many trillions of dollars of military expenditure saved by a supranational authority's abolition of war and by not having to renew deteriorating nuclear weapons.

The War on Terror would be discontinued, although the World Armed Force would guard against any possible future threat, and the nuclear powers would surrender their 23,574 decaying nuclear warheads – 12,987 of which are in the ex-USSR and any one of which could be hijacked or detonated at any time.

### Pessimistic Prospect in 13 Regions if there is no World State
If there is no World State – in defiance of the pattern of civilizations revealed by my study – then the outcome will still be an American domination of the world's 13 civilization-based regions: Europe; Japan; Oceania; China, Tibet; the Russian Federation; South America; Arab-Islam; Africa; India; South-East Asia; Central Asia; and of course North America. However, our view of the prospects of the world will be pessimistic in view of the lack of a 'peace dividend' and the need to continue military spending.

## Table 11.5: New People's Expansion and New God in 25 Civilizations

| Civilization | New people (stage 26) | Date of renewal (stage 29) | Heretical new god (stages 27–28) |
|---|---|---|---|
| 1. Indo-European Kurgan | Battle-Axe Kurgans (Bell-Beaker) | ca.1900–1750BCE | Ogma |
| 2. Mesopotamian | Assyrians | ca.1490–1000BCE | Ashur |
| 3. Egyptian | New Kingdom Thebans | ca.1576–1085BCE | Amon |
| 4. Aegean-Greek | Dorian Greeks | ca.1100–750BCE | Apollo |
| 5. Roman | Caesarian Principate | 30BCE–270BCE | Emperor's 'genius' |
| 6. Anatolian | Phrygians | ca.1125–900BCE | Cybele |
| 7. Syrian | Phoenicians | ca.1125–980BCE | Melqart/Astarte |
| 8. Israelite | Jews of Judah | ca.732–640BCE | Elohim |
| 9. Celtic | Christian Celts | ca.52–313 | Esus (or Yesu) as Jesus |
| 10. Iranian | Sasanians | ca.226–364 | Ahura Mazda |
| 11. European | Renaissance Humanists | ca.1555–1778 | Protestant God/Christ |
| 12. North-American | Universalists | ? | Universalist Light |
| 13. Byzantine-Russian | Russian Grand Duchy of Moscow | 1462–1689 | Russian Orthodox Christ |
| 14. Germanic-Scandinavian | Germanic tribes displaced by Huns | ca.375–476 | Arian Christ |
| 15. Andean | Peruvian Middle Horizon | ca.600–1200 | Doorway god |
| 16. Meso-American | Mayans | ca.300–900 | Kinich Ahu (or Itzamna) |
| 17. Arab | Ottomans | ca.1358–1683 | Sufi/Sunni Allah |
| 18. African | Muslims | ca.740–1500 | African Allah |
| 19. Indian | Muslims (Turkish Ghurids) | ca.1236–1526 | Indian Allah |
| 20. South-East-Asian | Indianised S.-E. Asians | ca.1287–1550 | Theravada Buddhism |
| 21. Japanese | Ashikaga/Muromachi Shogunate | ca.1391–1573 | Zen Buddhism |
| 22. Oceanian | S. American Long Ears | ca.1200–1500 | Sun-god |
| 23. Chinese | Ming dynasty | ca.1398–1644 | Neo-Confucianism |
| 24. Tibetan | Gelugpa (Dge-lugs-pa) Dalai Lamas | ca.1624–1720 | Tibetan Buddhism |
| 25. Central-Asian | All the Mongols | ca.1206–1370 | Tibetan Buddhism |

If there is no World State the consequences of the financial crisis will make money tight. The Syndicate will still control the world's natural energy resources.

Without the abolition of war, the clash between the Arab and North-American civilizations will continue. The War on Terror will drag on, and the nuclear-suitcase bombs will continue to be an unspoken threat. Bin Laden's successors will continue to try to revive the Caliphate. There will be conflict with Iran, which will continue to strive to become a nuclear power.

The world's population will increase to 9.4 billion, perhaps 10.5 billion by 2050,[8] putting a further strain on the world's natural resources, including food. Some oil will have dried up by 2030 (according to the UK Energy Research Centre).[9] US natural gas can be expected to dry up within 30–50 years.[10] The Syndicate will make huge profits from energy at the expense of humankind, and will attempt to federate the world by linking all regional Unions.

Before 2050, without a 'peace dividend,' there will be shortages of water and food, and mass migrations of peoples from former oil-rich regions, especially in the Islamic world; perhaps seeking natural resources. Civilizations at present in stage 46 can expect to be occupied by the time they reach stage 49. The North-American civilization will build a dominant, loose form of Roman Empire from 13 regions, and will do some of the occupying.

### The World State Will End When America's Stage 15 Ends
Whether there is an American-inspired World State with a supranational authority or an American domination of regions without a World State, the new order will not last. It will endure as long as stage 15 lasts, and after a lapse may be revived during America's stage 29. But it will not last forever.

As the North-American civilization progresses it will decline and disintegrate, as did the Roman Empire, from the failure of forces within and the success of enemies without. During such disintegration both a World State-cum-paradise and an American domination of regions in a troubled world will come to be seen as a Golden Age of peace, like the *Pax Romana* that flourished under Emperor Augustus, in which the arts prospered and the lot of humankind improved within the Roman world.

However, a World State would be more of a Golden Age and paradise than a world in which America dominated many regions.

A supranational authority would exist for only a while, but life under it would be more civilized than ever before. History would have progressed to Fukuyama's end-point of liberal democracy – the point beyond which Hegel felt there could be no further historical development although, as we have seen, the living civilizations would of course continue to pass through their stages and (in the case of most of them) approach their demise.

Liberty's peace, then, has two possible destinies: one that will fill humankind with optimism, in which all can share in Obama's – and all virtuous and benevolent Americans' – secret American Dream; and one which humankind will look upon with a degree of pessimism, in which the secret American Dream will never be realized and humankind will struggle as the United States dominates thirteen civilization-based regions.

Both destinies will light up the world for a while – the first to a greater degree than the second – before the rise and fall of living civilizations continues its relentless course.

# LIBERTY'S UNIVERSALIST DESTINY

W e have seen that America is within an expansionist phase, stage 15 of its rise-and-fall pattern. This stage succeeded an arrest in the growth of the North-American civilization due to a blow, the Civil War of 1861–5. This arrest began to be reversed in 1898 when, after the brief war with Spain over Cuba and the Philippines, America took control of Puerto Rico, Hawaii, Guam, and the Philippines (see chapter 1).

The feeling that America should remain true to its revolutionary roots and iso-lationist, and not be imperialistic or colonialist like the British, was a measure of the slowness of America's recovery from the shock of the Civil War. America sub-sequently presided over an imperial hegemony and reached American-supremacist superpowerdom, which Obama signaled it was time to give up.

I am now in a position to answer the question I asked on p.xii: what should America's direction be now?

## America's Direction: To Spread the American Dream to Humankind

In a sense, I have already answered this question. America should remain true to the ideals of its revolutionary roots and spread liberty and the benefits of the American Dream to all humankind as Obama quietly began to do in his first year of office. It should not endeavor to conquer the remaining tyrannies and impose democracy but should work for a voluntary choice by all the nation-states within the UN General Assembly to opt for a limited supranational authority that would abolish war and disarm, and bring in a World State and a *Pax Universalis*.

## The American Dream

The American Dream began with the Puritans who dreamt of freedom from religious persecution and cleared a space in the wilderness, worshipped God, and carved out a better world, from which their children would benefit even if they themselves did not. The American Dream at first had a spiritual dimension that was beyond personal gain. The dream of a Good Life turned into the dream of the Founding Fathers, of freedom and the enjoyment of 'Life, Liberty, and the pursuit of Happiness.'

Unlike other nations, America did not identify itself in terms of blood, language, religion, geography, or shared history, but in terms of ideals expressed in the 1776 Declaration of Independence and consolidated in the 1787 Federal Constitution, at the core of which was the American Dream of personal fulfillment, of fame or fortune, upward mobility, equality for all races, and what eventually expressed itself as home-ownership in the suburbs or a Good Life by the coast.[1]

The American Dream came to mean a house, car, beauty, youth and talent; wealth, fame, looks, health, and celebrity – goals to which Americans could aspire but which also applied to the rest of humankind. As the author F. Scott Fitzgerald wrote of American history and aspiration in 1937,

> 'I look at it – and think it is the most beautiful history in the world.
> It is the history of me and my people. And if I came here yesterday…I
> should still think so. It is the history of all aspiration – not just the
> American dream but the human dream.'[2]

## Liberty and Freedom are Universal

The Declaration of Independence, in which the American Dream is rooted, spoke of 'liberty,' and the American Dream is of freedom to strive for some of the above things.

'Liberty' and 'Freedom' complement each other. The Latin *libertas* suggests separation and independence from a previous condition, while the etymological root of 'freedom' suggests the rights of belonging in a community of free people.[3] Liberty implies separation from colonial masters, freedom implies connection in a new community. ('Free' and 'friend' probably have the same root as the Old-English word for 'love,' and a 'free' people is perhaps one 'bound in love and amity.' Perhaps individuals are only truly able to be free through mutual respect and regard, enshrined in a general consent to the rule of law, whether at local, national, inter-national or supranational level.)

The Founding Fathers' break with British colonialism and embracing of liberty led to a new connection as Americans and new immigrant arrivals enjoyed freedom. Liberty leads to freedom.

The secret American Dream has always been that liberty and freedom are universal, not just for the Americans. From the Declaration of Independence they have been the due of all humankind, and at one level the Statue of Liberty embodies their universality.

At a more hidden level, the Statue has a Freemasonic significance. It was a gift from French Freemasons to the American people to celebrate the revolution that threw up the Declaration of Independence in 1776 and the Freemasonic federal principle in statecraft that shaped the French Revolution of 1789. There was a Freemasonic dimension to the federal linking of the world's nation-states under Liberty – to which the Syndicate, the commercial élites that have worked for this linking, have not been blind.

The universality of Liberty has at one and the same time stood for the universality of revolutionary idealism and for the Freemasonic dedication to a *Novus Ordo Seclorum* ('new order of the ages'), the wording on the Great Seal of the United States: the birth of a 'New Atlantis' in the New World.

## A New Universalism

But the secret American Dream goes further. The universality of Liberty makes possible a new political and religious universalism, in which all humankind is free and equal, regardless of the God they worship.

The highest expression of political Universalism is the World State. Religious universalism draws on the essential Universalist truth of all religions, the divine Light common to all. The Christian Light of the World and transfiguration, the Islamic lamp-like Light of Allah, Buddhist enlightenment (for example Mahayana *sunyata*, Zen *satori*), Hindu Yogic *samadhi*, and the Taoist Void of Tao – all are one and the same religious and esoteric experience.[4]

At the level of ordinary membership, the lowest grades, Freemasonry, which has syncretistic roots in the early Egyptian, Canaanite, and Israelite religions, overtly acknowledges this. But at a more covert, occult, hidden level Freemasonry promotes Lucifer, the anti-Christian demiurge, the god of worldly power and money of which Albert Pike, the head of Freemasonry from 1858 to his death in 1891 and a secessionist leader in the Civil War, was a devotee,[5] and which the Syndicate honor. ('Yes, Lucifer is God,' Pike wrote in 1889 to 23 Freemasonic Supreme Councils and unfortunately Adonay [Jehovah] is also God.'[6]) The new Universalism gives Lucifer a wide berth.

## A Positive Tomorrow Universally Available

The American Dream in its widest meaning is the immigrants' dream of a Good Life under the benevolent shadow of Liberty, free from tyranny and persecution, with the opportunity to become comfortably off – the dream of a home in the suburbs, a secure job in a large corporation and a new car every few years, within a context of political tranquility.

The American Dream has passed into the secret American Dream of a positive tomorrow for all peoples, a dream that these benefits should be universally available to all humankind within the context of the political Universalism of a World State, and funded by the 'peace dividend' from disarmament and the abolition of war.

## America's Universalist Destiny

Destiny has been a concept in American expansion ever since 'manifest destiny,' later known as 'American Exceptionalism,' surfaced in 1839 and again in 1845: the idea that the United States had a special divinely-ordained, predetermined, and prov-idential destiny to lead the world, that it was head and shoulders above other nation-states in view of its ideals of liberty enshrined in the Declaration of Independence.

In fact, the political Universalism on which a World State can be founded can be freely chosen, as if a US President were standing at the double-crossroads of the Star (Stjernen; see p.xiii) and choosing the eighth radial path. Yet in a sense the President's choice may seem to be destined or preordained, for the path is there, to be taken or not as the President chooses.

As Obama said at the end of his Prague speech, 'Human destiny will be what we make of it.' In that sense he can still speak of America's Universalist *destiny*. It is a way forward that is already a possibility, an option. As we saw on p.183 Obama has already quietly chosen the eighth path, the new direction for American history that leads toward a World State. The question is: will the President take active steps to bring in a supranational authority and make a World State happen?

## Can a World State Really Happen?

If Obama does take steps to create a supranational authority, can the secret American Dream really be brought into being?

The present structure of global governance is inter-national, based on the relations *between* nations, and not supranational. Is it likely that the present system that includes the UN, the World Bank, the IMF, and the G20 can be fundamentally reformed to accommodate a completely new supranational level, above the UN?

Would the leaders of nation-states contemplate abolishing war and disarming, to obtain the 'peace dividend'? Would they not, with an eye to their own self-interest, simply ignore such a proposal? Are not the vested interests too strong? What nation-state's government would vote for a reduction in its own sovereignty? Would it not be more than a US President's job is worth to propose such a radical reform, to go before the UN General Assembly to make his case for a World Constitutional Convention? Would his poll ratings at home not plunge if he did that?

But such considerations were raised over the Lisbon Treaty of 2007, when 27 European nation-states – albeit after some wrangling – agreed to surrender some sovereignty and ratify the new constitution of the European Union, which brought no 'peace dividend' and augured instead the prospect of increased taxation.

A telling argument is: what is the cost to the world if such a radical reform is *not* proposed? The answer is of course: continued war, more War on Terror, over 24,000 nuclear weapons quietly decaying and becoming ever more unstable, nation-states like Iran trying to become nuclear powers, the perpetuation of financially straitened circumstances for most of humankind, and no participation in hope for the world's citizens, with many condemned to continue to scratch a living in an increasingly unstable world.

Quite simply, the US President *must* give it a try. He must go to the UN General Assembly and request that a World Constitutional Convention should be set up to establish a World Commission that can outlaw war, bring about full disarmament, and democratize the institutions of global governance and turn them into the institutions of partial world governance.

The rule of law which a World State would introduce has been called for by all the great figures of the 20th century, including Einstein, Russell, Truman, Eisenhower, Churchill, Gandhi, and Pope John Paul II.[7]

Eisenhower, the hero of my first poetic epic, *Overlord* (which is about the last year of the Second World War), said: 'The world no longer has a choice between force and law; if civilization is to survive, it must choose the rule of law.' He spoke of the American Dream in 1954 when President: 'The American Dream is a goal that can be achieved only in work and wise thought, in unity among men and faith in God.' Eisenhower's way of furthering the American Dream was to expand military investment (see pp.115–16) to spread wealth among American families who worked in military-related activities, giving them the opportunity to live comfortably.

George W. Bush, the hero of my second poetic epic, *Armageddon* (about the War on Terror), also believed in the American Dream. He said in 2002 when President: 'In order for all Americans to realize the American Dream, you've got to make sure every child has the necessary foundation to be good readers, good writers, good comprehenders.'[8] He saw education as the key to a later comfortable life. He also expanded military investment, which almost doubled during his time as President from just under $400 billion in 2000 to just over $700 billion in 2008[9] as he chased American supremacy through pre-emptive strikes.

In his first year of office President Obama pursued a different policy of universal peace and disarmament, as we saw in chapter 9.

### America's New Role as Philanthropic Benefactor

With the advent of Obama, America is in search of a new role. American supremacy has been dumped. US Secretary of State Dean Acheson said of the British Empire in 1962, 'Great Britain has lost an empire and has not yet found a role.'[10] America is now in a similar position of shedding an imperialist role – along with the influence of the Syndicate, the equivalent of the British pressure group, the Round Table, which encouraged British imperialism – and finding a new role as a philanthropic benefactor setting up a World State while controlling Syndicate involvement.

America's new role and way forward is to embrace an American-inspired limited supranational authority with the seven federal goals I have identified.

*Inter-National Rising and Falling Civilizations, Supranational World State*
I have said that the rise and fall of civilizations and the progress of nation-states will continue. Civilizations and nation-states operate at the inter-national level. Huntington's 'clash of civilizations,' between the Arab and North-American civilization, is at the inter-national level.

The World State is at the supranational level. Fukuyama, forecasting the 'end of history' in Hegel's sense of history's 'end-state' of political development, was writing of the supranational level. Of course civilizations would still continue at the inter-national level if the North-American civilization created a World Commission at the supranational level to pass a law to abolish war and introduce compulsory disarmament.

Both Huntington and Fukuyama were right. They wrote of different levels. Huntington wrote of the bottom (inter-national) half of the diagram/flow chart on p.199 while Fukuyama was writing of the top (supranational) half. It is important to grasp the interplay of levels as the United States, the most powerful inter-national nation-state, in its inter-national stage 15, founds a supranational *Pax Americana*, which would be a *Pax Universalis*.

Robert Kagan was also focusing on the inter-national level in *The Return of History and the End of Dreams*. Sensing that the expected international convergence after the Cold War had not happened, he saw Fukuyama's 'end of history' as an illusion, without considering how the conflicts between nations at the inter-national level could be legally resolved by a supranational World State.[11]

# The Secret American Dream's True Political and Religious Universalism

The secret American Dream is ultimately of the unity of all humankind, the long yearning for which has also been Liberty's dream – and the dream of the founders and proponents of Liberty, and of all benevolent Americans. True Universalism is different from self-serving Freemasonic universalism and Christian universalism, whose aims are to spread themselves to every nation-state.

Political Universalism offers a structured World State and limited federal goals that will best serve the interests of humankind. Religious Universalism has long been a goal of philosophers: identifying the essence of all the different religions and relating to this essence everywhere in the world in a combined spirit of unity and diversity.

In my study of history[12] I identify the essence of all religions as the divine Light referred to earlier (see p.223). The World State would bring in religious, and spiritual, Universalism as well as political Universalism, and through its new perspective a human being would be seen as having a soul and spirit, as in the Eastern religions, as well as a rational mind and body. There would be a paradigm shift and the human self would be seen as multilayered, able to receive in its universal being the divine Light which Dante, on his quest through the Dark Wood, eventually described in his *Paradiso*.

Such a new religious Universalism can be expected to be the 'new heretical religion' of the World State when the North-American civilization reaches its stage 26, the stage at which a 'new people' bring a 'new god' – a new religious focus – to a civilization, shortly before the renewal of the civilization in the expansionist stage 29.

## New Universalists

The 'new people' of stage 26 may mean either literally outsiders or invaders, or people who see the world in a radical new way. In the European civilization, following the Renaissance, which was a revival of another civilization's past culture (stage 24), the 'new people' were the Humanists, who grafted Protestantism onto the Catholic Light. In the same way, a revival of another civilization's past culture can be expected in stage 24 of the North-American civilization. As we saw on pp.217–18 I foresee a revival of the European empire's Universalism: the 'new people' will be Universalists, who will graft religious Universalism (along with a new multi-layered view of man) onto the American Protestant Light.

## Liberty

Liberty symbolizes the Light of religious Universalism for a united humankind. Like the Colossus at Rhodes, Liberty – 'Lady Libertas' – towers above the world with her torch, her Roman attire, and her radiate, seven-spiked solar crown suggesting illumination, clutching a keystone showing the date of the Declaration of Independence.

But Liberty also symbolizes political Universalism. Her left foot tramples on the broken shackles of the nationalism of nation-states, her right foot is raised to follow the eighth path.

I see beyond her noble Roman face the curve of a rainbow representing America's seven past bouts, or paths, of expansion, and as a whole symbolizing the new eighth path: the path of the unified spectrum, the onward thrust and growth of the North-American civilization as the benevolent bringer of political and spiritual unity to all the peoples of the world.

Liberty, Universalist goddess of the Light, holds up her torch to illumine the way forward, to light all humankind in a new union that is both physical and spiritual, like St. Augustine's 'City of God,' signifying that every human being has a soul that can progress at a spiritual level as well as a material body to feed and house in accordance with the American Dream, within a context of universal peace. The 'peace dividend' can create a new world community in which free souls live metaphysically as well as physically (albeit metaphorically) in Liberty's shadow.

Liberty's destiny beckons the US President to take the first step of setting up a supranational authority. Liberty's torch lights his way to the UN General Assembly in New York. The Universalism of a World State and of world citizens living under liberty is ahead – a Golden Age in which culture will flourish, in which unity underpins diversity.

I have had the vision of a new Universalism and it is now time for action. As the first World-Lord, the US President stands before the United Nations and requests the setting-up of a supranational World Commission with the structure and legal powers to outlaw war. The oppressed and the downtrodden reach out as the privileged watch events on their TV screens. The poor of the world, living on under $2 a day, sense that the secret American Dream is within their grasp.

Keep your nerve, Mr President. With a little belief and self-belief it can be done. We can do it. Take heart, you who live in the poorest slums: the secret American Dream can transform your lives and the Earth.

APPENDICES

# Data Relating to

# the World State

# APPENDIX I

# Nation-States' Populations as Percentages of World Population

Basis for Representation in the World Parliamentary Assembly
(see pp.204–6)

(Based on the July 1, 2009, estimate by the United Nations Department of
Economic and Social Affairs – Population Division.)

| Group* | Rank | Country/territory | Population | Last updated | Approx. %age of world pop. | Source |
|--------|------|-------------------|------------|--------------|----------------------------|--------|
| | | World | 6,788,400,000 | | 100 | US Census – International Programs Department |
| A | 1 | China | 1,333,910,000 | Nov 3, 2009 | 19.63 | Chinese population clock |
| A | 2 | India | 1,172,090,000 | Nov 3, 2009 | 17.25 | Indian population clock |
| A | 3 | United States | 307,855,000 | Nov 3, 2009 | 4.53 | Official USA population clock |
| C | 4 | Indonesia | 229,965,000 | | 3.38 | UN estimate |
| C | 5 | Brazil | 191,982,000 | Nov 3, 2009 | 2.83 | Official Brazilian population clock |
| C | 6 | Pakistan | 167,854,500 | Nov 3, 2009 | 2.47 | Official Pakistani population clock |
| C | 7 | Bangladesh | 162,221,000 | | 2.39 | UN estimate |
| C | 8 | Nigeria | 154,729,000 | | 2.28 | UN estimate |
| B | 9 | Russia | 141,881,000 | Nov 3, 2009 | 2.09 | Russian State Statistics Service |
| C | 10 | Japan | 127,560,000 | Oct 1, 2009 | 1.88 | Official Japan Statistics Bureau estimate |
| C | 11 | Mexico | 107,550,697 | | 1.58 | INEGI estimate National Population Statistics of Mexico |
| C | 12 | Philippines | 92,226,600 | Mid-2009 | 1.36 | National Statistics Office medium projection |
| C | 13 | Vietnam | 85,789573 | Apr 1, 2009 | 1.26 | Official preliminary results of the 2009 census |
| A | 14 | Germany | 82,002,000 | Dec 31, 2008 | 1.21 | Federal Statistical Office |
| C | 15 | Ethiopia | 79,221,000 | Jul 2008 | 1.17 | Ethiopia Central Statistics Agency |
| D | 16 | Egypt | 77,279,837 | Nov 3, 2009 | 1.14 | Official Egyptian population clock |
| D | 17 | Iran | 74,196,000 | | 1.09 | UN estimate |
| D | 18 | Turkey | 71,517,100 | Dec 31, 2008 | 1.05 | Turkish Statistical Institute estimate |

* See pp.204–6.

| Group* | Rank | Country/territory | Population | Last updated | Approx. %age of world pop. | Source |
|---|---|---|---|---|---|---|
| D | 19 | Democratic Republic of Congo | 66,020,000 | | 0.97 | UN estimate |
| B | 20 | France | 65,073,482 | Jan 1, 2009 | 0.96 | Official INSEE estimate. The figure for France without the overseas collectivities is 64,303,482 |
| D | 21 | Thailand | 63,389,730 | Dec 31, 2008 | 0.93 | Official Thai Statistics estimate |
| B | 22 | United Kingdom | 61,634,599 | Jan 1, 2009 | 0.91 | Eurostat estimate |
| A | 23 | Italy | 60,157,214 | Apr 2009 | 0.88 | Official ISTAT estimate |
| D | 24 | Myanmar (Burma) | 50,020,000 | | 0.74 | UN estimate |
| D | 25 | South Africa | 49,320,500 | Jul 1, 2009 | 0.73 | Statistics South Africa |
| D | 26 | South Korea | 48,333,000 | | 0.71 | UN estimate |
| D | 27 | Ukraine | 46,029,281 | Jul 1, 2009 | 0.68 | Official UKRSTAT estimate |
| A | 28 | Spain | 45,967,632 | Oct 1, 2009 | 0.68 | Official INE estimate |
| D | 29 | Colombia | 45,161,000 | Nov 3, 2009 | 0.66 | Official Colombian population clock |
| D | 30 | Tanzania | 43,739,000 | | 0.64 | UN estimate |
| D | 31 | Argentina | 40,134,425 | Jun 30, 2009 | 0.59 | Official INDEC estimate |
| D | 32 | Kenya | 39,802,000 | | 0.59 | UN estimate |
| D | 33 | Sudan | 39,154,490 | Apr 22, 2008 | 0.58 | 2008 Sudanese census |
| A | 34 | Poland | 38,100,700 | | 0.56 | Official Central Statistics Office of Poland |
| D | 35 | Algeria | 34,895,000 | | 0.51 | UN estimate |
| E | 36 | Canada | 33,831,000 | Nov 3, 2009 | 0.5 | Official Canadian population clock |
| E | 37 | Uganda | 32,710,000 | | 0.48 | UN estimate |
| E | 38 | Morocco | 31,629,000 | Nov 3, 2009 | 0.47 | Official Moroccan population clock |
| E | 39 | Iraq | 30,747,000 | | 0.45 | UN estimate |
| E | 40 | Nepal | 29,331,000 | | 0.43 | UN estimate |
| E | 41 | Peru | 29,132,013 | Jun 30, 2009 | 0.43 | Official INEI estimate |
| E | 42 | Venezuela | 28,536,000 | Nov 3, 2009 | 0.42 | Official Venezuelan population clock |
| E | 43 | Malaysia | 28,310,000 | Jul 31, 2009 | 0.41 | Statistics Department of Malaysia |
| E | 44 | Afghanistan | 28,150,000 | | 0.4 | UN estimate |
| E | 45 | Uzbekistan | 27,488,000 | | 0.4 | UN estimate |
| E | 46 | Saudi Arabia | 25,721,000 | | 0.38 | UN estimate |
| E | 47 | North Korea | 24,051,706 | Oct 2008 | 0.35 | UNFPA |
| E | 48 | Ghana | 23,837,000 | | 0.35 | UN estimate |
| E | 49 | Yemen | 23,580,000 | | 0.35 | UN estimate |
| E | 50 | Taiwan | 23,069,345 | Jun 30, 2009 | 0.34 | Official National Statistics Taiwan estimate |

| Group* | Rank | Country/territory | Population | Last updated | Approx. %age of world pop. | Source |
|---|---|---|---|---|---|---|
| E | 51 | Mozambique | 22,894,000 | | 0.34 | UN estimate |
| E | 52 | Australia | 22,040,000 | Nov 3, 2009 | 0.32 | Official Australian population clock |
| E | 53 | Syria | 21,906,000 | | 0.32 | UN estimate |
| A | 54 | Romania | 21,498,616 | Jan 1, 2009 | 0.32 | Eurostat estimate |
| E | 55 | Côte d'Ivoire | 21,075,000 | | 0.31 | UN estimate |
| E | 56 | Sri Lanka | 20,238,000 | | 0.3 | UN estimate |
| F | 57 | Madagascar | 19,625,000 | | 0.29 | UN estimate |
| F | 58 | Cameroon | 19,522,000 | | 0.29 | UN estimate |
| F | 59 | Angola | 18,498,000 | | 0.27 | UN estimate |
| F | 60 | Chile | 16,986,000 | Nov 3, 2009 | 0.25 | Official INE projection |
| A | 61 | Netherlands | 16,571,400 | Nov 3, 2009 | 0.24 | Official Netherlands population clock |
| F | 62 | Kazakhstan | 15,776,492 | Jul 1, 2009 | 0.23 | National Statistics Agency estimate |
| F | 63 | Burkina Faso | 15,757,000 | | 0.23 | UN estimate |
| F | 64 | Niger | 15,290,000 | | 0.23 | UN estimate |
| F | 65 | Malawi | 15,263,000 | | 0.22 | UN estimate |
| F | 66 | Cambodia | 14,805,000 | | 0.22 | UN estimate |
| F | 67 | Ecuador | 14,073,000 | Nov 3, 2009 | 0.21 | Official Ecuadorian population clock |
| F | 68 | Guatemala | 14,027.000 | | 0.21 | UN estimate |
| F | 69 | Mali | 13,010,000 | | 0.19 | UN estimate |
| F | 70 | Zambia | 12,935,000 | | 0.19 | UN estimate |
| F | 71 | Senegal | 12,534,000 | | 0.18 | UN estimate |
| F | 72 | Zimbabwe | 12,523,000 | | 0.18 | UN estimate |
| F | 73 | Chad | 11,274,106 | Jun 2009 | 0.17 | Chadian 2009 census |
| A | 74 | Greece | 11,257,285 | Jan 1, 2009 | 0.17 | Eurostat estimate |
| F | 75 | Cuba | 11,204,000 | | 0.16 | UN estimate |
| A | 76 | Belgium | 10,754,528 | Jan 1, 2009 | 0.16 | Eurostat estimate |
| A | 77 | Portugal | 10,627,250 | Jan 1, 2009 | 0.16 | Eurostat estimate |
| A | 78 | Czech Republic | 10,476,543 | Mar 31, 2009 | 0.15 | Czech Statistical Office |
| F | 79 | Tunisia | 10,327,800 | Jul 1, 2008 | 0.15 | National Statistics Institute of Tunisia |
| F | 80 | Dominican Republic | 10,090,000 | | 0.15 | UN estimate |
| F | 81 | Guinea | 10,069,000 | | 0.15 | UN estimate |
| F | 82 | Haiti | 10,033,000 | | 0.15 | UN estimate |
| A | 83 | Hungary | 10,031,208 | Jan 1, 2009 | 0.15 | Eurostat estimate |
| F | 84 | Rwanda | 9,998,000 | | 0.15 | UN estimate |
| F | 85 | Bolivia | 9,879,000 | | 0.15 | UN estimate |
| F | 86 | Serbia | 9,850,000 | | 0.14 | UN estimate |
| F | 87 | Belarus | 9,671,900 | Jan 1, 2009 | 0.14 | Official Statistics of Belarus |
| A | 88 | Sweden | 9,316,256 | Aug 31, 2009 | 0.14 | Statistics Sweden |
| F | 89 | Somalia | 9.133,000 | | 0.13 | UN estimate |

| Group* | Rank | Country/territory | Population | Last updated | Approx. %age of world pop. | Source |
|---|---|---|---|---|---|---|
| F | 90 | Benin | 8,935,000 | | 0.13 | UN estimate |
| F | 91 | Azerbaijan | 8,896,900 | Apr 1, 2009 | 0.13 | State Statistical Committee of Azerbaijan |
| A | 92 | Austria | 8,355,260 | Jan 1, 2009 | 0.12 | Eurostat estimate |
| F | 93 | Burundi | 8,303,000 | | 0.12 | UN estimate |
| F | 94 | Switzerland | 7,753,600 | Aug 31, 2009 | 0.11 | Official Switzerland Statistics estimate |
| A | 95 | Bulgaria | 7,606,551 | Jan 1, 2009 | 0.11 | Eurostat estimate |
| G | 96 | Honduras | 7,466,000 | | 0.11 | UN estimate |
| G | 97 | Israel | 7,459,900 | Aug 31, 2009 | 0.11 | Israeli Central Bureau of Statistics |
| A | 98 | Hong Kong | 7,008,900 | Dec 31, 2008 | 0.103 | Hong Kong Census and Statistics Department |
| G | 99 | Tajikistan | 6,952,000 | | 0.102 | UN estimate |
| G | 100 | Papua New Guinea | 6,732,000 | | 0.099 | UN estimate |
| G | 101 | Togo | 6,619,000 | | 0.097 | UN estimate |
| G | 102 | Libya | 6,420,000 | | 0.094 | UN estimate |
| G | 103 | Paraguay | 6,349,000 | | 0.093 | UN estimate |
| G | 104 | Laos | 6,320,000 | | 0.093 | UN estimate |
| G | 105 | Jordan | 6,316,000 | | 0.093 | UN estimate |
| G | 106 | El Salvador | 6,163,000 | | 0.091 | UN estimate |
| G | 107 | Nicaragua | 5,743,000 | | 0.085 | UN estimate |
| G | 108 | Sierra Leone | 5,696,000 | | 0.084 | UN estimate |
| A | 109 | Denmark | 5,519,441 | Jun 30, 2009 | 0.081 | Statistics Denmark |
| G | 110 | Kyrgyzstan | 5,482,000 | | 0.081 | UN estimate |
| A | 111 | Slovakia | 5,413,548 | Mar 31, 2009 | 0.08 | Statistics Slovakia |
| A | 112 | Finland | 5,349,200 | Nov 4, 2009 | 0.079 | Official Finnish Population clock |
| G | 113 | Turkmenistan | 5,110,000 | | 0.075 | UN estimate |
| G | 114 | Eritrea | 5,073,000 | | 0.075 | UN estimate |
| G | 115 | Singapore | 4,987,600 | Mid-2009 | 0.073 | Statistics Singapore |
| G | 116 | Norway | 4,843,700 | Nov 4, 2009 | 0.071 | Official Norwegian population clock |
| G | 117 | United Arab Emirates | 4,599,000 | | 0.068 | UN estimate |
| G | 118 | Costa Rica | 4,579,000 | | 0.067 | UN estimate |
| A | 119 | Ireland | 4,459,300 | Apr 1, 2009 | 0.065 | Irish Central Statistics Office estimate |
| G | 120 | Croatia | 4,435,056 | Jan 1, 2009 | 0.065 | Eurostat estimate |
| G | 121 | Central African Republic | 4,422,000 | | 0.065 | UN estimate |
| G | 122 | Georgia | 4,385,400 | Jan 1, 2009 | 0.065 | Statistics Georgia |
| G | 123 | New Zealand | 4,336,100 | Nov 4, 2009 | 0.064 | Official New Zealand population clock |
| G | 124 | Lebanon | 4,224,000 | | 0.062 | UN estimate |

| Group* | Rank | Country/territory | Population | Last updated | Approx. %age of world pop. | Source |
|---|---|---|---|---|---|---|
| I | 125 | Puerto Rico | 3,982,000 | | 0.059 | UN estimate |
| G | 126 | Bosnia and Herzegovina | 3,767,000 | | 0.055 | UN estimate |
| I | 127 | Palestine | 3,761,646 | Dec 1, 2007 | 0.055 | 2007 Palestinian Bureau Census |
| G | 128 | Republic of the Congo | 3,683,000 | | 0.054 | UN estimate |
| G | 129 | Moldova | 3,567,500 | Jan 1, 2009 | 0.053 | National Bureau of Statistics of Moldova |
| G | 130 | Liberia | 3,476,608 | Mar 21, 2008 | 0.051 | 2008 Population and Housing Census |
| G | 131 | Panama | 3,454,000 | | 0.051 | UN estimate |
| G | 132 | Uruguay | 3,361,000 | | 0.049 | UN estimate |
| G | 133 | Lithuania | 3,349,872 | Jan 1, 2009 | 0.049 | Eurostat estimate |
| G | 134 | Mauritania | 3,291,000 | | 0.048 | UN estimate |
| G | 135 | Armenia | 3,230,100 | Jan 1, 2008 | 0.048 | |
| G | 136 | Albania | 3,170,000 | Jan 1, 2008 | 0.047 | |
| G | 137 | Kuwait | 2,985,000 | | 0.44 | UN estimate |
| G | 138 | Oman | 2,845,000 | | 0.042 | UN estimate |
| G | 139 | Jamaica | 2,719,000 | | 0.04 | UN estimate |
| G | 140 | Mongolia | 2,671,000 | | 0.039 | UN estimate |
| A | 141 | Latvia | 2,254,000 | Sep 2009 | 0.033 | Official Statistics of Latvia |
| G | 142 | Namibia | 2,171,000 | | 0.032 | UN estimate |
| G | 143 | Lesotho | 2,067,000 | | 0.03 | UN estimate |
| H | 144 | Republic of Macedonia | 2,048,620 | Jan 1, 2009 | 0.03 | Eurostat estimate |
| A | 145 | Slovenia | 2,048,480 | Nov 4, 2009 | 0.03 | Official Slovenian population clock |
| H | 146 | Botswana | 1,950,000 | | 0.029 | UN estimate |
| H | 147 | Gambia | 1,705,000 | | 0.025 | UN estimate |
| H | 148 | Guinea-Bissau | 1,611,000 | | 0.024 | UN estimate |
| H | 149 | Gabon | 1,475,000 | | 0.022 | UN estimate |
| H | 150 | Qatar | 1,409,000 | | 0.021 | UN estimate |
| A | 151 | Estonia | 1,340,415 | Jan 1, 2009 | 0.02 | |
| H | 152 | Trinidad and Tobago | 1,339,000 | | 0.02 | UN estimate |
| H | 153 | Mauritius | 1,288,000 | | 0.019 | UN estimate |
| H | 154 | Swaziland | 1,185,000 | | 0.017 | UN estimate |
| H | 155 | East Timor | 1,134,000 | | 0.017 | UN estimate |
| H | 156 | Djibouti | 864,000 | | 0.013 | UN estimate |
| H | 157 | Fiji | 849,000 | | 0.012 | UN estimate |
| A | 158 | Cyprus | 793,963 | Jan 1, 2009 | 0.012 | Eurostat estimate |
| H | 159 | Bahrain | 791,000 | | 0.012 | UN estimate |
| H | 160 | Guyana | 762,000 | | 0.011 | UN estimate |

| Group* | Rank | Country/territory | Population | Last updated | Approx. %age of world pop. | Source |
|---|---|---|---|---|---|---|
| H | 161 | Bhutan | 697,000 | | 0.01 | UN estimate |
| H | 162 | Comoros | 676,000 | | 0.01 | UN estimate |
| H | 163 | Equatorial Guinea | 676,000 | | 0.01 | UN estimate |
| H | 164 | Montenegro | 624,000 | | 0.009 | UN estimate |
| J | 165 | Macau | 546,200 | Mar 31, 2009 | 0.008 | Macau Statistics and Census Service |
| H | 166 | Solomon Islands | 523,000 | | 0.008 | UN estimate |
| H | 167 | Suriname | 520,000 | | 0.008 | UN estimate |
| J | 168 | Western Sahara | 513,000 | | 0.008 | UN estimate |
| H | 169 | Cape Verde | 506,000 | | 0.007 | UN estimate |
| A | 170 | Luxembourg | 493,500 | Jan 1, 2009 | 0.007 | Eurostat estimate |
| A | 171 | Malta | 413,627 | Jan 1, 2009 | 0.006 | Eurostat estimate |
| H | 172 | Brunei | 400,000 | | 0.006 | UN estimate |
| H | 173 | Bahamas | 342,000 | | 0.005 | UN estimate |
| H | 174 | Belize | 322,100 | Jun 30, 2008 | 0.005 | Statistical Institute of Belize |
| H | 175 | Iceland | 319,246 | Jul 1, 2009 | 0.005 | Statistics Iceland |
| H | 176 | Maldives | 309,000 | | 0.005 | UN estimate |
| H | 177 | Barbados | 256,000 | | 0.004 | UN estimate |
| H | 178 | Vanuatu | 240,000 | | 0.004 | UN estimate |
| J | 179 | Netherlands Antilles | 198,000 | | 0.003 | UN estimate |
| H | 180 | Samoa | 179,000 | | 0.003 | UN estimate |
| J | 181 | Guam | 178,000 | | 0.003 | UN estimate |
| H | 182 | St. Lucia | 172,000 | | 0.003 | UN estimate |
| H | 183 | São Tomé and Principe | 163,000 | | 0.002 | UN estimate |
| H | 184 | Federated States of Micronesia | 111,000 | | 0.002 | UN estimate |
| J | 185 | US Virgin Islands | 110,000 | | 0.002 | UN estimate |
| H | 186 | St. Vincent and the Grenadines | 109,000 | | 0.002 | UN estimate |
| J | 187 | Aruba | 107,000 | | 0.002 | UN estimate |
| H | 188 | Grenada | 104,000 | | 0.002 | UN estimate |
| H | 189 | Tonga | 104,000 | | 0.002 | UN estimate |
| H | 190 | Kiribati | 98,000 | | 0.001 | UN estimate |
| J | 191 | Jersey | 89,300 | Dec 31, 2006 | 0.001 | States of Jersey Statistics Unit |
| H | 192 | Antigua and Barbuda | 88,000 | | 0.001 | UN estimate |
| J | 193 | Northern Mariana Islands | 87,000 | | 0.001 | UN estimate |
| H | 194 | Andorra | 86,000 | | 0.001 | UN estimate |
| H | 195 | Seychelles | 84,000 | | 0.001 | UN estimate |

| Group* | Rank | Country/territory | Population | Last updated | Approx. %age of world pop. | Source |
|---|---|---|---|---|---|---|
| J | 196 | Isle of Man | 80,000 | | 0.001 | UN estimate |
| H | 197 | Dominica | 67,000 | | 0.001 | UN estimate |
| J | 198 | American Samoa | 67,000 | | 0.001 | UN estimate |
| J | 199 | Bermuda | 65,000 | | 0.001 | UN estimate |
| H | 200 | Marshall Islands | 62,000 | | 0.001 | UN estimate |
| J | 201 | Guernsey | 61,811 | Mar 1, 2007 | 0.001 | UN estimate: Series A, Table 2 |
| J | 202 | Greenland | 57,000 | | 0.001 | UN estimate |
| J | 203 | Cayman Islands | 56,000 | | 0.001 | UN estimate |
| H | 204 | St. Kitts and Nevis | 52,000 | | 0.001 | UN estimate |
| J | 205 | Faroe Islands | 49,006 | Aug 1, 2009 | 0.001 | Official statistics of the Faroe Islands |
| H | 206 | Liechtenstein | 35,593 | Jan 1, 2009 | 0.0005 | |
| H | 207 | Monaco | 33,000 | | 0.0005 | UN estimate |
| J | 208 | Turks and Caicos Islands | 33,000 | | 0.0005 | UN estimate |
| J | 209 | Gibraltar | 31,000 | | 0.0005 | UN estimate |
| H | 210 | San Marino | 30,800 | Jan 1, 2008 | 0.0005 | |
| J | 211 | British Virgin Islands | 23,000 | | 0.0003 | UN estimate |
| J | 212 | Cook Islands | 20,000 | | 0.0003 | UN estimate |
| H | 213 | Palau | 20,000 | | 0.0003 | UN estimate |
| J | 214 | Anguilla | 15,000 | | 0.0002 | UN estimate |
| H | 215 | Tuvalu | 10,000 | | 0.0001 | UN estimate |
| H | 216 | Nauru | 10,000 | | 0.0001 | UN estimate |
| J | 217 | Montserrat | 5,900 | | 0.0001 | UN estimate |
| J | 218 | St. Helena | 4,500 | | 0.0001 | UN estimate |
| J | 219 | Falkland Islands | 3,000 | | 0.00005 | UN estimate |
| J | 220 | Niue | 1,500 | | 0.00003 | UN estimate |
| J | 221 | Tokelau | 1,200 | | 0.00003 | UN estimate |
| H | 222 | Vatican City | 800 | | 0.00002 | UN estimate |
| J | 223 | Pitcairn Islands | 50 | | 0.000001 | UN estimate |
| K* | 224–231 | see note below | | | | |

* K = Eight disputed territories not on this UN-based list: Abkhazia, Chechnya, Kashmir, Kosovo, Nagomo-Karabakh, South Ossetia, Tibet, Transnistria.

# 18 Sub-Regions and 209 Nation-States

Basis for Representation in the World Senate (see pp.206–7)

(The 209 nation-states comprise 192 UN nation-states; 16 related and disputed territories;and Taiwan, which was not in the UN in 2009.)

---

**AFRICA**
**Northern Africa**

| | | |
|---|---|---|
| Algeria | Morocco | Western Sahara |
| Egypt | Sudan | |
| Libya | Tunisia | |

---

**Western Africa**

| | | |
|---|---|---|
| Benin | Guinea | Nigeria |
| Burkina Faso | Guinea-Bissau | Senegal |
| Cape Verde | Liberia | Sierra Leone |
| Côte d'Ivoire | Mali | Togo |
| Gambia | Mauritania | |
| Ghana | Niger | |

---

**Eastern Africa**

| | | |
|---|---|---|
| Burundi | Malawi | Somalia |
| Comoros | Mauritius | Tanzania |
| Djibouti | Mayotte | Uganda |
| Eritrea | Mozambique | Zambia |
| Ethiopia | Réunion | Zimbabwe |
| Kenya | Rwanda | |
| Madagascar | Seychelles | |

---

**Middle Africa**

| | | |
|---|---|---|
| Angola | Congo | Equatorial Guinea |
| Cameroon Republic of | Congo, Democratic Republic of | Gabon |
| Central African Republic | Chad | São Tomé and Principe |

---

**Southern Africa**

| | | |
|---|---|---|
| Botswana | Namibia | Swaziland |
| Lesotho | South Africa | |

---

**AMERICAS**
**Northern America**

| | |
|---|---|
| Canada | United States |

**Central America**

| | | |
|---|---|---|
| Belize | Guatemala | Nicaragua |
| Costa Rica | Honduras | Panama |
| El Salvador | Mexico | |

**Caribbean**

| | | |
|---|---|---|
| Antigua and Barbuda | Grenada | Puerto Rico |
| Bahamas | Guadeloupe | St. Kitts and Nevis |
| Barbados | Haiti | St. Lucia |
| Cuba | Jamaica | St. Vincent and the |
| Dominica | Martinique | Grenadines |
| Dominican Republic | Netherlands Antilles | Trinidad and Tobago |

**South America**

| | | |
|---|---|---|
| Argentina | Ecuador | Suriname |
| Bolivia | French Guiana | Uruguay |
| Brazil | Guyana | Venezuela |
| Chile | Paraguay | |
| Colombia | Peru | |

**ASIA**
**Western Asia**

| | | |
|---|---|---|
| Armenia | Israel | Qatar |
| Azerbaijan | Jordan | Saudi Arabia |
| Bahrain | Kuwait | Syria |
| Cyprus | Lebanon | Turkey |
| Georgia | Oman | United Arab Emirates |
| Iraq | Palestinian Territory | Yemen |

**South-Central Asia**

| | | |
|---|---|---|
| Afghanistan | Kazakhstan | Sri Lanka |
| Bangladesh | Kyrgyzstan | Tajikistan |
| Bhutan | Maldives | Turkmenistan |
| India | Nepal | Uzbekistan |
| Iran | Pakistan | |

**South-East Asia**

| | | |
|---|---|---|
| Brunei | Malaysia | Thailand |
| Cambodia | Myanmar | Timor-Leste |
| Indonesia | Philippines | Vietnam |
| Laos | Singapore | |

**East Asia**

| | | |
|---|---|---|
| China | Japan | Mongolia |
| China, Hong Kong | Korea, North | Taiwan |
| China, Macao | Korea, South | |

## EUROPE
**Northern Europe**

| | | |
|---|---|---|
| Channel Islands | Iceland | Norway |
| Denmark | Ireland | Sweden |
| Estonia | Latvia | United Kingdom |
| Finland | Lithuania | |

**Western Europe**

| | | |
|---|---|---|
| Austria | Germany | Monaco |
| Belgium | Liechtenstein | Netherlands |
| France | Luxembourg | Switzerland |

**Eastern Europe**

| | | |
|---|---|---|
| Belarus | Moldova | Russia |
| Bulgaria | Poland | Slovakia |
| Czech Republic | Romania | Ukraine |
| Hungary | | |

**Southern Europe**

| | | |
|---|---|---|
| Albania | Italy | Portugal |
| Andorra | Kosovo | San Marino |
| Bosnia and Herzegovina | Macedonia | Serbia |
| Croatia | Malta | Slovenia |
| Greece | Montenegro | Spain |

## OCEANIA

| | | |
|---|---|---|
| Australia | Kiribati | Papua New Guinea |
| Federated States of Micronesia | Marshall Islands | Samoa |
| | Nauru | Solomon Islands |
| Fiji | New Caledonia | Tonga |
| French Polynesia | New Zealand | Tuvalu |
| Guam | Palau | Vanuatu |

# APPENDIX III

# Bin Laden's / Al-Qaeda's Historical Attempts to Acquire Weapons of Mass Destruction and Unleash Armageddon in the United States

which the World State must Prevent (see p.87)

(In 2009 there were 23,573 nuclear warheads in the world, of which the Russians had 12,987. Source: guardian.co.uk. Given the chaotic state of the ex-Soviet Union in the 1990s, it is not surprising if a small number of these fell into Mafia hands, for sale to bin Laden and al-Qaeda.)

| Date | Type | Event | Source |
|---|---|---|---|
| 1992 | Nuclear | Bin Laden purchased highly enriched uranium stolen from Valendaba, a nuclear manufacturing facility near Pretoria, South Africa. Testimony concerning bin Laden's acquisition of nuclear weapons and materials while living in Sudan and his setting-up of a lab in Khartoum to make nuclear weapons was provided by former al-Qaeda operatives in *United States v. Usama bin Laden, et. al.*, S(10) 98 Cr. (LBS), Southern District of New York, 2001. | Gordon Thomas, 'Los Malerines de Osama,' El Mundo, September 23, 2001; Paul L. Williams, *The Al Qaeda Connection*, p.28. |
| 1993–4 | Nuclear/ Radio-logical | Jamal Ahmed al-Fadl claimed that, on behalf of bin Laden, he had made arrangements for the purchase of uranium for nuclear weapons for $1 million and had it delivered to the training camps in Afghanistan. | Kimberly McCloud and Matthew Osborne, 'WMD Terrorism and Usama Bin Laden,' CNS Report, November 20, 2001. |
| After 1994 and by August 1996 | Nuclear | Bin Laden paid a group of Chechens $30 million in cash and two tons of opium in exchange for approximately 20 nuclear warheads. | Riyad Alam al-Din, 'Report Links Bin Laden, Nuclear Weapons,' *Al-Watan al-Arabi*, November 23, 1998; Emil Torabi, 'Bin Laden's Nuclear Weapons,' *Muslim Magazine* (winter 1998). |
| After 1996 | Nuclear | Bin Laden paid more than £2 million to a middleman in Kazakhstan for a suitcase bomb. | Marie Calvin, 'Holy War with US in His Sights,' *Times* (London), August 16, 1998. |

| Date | Type | Event | Source |
|------|------|-------|--------|
| 1996–8 | Chemical | Bin Laden bought CW (chemical weapons) over a two-year period prior to 1998 from European states and the former Soviet Union. This information comes from the testimony of a jihad leader arrested on August 20, 1998, in Baku, Azerbaijan. | Muhammad Salah, 'Bin Laden Front Reportedly Bought CBW from E. Europe,' *Al-Hayah*, April 20, 1999; Muhammad Salah, 'US Said Interrogating Jihadist over CBW,' *Al-Hayah*, April 21, 1999. |
| May 1997 | Nuclear | General Aleksandr Lebed, Yeltsin's former security secretary, told members of the US House of Representatives that 84 nuclear-suitcase bombs were missing. Out of 132 produced he could only account for 48. He said that some of the missing bombs might be in the hands of Muslim extremists. | Scott Parish, 'Are Suitcase Nukes on the loose? The Story behind the Controversy,' Center for Nonproliferation Studies, Monterey Institute of International Studies, Monterey, California, November 1997. |
| Before Oct 1997 | Nuclear | Bin Laden purchased 48 nuclear-suitcase bombs from the Russian Mafia. | 'Al-Majallah Obtains Serious Information of Al-Qaeda's Attempt to Acquire Nuclear Arms,' *Al-Majallah* (London-based Saudi weekly), September 8, 2002. |
| Before 1998 | Nuclear | Abdul Qadeer Khan was alleged to have supplied bin Laden with nuclear suicide bombs. They were looked after by Pakistani nuclear engineers and ISI generals, who were paid $60–100 million by bin Laden. | 'Pakistan Scientist Brokered North Korea Deal,' NBC News, October 18, 2002. Also Mishra, 'Nuclear Scientific Community of Pakistan.' Also John M Curtis, 'Pakistan's Bomb Maker,' *Online Columnist.com*, January 5, 2003, http://www.onlinecolumnist.com/01503.htm. |
| Before 1998 | Nuclear | Via al-Qaeda agents bin Laden bought 12–15 kg (26–33lb) of uranium-235 for $75 million from a Ukrainian arms dealer, Semion Mogilevich, and 20 kg (44lb) of uranium-236 enriched 85 percent. | Ryan Mauro, 'Terrorist Possession of Weapons of Mass Destruction,' *World Threats*, Monthly Analysis, February 2003, http://www.worldthreats.vcon/monthly%20analysis/MA%202003.htm Also Robert Friedman, 'The Most Dangerous Mobster in the World,' *Village Voice*, May 22, 1998. |
| Before 1998 | Nuclear | Via al-Qaeda agents bin Laden bought two bars of enriched uranium-138 from Egyptian black-marketer Ibrahim Abd in Hamburg, Germany. | Ryan Mauro, 'The Next Attack on America,' *World Threats*, November 27, 2003, http://www.freepublic.com/focus/f-news/1020690/posts. Also 'Bin Laden buys Nuclear Materials,' *World Net Daily*, November 26, 2003. |
| 1997–8 | Chemical/ Biological | Islamic extremists, including al-Qaeda operatives, were trained in secret camps near Baghdad in the use of CBWs (chemical and biological weapons) by instructors from Iraq's secret military intelligence Unit 999. | Gwynne Roberts, 'Militia Defector Claims Baghdad Trained Al-Qaeda Fighters in Chemical Warfare,' *Sunday Times* (London), July 14, 2002. |

| Date | Type | Event | Source |
|------|------|-------|--------|
| Oct 1997 | Chemical/ Biological | A meeting was held in Sudan between bin Laden, Ayman al-Zawahiri, and Hasan al-Turabi, leader of Sudan's National Islamic Front regime, about the construction of a CBW factory. | Jihad Salim, 'Report on Bin Laden, Zawahiri, Afghans,' *Al-Watan al-Arabi*, February 16, 2001. |
| 1998 | Nuclear/ Radio- logical | Russian Intelligence blocked an attempt by bin Laden to purchase Soviet-origin uranium. | Earl Lane and Knut Royce, 'Nuclear Aspirations? Sources: Bin Laden Tried to Obtain Enriched Uranium,' *Newsday*, September 19, 2001. |
| 1998 | Chemical/ Biological | From looters in Kabul a reporter obtained two computers that had been found in an abandoned al-Qaeda safe house. One of the computers contained a file describing 'plans to launch a chemical and biological weapons program.' Bin Laden's deputy al-Zawahiri reportedly created the documents describing his CBW program, code-named 'Curdled Milk.' The document included work on a pesticide-nerve agent that was tested on rabbits and dogs. Al-Zawahiri was assisted by Midhat Mursi (aka Abu Khabbab), a chemical engineer. | Alan Culluson and Andrew Higgins, 'Computer in Kabul Holds Chilling Memos,' *Wall Street Journal*, December 31, 2001; 'Report: Al Qaeda Computer Had Plans for Bio-Weapons,' Reuters, December 21, 2001. |
| May 1998 | Chemical/ Biological | Al-Qaeda purchased three CBW factories in the former Yugoslavia and hired a number of Ukrainian chemists and biologists to train its members. | Guido Olimpio, 'Islamic Group Said Preparing Chemical Warfare on he West,' *Corriere della Sera*, July 8, 1998; Yossef Bodansky, *Bin Laden: The Man Who Declared War on America* (New York: Prima, 2001), 326. |
| August 1998 | Chemical | The CIA discovered that bin Laden had attempted to acquire unspecified CW for use against US troops in the Persian Gulf. | Barry Schweid, 'US Suggests Iraq Got Weapons from Sudan,' *Record* (New Jersey), August 27, 1998. |
| Sept 1998 | Nuclear/ Radio- logical | Mamdouh Mahmud Salim, an al-Qaeda operative, was arrested in Munich, Germany, for trying to purchase nuclear material, including highly enriched uranium. | Benjamin Weiser, 'US Says Bin Laden Aide Tried to Get Nuclear Weapons,' *New York Times*, September 26, 1998. |
| Sept 1998 | Chemical | Wadi al-Hajj, a Lebanese national, is arrested in Arlington, Texas for perjury. The FBI contends that he had lied about his affiliation with bin Laden and that he was involved in procuring WMD for al-Qaeda. | CNN, December 20, 1998. |
| Dec 1998 | Chemical/ Nuclear | In an interview with *Time* magazine, bin Laden said that acquiring weapons of any type, including chemical and nuclear, is a Muslim 'religious duty.' | 'Interview with bin Laden,' *Time*, December 24, 1998. |
| 1999 | Chemical | Afghan sources maintained that bin Laden made use of a plant in Charassiab, a district south of Kabul, to produce CW. | 'Afghan Alliance – UBL trying to Make Chemical Weapons,' *Parwan Payam-e Mojahed*, December 23, 1999. |

| Date | Type | Event | Source |
|------|------|-------|--------|
| April 1999 | Biological | Bin Laden obtained BW substances through the mail from former Soviet Union republics (the Ebola virus and salmonella bacterium), from East Asia (anthrax-causing bacteria), and from the Czech Republic (botulinum toxin). | Al J. Venter, 'Elements Loyal to Bin Laden Acquire Biological Agents "Through the Mail,"' *Jane's Intelligence Review* (August 1999); Khalid Sharaf al-Din, 'Bin Laden Men Reportedly Possess Biological Weapons,' *Al-Sharq al-Awsat*, March 6, 1999. |
| July 1999 | Chemical/ Biological | An Islamist lawyer testified that al-Qaeda has CBW and will likely use such weapons against the United States. | 'Islamist Lawyer on Bin Laden, Groups,' *Al-Sharq al-Awsat*, July 12, 1999. |
| Before 2000 | Biological | Al-Qaeda operatives bought anthrax and plague from arms dealers in Kazakhstan. | Paul Daley, 'Report Says UBL-Linked Terrorist Groups Possess "Deadly" Anthrax, Plague Viruses,' *Melbourne Age*, June 4, 2000. |
| Feb 2000 | Chemical | Italian police foil a plot by nine Moroccans, with ties to al-Qaeda, to poison the water supply of the US Embassy in Rome with a cyanide compound. | Eric Croddy *et al.*, 'Chemical Terrorist Plot in Rome?,' CNS Research Story March 11, 2002. |
| Late 2000 | Nuclear | The intelligence agency of an unnamed European country intercepted a shipment – originating in Kazakhstan, Russia, Turkmenistan and the Ukraine – of approximately 20 nuclear warheads intended for bin Laden and the Taliban regime of Afghanistan. | 'Arab Security Sources Speak of a New Scenario for Afghanistan: Secret Roaming Networks That Exchange Nuclear Weapons for Drugs,' *Al-Sharq al-Awsat*, December 24, 2000. |
| 2001 | Biological | Various sources maintained that Mohammed Atta, the leader of the September 11 hijackers, was provided with a vial of anthrax by an Iraqi intelligence agent at a meeting in Prague. | Kreindler and Kreindler 9/11 lawsuit; 'Prague Discounts an Iraqi Meeting,' *New York Times*, October 21, 2001; 'Czechs Retract Iraq Terror Link,' United Press International, October 20, 2001. |
| 2001 | Biological | Ahmed Ressam, arrested in a plot to bomb Los Angeles International Airport, testified that bin Laden is interested in using low-flying aircraft to disperse BW agents over major US metropolitan areas. | 'Bin Laden's Biological Threat,' BBC, October 28, 2001. |
| 2001 | Biological | Documents found in Afghanistan revealed that al-Qaeda was conducting research on using botulinum toxin to kill 2,000 people. | 'Al Qaeda Tested Germ Weapons,' Reuters, January 1, 2002. |
| 2001 | Chemical | Ahmed Ressam claimed to witness the gassing of a dog with cyanide in an al-Qaeda training camp. | Pamela Hess, 'Al-Qaeda May Have Chemical Weapons,' United Press International, August 19, 2002. |
| Feb 2001 | Chemical | After receiving warnings from an Arab embassy in Islamabad, Pakistan, the US aborted a planned air strike against Afghanistan for fear of a chemical attack by al-Qaeda. | Sa'id al-Qaysi, 'US Said Aborted Planned Attack on Bin Laden for Fear of "Chemical Strike,"' *Al-Watan al-Arabi*, February 16, 2001. |

| Date | Type | Event | Source |
|------|------|-------|--------|
| Feb 2001 | Chemical | Bin Laden's élite 055 Brigade reorganized under the leadership of Midhat Mursi, a.k.a. Abu Khabab, an Eyptian and expert in sarin gas production. | Sa'id al-Qaysi, 'US Said Aborted Planned Attack on Bin Laden for Fear of "Chemical Strike,"' *Al-Watan al-Arabi*, February 16, 2001. |
| April 2001 | Nuclear/ Radio-logical | Ivan Ivanov claimed to have met with bin Laden in China to discuss the establishment of a company to buy nuclear waste. Ivanov was then approached by a Pakistani chemical engineer interested in buying nuclear fuel rods from the Bulgarian Kozlodui reactor. | Adam Nathan and David Leppard, 'Al-Qaeda's Men Held Secret Meetings to Build "Dirty Bomb,"' *Sunday Times* (London), October 14, 2001. |
| Since summer 2001 | Chemical/ Biological/ Nuclear | Iraqi military instructors provided training to 150–250 al-Qaeda operatives in northern Iraq in the use of CBW and the handling of nuclear devices. | 'Abu Nidal's Nemesis,' DEBKAfile (Jerusalem), August 20, 2002. |
| Oct 2001 | Nuclear | Mossad arrested an al-Qaeda operative with backpack containing a tactical nuclear weapon at the checkpoint in Ramallah. | United Press International, December 21, 2001. First reports spoke of a radiological bomb. |
| Before Nov 2001 | Chemical | CNN releases al-Qaeda videotapes that show dogs being killed by unidentified toxic chemicals, which experts believe could be either a crude nerve agent or hydrogen cyanide gas. | *Insight*, CNN, August 19, 2002. |
| Before Nov 2001 | Biological | US officials discovered documents concerning the aerial dispersal of anthrax via balloon within the Kabul office of Pakistani scientist Dr Bashiruddin Mahmood. | 'Sketches of Anthrax Bomb Found in Pakistani Scientist's Office,' Rediff.com, November 28, 2001. |
| Before Nov 2001 | Nuclear/ Biological/ Chemical | Two Pakistani scientists shared nuclear, biological, and chemical weapons information with bin Laden, who said that the nuclear material had been provided by the Islamic Movement of Uzbekistan. | Toby Hamden, 'Rogue Scientists Gave Bin Laden Nuclear Secrets,' *Daily Telegraph* (London), December 13, 2001; Peter Baker, 'Pakistani Scientist Who Met Bin Laden Failed Polygraphs, Renewing Suspicions,' *Washington Post*, March 3, 2002; Susan B. Glasser and Kamra Khan, 'Pakistan Continues Probe of Nuclear Scientists,' *Washington Post*, November 14, 2001. |
| Nov 2001 | Chemical/ Nuclear | In an interview bin Laden declared: 'We have chemical and nuclear weapons as a deterrent, and if America uses them against us, we reserve the right to use them.' | Hamid Mir, 'Osama Claims He Has Nukes: If US Uses N-Arms It Will Get Some Response,' *Dawn* (Pakistan), November 10, 2001. |
| Nov 2001 | Nuclear | Evidence obtained from the offices of *Ummah* Tameer E-Nau of Kabul shows that a nuclear weapon may have been shipped to the US from Karachi in a cargo container. | Arnaud de Borchgrave, 'Al Qaeda's Nuclear Agenda Verified,' *Washington Times*, December 10, 2001. |

| Date | Type | Event | Source |
|---|---|---|---|
| Nov 2001 | Nuclear | Bin Laden acquired a Russian-made suitcase nuclear weapon from Central Asian sources. The weapon was reported to weigh 8kg (17lb) and to possess at least 2kg (4.4lb) of fissionable uranium and plutonium. The report said the device, with serial number 9999 and a manufacturing date of October 1998, could be set off by a cellphone signal. This weapon, according to sources, had been forward-deployed to the US. | 'N-weapons May Be in US Already,' *Daily Telegraph* (Sydney, Australia), November 14, 2001. |
| Nov 2001 | Nuclear | A *Times* (London) reporter discovered a blueprint for a 'Nagasaki bomb' in an abandoned al-Qaeda house in Kabul. | 'Nuke Plans Found; Brit Paper Discovers Details of Weapons in Kabul Safe House,' *Toronto Sun*, November 15, 2001; Hugh Dougherty, 'Afghan Nuclear Weapons Papers "May Be Internet Spoofs,"' *Press Association*, November 19, 2001. |
| Nov 2001 | Nuclear | A 'superbomb' manual that addresses the physics of nuclear weapons and dirty bombs was discovered in a safe house in Afghanistan. | 'Osama Bin Laden's Bid to Acquire Weapons of Mass Destruction Represents the Greatest Threat That Western Civilization Has Faced,' *Mail on Sunday* (London), June 23, 2002. |
| Dec 2001 | Radio-logical | Uranium-235 was found in a lead-lined canister in Kandahar. | Barbie Dutter and Ben Fenton, 'Uranium and Cyanide Found In Drums at Bin Laden's Base,' *Daily Telegraph* (London), December 24, 2001. |
| Late 2001 | Biological | US intelligence agents uncovered evidence in Afghanistan that one or more Russian scientists were helping al-Qaeda develop biological weapons, including anthrax. | Jeffrey Bartholet, 'Terrorist Sleeper Cells,' *Newsweek*, December 9, 2001. |
| Late 2001 | Biological | Al-Zawahiri's home in Kabul tested positive for traces of anthrax, as did 5 of 19 al-Qaeda labs in Afghanistan. | 'Al-Qaeda: Anthrax found in Al-Qaeda Home,' Global Security Newswire, December 10, 2001; Judith Miller, 'Labs Suggest Al Qaeda Planned to Build Arms, Officials Say,' *New York Times*, September 14, 2001. |
| Late 2001 | Biological | John Walker Lindh told interrogators that a biological attack was expected to be part of a 'second wave' of al-Qaeda attacks. | 'Walker Lindh: Al Qaeda Planned More Attacks,' CNN, October 3, 2002. |
| 2002 | Chemical | The facility of Ansar al-Islam, a radical Islamist group operating in northern Iraq with ties to al-Qaeda, produced a form of cyanide cream that kills on contact. | William Safire, 'Tying Saddam to Terrorist Organizations,' *New York Times*, August 25, 2002. |
| Jan–June 2002 | Biological | Ansar al-Islam had conducted experiments with ricin, a deadly toxin, on at least one human subject. | 'US Knew of Bio-Terror Tests in Iraq,' BBC News, August 20, 2002; 'US Monitors Kurdish Extremists,' Fox News, August 21, 2002; Isma'il Zayir, 'Ansar al-Islam Group Accuses [Jalal] Talabani of Spreading Rumors About Its Cooperation with Al-Qaeda,' *Al Hayah*, August 22, 2002. |

| Date | Type | Event | Source |
|---|---|---|---|
| Jan 2002 | Nuclear | Diagrams of US nuclear power plants were discovered in abandoned al-Qaeda camps and facilities in Afghanistan. | Bill Gertz, 'Nuclear Plants Targeted,' *Washington Times*, January 31, 2002; John J. Lumpkin, 'Diagrams Show Interest in Nuke Plants,' Associated Press, January 30, 2002. |
| Feb 2, 2002 | Chemical/ Biological | CIA director George Tenet informed the Senate that bin Laden has displayed a strong interest in CW and that his operatives have been 'trained to conduct attacks with toxic chemicals or biological toxins.' | Pamela Hess, 'Al Qaeda May Have Chemical Weapons,' United Press International, August 19, 2002. |
| Before March 2002 | Biological | US forces discovered a BW laboratory under construction near Kandahar. It had been abandoned by al-Qaeda. The laboratory was being built to produce anthrax. | Dominic Evans, 'US Troops Found Afghan Biological Lab,' Reuters, March 22, 2002; Michael R. Gordon, 'US Says It found Al Qaeda Lab Being Built to Produce Anthrax,' *New York Times*, March 23, 2002. |
| April 2002 | Radio- logical | Abu Zubayda said that al-Qaeda possesses the ability to produce a radiological weapon and already has one in the US. | Jamie McIntyre, 'Zubayda: al Qaeda Had "Dirty Bomb" Know-How,' CNN, April 22, 2002; 'Al-Qaeda Claims "Dirty Bomb" Know-How,' BBC, April 23, 2002. |
| May 2002 | Radio- logical | US citizen Abdullah al-Muhaji (formerly Jose Padilla) was arrested in Chicago. He had been involved with al-Qaeda in a plan for a radiological bomb attack on the US. | Dan Eggen and Susan Schmidt, "Dirty Bomb" Plot Uncovered, US Says: Suspected Al Qaeda Operative Held as "Enemy Combatant,"' *Washington Post*, June 11, 2002. |
| May 2002 | Chemical | During the arrest of Sami Uthman, a Lebanese national who moved to the US and became an imam at a mosque in Seattle, police officials found papers by London-based al-Qaeda recruiter Sheikh Abu Hamza al-Masri, firearms, military manuals, and 'instructions on poisoning water sources.' | Patrick J. McDonnell and Josh Meyer, 'Links to Terrorism Probed in Northwest,' *Los Angeles Times*, July 13, 2002. |
| Before June 2002 | Chemical/ Biological | Al-Qaeda's 5,000-page *Encyclopedia of Jihad* is devoted to construction of CBW (chemical and biological weapons). | 'Osama Bin Laden's Bid to Acquire Weapons of Mass Destruction Represents the Greatest Threat That Western Civilization Has Faced,' *Mail on Sunday* (London), June 23, 2002. |
| June 3, 2002 | Radio- logical | Bin Laden tried to acquire 5kg (11lb) of radioactive thallium from measuring devices on decommissioned Russian submarines, but Russia's Federal Security Service claimed to have blocked the sale. | 'Insider Notes,' United Press International, June 3, 2002. |
| Before July 2002 | Chemical | CNN correspondent Mike Boettcher reports that US intelligence agencies discovered evidence of recent purchases of cyanide by al-Qaeda operatives. | *Wolf Blitzer Reports*, CNN, July 31, 2002. |

| Date | Type | Event | Source |
|------|------|-------|--------|
| July 18, 2002 | Biological | Stephen Younger, director of the Defense Threat Reduction Agency, testified that al-Qaeda's interest in BW focused mainly on anthrax. | 'Weapons Worries,' CBS News, July 18, 2002. |
| Sep 13, 2002 | Chemical/ Biological | Laboratory equipment found near Kandahar supports the assessment that al-Qaeda has acquired the necessary ingredients for 'a very limited production of biological and chemical agents.' | Judith Miller, 'Lab Suggests Al Qaeda Planned to Build Arms, Officials Say,' *New York Times*, September, 14, 2002. |
| Oct or Nov 2002 | Chemical | The Islamist group Asbat al-Ansar, a Lebanon-based Sunni group affiliated with al-Qaeda, obtained the nerve agent VX from Iraq. | Barton Gellman, 'US Suspects Al Qaeda Got Nerve Gas Agent from Iraqis,' *Washington Post*, December 12, 2002. |
| Nov 9, 2002 | Chemical | British security officials arrested three agents of al-Qaeda who were planning a cyanide attack on the London subway. | Hala Jaber and Nicholas Rufford, 'MI5 Foils Poison-Gas Attack on Tube,' *Sunday Times* (London), November 17, 2002. |
| After March 2, 2003 | Nuclear | Khalid Sheikh Mohammed was apprehended on March 1, 2003. He and other al-Qaeda defectors and informants claimed that bin Laden had announced his intention to detonate nuclear-suitcase bombs in at least seven and possibly ten US cities. | Patrick J. McDonnell and Josh Meyer, 'Links to Terrorism Probed in Northwest,' *Los Angeles Times*, July 13, 2002. |
| Before 2004 | Nuclear/ Radio-logical | Bin Laden dispatches envoys to several eastern European countries to purchase enriched uranium. | 'Arab Security Sources Speak of a New Scenario for Afghanistan: Secret Roaming Networks that Exchange Nuclear Weapons for Drugs,' *Al-Sharq al-Awsat*, December 24, 2004. |
| March 3, 2004 | Nuclear | In an interview with Pakistani journalist Hamid Mir, Ayman al-Zawahiri claimed that al-Qaeda possessed nuclear weapons. Zawahiri told Mir that al-Qaeda agents had been sent to 'Moscow, Tashkent, and other countries in Central Asia' to buy portable nukes. | Max Delany, 'Under Attack from Al-Qaeda,' *Moscow News*, March 3, 2004. |
| Sept 2004 | Radio-logical | Midhat Mursi, an al-Qaeda affiliate, managed chemical laboratories in Afghanistan for the manufacturing of radiological bombs. Mursi used the alias 'Abu Khabab' and remained in contact with Ayman al-Zawahiri. | Muhammad Wajdi Qandyl, 'Secret Weapons of Mass Destruction and al Qaeda,' *Al-Akhbar* (Cairo), January 18, 2004. |
| Nov 2004 | Nuclear | Sharif al-Masri, a key al-Qaeda operative, informed authorities that bin Laden has arranged to smuggle nuclear supplies and tactical weapons into Mexico. | 'Al Qaeda Wants to Smuggle N-Material to US,' *Nation*, November 17, 2004. |

| Date | Type | Event | Source |
|---|---|---|---|
| Before Nov 2005 | Nuclear/ Radio- logical | Bin Laden purchased seven enriched-uranium rods from Ukrainian arms dealer Semion Mogilevich. | Uthman Tizghart, 'Does Bin Laden Really Possess Weapons of Mass Destruction? Tale of Russian Mafia Boss Semion Mogilevich Who Supplied Bin Laden with the Nuclear "Dirty Bomb,"' Al-Majallah (London), November 25, 2005. |
| Feb 17, 2005 | Nuclear | CIA director Porter Goss said that it remains only a matter of time before al-Qaeda attempts to use weapons of mass destruction, including tactical nuclear bombs, against the US. His remarks were upheld by FBI director Robert Mueller. | CNN, February 17, 2005. |
| April 20,2005 | Nuclear | Intelligence agents confirmed that Abu Musab Zarqawi has obtained a nuclear device or is preparing a radiological explosive for an attack. The nuclear device/ dirty nuke is being stored in Afghanistan. | Bill Gertz, 'Reports Reveal Zarqawi's Nuclear Threat,' Washington Times, April 20, 2005. |

Source: Kimberley McCloud, Gary A. Ackerman and Jeffrey M. Bale, 'Chart: Al Qaeda's WMD Activities,' Center for Nonproliferation Studies, Monterey Institute of International Studies, January 21, 2003. Revised and enlarged by Paul L. Williams. Enlarged and edited by Nicholas Hagger.

# APPENDIX IV

# Maps relating to American Superpowerdom

Illustrations of the extent of American Military Influence at the beginning of the coming World State

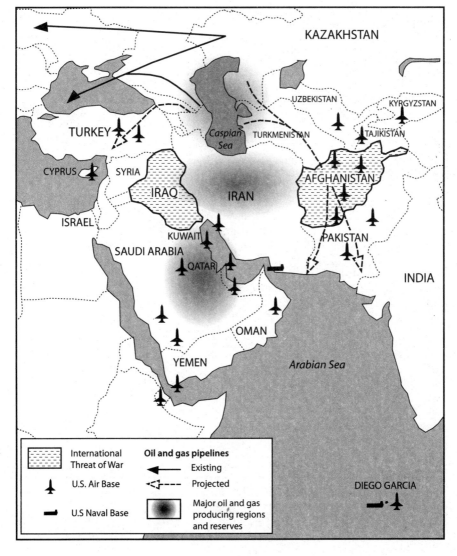

1. US Bases near Afghanistan, Iraq, and the Caspian, 2003

**2. US Military Bases, 2002** (see pp.78–9, 100)

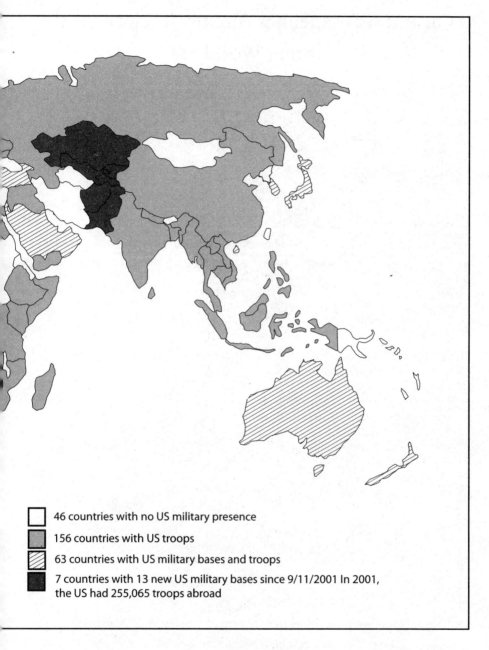

46 countries with no US military presence

156 countries with US troops

63 countries with US military bases and troops

7 countries with 13 new US military bases since 9/11/2001 In 2001, the US had 255,065 troops abroad

Based on: Department of Defense, 'Base Structure Report, FY 2001' and 'Active Duty Military Personnel Strengths by Regional Area and by Country, Dec 31, 2001,' Zoltan Grossman, 'War and New US Military Bases' in *CounterPunch*, Feb 2, 2002; and *Monthly Review*, 2002.

# Oil and Gas Pipelines Already in Place for the coming World State

# 1. World Distribution of Oil and Gas pipelines

This map reveals the scale of global pipeline projects (see ch.8 and p.158).

# 2. Oil Pipelines by Continent

## Africa
Chad–Cameroon pipeline
Petronet
Sumed pipeline
Tazama pipeline

## Asia
Afghanistan oil pipeline (see Trans-Afghan)
Alashankou–Dushanzi crude oil pipeline
Baku–Chechnya–Novorossiysk pipeline
Baku–Supsa pipeline
Baku–Tbilisi–Ceyhan pipeline
Caspian Pipeline Consortium
Eastern Siberia–Pacific Ocean (ESPO) oil
    pipeline (planned)
Kabrai–Dhanbad cutter pipeline
Kazakhstan–China oil pipeline
Kirkuk–Banias pipeline (defunct since
    2003)
Kirkuk–Ceyhan oil pipeline
Kirkuk–Haifa oil pipeline (planned)
Mumbai–Manmad pipeline
Sakhalin-2 pipeline
Samsun–Ceyhan pipeline
Sino-Burma pipelines
South–North Pipeline Korea
Tengiz (Kazakhstan)–Novorossiysk
    pipeline
Trans-Afghan oil pipeline
    (Turkmenistan/Chardhzou–
    Afghanistan–Pakistan–India)
Trans-Arabian Pipeline, aka Tapline
    (defunct)
Trans-Caspian oil pipeline (planned)
Trans-Israel pipeline
Trans-Korea pipeline
West-Qurna pipeline (planned)

## Europe
AMBO pipeline (see Trans-Balkan)
Baltic pipeline system
Brent system
Burgas–Alexandroupoli pipeline (see
    Trans-Balkan)
CLH pipelines – Spain
Druzhba pipeline
Forties pipeline system
Grozny–Tuapse pipeline

Ninian pipeline
Odessa–Brody pipeline
Pan-European pipeline
Transalpine pipeline
Trans-Balkan oil pipeline (Baku–Ceyhan–
    Burgas–Alexandropouli/Vlore)

## North America
Big Inch
Calnev pipeline
Colonial pipeline
Keystone pipeline (proposed)
Lakehead pipeline
Minnesota pipeline
North Dakota system
Portland–Montreal Pipe Line
Trans-Alaska pipeline system
Yellowstone pipeline

## Latin America
Activo de Burgos pipeline network –
    Mexico
Burgos–Monterrey pipeline – Mexico
Cadereyta pipeline – Mexico
ECOPETROL pipelines – Colombia
OCP Pipeline – Ecuador
OIL TANKING pipeline – Argentina
PDVSA pipelines – Venezuela
PEMEX pipelines – Mexico
PETROANDINA pipeline – Argentina
    (under construction)
Recope pipelines – Costa Rica
San Fernando pipeline – Mexico
SOTE pipeline – Ecuador
Tamazunchale pipeline – Mexico
TGN pipeline network – Argentina
TGI pipeline network – Colombia
TGS pipeline network – Argentina
Trans-Isthmian pipeline – Panama
Transpetro pipelines – Brazil

# 3. Natural Gas Pipelines by Continent

## Africa
Trans-Saharan gas pipeline (Nigeria–
  Niger–Algeria–Tunisia, planned)
West African gas pipeline

## Asia
Altai gas pipeline (planned)
Arab gas pipeline
Bukhara–Tashkent–Bishkek–Almaty
  pipeline
Central Asia-Center gas pipeline system
Central Asia-China gas pipeline
Dolphin gas project
Iran–Armenia natural gas pipeline
Iran–Pakistan–India gas pipeline
  (planned)
Iran–Turkey pipeline
Korpezhe–Kurt Kui pipeline
Myanmar–Thailand pipelines (3)
Peninsular gas pipeline
Sakhalin-2 pipeline
Shaan-Jing pipeline
South Caucasus (Baku–Tbilisi–Erzurum)
  pipeline
Trans-Caspian gas pipeline (Kazakhstan–
  Baku–Tbilisi–Ceyhan, planned)
Trans-Thailand Malaysian gas pipeline
Trans-Afghan (i.e. Turkmenistan–
  Afghanistan–Pakistan–India) gas
  pipeline (planned)
Trans-Ukraine gas pipeline
West–East gas pipeline
Yadana pipeline
Zhongxian–Wuhan pipeline

## Europe
Baltic Gas Interconnector – Germany,
  Denmark and Sweden (planned)
Baltic Pipe (planned)
Balticconnector (planned)
BBL pipeline
Blue Stream pipeline
CATS pipeline
ENAGAS pipeline – Spain
Europipe I
Europipe II
FLAGS

Franpipe
Frigg UK system
Fulmar gas pipeline
GALSI
Gazela pipeline
Greece–Italy pipeline (planned)
Greenstream pipeline
Interconnector
JAGAL
Langeled pipeline – Northwestern
  Europe
Maghreb–Europe gas pipeline
Medgaz (under construction)
MIDAL
Nabucco pipeline (planned)
NEL pipeline (planned)
Netra
NOGAT Pipeline System Nord Stream –
  North-European gas pipeline (planned)
OPAL pipeline (planned)
Progress pipeline
Rehden–Hamburg gas pipeline
Skanled (planned)
South-German natural gas pipeline
South-Stream – Russia–Bulgaria–
  Italy / Austria (planned)
South-Wales gas pipeline
Soyuz pipeline
Statpipe
STEGAL
Trans-Adriatic pipeline (planned)
Trans-Austria gas pipeline
Trans-Europa Naturgas pipeline
Trans-Mediterranean pipeline
Transitgas pipeline
Turkey–Greece pipeline
Tyra West – F3 pipeline
Vesterled
WEDAL
White Stream
Yamal–Europe pipeline
Zeepipe

## North American Gas Pipelines

Interstate (interprovincial in Canada) pipelines are regulated by the Federal Energy Regulatory Commission (FERC) in the United States and the National Energy Board in Canada. Intrastate / intraprovincial pipelines are regulated by state, provincial, or other local jurisdictions.

FERC requires most interstate pipelines to maintain an interactive website with standardized information regarding their operations under a heading of 'Informational Postings.' The exact legal name of each company appears below. Many of these companies are wholly owned subsidiaries of larger publicly-traded companies.

### Canada
Alliance Pipeline Limited Partnership
Brunswick Pipline (Emera Incorporated)
Foothills Pipeline Ltd
Maritimes & Northeast pipeline
Sable Offshore Energy Inc (SOEI)
TransCanada PipeLines, LP
TransQuebec & Maritimes pipeline
WestCoast Energy Inc

### Mexico
Activo de Burgos – pipeline network
Burgos–Monterrey pipeline
Cadereyta pipeline
San Fernando pipeline
Tamazunchale pipeline

### United States: Major Interstate Gas Pipelines
Alaskan Natural gas pipeline (planned)
Alliance Pipeline LP
ANR Pipeline Company – formerly Michican Wisconsin
CenterPoint Energy Gas Transmission Company
CenterPoint Energy – Mississippi River, formerly Mississippi River Transmission
Colorado Interstate Gas Company
Columbia Gas Transmission Corporation
Columbia Gulf Transmission Company
Dominion Transmission Inc. – formerly Consolidated Gas Transmission
East Tennessee Natural Gas Company
El Paso Natural Gas Company

Florida Gas Transmission Company
Gas Transmission Northwest Corporation – formerly Pacific Gas Transmission
Great Lakes Gas Transmission Limited Partnership
Gulf South Pipeline Company LP – for United Gas Pipeline Company
Kern River Gas Transmission Company
Kinder Morgan Interstate Gas Transmission LLC – owned by Kinder Morgan Energy Partners, formerly Kansas Nebraska and KN Energy
Maritimes & Northeast Pipeline LLC
Midwestern Gas Transmission Company
National Fuel Gas Supply Corporation
Natural Gas Pipeline Company of America
Northern Border Pipeline Company
Northern Natural Gas Company
Northwest Pipeline Corporation
Panhandle Eastern Pipe Line Company LP
Questar Pipeline Company
Questar Southern Trails Pipeline Company
Rockies Express Pipeline
Southern Natural Gas Company
Southern Star Central Gas Pipeline Inc.
Tennessee Gas Pipeline Company
Texas Eastern Transmission LP
Texas Gas Pipe Line Corporation
Texas Gas Transmission LLC
Texas–Ohio Pipeline Inc.
Trailblazer Pipeline Company
Transcontinental Gas Pipe Line Corporation

Transwestern Pipeline Company LLC
Trunkline Gas Company LLC
Viking Gas Transmission Company
Williston Basin Interstate Pipeline Co.

## United States: Minor Interstate Gas Pipelines

ANR Storage Company
Arkansas Western Pipeline LLC
Black Marlin Pipeline Company
Blue Dolphin Pipe Line Company
    Company LP
Blue Lake Gas Storage Company
Boundary Gas Incorporated
B-R Pipeline Company
Canyon Creek Compression Company
Caprock Pipeline Company
Carolina Gas Transmission, a SCANA
    Company (formerly SCG Pipeline
    Inc./South Carolina Pipeline Corp.)
Centra Pipelines Minnesota Inc.
Central Kentucky Transmission Company
Central New York Oil And Gas Company
    LLC
Chandeleur Pipe Line Company
Cheyenne Plains Gas Pipeline Company
    LLC
Clear Creek Storage Company LLC
Cotton Valley Compression LLC
Crossroads Pipeline Company
Dauphin Island Gathering Partners
Destin Pipeline Company LLC
Discovery Gas Transmission LLC
Distrigas Corporation
Dominion South Pipeline Co. LP
Eastern Shore Natural Gas Company
Egan Hub Storage LLC
Enbridge Pipelines (Alatenn) LLC
    (formerly Alabama-Tennessee)
Enbridge Pipelines (Kpc)
Enbridge Pipelines (Midla) LLC (formerly
    Mid-Louisiana)
Energy West Development Inc.
Equitrans LP
Freebird Gas Storage LLC
Garden Banks Gas Pipeline LLC
Gas Gathering Corporation
Gasdel Pipeline System Inc.
Gas Transmission Northwest Corp.
Granite State Gas Transmission Inc.
Great Lakes Gas Transport LLC
Guardian Pipeline LLC

Gulf States Transmission Corporation
Honeoye Storage Corporation
Horizon Pipeline Company LLC
Inland Gas Company
Iroquois Gas Transmission System LP
Kentucky West Virginia Gas Company
KO Transmission Company
Louisiana-Nevada Transit Company
Markwest New Mexico LP (Pinnacle)
Michigan Consolidated Gas Company
Michigan Gas Storage Company
Midwest Gas Storage Inc. Millennium
    Pipeline
MIGC Inc.
Mississippi Canyon Gas Pipeline LLC
Missouri Interstate Gas LLC
Mobile Bay Pipeline Company
Mojave Pipeline Company
Ngo Transmission Inc.
Nora Transmission Company
Nornew Energy Supply Inc.
Norteño Pipeline Company
North Baja Pipeline LLC
North Penn Gas Company
Oktex Pipeline Company
Overthrust Pipeline Company
Ozark Gas Transmission LLC
Pacific Interstate Transmission Company
Paiute Pipeline Company
Penn-York Energy Corporation
Petal Gas Storage LLC
Phillips Gas Pipeline Company
Pine Needle LNG Company LLC (peak
    shaving storage – not an import
    terminal)
Portland General Electric Company
Portland Natural Gas Transmission
    System
Puget Sound Energy Inc.
Richfield Gas Storage System
Riverside Pipeline Company LP
Sabine Pipe Line Company LLC
Saltville Gas Storage Company LLC
Sea Robin Pipeline Company LLC
Southwest Gas Storage Company
Steuben Gas Storage Company
U S G Pipeline Company
T C P Gathering Co.
Total Peaking Services LLC
TransColorado Gas Transmission
    Company
Trans-Union Interstate Pipeline LP
Tuscarora Gas Transmission Company

Vector Pipeline LP
Venice Gathering System LLC
Washington Natural Gas Company
Western Gas Interstate Company
Western Transmission Corporation
Westgas Interstate Inc.
West Texas Gas Inc.
Wyoming Interstate Company Ltd
Young Gas Storage Company Ltd

## Predominantly Offshore Gas Pipelines

Black Marlin Pipeline Co.
Chandeleur Pipeline Co.
Dauphin Island Gathering Partners
Destin Pipeline Co. LLC
Discovery Gas Transmission LLC
Enbridge Pipelines (UTOS) LLC
Garden Banks Gas Pipeline LLC
Gulfstream Natural Gas System LLC
High Island Offshore System LLC
Mississippi Gas Canyon Pipeline LLC
Nautilus Pipeline Co. LLC
Pacific Interstate Offshore Company
Panther Interstate Pipeline Energy LLC
Pacific Offshore Pipeline Company
Sea Robin Pipeline Co.
Shell Offshore Inc.
Stingray Pipeline Co. LLC
Venice Gathering System LLC

## LNG (Liquefied Natural Gas) Import/Export Terminals

Distrigas Of Massachusetts LLC
Dominion Cove Point LNG LP
Gulf Gateway Deepwater Port
Keyspan LNG LP (Alng)
Phillips Alaska Natural Gas Corporation and Marathon Oil Company
Southern LNG Inc.
Trunkline LNG Company LLC

## Hinshaw Pipelines

Although these pipelines convey gas in interstate commerce, they are subject to state, not Natural Gas Act, regulation.
Atlanta Gas Light Company
Cobra Pipeline Company Ltd
East Ohio Gas Company
Empire State pipeline
Michigan Consolidated Gas Company
Nornew Energy Supply Inc.
Northern Illinois Gas Company (Nicor Gas)
Pacific Gas and Electric Company

## South American Gas Pipelines

Camisea Pipeline – Peru
Cruz del Sur pipeline
ECOPETROL pipelines – Colombia
Gas Andes pipeline – Chile
Gas Atacama pipeline – Chile
Gasbol pipeline – Brazil
Gasoriente pipeline – Colombia
GASUN
Gran Gasoducto del Sur
OCP Pipeline – Ecuador GASENE
Paraná–Uruguayana pipeline
Recope Pipelines – Costa Rica
SOTE Pipeline – Ecuador
TGI Pipeline Network – Colombia
TGN Pipeline Network – Argentina
TGS Pipeline Network – Argentina
Trans-Caribbean pipeline (planned)
Trans-Isthmian pipeline – Panama
Urucu–Manaus pipeline
Yabog pipeline

## Oceania Gas Pipelines

Dampier to Bunbury natural gas pipeline
SEAgas pipeline

# 4. Maps of Pipelines Referred to in the Text

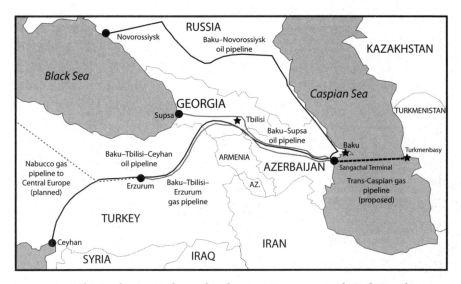

(a) Four Oil Pipelines: Baku–Chechnya–Novorossiysk Oil Pipeline; Baku–Supsa Oil Pipeline; Baku–Tbilisi–Erzurum Oil Pipeline; and Baku–Tbilisi–Ceyhan Oil Pipeline (see pp.130–1, 145)

(b) **Trans-Balkan Oil Pipeline** (see p.131)

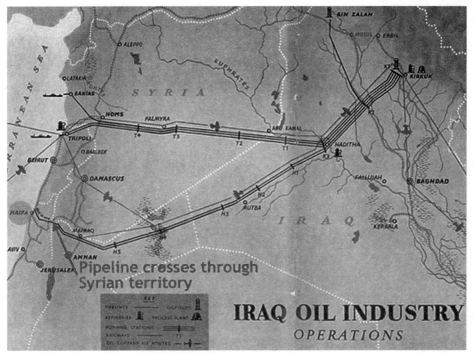

(c) A Historical Map of Proposed Reconstruction of Kirkuk–Haifa Oil
Pipeline (see p.142)

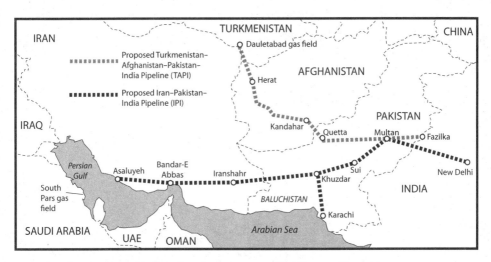

(d) Trans-Afghan Gas Pipeline (TAP) or Turkmenistan–Afghanistan–
Pakistan–India Gas Pipeline (TAPI); and Iran–Pakistan–India (IPI)
Gas Pipeline (see pp.132, 134, 138–9, 148, 163)

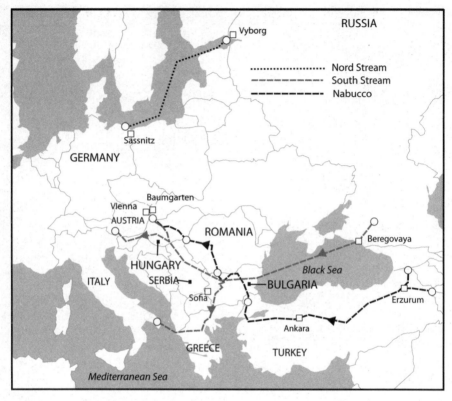

(e) **Planned Routes of Russian Nord Stream (top) and South Stream (middle) Gas Pipelines and US Nabucco Gas Pipeline (bottom)**
(see p.146)

# List of Websites Supporting Data/Maps

# A World State in Waiting

The United Nations Millennium Summit, the largest gathering in history of world leaders, brought together 149 Heads of State and Government and high-ranking officials from over 40 other countries. (New York, September 6, 2000. United Nations Photo by Terry Deglau / Eastman Kodak.)

**Front row, from left:**
1. Olusegun Obasanjo, President of Nigeria
2. Alyaksandr Lukashenka, President of Belarus
3. Ali Abul Ragheb, Prime Minister of Jordan
4. King Abdullah II Bin Al Hussein of Jordan
5. Heydar Alirza ogly Aliyev, President of Azerbaijan
6. Robertt S. Kocharian, Presient of Armenia
7. Tony Blair, Prime Minister of the UK
8. Jacques Chirac, President of France
9. William J. Clinton, President of the United States
10. Taija Halonen, President of Finland
11. Kofi Annan, Secretary-General of the United Nations
12. Sam Nujoma, President of Namibia
13. Jiang Zemin, President of China
14. Vladimir V. Putin, President of the Russian Federation
15. Fernando de la Rua, President of Argentina
16. Thomas Klestil, President of Austria
17. Sir Orville Turnquest, Governor General of the Bahamas
18. King Harald V of Norway
19. Jens Stoltenberg, Prime Minister of Norway
20. Kim Dae-jung, President of the Republic of Korea
21. K. H. Abdurrahman Wahid, President of Indonesia

**Second row:**
22. Denis Sassou Nguesso, President of the Congo
23. Andres Pastrana Arango, President of Colombia
24. Antonio Mascarenhas Monteiro, President of Cape Verde
25. Sultan Hassanal Bolkiah Muizznddin Waddaulah of Brunei
26. Festus G. Mogae, President of Botswana
27. Flt-Lt Jerry John Rawlings, President of Ghana
28. Gerhard Schroeder, Federal Chancellor of Germany
29. Harri Uolkeri, President, 55th session of the General Assembly
30. Louise Frechette, Deputy Secretary-General of the UN
31. Theo-Ben Guirab, President of the 54th session of GS
32. Yoshiro Mori, Prime Minister of Japan
33. Fidel Castro Ruz, President of Cuba
34. Alija Izetbegovic, Chairman of the Presidency of Bosnia and Herzegovina
35. Peter Stoyanov, President of Bulgaria
36. Thabo Mbeki, President of South Africa
37. Ricardo Lagos Escobar, President of Chile
38. Colonel Azali Assoumani, President of Comoros

**Third row:**
39. Eduard A Shevardnadze, President of Georgia
40. El Hadj Omar Bongo, President of Gabon
41. Teodore Obiang Nguema Mbasogo, President of Equatorial Guinea
42. Gustavo Noboa Bejarano, President of Ecuador
43. Ismail Oman Guelleh, President of Djibouti
44. Jean Chretien, Prime Minister of Canada
45. Glafcos Clerides, President of Cyprus
46. Miguel Angel Rodriguez, President of Costa Rica

47. Crown Prince Abdullah Bin Abdul Aziz Al-Saud of Saudi Arabia
48. Crown Prince Moulay Rachid of Morocco
49. Marco Antonio de Oliveira Maciel, Vice-President of Brazil
50. Stjepan Mesic, President of Croatia
51. Vaclav Havel, President of the Czech Republic
52. Giuliano Amato, Prime Minister of Italy
53. Hipolito Mejia Dominguez, President, the Dominican Republic
54. Francisco Guillermo Flores Perez, President of El Salvador
55. Isaias Afwerki, President of Eritrea
56. Colonel Yahya A.J.J. Jammeh, President of the Gambia
57. Alfonso Portillo Cabrera, President of Guatemala

**Fourth row:**
58. Joaquim Alberto Chissano, President of Mozambique
59. Leo A. Falcam, President, Federated States of Micronesia
60. Maaouya Ould Sid' Ahmed Taya, President of Mauritania
61. Alpha Oumar Konare, President of Mali
62. Bakili Muluzi, President of Malawi
63. Valdas Adamkus, President of Lithuania
64. Teburoro Tito, President of Kiribati
65. Nursultan A. Nazarbaev, President of Kazakhstan
66. Carlos Roberto Flores Facusse, President of Honduras
67. Bharrat Jagdeo, President of Guyana
68. Bernard Dowiyogo, President of Nauru
69. Rene Preval, President of Haiti
70. Ferenc Madi, President of Hungary
71. Daniel Toroitich arap Moi, President of Kenya
72. Vaira Vlke Freiberga, President of Latvia
73. Didier Ratsiraka, President of Madagascar
74. Maumoon Abdul Gayoom, President of the Maldives
75. Kessai Note, President of the Marshall Islands
76. Ernesto Zedillo, President of Mexico
77. Natsagiyn Bagabandi, President of Mongolia

**Fifth row:**
78. Boris Trajkovski, President of Macedonia
79. General Omer Hassan Ahmed Al-Bashir, President, Sudan
80. Milan Kucan, President of Slovenia
81. Abdoulaye Wade, President of Senegal
82. Miguel dos Anjos da Cunha Lisboa Trovoada, President of São Tomé and Principe
83. Charles Antrobus, Governor-General of Saint Vincent and the Grenadines
84. Emil Constantineseu, President of Romania
85. Sheik Hamad bin Khalifa Al-Thani, Amir of Qatar
86. Joseph E. Estrada, President of the Philippines
87. Arnoldo Aleman Lacayo, President of Nicaragua
88. King Mswati III of Swaziland
89. Aleksander Kwasniewski, President of Poland
90. Petru Lucinschi, President of Moldova
91. Maria Dornenica Michelotti, Captain Regent of San Marino
92. Gian Marco Marcucci, Captain Regent of San Marino
93. Alhaji Ahmad Tejan Kabban, President of Sierra Leone

94. Abdikassim Salad Hassan, President of Somalia
95. Emomali Rakhmonov, President of Tajikistan
96. General Gnassingbe Eyadema, President of Togo

**Sixth row:**

97. Lester B. Bird, Prime Minister of Antigua and Barbuda
98. Julio Cesar Franco, Vice-President of Paraguay
99. Sayyed Faisul Bin Ali Bin Faisul Al-Said, Minister for National Heritage and Culture of Oman
100. Abdelaziz Boutefika, President of Algeria
101. Burhanuddin Rabbani, President of Afghanistan
102. Tran Duc Luong, President of Vietnam
103. Jorge Batlle Ibanez, President of Uruguay
104. John Howard, Prime Minister of Australia
105. Zine El Abidine Ben Ali, President of Tunisia
106. Sheikh Hamad Bin Mohammad Al-Sharqi, Vice-President of United Arab Emirates
107. Ahmet Necdet Sezer, President of Turkey
108. Leonid D. Kuchma, President of Ukraine
109. Hugo Chavez Frias, President of Venezuela
110. Field Marshal Ali Abdullah Saleh, President of Yemen
111. Robert G. Mugabe, President of Zimbabwe
112. Rexhep Meidani, President of Albania
113. Crown Prince Albert of Monaco
114. Arturo Vallarino, First Vice-President of Panama
115. Jules Rattankoemar Ajodhia, Vice-President of Suriname

**Seventh row:**

116. David Oddsson, Prime Minister of Iceland
117. Keith C. Mitchell, Prime Minister of Grenada
118. Meles Zenawi, Prime Minister of Ethiopia
119. Nagoum Yamassoum, Prime Minister of Chad
120. Yeshey Zimba, Head of Government of Bhutan
121. Guy Verhofstadt, Prime Minister of Belgium
122. Sheikh Mohammed Bin Mubarak Al-Khalifa, Foreign Minister of Bahrain
123. Edward Fenech Adaini, Prime Minister of Malta
124. Yasser Arafat, President of the Palestinian Authority
125. Percival James Patterson, Prime Minister of Jamaica
126. Angelo Cardinal Sodano, Prime Minister of the Holy See
127. Ehud Barak, Prime Minister of Israel
128. Sheikh Hasina, Prime Minister of Bangladesh
129. Said Musa, Prime Minister of Belize
130. Amre Moussa, Foreign Minister of Egypt
131. Mart Siimann, Prime Minister of Estonia
132. Costas Simitis, Prime Minister of Greece
133. Lamine Sidime, Prime Minister of Guinea
134. Bertie Ahern, Prime Minister of Ireland

**Eighth row:**

135. Barak T. Sope Maautamate, Prime Minister of Vanuatu
136. Basdeo Panday, Prime Minister of Trinidad and Tobago
137. Goran Persson, Prime Minister of Sweden
138. Mikulas Dzurinda, Prime Minister of Slovakia
139. Denzil Douglas, Prime Minister of Saint Kitts and Nevis
140. Antonio Guterres, Prime Minister of Portugal
141. General Pervez Musharraf, Chief Executive of Pakistan
142. Wim Kok, Prime Minister of the Netherlands
143. Pakalitha Bethuel Mosisili, Prime Minister of Lesotho
144. Marc Forne Molne, Chief of Government of Andorra
145. Mario Frick, Prime Minister of Liechtenstein
146. Girija Prasad Koirala, Prime Minister of Nepal
147. Helen Clark, Prime Minister of New Zealand
148. Sir Mekere Morauta, Prime Minister of Papua New Guinea
149. Kenny D. Anthony, Prime Minister of Saint Lucia
150. Goh Chok Tong, Prime Minister of Singapore
151. Jose Maria Aznar, President of the Government of Spain
152. Prince Ulukalala Lavaka Ata, Prime Minister of Tonga
153. Ionatana Ionatana, Prime Minister of Tuvalu

**Ninth row:**

154. Lakshman Kadirgamar, Foreign Minister, Sri Lanka
155. Sabo Nassirou, Foreign Minister of Niger
156. Datuk Seri Syed Hamid Albar, Foreign Minister, Malaysia
157. Monie R. Captan, Foreign Minister of Liberia
158. Sheikh Sabah Al-Ahmad Al-Jaber Al-Sabah, Foreign Minister of Kuwait
159. Claude Morel, Representative of the Seychelles
160. Yerodia Abdoulaye Ndombasi, Foreign Minister of Democratic Republic of the Congo
161. Marcel Metefara, Foreign Minister of Central African Republic
162. Selim Tadmoury, Permanent Representative of Lebanon
163. Joao Bernardo de Miranda, Foreign Minister of Angola
164. Jakaya Mrisho Kikwete, Foreign Minister of United Republic of Tanzania
165. Somsavat Lengsavad, Deputy Prime Minister and Minister for Foreign Affairs of Lao People's Democratic Republic
166. Surin Pitsuwan, Foreign Minister of Thailand
167. Billie Miller, Deputy Prime Minister of Barbados
168. Farouk Al-Shara', Foreign Minister of Syria
169. Iaia Djalo, Foreign Minister of Guinea-Bissau
170. Michel Kafando, Representative of Burkina Faso
171. Tariq Aziz, Deputy Prime Minister of Iraq
172. Anund P. Neewoor, Representative of Mauritius
173. Jean-Claude Juncker, Prime Minister of Luxembourg
174. Tuiloma Neroni Slade, Representative of Samoa
175. Severin Ntahomvukiye, Foreign Minister of Burundi
176. Charles Providence Gomis, Foreign Minister of Côte d'Ivoire
177. Jeremiah Mancle, Charge d'Affaires, Solomon Islands
178. Murathek C. Imanaliev, Foreign Minister of Kyrgyzstan
179. Abdurrahman Mohamed Shalghem, Foreign Minister, Libya
180. Win Aung, Foreign Minister of Myanmar
181. Baryr Berdyev, Foreign Minister of Turkmenistan

# Notes and Sources

### Epigraph
1. Wendell L. Willkie, *One World*, p.165.

### Prologue
1. The traditional seven seas are the Mediterranean Sea (including the Tyrrhenian and Aegean), the Adriatic Sea, the Black Sea, the Red Sea, the Arabian Sea, the Persian Gulf, and the Caspian Sea. The seven continents are Asia, Africa, North America, South America, Antarctica, Europe, and Australia. (To arrive at seven rather than five, North and South America have to be separated and Antarctica included.)
2. See http://www.statueofliberty.org/Fun_Facts.html.
3. See http://en.wikipedia.org/wiki/Colossus_of_rhodes.
4. See http://en.wikipedia.org/wiki/Colossus_of_rhodes.
5. *Anthologia Graeca*, 4, p.171, ed. Hermann Beckby, Munich, 1957.
6. Some thought has been given as to whether the omission of the comma was a bronze-worker's error or a deliberate mistake. Emma Lazarus was addressing the ancient lands of Europe, saying in effect, "You can keep your pomp but give America your poor." The omission of the comma creates an imperative that may address the people of Europe, saying in effect, "You can keep your ancient lands and pomp, but give America your poor." It has been suggested that Liberty is addressing the American people and is urging an imperialistic destiny: "Keep (i.e. hang on to) the ancient lands that you have occupied." This is unconvincing as America had very few colonial possessions before 1883, about which there was little "storied pomp." The missing comma is likely to be an error rather than a deliberate change of meaning.
7. James Truslow Adams, *The Epic of America*, p.404.
8. Donald Rumsfeld, interview with *Al-Jazeera* TV, February 25, 2003, press release, Department of Defense.
http://www.defense.gov/transcripts/transcript.aspx?transcriptid=1946
9. See www.empirenotes.org.
10. President George W. Bush speaking at a press conference held at the White House on April 13, 2004,
http://www.nytimes.com/2004/04/13/politics/13CND-BTEX.html.
11. See www.planetware.com/hillerod/gribskov-dk-z-hilg.htm.
12. Remarks by President Obama to the UN General Assembly in New York on September 23, 2009,
http://www.whitehouse.gov/the_press_office/Remarks-by-the-President-to-the-United-Nations-General-Assembly.

## Chapter 1: Liberty's Colonial Empire

1. See http://www.historynet.com/spanish-american-war-raid-on-cienfuegos.htm.
2. Joy Hakim, *History of US: Book Eight, An Age of Extremes*.
3. *The World of 1898: The Spanish–American War*, Hispanic Division, Library of Congress. See http://www.loc.gov/rr/hispanic/1898/.
4. Leslie W. Walker, 'Guam's Seizure by the United States in 1898.' *The Pacific Historical Review*, University of California Press, 14 (1) pp.1–12. See http://www.jstor.org/stable/3634509.
5. 'Chronology of Puerto Rico in the Spanish–American War' in *The World of 1898: The Spanish-American War*, Hispanic Division, Library of Congress. See http://www.loc.gov/rr/hispanic/1898/chronpr.html.
6. See http://www.census.gov/population/www/proas/pr_ia_hist.html.
7. Fred Harrington, article in *The Mississippi Valley Historical Review*, vol. 22, No.2 (Sep 1935), pp.211–30. Originally published in David Claypoole's American *Daily Advertiser* on September 19, 1796: 'The Address of General Washington to the People of the United States on his Declining of the Presidency of the United States,' the letter was almost immediately reprinted in newspapers across the country and later in a pamphlet form. The work was later named a 'Farewell Address,' as it was Washington's valedictory after 45 years of service to the new republic, first during the Revolution as commander-in-chief of the Continental Army and later as the nation's first president.
8. See http://www.msc.edu.ph/centennial/benevolent.html.
9. *San Francisco Call*, April 15, 1899; quoted in Stuart Creighton Miller, *Benevolent Assimilation*, p.89.
10. Miller, *op. cit.*, p.220.
11. Quoted in Miller, *op. cit.*, p.207.
12. Mark Twain, Letter to the Editor, *New York Herald*, October 15, 1900.
13. Max Boot 'American Imperialism? No Need to Run Away from the Label.' USA Today, http://www.cfr.org/publication.html?id=5934.
14. Max Boot, 'Neither New nor Nefarious: The Liberal Empire Strikes Back.' *Current History* 102 (667). http://www.mtholyoke.edu/acad/intrel/bush/boot.htm.
15. Samuel Flagg Benis, *A Diplomatic History of the United States*; quoted in Miller, *op. cit.*, p.3.
16. Samuel E. Morrison and Henry Steele Commager, *The Growth of the American Republic*, ii, p.406.
17. For the early 20th-century interventions, see Amaury de Riencourt, *The American Empire*, p.29.
18. De Riencourt, *op. cit.*, pp.29–30.

## Chapter 2: Liberty's Interrupted Isolation: Interventions in Europe

1. Nicholas Hagger, *The Secret Founding of America*, pp.136–9.
2. Niall Ferguson, *Colossus: The Rise and Fall of the American Empire*, pp.62, 318.
3. George Black, *The Good Neighbor*, p.42.
4. Roland Hugins, *The Possible Peace*, 1916 edition, p.170. See http://books.google.com/books?id=lmf2XYVnSeQC&printsec=frontcover&dq=roland+hugins&cd=1#v=onepage&q=&f=false.
5. Quoted in Stanley Karnow, *Vietnam: A History*; and in Ferguson, *op. cit.*, pp.65–6.
6. Until recently these figures were available on the United States Department of Veteran Affairs website, http://www1.va.gov/vetdata/.


## Chapter 3: Liberty's Imperial Hegemony

1. See http://modern-us-history.suite101.com/article.cfm/churchill-warns-of-iron-curtain-in-europe.
2. Michael Kort, *The Colombia Guide to the Cold War*, p.3.
3. For the spread of the Soviet empire, see Brian Crozier, *Soviet Imperialism, How to Contain It*, London: Temple Smith, 1978.
4. John Spanier, *The Truman–MacArthur Controversy and the Korean War*.
5. Mathew Aid, *The Secret Sentry: The Untold History of the National Security Agency*.
6. Norman Livergood, 'The New US–British Oil Imperialism': http://www.hermes-press.com/impintro1.htm.
7. Christine Toomey, 'Revealed: Pact's Blitzkrieg Plan to Invade West,' *Sunday Times*, March 28, 1993.
8. Ronald Reagan, 'Remarks at the Brandenburg Gate.' Ronald Reagan Presidential Foundation, see http://www.reagan.utexas.edu/archives/speeches/1987/061287d.htm. See also Dinesh D'Souza, 'How Reagan Won the Cold War,' *National Review*, November 24, 1997; adapted from D'Souza's book *Ronald Reagan: How an Ordinary Man Became an Extraordinary Leader*.
9. Margaret Thatcher, speaking at the Clare Boothe Luce Lecture, Washington D.C. on September 23, 1991.
10. See Dinesh D'Souza, 'How Reagan Won the Cold War.' http://www.nationalreview.com/flashback/dsouza200406061619.asp.
11. Craig Calhoun, 'Cold War.' chapter in *Dictionary of the Social Sciences*, Oxford University Press, 2002. See also http://social.jrank.org/pages/1660/Cold-War.html.
12. Walter LaFeber in *The Reader's Companion to American History*, ed. Eric Fonar and John Arthur Garraty, p.1.

## Chapter 4: Liberty's Federal Unification

1. Hagger, *The Secret Founding of America*.
2. Cited in Edwin B. Bronner, *William Penn's 'Holy Experiment': The Founding of Pennsylvania, 1681–1701*, p.6; and quoted in Frank Lambert, *The Founding Fathers and the Place of Religion in America*, pp.100–2.
3. Arthur Quinn, *A New World: An Epic of Colonial America from the Founding of Jamestown to the Fall of Quebec*, p.339.
4. Hagger, *The Secret Founding of America*, ch.4.
5. N.B. Cockburn, *The Bacon Shakespeare Question: The Baconian Theory Made Sane*, p.242.
6. For fuller details see Hagger, *The Secret Founding of America*, pp.89–100.
7. See Hagger, *The Secret History of the West*, pp.80–1.
8. *The letters of John Chamberlain*, ed. N.E. McClure.
9. Charlotte C. Stopes, *The Life of Henry, Third Earl of Southampton*, pp.361–2.
10. See Hagger, *The Secret History of the West*, ch.3.
11. Anderson's *Constitution* is reproduced in Hagger, *The Secret Founding of America*, pp.225–30.
12. Michael Baigent and Richard Leigh, *The Temple and The Lodge*, pp.201–3.
13. The Albany Plan of Union is reproduced in Hagger, *The Secret Founding of America*, pp.231–4.
14. John Daniel, *Scarlet and the Beast*, vol. I, p.166; and Hagger, *The Secret History of the West*, pp.234–40.
15. Michael Baigent, Richard Leigh and Henry Lincoln, *The Holy Blood and The Holy Grail*, p.149.
16. William T. Still, *New World Order: The Ancient Plan of Secret Societies*, p.61; see Hagger, *The Secret Founding of America*, p.301, n.31 for fuller details.
17. Hagger, *The Secret Founding of America*, pp.136–40.
18. Henry C. Clausen, *Masons Who Helped Shape Our Nation*, p.82.
19. For a picture of the Freemasonic rising sun, see Richard B. Morris, *The Framing of the Federal Constitution, Handbook 103*, pp.10–11.
20. Daniel, *op. cit.*, p.296. See also http://spillspace.com/2009/capital-geometry/.
21. For fuller details see Hagger, *The Secret Founding of America*, pp.164–5.

## Chapter 5: Liberty's Western Empire: Continental Expansion Westward

1. Thomas Jefferson, letter to George Rogers Clark, December 25, 1780, in *The Papers of Thomas Jefferson*, iv, pp.237–8. Compare Jefferson's letter to Madison, April 27, 1809, in James Morton Smith, ed., *The Republic of Letters: The Correspondence between Thomas Jefferson and James Madison, 1776–1826*, vol. iii, p.1586, where he writes of having 'such an empire for liberty as she has never surveyed since the creation.'
2. James Truslow Adams, *The Epic of America*, pp.114–15.
3. Richard Sylla, 'Shaping the US Financial System, 1690–1913: The Dominant

Role of Public Finance' in Richard Tilly and Gabriel Tortella, eds., *The States, The Financial System and Economic Modernization*, Cambridge, 1999, pp.259ff; quoted in Niall Ferguson, *Colossus, The Rise and Fall of the American Empire*, p.37.

4. See http://www.city-data.com/states/Michigan-Population.html.
5. John L. O'Sullivan, 'Annexation,' *United States Magazine and Democratic Review*, 17(1) (July–August 1845): 5–10; see http://web.grinnell.edu/courses/HIS/f01/HIS202-01/Documents/Osullivan.html.
6. Howard Zinn, *A People's History of the United States 1492–Present*, p.151.
7. Trevor B. McCrisken, 'Exceptionalism: Manifest Destiny,' in *Encyclopaedia of American Foreign Policy*, vol. 2, p.68.
8. See http://www.gseis.ucla.edu/courses/ed253a/american-exceptionalism.htm.
9. Francis Parkman, *The Conspiracy of Pontiac* (1851); quoted in Philip Fisher, *Hard Facts: Setting and Form in the American Novel*, p.26.
10. See Russell Thornton, *American Indian Holocaust*, pp.48–9.
11. Dana Priest, *The Mission: Waging War and Keeping Peace with America's Military*, p.70.
12. For fuller details see Hagger, *The Secret Founding of America*, pp.180–4.
13. Daniel, *op. cit.*, p.542; James Perloff, *The Shadows of Power, The Council on Foreign Relations and the American Decline*, p31.

## Chapter 6: Liberty's Supremacy: Superpowerdom and World Empire

1. See www.globalsecurity.org/military/world/spending.htm.
2. Robert M. Gates, 'A Balanced Strategy: Reprogramming the Pentagon for a New Age,' in www.foreignaffairs.com/articles/63717/robert-m-gates/a-balanced-strategy; and *Weighing the US Navy Defense & Security Analysis*, vol. 17, Issue 3, December 2001, pp.259–65.
3. Chalmers Johnson, reference to 'the NATO Watch Committee, the International Network for the Abolition of Foreign Military Bases,' see http://www.globalpolicy.org/component/content/article/153/26325.html.
4. See http://top-10-list.org/2010/01/11/te-upcoming-world-economies/ and http://www.economywatch.com/economies-in-top/
5. See Huntington, 'The Lonely Superpower'; http://www.univercidade.br/uc/cursos/graduacao/ri/pdf/textosesp/ForeignAffairsTheLonely.pdf.
6. Dr John Coleman, *Diplomacy by Deception*, p.47.
7. See http://www.firethistime.org/contemptchrono.htm.
8. See http://www.firethistime.org/contemptchrono.htm.
9. Coleman, *op. cit.*, p.49.
10. Coleman, *op. cit.*, p.49.
11. Coleman, *op. cit.*, pp.49–50.

12. Coleman, *op. cit.*, p.50.

13. Coleman, *op. cit.*, p.51.

14. See http://www.firethistime.org/contempchrono.htm for all the figures. The Soviet Union received $1b from Saudi Arabia and $4b in loans in emergency aid from Saudi Arabia, Kuwait and UAE. China received a loan of $140m. The US paid the UN $187m, half the debt it owed the UN in unpaid dues. See the same website for the 52–47 vote and the number of men.

15. See http://news.bbc.co.uk/onthisday/hi/dates/stories/february/28/newsid_2515000/2515289.stm.

16. Peter L. Bergen, *Holy War, Inc. Inside the Secret World of Osama bin Laden*, pp.49–50.

17. See http://www.telegraph.co.uk/news/main.jhtml?xml=/news/2001/12/02/wkand02.xml and http://www.telegraph.co.uk/news/worldnews/asia/afghanistan/1364045/Bin-Laden-paid-68m-for-loyalty-of-Taliban.html.

18. Simon Reeve, *The New Jackals: Osama bin Laden and the Future of Terrorism*, extracted in the British press, e.g. *News of the World*, September 16, 2001. See also Adam Robinson, *Bin Laden: Behind the Mask of Terror*.

19. Osama bin Laden, October 21, 2001, in *Messages to the World: The Statements of Osama bin Laden*, ed. Bruce Lawrence, p.121; letter from al-Zawahiri (bin Laden's deputy) to al-Zarqawi, July 9, 2005, released by the US Office of the Director of National Intelligence on October 11, 2005.

20. *Messages to the World: The Statements of Osama bin Laden, op. cit.*, pp.23–30.

21. For the list, see the Appendix, pp.242–50, which can also be found in Hagger, *Armageddon*, pp.582–95.

22. Yossef Bodansky, *Bin Laden, The Man who Declared War on America*, pp.329–31.

23. See http://www.guardian.co.uk/news/datablog/2009/sep/06/nuclear-weapons-world-us-north-korea-russia-iran. The USSR high for nuclear weapons was in 1985 (45,000). See Hagger, *The World Government*, ch.6 for more detailed coverage. As regards the number of US nuclear weapons, in early May 2010 the US Secretary of State Hillary Clinton declassified the size of the US nuclear arsenal to galvanize efforts to rid the world of nuclear weapons. She revealed that the Pentagon's figures show that the US stockpile consisted of 5,113 nuclear warheads and 'several thousand' more retired warheads awaiting dismantling.

24. Paul L. Williams, *The Al Qaeda Connection*, p.99.

25. *Washington Post*, December 23, 2001.

26. Several nations by October 7, 2001; 18 nations by December 20, 2001; later swelled to 53 contributing nations.

27. Richard Miniter, *Shadow War, The Untold Story of How America Is Winning the War on Terror*, p.20.

28. Miniter, *op. cit.*, pp.20–2. An Icelandic documentary film shown in New York in 2010, *Feathered Cocaine*, claimed that bin Laden had been living in a guarded compound north of Tehran with his wife, several children, and grandchildren

since 2003, protected by the Iranian regime. See report 'Bin Laden 'is living in luxury in Tehran'' in London *Daily Mail*, May 6, 2010.

29. *Washington Post*, see http://www.washingtonpost.com/wp-srv/inatl/longterm/iraq/timeline/062793.htm. See also http://everything2.com/title/The+plot+to+kill+George+Bush.

30. See http://www.rense.com/general67/comdt.htm.

31. The owner of a Chinese bank who claims to have stumbled across this on a computer screen, in direct conversation with the author.

32. Richard A. Clarke, *Against All Enemies*, p.32.

33. Stephen Hayes, *The Connection*, p.83.

34. See http://georgewbush-whitehouse.archives.gov/nsc/nss/2006/sectionV.html.

35. See http://transcripts.cnn.com/2002/ALLPOLITICS/01/29/bush.speech.txt/.

36. See http://georgewbush-whitehouse.archives.gov/news/releases/2001/09/20010920-8.html.

37. Alireza Jafarzadeh, *The Iran Threat*, pp.113–14.

38. See http://abcnews.go.com/Blotter/IraqCoverage/story?id=1692347&page=1.

39. London *Sunday Times*, January 24, 2010.

40. See http://www.channel4.com/news/articles/world/asia_pacific/exclusive+iran+supplies+weapons+to+taliban/3582967.

41. London *Sunday Times*, March 21, 2010, p.26, 'Iran teaches Taliban art of ambush.'

42. London *Daily Telegraph*, April 1, 2010, 'Anger as Iran tries to broker Shia coalition to rule Iraq.'

43. *Joint Vision, 2020, America's Military – Preparing for Tomorrow*, US Department of Defense.
See http://www.dtic.mil/doctrine/jel/jfq_pubs/1225.pdf and http://www.defense.gov/news/newsarticle.aspx?id=45289.

44. F. William Engdahl, *Full Spectrum Dominance: Totalitarian Democracy in the New World Order*, p.vii.

45. See http://www.globalresearch.ca/index.php?context=va&aid=5564 and http://sirenschronicles.com/2009/05/14/how-many-military-bases-do-we-have-around-the-world/ and reference to Chalmers Johnson and 'the NATO Watch Committee, the International Network for the Abolition of Foreign Military Bases'; see also *Base Structure Report (A Summary of DoD's Real Property Inventory)*, US Department of Defense, Office of the Deputy Under Secretary of Defense (Installations & Environment) Fiscal Year 2003 baseline; quoted in 'Military of the United States,' Wikipedia, http://en.wikipedia.org/wiki/Military_of_the_United_States: 'As of 2005, the US occupied over 700 military bases in over 36 countries worldwide.' See also http://www.globalpolicy.org/component/content/article/153/26325.html.

46. Juan Gelman, 'Terratenientes.' *Rebelion*, February 26, 2007, see http://www.rebelion.org/noticia.php?id-47353.

47. Joseph Curl, 'US Eyes Cuts at Germany, S. Korea Bases,' *Washington Times*, February 12, 2003; quoted in Ferguson, *op. cit.*, p.16.

48. *Statistical Abstract of the United States*, 2002, table 495; quoted in Ferguson, *op. cit.* p.16.

49. Hugh d'Andrade and Bob Wing's 2002 Map 1 entitled 'US Military Troops and Bases Around the World: The Cost of "Permanent War."' *War Times*, Issue 5, p.5, September 2, 2005. See http://www.globalresearch.ca/index.php?context=va&aid=5564.

50. See http://www.globalpolicy.org/component/content/article/153/26325.html.

51. Robert Kagan, *The Return of History and the End of Dreams*, p.91.

52. See http://www.airforce-magazine.com/MagazineArchive/Magazine%20Documents/2009/May%202009/0509facts_fig.pdf.

53. See http://www.globalresearch.ca/index.php?context=va&aid=5564.

54. *New York Times*, February 26, 2003; quoted in Ferguson, *op. cit.*, p.16.

55. Ferguson, *op. cit.*, p.16.

56. See http://www.brookings.edu/~/media/Files/Programs/FP/afghanistan%20index/index.pdf, p.10, figure 1.10.

57. See http://www.huffingtonpost.com/2009/02/24/us-troops-to-leave-iraq-b_n_169582.html and http://www.cnn.com/2009/POLITICS/02/27/obama.troops/index.html.

58. See www.democraticunderground.com.

59. Gregg Easterbrook, 'America Power Moves Beyond the Mere Super,' *New York Times*, April 27, 2003; quoted in Ferguson, *op. cit.*, p.16.

60. Paul Kennedy, 'Power and Terror,' London *Financial Times*, September 3, 2002; quoted in Ferguson *op. cit.*, p.16.

61. 'Summary of the Annual Review of Developments in Globalization and Regional Integration in the Countries of the ESCWA Region.' See http://www.escwa.un.org/information/publications/edit/upload/grid-02-2.pdf.

62. See http://globalization.kof.ethz.ch/. See also http://www.investinflanders.com/en/news_details/default.aspx?id=34270fc1-752e-4a25-87a2-d5644d4a6010&news=Belgium+world's+most+globalized+country&parent=af2ecb9b-ab1b-42d4-acd9-7e377bcd80b8 and http://www.eu-digest.com/2009/02/flanders-investment-and-trade-belgium.html.

63. See http://www.atkearney.com/index.php/Publications/globalization-index.html.

64. See https://www.cia.gov/library/publications/the-world-factbook/rankorder/2078rank.html?countryName=United%20States&countryCode=us&regionCode=na&rank=4#us.

65. See http://www.answerbag.com/q_view/53199:http://

antrhow.palomar.edu/language/language_1.htm.

66. See http://www.reuters.com/article/ousiv/idUSTRE52966Z20090310.
67. See 'A Global Retreat as Economies Dry Up.'
http://www.washingtonpost.com/wp-dyn/content/article/
2009/03/04/AR2009030404221.html.
Also see 'Economic Crisis Poses Threat to Global Stability.'
http://www.npr.org/templates/story/story.php?storyId=100781975.

## Chapter 7: Liberty's Commercial *Élites* Before 1989: The Birth of the New World Order

1. Derek Wilson, *Rothschild: A Story of Wealth and Power*, pp.9–33; Frederic Morton, *The Rothschilds, A Family Portrait*, pp.17–36; Count Egon Caesar Corti, *The Rise of the House of Rothschild*, pp.1–26; George Armstrong, *The Rothschild Money Trust*, pp.21–2.
2. George Armstrong, *The Rothschild Money Trust*, p.21; Wilson, *op. cit.*, p.32.
3. Corti, *op. cit.*, p.402; Morton, *op. cit.*, p.17.
4. For full details, see Hagger, *The Secret History of the West*, ch.5.
5. For full details, see Hagger, *The Secret History of the West*, ch.5.
6. Armstrong, *op. cit.*, p.24.
7. Niall Ferguson, *The World's Banker: The History of the House of Rothschild*, pp.103–5.
8. Armstrong, *op. cit.*, p.35.
9. Morton, *op. cit.*, pp.150–2.
10. For full details, see Hagger, *The Syndicate*, ch.2, note 36 (pp.343–9).
11. Emanuel M. Josephson, *The 'Federal' Reserve Conspiracy and Rockefeller*, p.75.
12. Emanuel M. Josephson, *The Truth about Rockefeller, Public Enemy No. 1*, pp.2, 54.
13. David Allen Rivera, *Final Warning: A History of the New World Order*, p.65.
14. Ron Chernow, *Titan: The Life of John D. Rockefeller Sr.*, p.557.
15. Josephson, *The 'Federal' Reserve Conspiracy and Rockefeller*, pp.74–5.
16. See Hagger, *The Secret History of the West*, pp.435–9; and Hagger, *The Secret Founding of America*, p.193.
17. For the full story, see Hagger, *The Secret History of the West*, ch.7. See also *The Syndicate*, pp.20–2.
18. See Hagger, *The Secret Founding of America*, p.193.
19. Michael Baigent, Richard Leigh, and Henry Lincoln, *The Messianic Legacy*, p.187; John Daniel, *Scarlet and the Beast*, vol. 1, pp.572–3.
20. Emanuel M. Josephson, *Rockefeller: 'Internationalist,' The Man Who Misrules the World*, pp.204–31, particularly p.212; Josephson, *The Truth about Rockefeller, Public Enemy No. 1*, pp.44, 133.
21. John Loftus and Mark Aarons, *The Secret War against the Jews*, p.168.
22. See Hagger, *The Syndicate*, pp.60–1.
23. James Perloff, *The Shadows of Power: The Council on Foreign Relations and the American Decline*, p.64; Rivera, *op. cit.*, p.93.
24. Perloff, *op. cit.*, p.64: 'It [the CFR] worked in secret and was underwritten by

the Rockefeller Foundation.'

25. Rivera, *op. cit.*, p.94.

26. For full details see Perloff, *op. cit.*, pp.111, 145, 158–9, 168; and 7, 104, 110.

27. Perloff, *op. cit.*, p.55.

28. For a poetic treatment of this decision, see Hagger, *Overlord*, book 9; and in verse drama see Hagger, *The Warlords* (published in 1995, also in *Collected Verse Plays*).

29. Des Griffin, *Descent into Slavery?*, pp.137–8. See also http://www.popmartian.com/mcelwaine/7th-coming/30_plus/The%20 Dr.%20Beter%20Audio-Letter%20INTELLIGENCE%20REPORTS/ ww2cause.txt: 'Nelson Rockefeller made sure that President Roosevelt's preparations for the war were co-ordinated precisely with the Rockefeller machinations overseas, including Hitler's build-up on the one hand and the plotting of the Pearl Harbor on the other.' For further details see Hagger, *The Syndicate*, pp.385–6.

30. Perloff, *op. cit.*, p.82.

31. Laurence H. Shoup and William Minter, *Imperial Brain Trust*, p.35.

32. Norman D. Livergood, *The New US–British Oil Imperialism*: http://www.hermes-press.com/impintro1.htm, pp.7–8.

33. Perloff, *op. cit.*, p.72.

34. The Rockefeller involvement can be gauged from David Rockefeller's involvement as secretary.

35. Townsend Hoopes and Douglas Brinkley, *FDR and the Creation of the UN*, pp.130–2. For Hiss as a Soviet spy, see Perloff, *op. cit.*, p.70; Rivera, *op. cit.*, p.166.

36. Josephson, *Rockefeller 'Internationalist.' The Man Who Misrules the World*, pp.237, 391.

37. Hoopes and Brinkley, *op. cit.*, p.176.

38. Rivera, *op. cit.*, p.93.

39. Rivera, *op. cit.*, p.166; Perloff, *op. cit.*, p.72.

40. Perloff, *op. cit.*, p.43.

41. Coleman, *op. cit.*, p.138.

42. William Jasper, *Global Tyranny...Step by Step: The United Nations and the Emerging New World Order*, p.239.

43. Stanley Weintraub, *MacArthur's War: Korea and the Undoing of an American Hero*, pp.157–8.

44. Josephson, *Rockefeller 'Internationalist.' The Man Who Misrules the World*, p.419; Josephson, *The 'Federal' Reserve Conspiracy and Rockefeller*, p.135.

45. See http://news.bbc.co.uk/onthisday/hi/dates/stories/april/11/ newsid_3708000/3708197.stm and Joseph C. Goulden, *Korea: The Untold Story of the War*.

46. Josephson, *Rockefeller 'Internationalist.' The Man Who Misrules the World*, p.24.

47. Armstrong, *op. cit.*, p.36.

48. Kennett Love, *Suez: The Twice-Fought War*, pp.557–8; and Robert Hendershot,

*Family Spats:Perception, Illusion and Sentimentality in the Anglo-American Special Relationship*. For background see http://history.sandiego.edu/gen/text/suez.html

49. *Suez 1956*: http://history.sandiego.edu/gen/text/suez.html
50. Official Report of the House of Lords, November 7, 1957; Vol. 206, c.192. See http://hansard.millbanksystems.com/commons/1957/dec/20/foreign-affairs.
51. Eisenhower, farewell address on radio and TV, January 17, 1961, Public Papers of the Presidents of the United States at http://www.presidency.ucsb.edu/ws/
52. Charles Griffin, 'New Light on Eisenhower's Farewell Address.' *Presidential Studies Quarterly*, 22 (1992), pp.469–79.
53. Livergood, *op. cit.*, pp.7–8.
54. Andrew Rotter, *The Causes of the Vietnam War*, http://www.english.illinois.edu/MAPS/vietnam/causes.htm.
55. Josephson, *The 'Federal' Reserve Conspiracy and Rockefeller*, p.292.
56. Josephson, *The 'Federal' Reserve Conspiracy and Rockefeller*, p.292.
57. Josephson, *The 'Federal' Reserve Conspiracy and Rockefeller*, p.292.
58. John Cotter, *A Study in Syncretism*, p.105.
59. Robert Gaylon Ross Sr., *Who's Who of the Elite*, pp.224–33.
60. Josephson, *The 'Federal' Reserve Conspiracy and Rockefeller*, pp.284–5, 183.
61. Josephson, *The 'Federal' Reserve Conspiracy and Rockefeller*, pp.284–5, 183. See also http://www.capital-flow-analysis.com/investment-tutorial/case_1w.html.
62. Gary Allen and Larry Abraham, *None Dare Call It Conspiracy*, p.104.
63. A seven-paragraph article republished in *The Militant*, October 14, 1996: http://www.themilitant.com/1996/6036/6036_33.html
64. Josephson, *The 'Federal' Reserve Conspiracy and Rockefeller*, pp.292–3.
65. Josephson, *The 'Federal' Reserve Conspiracy and Rockefeller*, pp.292–3.
66. Perloff, *op. cit.*, p.145; Myer Kutz, *Rockefeller Power*, p.6.
67. Livergood, *op. cit.*, p9.
68. Desmond McForan, *The World Held Hostage*, pp.30–65, 93–5, 131–40, 153–6.
69. McForan, *op. cit.*, p.xiv.
70. McForan, *op. cit.*, pp.125–6.
71. *American Free Press*, June 28, 2010, p.10.

## Chapter 8: Liberty's Commercial *Élites* After 1989: The Rise of the New World Order

1. Coleman, *op. cit.*, p.49.
2. Woodrow Wilson, address to Congress, January 8, 1918, in *Papers Relating to the Foreign Relations of the United States, 1918: Supplement I, The World War* (2 vols., Washington, DC, US Government Printing Office, 1933), I, pp.15–16. See http://www.historyplace.com/speeches/wilson-points.htm.
3. A. Ralph Epperson, *The New World Order*, p.xiv; quoting Jean-Michel

Angebert, *The Occult and the Third Reich*, p.192.

4. Nelson A. Rockefeller, *The Future of Federalism*, serialized extract, 'Federalism and Free World Order.' May 1962. See http://streitcouncil.org/uploads/PDF/F&U-%201962-%20May-%20Rockefeller-%20federalism%20and%20free%20world%20order.pdf.

5. Richard Nixon, *Foreign Affairs*, October 1967 issue.

6. Hagger, *The Syndicate*, pp.120–21, 132.

7. All these quotations about the New World Order are sourced in Hagger, *The Syndicate*, pp.121–2.

8. *Spotlight*, April 22, 1996, pp.4–5: 'Sources have told the *Spotlight* Chernomyrdin and David Rockefeller are secret partners in Russian energy combines.'

9. Coleman, *op. cit.*, p.49.

10. *American Free Press*, January 26, 2004.

11. See http://tbpipeline.com/project/milestones.

12. Coleman, *op. cit.*, p.51.

13. Bergen, *op. cit.*, pp.48–9; *American Free Press*, October 15, 2001, pp.1–3; London *Daily Mail*, September 24, 2001, pp.3–4.

14. Bergen, *op. cit.*, pp.48–9.

15. *American Free Press*, January 7, 2002; 14 January 2002.

16. Sherman H. Skolnick, 'America's Reichstag Fire': http://www.world-action.co.uk/reichstag.html.

17. Bergen, *op. cit.*, pp.82–3.

18. Craig Unger, *House of Bush, House of Saud*, pp.1–17.

19. *Portman Papers*, January 2003, p.12; several issues of the *American Free Press* around that time.

20. See http://www.telegraph.co.uk/news/worldnews/asia/afghanistan/1360616/Bin-Laden-may-never-be-caught.html.

21. *American Free Press*, July 21, 2003.

22. Sherman H. Skolnick, *US Government Prior Knowledge of Emergency*, 9.11.2001, www.skolnicksreport.com/pkem.html.

23. John J. Lumpkin, Associated Press: 'Officials at the Chantilly, Va.-based National Reconnaissance Office had scheduled an exercise that morning in which a small corporate jet would crash into one of the four towers at the agency's headquarters building after experiencing a mechanical failure.' See http://www.oilempire.us/nro.html.

24. *American Free Press*, November 11, 2002.

25. See http://www.historycommons.org/timeline.jsp?before_9/11=militaryExercises&timeline=complete_911_timeline.

26. See interview with Richard Gage, http://www.youtube.com/watch?v=ssuAMNas1us and http://www.americanfreepress.net/html/911architectsfortruth_32509.html.

27. See http://whatreallyhappened.com/WRHARTICLES/silverstein_wtc.html and http://whatreallyhappened.com/WRHARTICLES/silverstein.html.

28. *American Free Press*, December 10, 2001.

29. *American Free Press*, August 12, 2002.
30. See http://greenyes.grrn.org/2001/02/msg00097.html; http://www.aspectenterprise.com/about_aspect/advisery.php; and http://usacc.org/contents.php?cid=32;
31. *American Free Press*, October 8, 2001.
32. Jim Tucker, *Bilderberg Diary*, p.9.
33. Clarke, *op. cit.*, p.32.
34. George Soros, *The Bubble of American Supremacy*, p.vii.
35. See http://bushstole04.com/monetarysystem/rothschild_bank.htm.
36. *American Free Press*, April 21, 2002, May 12, 2002.
37. *American Free Press*, July 21, 2003.
38. *American Free Press*, January 26, 2004.
39. See http://www.bp.com/sectiongenericarticle.do?categoryId=9014823&contentId=7027814.
40. See http://en.wikipedia.org/wiki/Baku%E2%80%93Tbilisi%E2%80%93Ceyhan_pipeline and http://www.gasandoil.com/goc/company/cnc23849.htm.
41. See http://www.itar-tass.com/eng/level2.html?NewsID=13236773&PageNum=0 and http://en.wikipedia.org/wiki/Baku–Tbilisi–Ceyhan_pipeline.
42. See http://www.azerbaijan.az/_Economy/_OilStrategy/oilStrategy_05_e.html.
43. See http://www.oxfordenergy.org/pdfs/NG25.pdf and http://www.caucaz.com/home_eng/depeches.php?idp=1064.
44. For points in this paragraph and the next three paragraphs see F. William Engdahl, 'Ukraine and a Tectonic Shift in Heartland Power.' http://en.rian.ru/valdai_foreign_media/20100323/158285355.html.
45. *Encyclopedia Britannica*, 15th ed., 1974–91, entry for 'Khazars' says: 'The most striking characteristic of the Khazars was the apparent adoption of Judaism by the *khagan* [ruler] and the greater part of the ruling class in about 740. The circumstances of the conversion remain obscure, the depth of their adoption of Judaism difficult to assess; the fact itself, however, is undisputed and unparalleled in the history of central Eurasia. A few scholars have even asserted that the Judaized Khazars were the remote ancestors of many of the Jews of eastern Europe and Russia.'
46. 'Final destination Iran?,' *Sunday Herald Scotland*, March 14, 2010, see http://www.heraldscotland.com/news/world-news/final-destination-iran-1.1013151. See also *American Free Press*, April 5, 2010.
47. See video of Representative Paul Kanjorski, http://www.youtube.com/watch?v=pD8viQ_DhS4, accessed on 9.3.2010.
48. See http://bushstole04.com/monetarysystem/rothschild_bank.htm.
49. See http://www.templeinstitute.org/megillat-bush.htm.
50. James (Jim) P. Tucker, 'Bilderberg Surreptitiously Pushes Global Treasury Department,' *American Free Press*, March 22, 2010.
51. James P. Tucker, *American Free Press*, April 12–19, 2010, p.3.
52. William Engdahl, 'Gulf Oil Spill 'Could Go Years' If Not Dealt With,' June 10, 2010, http://www.engdahl.oilgeopolitics.net/print/Gulf%20Oil%20Spill.pdf.

53. 'Will Gulf Calamity Lead to Rothschild Financial Takeover?' The *American Free Press*, June 28, 2010, p.9.

## Chapter 9: The Secret American Dream: America's Philanthropic Mission

1. Jules Dufour, Global Research, 'Review Article: The Worldwide Network of US Military Bases.' July 1, 2007. See http://www.globalpolicy.org/component/content/article/153/26325.html.
2. See http://www.globalpolicy.org/component/content/article/153/26325.html.
3. Michael Ignatieff, 'The American Empire: The Burden.' *New York Times Magazine*, January 5, 2003, Section 6. Robert Kagan, 'The Benevolent Empire.' *Foreign Policies*, Summer 1998, pp.24–34.
4. Ziauddin Sardar and Merryl Wyn Davies, *American Dream, Global Nightmare*, p.vi.
5. *The Global 2000 Report to the President* was unveiled at a press conference by US Secretary of State Edmund Muskie on July 24, 1980. It was accepted by President Carter.
6. *The Global 2000 Report to the President*, pp.41–2. See http://www.globalpolicy.org/component/content/article/153/26325.html.
7. *American Free Press*, February 15, 2010, referring to the Attorney Ezili Danto.
8. F. William Engdahl, 'The Fateful Geological Prize Called Haiti.' See http://www.engdahl.oilgeopolitics.net/Geopolitics___Eurasia/Prize_Haiti/prize_haiti.html
9. Paul Kennedy, *The Rise and Fall of the Great Powers*, pp.360–61, 515–21.
10. Michael J. Panzner, *When Giants Fall*, p.xi.
11. See http://alfin2100.blogspot.com/2008/12/2010-good-bye-usa-hello-split-america.html. For Igor Panarin's prediction that the US would break up in 2010 see http://online.wsj.com/article/SB123051100709638419.html.
12. Hagger, *The Fire and the Stones* (1991); updated as *The Light of Civilization* and *The Rise and Fall of Civilizations*. These works set out Hagger's historical Universalism.
13. Samuel P. Huntington, *The Clash of Civilizations and the Remaking of World Order*.
14. Huntington, *op. cit.*, pp.254–8.
15. Huntington, *op. cit.*, p.310.
16. For an interesting angle on Hegel's end of history, see http://www.historicalinsights.com/dave/hegel.html.
17. See http://hubpages.com/hub/Murder-Tyranny-and-The-Bilderberg-Group.
18. See http://sirsatire.wordpress.com/2008/10/17/bilderberg-group-gives-obama-green-light/?referer=sphere_related_content/.
19. See http://www.city-data.com/forum/elections/226335-candidates-who-council-foreign-relations-members.html.
20. See http://www.rense.com/general80/obmw.htm.
21. See http://www.rense.com/general80/obmw.htm.

22. See http://troyspace2.wordpress.com/2008/04/23/royal-arch-cryptic-knights-templar-masons-solomons-temple-rebuilders-revealed/. Also see http://forums.islamicawakening.com/showthread.php?t=18470.

23. See http://www.suntimes.com/news/politics/obama/familytree/545460,BSX-News-wotreea09.article.

24. See http://www.associatedcontent.com/article/639903/barack_obama_is_related_to_george_w_pg2.html?cat=9.

25. See http://www.guardian.co.uk/world/2009/jun/04/barack-obama-speech-cairo-israel.

26. *Our Creative Diversity: Report of the World Commission on Culture and Development*, summary version, UNESCO, Paris, 1996, p.16. See http://unesdoc.unesco.org/images/0010/001055/105586e.pdf.

27. See http://www.guardian.co.uk/world/2009/jun/04/barack-obama-keynote-speech-egypt.

28. See http://www.guardian.co.uk/world/2009/sep/23/barack-obama-un-speech.

29. See http://www.msnbc.msn.com/id/34360743/.

30. See http://www.huffingtonpost.com/2009/04/05/obama-prague-speech-on-nu_n_183219.html.

31. See http://www.huffingtonpost.com/2009/04/05/obama-prague-speech-on-nu_n_183219.html.

32. See http://news.bbc.co.uk/1/hi/8389849.stm.

33. See http://www.whitehouse.gov/the-press-office/remarks-president-troops.

34. London *The Daily Telegraph* online, April 12, 2010, see http://www.telegraph.co.uk/news/worldnews/northamerica/usa/barackobama/7583173/Al-Qaeda-trying-to-secure-nuclear-weapons-says-Barack-Obama.html. See also http://news.bbc.co.uk/1/hi/8614695.stm.

35. See http://www.cfr.org/publication/21889/obamas_speech_at_the_nuclear_security_summit_april_2010.html

36. See http://obama.3cdn.net/4465b108758abf7a42_a3jmvyfa5.pdf.

37. See http://www.guardian.co.uk/environment/2009/dec/17/un-leaked-report-copenhagen-3c.

38. See http://preventdisease.com/news/09/061709_geoengineering.shtml.

39. See http://www.america.gov/st/peacesec-english/2009/May/20090507095154dmslahrellek0.7992975.html.

40. See http://www.caadp.net/news/?p=92.

41. See http://www.caadp.net/news/?p=92.

42. For the differences between the Roadmap Act and the Global Food Security Act, see http://www.friendsofwfp.org/site/c.hrKJIXPFIqE/b.5259725/k.FBC6/Current_Legislation.htm.

43. See http://obama-mamas.com/blog/?p=1670.

44. See http://news.bbc.co.uk/1/hi/7977939.stm.

45. Senate Report 1110-331 – *The Global Poverty Act of 2007*, see

http://www.govtrack.us/congress/bill.xpd?bill=s110-2433.

46. See http://www.aim.org/aim-column/obamas-global-tax-proposal-up- for-senate-vote/.

47. The World Bank, *Understanding Poverty, 2007*; see
http://web.worldbank.org/WBSITE/EXTERNAL/TOPICS/
EXTPOVERTY/0,,contentMDK:20153855~menuPK:373757~pagePK:148956
~piPK:216618~theSitePK:336992,00.html.

48. See http://www.guardian.co.uk/world/2009/jun/04/barack-obama-keynote-speech-egypt.

49. See http://www.guardian.co.uk/world/2009/sep/23/barack-obama-un-speech.

50. See http://www.msnbc.msn.com/id/34360743/.

51. See http://www.state.gov/t/isn/c10390.htm.

52. See http://www.state.gov/t/isn/c18406.htm.

53. See http://www.huffingtonpost.com/2009/04/05/obama-prague-speech-on-nu_n_183219.html and http://netindian.in/news/2010/04/04/0006031/pm-attend-obamas-summit-nuclear-security-april-12-13.

54. See http://obama.3cdn.net/4465b108758abf7a42_a3jmvyfa5.pdf.

55. See http://www.guardian.co.uk/environment/2009/dec/17/un-leaked-report-copenhagen-3c.

56. See http://preventdisease.com/news/09/061709_geoengineering.shtml.

57. See http://www.america.gov/st/peacesec-english/2009/May/20090507095154dmslahrellek0.7992975.html.

58. See http://www.caadp.net/news/?p=92.

59. See http://www.friendsofwfp.org/site/c.hrKJIXPFIqE/b.5259725/k.FBC6/Current_Legislation.htm.

60. See http://news.bbc.co.uk/1/hi/7977939.stm.

61. See http://www.crossroad.to/Quotes/law/global/poverty-act.htm.

62. See http://abcnews.go.com/Politics/State_of_the_Union/state-of-the-union-2010-president-obama-speech-transcript/story?id=9678572.

63. See http://casey.senate.gov/newsroom/press/release/?id=936E5863-FDED-4E20-AD01-61C71EA48E0B.

64. See http://www.cfr.org/publication/18306/obamabiden_new_energy_for_america_plan_january_2009.html?breadcrumb=/publication/by_type/dor.

65. See http://www.govtrack.us/congress/bill.xpd?bill=h111-1.

66. See http://www.financialstability.gov/docs/fact-sheet.pdf.

67. See http://www.circ.ahajournals.org/cgi/content/full/101/16/2015 and http://www.barackobama.com/pdf/issues/HealthCareFullPlan.pdf.

68. See http://abcnews.go.com/Politics/State_of_the_Union/state-of-the-union-2010-president-obama-speech-transcript/story?id=9678572.

69. See http://www.guardian.co.uk/world/2009/jun/04/barack-obama-keynote-speech-egypt.

70. See http://www.guardian.co.uk/world/2009/sep/23/barack-obama-un-speech.

71. See http://www.msnbc.msn.com/id/34360743/.

72. See http://abcnews.go.com/Politics/State_of_the_Union/state-of-the-union-2010-president-obama-speech-transcript/story?id=9678572.
73. See http://www.huffingtonpost.com/2009/04/05/obama-prague-speech-on-nu_n_183219.html.
74. See http://www.cfr.org/publication/18306/obamabiden_new_energy_for_america_plan_january_2009.html?breadcrumb=/publication/by_type/dor.
75. See http://www.govtrack.us/congress/bill.xpd?bill=h111-1.
76. See http://www.circ.ahajournals.org/cgi/content/full/101/16/2015 and http://www.barackobama.com/pdf/issues/HealthCareFullPlan.pdf.
77. See http://www.govtrack.us/congress/bill.xpd?bill=h111-1.
78. See http://www.govtrack.us/congress/bill.xpd?bill=h111-1.
79. See http://www.financialstability.gov/docs/fact-sheet.pdf.
80. See http://www.govtrack.us/congress/bill.xpd?bill=h111-1.
81. See http://www.nytimes.com/2009/01/20/us/politics/20text-obama.html.
82. See http://www.guardian.co.uk/world/2009/jun/04/barack-obama-speech-cairo-israel.
83. See http://www.nytimes.com/2009/09/24/us/politics/24prexy.text.html.
84. *American Free Press*, February 22, 2010.
85. See http://www.time.com/time/world/article/0,8599,1889512,00.html.
86. See http://whitehouse.georgewbush.org/news/2005/012005.asp.
87. See http://www.independent.co.uk/opinion/commentators/henry-kissinger-the-world-must-forge-a-new-order-or-retreat-to-chaos-1451416.html.
88. 'Green lobby attacks Obama as he approves offshore hunt for oil.' London *Daily Telegraph,* April 1, 2010.
89. See http://www.huffingtonpost.com/2009/01/20/president-obamas-inaugura_n_159370.html.
90. See http://www.huffingtonpost.com/2009/04/05/obama-prague-speech-on-nu_n_183219.html.
91. See http://browse.guardian.co.uk/search?search=OBAMA+ORDERS+NEW+NUCLEAR+REVIEW&search_target=/search&fr=cb-guardian
92. http://news.bbc.co.uk/1/hi/world/europe/8589385.stm. See also London *Daily Mail*, March 27, 2010.
93. See http://www.msnbc.msn.com/id/34360743/.
94. The conclusion in Hagger, *The World Government*, Parts One and Two. This work sets out Hagger's political Universalism.

## Chapter 10: How the World State Might Look and How It Could Be Funded

1. See Hagger, *The Secret History of the West* and *The Syndicate*, which between them cover many 20th-century revolutions.
2. Saba Riazati, 'A Closer Look: Professor Seeks Stronger UN.' *The Daily Bruin*, October 18, 2006.
3. Rivera, *op. cit.*, p.89; Carroll Quigley, *Anglo-American Establishment*, pp.117ff.

4. Rivera, *op. cit.*, p.91.
5. Lindsay Jenkins, *Britain Held Hostage*, p.47; and Dr Adrian Krieg, *July 4th, 2016, The Last Independence Day*, p.26.
6. Rivera, *op. cit.*, p.177.
7. Rivera, *op. cit.*, p.186.
8. Dr John Coleman, *Conspirators' Hierarchy: The Story of the Committee of 300*, p.13.
9. Rivera, *op. cit.*, p.190.
10. See James P. Tucker, *American Free Press*, April 12–19, 2010, p.3.
11. Hagger, *The World Government*, chs.3 and 4.
12. For a full list, see Hagger, *The World Government*, Appendix, B6, based on http://answers.google.com/answers/threadview?id=55124.
13. See http://home.att.net/~howingtons/dem/truman.html.
14. Grenville Clark and Louis Sohn, *World Peace Through World Law*, 3rd edition enlarged, pp.1–370.
15. For full details, see pp.204–6.
16. For full details, see pp.208–9.
17. For full details, see pp.206–7.
18. For alternative totals of global military spending in 2008, see http://daga.dhs.org/icp/faithpeace/2009/90220a.htm for $1.4727 trillion; see http://en.wikipedia.org/wiki/List_of_countries_by_military_expenditures for $1.47 trillion; see http://www.globalissues.org/article/75/world-military-spending#WorldMilitarySpending for $1.464 trillion (quoting the Stockholm International Peace Research Yearbook, 2009); and see http://news.therecord.com/article/550332 for $1.46 trillion.

## Chapter 11: Liberty's World State: Life Under Universal Peace

1. For a full explanation of the glacial-interglacial cycle and its impact on our time, see Hagger, *The New Philosophy of Universalism*, pp.136–43.
2. See list http://en.wikipedia.org/wiki/List_of_countries_by_population#cite_note-unpop-3.
3. Hagger, *Collected Poems 1958–2005*, pp.93–4.
4. Hagger, *The Fire and the Stones*; updated as *The Light of Civilization* and *The Rise and Fall of Civilizations*.
5. See Hagger, *The Rise and Fall of Civilizations*, pp.536 and 111–22 for full details.
6. See Hagger, *The Rise and Fall of Civilizations*, pp.545–6, and 282–90 and 293–8 for full details.
7. See Hagger, *The Rise and Fall of Civilizations*, pp.539 and 183–90.
8. See http://esa.un.org/unpp/. See also http://www.un.org/esa/population/publications/wpp2008/pressrelease.pdf *The Global 2000 Report to the President*, p.41, forecast that the world population would be ten billion in 2030.
9. See http://www.ukerc.ac.uk/support/tiki-index.php?page=Global+Oil+Depletion.

10. See http://www.need.org/needpdf/infobook_activities/SecInfo/NGasS.pdf.

## Epilogue: Liberty's Universalist Destiny

1. Jim Cullen, *The American Dream*, chs.1–6.
2. Quoted in Cullen, op. cit., p.183.
3. David Hackett Fischer, *Liberty and Freedom*, p.5.
4. See Hagger, *The Fire and the Stones,* Part One, and *The Light of Civilization* for full coverage of the tradition of religious Universalism. These works set out Hagger's religious Universalism.
5. See Hagger, *The Secret Founding of America*, pp.177–85.
6. Quoted in Edith Starr Miller, *Occult Theocrasy*, vol.1, p.221; also quoted in John Daniel, *Scarlet and the Beast*, vol.1, pp.393–4. Pike's letter was read on July 14, 1889, at the annual Congress of 23 Grand Lodge Supreme Councils in Paris. The letter was recorded by A.C. De La Rive in *La Fin et l'Enfant dans la Franc-Maçonnerie Universelle*. The reading was noted in a letter in an English Masonic periodical, *The Freemason,* on January 19, 1935.
7. See Hagger, *The World Government*, Prologue and ch.2 for quotations.
8. George W. Bush, speech to Pennsylvania State University, April 2, 2002.
9. See http://www.globalissues.org/article/75/world-military-spending#USMilitarySpending.
10. See http://quotationsbook.com/quote/12281/.
11. Robert Kagan, *The Return of History and the End of Dreams*, pp.3-10.
12. Hagger, *The Fire and the Stones*, updated as *The Light of Civilization* and *The Rise and Fall of Civilizations*.

# Bibliography

Adams, James Truslow, *The Epic of America*, Boston: Little, Brown & Co. 1931; Simon Publications, 2001.

Aid, Matthew, *The Secret Sentry: The Untold History of the National Security Agency*, Bloomsbury, 2010.

Allen, Gary and Abraham, Larry, *None Dare Call It Conspiracy*, Concord Press, 1972.

*Anthologia Graeca*, ed. Hermann Beckby, Heimeran, Munich 1957.

Armstrong, George, *The Rothschild Money Trust*, Omni Publications, California, 1940.

Baigent, Michael, Leigh, Richard and Lincoln, Henry, *The Holy Blood and the Holy Grail*, Corgi Books, 1982.

—, *The Messianic Legacy*, Corgi Books, 1987.

Baigent, Michael and Leigh, Richard, *The Temple and the Lodge*, Arcade, 1989.

Bemis, Samuel Flagg, *A Diplomatic History of the United States*, New York, 1955.

Bergen, Peter L., *Holy War Inc.: Inside the Secret World of Osama bin Laden*, Weidenfeld and Nicolson, London, 2001/Phoenix 2002.

Black, George, *The Good Neighbor: How the United States Wrote the History of Central America and the Caribbean*, New York, 1988.

Bobbitt, Philip, *The Shield of Achilles*, London: Allen Lane, 2002.

Bodinsky, Yossef, *Bin Laden, The Man Who Declared War on America*, Forum, 1999.

Bronner, Edwin B, *William Penn's 'Holy Experiment': The Founding of Pennsylvania, 1681–1701*, New York, 1962.

Calhoun, Craig, *Dictionary of the Social Sciences*, Oxford University Press, 2002.

Chernow, Ron, *Titan: The Life of John D. Rockefeller Sr.*, Little, Brown, 1998.

Clark, Grenville, and Sohn, Louis, *World Peace Through World Law*, third edition enlarged, Harvard University Press, 1966.

Clarke, Richard A., *Against All Enemies: Inside America's War on Terror*, Free Press, 2004.

Clausen, Henry C., *Masons Who Helped Shape Our Nation*, Washington, 1976.

Cockburn, N.B., *The Bacon Shakespeare Question: The Baconian Theory Made Sane*, Biddles, 1998.

Coleman, Dr John, *Conspirators' Hierarchy: The Story of the Committee of 300*, America West Publishers, POBox 2208, Carson City, NV 89702, 1992.

—, *Diplomacy by Deception*, Joseph Publishing Co., Nevada, 1993.

Corti, Count Egon Caesar, *The Rise of the House of Rothschild*, Western Islands, USA, 1928, 1972.

Cotter, John, *A Study in Syncretism*, Canadian Intelligence Publications, 1979.

Crozier, Brian, *Soviet Imperialism, How to Contain It*, London; Temple Smith, 1978.

Cullen, Jim, *The American Dream: A Short History of an Idea that Shaped a Nation*, Oxford University Press, 2003.

Daniel, John, *Scarlet and the Beast*, vol. I, JKI Publishing, 1995.
D'Souza, Dinesh, *Ronald Reagan: How an Ordinary Man became an Extraordinary Leader*, Touchstone, New York, 1999.
*Encyclopaedia of American History*, vol. 2, New York: Charles Scribner's Sons, 2002.
Engdahl, F. William, *Full Spectrum Dominance: Totalitarian Democracy in the New World Order*, edition.engdahl, 2009.
Epperson, A. Ralph, *The New World Order*, Publius Press, 1990.
Ferguson, Niall, *Colossus: The Rise and Fall of the American Empire*, Allen Lane, 2004.
—, *The World's Banker: The History of the House of Rothschild*, Weidenfeld & Nicolson, London, 1998.
Fischer, David Hackett, *Liberty and Freedom*, Oxford University Press, 2005.
Fisher, Philip, *Hard Facts: Setting and Form in the American Novel*, Oxford University Press, 1985.
Fonar, Eric and Garraty, John Arthur, *The Reader's Companion to American History*, Houghton Mifflin Books, 2002.
Fukuyama, Francis, *The End of History and the Last Man*, Hamish Hamilton, 1992.
*Global Future, Time to Act: Report to the President*, University of Michigan Library, 1981.
*Global 2000 Report to the President, The: Entering the Twenty-First Century*, Penguin 1982; British Library book reference no. X.520/29289.
Goulden, Joseph C., *Korea: The Untold Story of the War*, McGraw-Hill, 1984.
Griffin, Des, *Descent into Slavery?*, Emissary Publications, USA, 1993.
Hagger, Nicholas, *Armageddon, The Triumph of Universal Order, An Epic Poem on the War on Terror and of Holy War Crusaders*, O Books, 2010.
—, *Collected Poems*, O Books, 2006.
—, *Collected Verse Plays*, O Books, 2007.
—, *The Fire and the Stones*, Element, 1991.
—, *Overlord, The Triumph of Light 1944–45*, O Books, 2006.
—, *The Light of Civilization*, O Books, 2006.
—, *The New Philosophy of Universalism*, O Books, 2009.
—, *The Rise and Fall of Civilizations*, O Books, 2008.
—, *The Secret Founding of America*, Watkins Publishing, 2007.
—, *The Secret History of the West*, O Books, 2005.
—, *The Syndicate*, O Books, 2004.
—, *The Warlords, From D-Day to Berlin*, Element, 1995.
—, *The World Government*, O Books, 2010.
Hakim, Joy, *History of US: Book Eight, An Age of Extremes*, New York: Oxford University Press, 1994.
Hayes, Stephen F., *The Connection*, HarperCollins, 2004.
Hendershot, Robert, *Family Spats: Perception, Illusion, and Sentimentality in the Anglo-American Special Relationship*, VDM Verlag Dr. Muller, 2008.
Hoopes, Townsend and Brinkley, Douglas, *FDR and the Creation of the UN*, Yale University Press, 1997.

Hugins, Roland, *The Possible Peace: A Forecast of World Politics After the Great War*, 1916/BiblioBazaar 2009.

Huntington, Samuel P., *The Clash of Civilizations and the Remaking of World Order*, Simon & Schuster, 1996.

Jafarzadeh, Alireza, *The Iran Threat, President Ahmadinejad and the Coming Nuclear Crisis*, Palgrave McMillan, New York, 2007.

Jasper, William F., *Global Tyranny... Step by Step: The United Nations and the Emerging New World Order*, Western Islands, USA, 1992.

Jenkins, Lindsay, *Britain Held Hostage: The Coming Euro-Dictatorship*, Orange State Press, Washington, 1997.

Josephson, Emanuel M., *Rockefeller: 'Internationalist,' The Man who Misrules the World*, Chedney Press, New York, 1952.

—, *The 'Federal' Reserve Conspiracy and Rockefeller*, Chedney Press, New York, 1968.

—, *The Truth about Rockefeller, Public Enemy No. 1*, Chedney Press, New York, 1964.

Kagan, Robert, *The Return of History and the End of Dreams*, Atlantic Books, 2008.

Karnow, Stanley, *Vietnam: A History*, London: Pimlico, 1994.

Kennedy, Paul, *The Rise and Fall of the Great Powers*, Unwin Hyman, 1988.

Kort, Michael, *The Colombia Guide to the Cold War*, Colombia University Press, 2001.

Krieg, Dr Adrian, *July 4th, 2016: The Last Independence Day*, Hallberg, 2000.

Kutz, Myer, *Rockefeller Power*, Pinnacle Books, New York, 1974.

Lambert, Frank, *The Founding Fathers and the Place of Religion in America*, Princeton University Press, 2003.

Lawrence, Bruce, ed., *Messages to the World: The Statements of Osama bin Laden*, Verso, 2005.

Loftus, John and Aarons, Mark, *The Secret War against the Jews*, St. Martin's Press, New York, 1994.

Love, Kennett, *Suez: The Twice-Fought War*, McGraw Hill, 1969.

McForan, Desmond, *The World Held Hostage*, Oak-Tree Books, 1986.

Miller, Edith Starr, *Occult Theocrasy*, vol.1, 1933; Christian Book Club of America, Hawthorne, CA, 1980.

Miller, Stuart Creighton, *'Benevolent Assimilation:' The American Conquest of the Philippines, 1899–1903*, Yale University Press 1982.

Miniter, Richard, *Shadow War: The Untold Story of How America Is Winning the War on Terror*, Regnery Publishing, Inc., 2004.

Morris, Richard B., *The Framing of the Federal Constitution, Handbook 103*, Division of Publications, National Park Service, US Department of the Interior, 1986.

Morrison, Samuel E., and Commager, Henry Steele, *The Growth of the American Republic*, 2 vols, New York, Oxford University Press, 1953.

Morton, Frederic, *The Rothschilds: A Family Portrait*, Atheneum, New York, 1962.

Panzner, Michael J., *When Giants Fall*, John Wiley & Sons, 2009.

Perloff, James, *The Shadows of Power: The Council on Foreign Relations and the American Decline*, Western Islands, USA, 1988.

Priest, Dana, *The Mission: Waging War and Keeping Peace with America's Military*, New York, 2003.

Quigley, Carroll, *Anglo-American Establishment*, Emissary Publications, USA, 1981.

Quinn, Arthur, *A New World: An Epic of Colonial America from the Founding of Jamestown to the Fall of Quebec*, Faber and Faber, 1994.

Reeve, Simon, *The New Jackals: Osama bin Laden and the Future of Terrorism*, Carlton Books Ltd, 2001.

Riencourt, Amaury de, *The American Empire*, New York: The Dial Press, 1968.

Rivera, David Allen, *Final Warning: A History of the New World Order*, Rivera Enterprises, 1984–94.

Robinson, Adam, *Bin Laden: Behind the Mask of Terror*, Mainstream, UK, 2001.

Rockefeller, Nelson A., *The Future of Federalism*, Harvard University Press, 1962.

Ross, Robert Gaylon Sr., *Who's Who of the Elite*, RIE, HCR1, Box 516, Spicewood, Texas 78669-9549, 1995.

Sardar, Ziauddin and Davies, Merryl Wyn, *American Dream, Global Nightmare*, Icon Books, 2004.

Sharansky, Natan, *The Case for Democracy*, Public Affairs, New York, 2004.

Shoup, Laurence H. and Minter, William, *Imperial Brain Trust: The Council on Foreign Relations and United States Foreign Policy*, New York, Monthly Review Press., 1978.

Smith, James Morton, ed., *The Republic of Letters: The Correspondence between Thomas Jefferson and James Madison, 1776–1826*, vol. iii, New York: W.W. Norton, 1994.

Soros, George, *The Bubble of American Supremacy*, Weidenfeld & Nicolson, 2004.

Spanier, John, *The Truman–MacArthur Controversy and the Korean War*, W.W. Norton & Company, 1965.

Still, William T., *New World Order: The Ancient Plan of Secret Societies*, Huntington House Publishers, 1990.

Stopes, Charlotte C., *The Life of Henry, Third Earl of Southampton*, Cambridge University Press, England, 1922.

Tucker, Jim, *Bilderberg Diary*, American Free Press, 2005.

Unger, Craig, *House of Bush, House of Saud*, Gibson Square Books, 2004.

Von Bülow, Andreas, *The CIA and September 11*, Piper Verlag, 2004.

Weintraub, Stanley, *MacArthur's War: Korea and the Undoing of an American Hero*, Simon & Schuster, 2008.

Williams, Paul L., *The Al Qaeda Connection*, Prometheus Books, 2005.

Willkie, Wendell L., *One World*, Cassell, 1943.

Wilson, Derek, *Rothschild: A Story of Wealth and Power*, Mandarin, London 1988.

Zinn, Howard, *A People's History of the United States 1492–Present*, HarperCollins Publishers, New York, 2005.

# Index